STRANGERS TO THESE SHORES

HOUGHTON MIFFLIN COMPANY   BOSTON

DALLAS   GENEVA, ILLINOIS   HOPEWELL, NEW JERSEY
PALO ALTO   LONDON

STRANGERS TO THESE SHORES

RACE AND ETHNIC RELATIONS
IN THE UNITED STATES

VINCENT N. PARRILLO

THE WILLIAM PATERSON COLLEGE
OF NEW JERSEY

Library of Congress Catalog Card Number: 79–87856

ISBN: 0-395-28562-3

TO MY ITALIAN-AMERICAN FATHER

AND MY IRISH-AMERICAN MOTHER

CONTENTS

(vii)

CHAPTER SEVEN

THE ASIAN IMMIGRANTS / 267

CHAPTER EIGHT

OTHER NON-WESTERN IMMIGRANTS / 315

CHAPTER NINE

BLACKS IN AMERICA / 345

CHAPTER TEN
THE HISPANIC IMMIGRANTS / 393

CHAPTER ELEVEN
THE AMERICAN MOSAIC / 433

APPENDIX
IMMIGRATION BY COUNTRY
FOR DECADES 1820–1977 / 469

PREFACE

Strangers to These Shores is a primary text for courses in race and ethnic relations, with a focus on the United States. This book evolved as an effort to provide a comprehensive overview of major sociological theories and concepts regarding the interaction between dominant and minority groups, as well as a sociohistorical account of the experiences of many different groups in this country. The intent has been to offer a readable and manageable text, giving students both a solid foundation in this field and an insight into the complexity of the social fabric that constitutes American society.

The first three chapters present a conceptual and theoretical overview of the subject area, giving students a basis from which to examine the experiences of the minority groups that are discussed in subsequent chapters. A variety of perspectives are presented to show the full range of positions on the subject. Instructors may wish to emphasize their own perspectives throughout the book. The overview provides a general frame of reference rather than a detailed analysis; for a more comprehensive examination of any subject discussed in this book, the reader should consult the sources listed in the notes and suggested readings at the end of each chapter.

After some introductory concepts in the first chapter, we consider in Chapter 2 the present understanding about prejudice and discrimination and their possible causes, manifestations, and interrelationships. Patterns of ingroup responses to outgroups, and outgroup responses to ingroups, provide the next focus. Chapter 3 explores some of the theories that offer explanations for the various reactions that occur when different peoples come into contact with one another. Particular attention is paid to differences in power, race, culture, and social class. In the last section of this chapter we look at the dominant group's various expectations about how minority groups should integrate into its society.

Chapters 4 through 10 offer the reader some insights into the experiences of a wide array of racial and ethnic minorities. In-depth studies of the cultural orientations and histories of each minority are not possible, for that would take far more space than the length of this book permits. Instead, a brief overview of the experiences of each group is presented to demonstrate the diversity of peoples within the United States and to illustrate the concepts and theories discussed in the first part of the book. Not every racial and ethnic group is discussed, but enough have been included to be illustrative of the diversity among Americans.

At the end of the book we examine some other theoretical approaches for understanding the similarities and differences in the groups discussed. An analysis of the so-called ethnic reawakening, the variety of forms of ethnic behavior, and ethnic stratification completes our study of racial and ethnic minorities.

Many people helped in the writing of this book. I am indebted to my colleagues—Maboud Ansari, Joseph Brandes, Forrest Pritchett, and Paul Vouras—for their suggestions and encouragement. Don A. Edwards provided excellent editorial assistance in making this book more readable, and Lynn Culley worked many long hours typing the several drafts of the manuscript. Thanks also go to Debbie Itzie and Michele Valentino, who helped me in preparing the manuscript.

I would like to thank the following students of mine whose excellent immigrant tape projects provided the excerpts found in chapters 4 through 10: Bruce Bisciotti, Doris Brown, Hermione Cox, Milly Gottlieb, Daniel Kazan, David Lenox, Sarah Martinez, Chairath Phaladiganon, Terrence Royful, Michelle Schwartz, Geri Squire, Luba Tkatchov, and Leo Uebelein. Their contributions bring a very human touch to the study of minority peoples.

The following reviewers provided helpful comments as the book was being written: Nijole V. Benokraitis, University of Baltimore; Phyllis L. Fleming, University of Minnesota, Twin Cities; George Gross, Northern Michigan University; Patrick H. McNamara, The University of New Mexico; William H. Martineau, College of William and Mary; Chad Richardson, Pan American University; and Marios Stephanides, Spalding College. Stanford M. Lyman, of the New School for Social Research, offered valuable criticism and guidance, for which I am especially grateful.

On a personal note, I want to thank my wife, Beth, for her patience and understanding during the researching and writing of this book. Any author or author's spouse will appreciate that the demands and sacrifices that must be made for a project such as this are substantial.

V. N. P.

ONE

THE STUDY OF MINORITIES

Ethnicity has always been an important factor in human behavior, but in recent years, many people have rediscovered personal meaning in their ethnic identity. Many Americans, particularly those whose family backgrounds go back three or more generations in this country, are suddenly taking a greater interest in their heritage. The ever-increasing amount of scholarly and popular literature, media coverage, and college instruction in this field is further testimony to this rediscovery.

In spring 1977, the spectacular success of the televised version of Alex Haley's book *Roots* prompted many Americans of all races to learn more about their own heritage. Since that telecast, thousands of Americans have crowded into archives or journeyed overseas to reclaim a heritage that has been somewhat bleached away by the assimilation process. Mostly young, third-generation Americans, these individuals are redefining the meaning of *American* as they seek to learn more about their roots.

Many sociologists have also taken an increased interest in studying racial and ethnic groups and their interrelationships with society as a whole. This trend, no doubt, is partly just symptomatic of the times, but it is probably largely a reflection of the fact that today's sociologists are more committed to playing an important role in society, particularly by resolving social problems rather than just explaining them.[1]

THE STRANGER AS A SOCIAL PHENOMENON

To understand intergroup relations, we must recognize that differences among various peoples cause each group to look upon other groups as strangers. Among isolated peoples, the arrival of a stranger has always been a momentous occasion, often eliciting strong emotional responses. Reactions might range from warm hospitality to conciliatory or protective ceremonies to hostile acts. In an urbanized and mobile society, the stranger often still evokes similar responses. From the Tiwi of northern Australia, who consistently killed intruders, to the nativists of any country or time, who continually strive to keep out "undesirable elements," the underlying premise is the same: the outsiders are not human enough to share the land and resources with the "chosen people" already there.

By definition, the *stranger* is not only an outsider but also someone different and personally unknown. People perceive strangers primarily through *categoric knowing*, the classification of others based on limited information obtained visually and perhaps verbally.[2] On the basis of scanty information, people make judgments and generalizations, confusing an individual's characteristics with typical group-member characteristics. For instance, if a visiting Swede asks for tea rather than coffee, the host might incorrectly conclude that all Swedes dislike coffee.

Immigrants, first-generation Americans of different racial and ethnic groups, have been perceived as a particular kind of stranger: one who intends to stay. As the presence of immigrants became less of a novelty, fear, suspicion, and distrust often replaced the natives' initial curiosity. The strangers often remained strangers as each group sought its own kind for personal interaction.

The role of a stranger can be analyzed regardless of the particular period in history. Georg Simmel (1858–1918) theorized that strangers represent both *nearness*, because they are physically close, and *remoteness*, because they react differently to the immediate situation and have different values and ways of doing things.[3] The stranger is both inside· and outside: physically present and participating, but also outside the situation, being from another place.

The native perceives the stranger in an abstract, typified way. That is, the individual becomes the *totality*, or stereotype, of the group. The stranger, however, perceives the natives in concrete, individual terms. Simmel suggests that strangers have a higher degree of objectivity about the natives because the strangers' geographical mobility reflects mobility in their minds as well. The stranger is free from indigenous habit, piety, and precedent. Furthermore, because strangers do not participate fully in society, they have a certain mental detachment, causing them to see things more objectively.

Simmel approaches the role of the stranger through an analysis of the formal structures of life. In contrast, Alfred Schutz — himself an immigrant to the United States — analyzes the stranger as lacking "intersubjective understanding."[4] By this he means the reciprocity of perspectives among those from the same social world. Because this is a shared world, it is an intersubjective one. For the native, then, every social situation is a coming together not only of roles and identities, but also of shared realities — the intersubjective structure of consciousness. What is taken for granted by the native is problematic to the stranger. In a familiar world, people live through the day by responding to daily routine without questioning or reflection. To strangers, however, every situation is new and is therefore experienced as a crisis.

Strangers experience a "lack of historicity" — a lack of the shared memory of those with whom they live. Human beings who interact together over a period of time "grow old together"; strangers, however, are "young," being newcomers, and they experience at least an approximation of the freshness of childhood. They are aware of things that go unnoticed by the natives, such as their customs, social institutions, appearance, and life style.

Sometimes the stranger may be the comical butt of jokes because of unfamiliarity with the everyday routine of life in this new setting. In time, however, strangers take on the natives' perspective; the strangers' consciousness is lowered because the freshness of their perceptions is lost. Also, the natives' abstract typifications about the strangers become more concrete through social interaction. As Schutz says, "The vacant frames become occupied by vivid experiences." As acculturation takes place, the native begins to view the stranger more concretely and the stranger becomes less questioning about daily activities. Use of the term *naturalized citizen* takes on a curious connotation when examined from this perspective, as it implies that people are in some way odd or unnatural until they have taken on the characteristics of the natives.

As its title suggests, this book is about many strangers who came to the United States in search of a better life. Through an examination of sociological theory and the experiences of many racial and ethnic groups, the story of how the stranger perceives and is received will be continually retold. The adjustment from stranger to neighbor may be viewed as movement along a continuum, but this continuum is not cyclical nor is assimilation inevitable. Rather, it is the process of social interaction among different groups of people.

ETHNOCENTRISM

An understanding of the concept of the stranger is important in order to understand *ethnocentrism*, a term meaning the "view of things in which one's own group is the center of everything, and all others are scaled and rated with reference to it."[5] Ethnocentrism thus refers to people's tendency to identify with their own ethnic or national group as a means of fulfilling their needs for group belongingness and security. (The word is derived from two Greek words: *ethnos*, meaning nation, and *kentron*, meaning center.) As a result of ethnocentrism, people usually view their own cultural values as somehow more real and thus superior to those of other groups, and they prefer their own way of doing things. Unfortunately for human relations, such ethnocentric thought is often extended until it negatively affects attitudes and emotions toward those who are perceived as different.

Sociologists define *ingroup* as a group to which individuals belong and feel loyalty; thus everyone — whether a member of a majority group or a minority group — is part of an ingroup. *Outgroups* are defined, in relation to ingroups, as groups consisting of all people who are not members of one's ingroup. Studying majority groups as ingroups helps to understand their reactions to strangers of another race or culture entering their society. Similarly, considering minority groups as ingroups enables us to understand their efforts to maintain their ethnic identity and solidarity in the midst of the dominant culture.

There is ample evidence about people from past civilizations who have regarded other cultures as inferior, incorrect, or immoral. This assumption that *we* are better than *they* generally results in outgroups becoming objects of ridicule, contempt, or hatred. Such attitudes may lead to stereotyping, prejudice, discrimination, and even violence. What actually does occur depends upon many factors, including structural and economic conditions, which will be discussed in subsequent chapters.

Despite its ethnocentric beliefs, the ingroup does not *always* view the outgroup as inferior. There are numerous documented cases of groups who have retained their values and standards while recognizing the superiority of another group in some specific areas.[6] Also, countless people reject their own ingroup by being "voluntary exiles, expatriates, outgroup emulators, social climbers, renegades, and traitors."[7] An outgroup may become a *positive reference group* — that is, it may serve as an exemplary model — if members of the ingroup perceive it as having a conspicuous advantage over them in terms of survival or adaptation to the environment, success in warfare, a stronger political structure, greater wealth, or a higher occupational status.[8]

Ethnocentrism is an important factor in determining minority-group status in society, but because of many variations in intergroup relations, it alone cannot explain the causes of prejudice. For example, majority-group members may view minority groups with suspicion, but not all minority groups become the targets of extreme prejudice and discrimination.

Some social-conflict theorists argue that when the ingroup perceives the outgroup as a real threat competing for scarce resources, the ingroup reacts with increased solidarity, ethnocentrism, and hostility toward the outgroup.[9] According to this view, ethnocentrism can lead to prejudice, discrimination, and hostility, the degree of which depends upon several economic and geographic considerations. It would thus appear that ethnocentrism leads to negative consequences when the ingroup feels threatened. One counterargument to this view would be that ethnocentric attitudes — thinking that because others are different, they are thus a threat — initially caused the problem. However, the major difficulty with this approach is that it does not explain variations in the frequency, type, or intensity of intergroup conflict from one society to the next or between different immigrant groups and the ingroup.

IN THE UNITED STATES

An ethnocentric attitude is often not deliberate, but instead an outgrowth of growing up and living within a familiar environment. Consider, for example, that Americans have labeled their major-league

❦❦❦

FIGURE 1.1

"FREE TRADE LUNCH"

The immigrant laborer was seen as an economic threat. Here English, Italian, Mexican, Russian, and German immigrants are shown devouring meat, which symbolizes American workingmen's wages, and bread, which symbolizes prosperity. In the background, immigrants are shown preventing the American laborer from entering the restaurant to get his share of the free lunch. Cartoon appeared in *Judge*, July 28, 1888. (The Distorted Image, Anti-Defamation League. John and Selma Appel Collection)

baseball championship games a *World Series*, although until recently, not even Canadian teams were included in an otherwise exclusively United States professional sports program. *American* is another word we use — even in this book — to identify ourselves to the exclusion of people in other parts of North and South America. The Organization of American States (OAS), which consists of countries in both North and South America, should remind us that others are equally entitled to call themselves Americans.

At one point in this country's history, many state and national leaders identified their expansionist goals as a "manifest destiny," as if Divine Providence had ordained specific boundaries for the United States. Indeed, many a member of the clergy has preached a fiery sermon over the years regarding God's special plans for this country, and all presidents have invoked the Deity in their inaugural addresses for special assistance to this country.

IN OTHER TIMES AND LANDS

Throughout history, people of many cultures have demonstrated an ethnocentric view of the world. For example, the British once believed they were obliged to carry the "white man's burden" in "civilizing" the nonwestern world. Yet two thousand years earlier, the Romans thought natives of Britain to be an inferior people, as indicated in this excerpt from a letter written by the orator Cicero to his friend Atticus:

> Do not obtain your slaves from Britain because they are so stupid and so utterly incapable of being taught that they are not fit to form a part of the household of Athens.

The Greeks, whose civilization predated the Roman Empire, considered all those around them — Persians, Egyptians, Macedonians, and others — distinctly inferior and called them barbarians (*barbarikos*), a Greek word describing those who did not speak Greek as making noises that sounded like *bar-bar*.

Religious chauvinism blended with ethnocentrism in the Middle Ages when the Crusaders, spurred on by their beliefs, considered it their duty to free the Holy Land from the control of the "infidels." They traveled a great distance, by land and sea, taking with them horses, armor, and armaments, to wrest control from the native inhabitants because the "infidels" had the audacity to follow the teachings of Mohammed rather than Jesus. On their journey across Europe, the Crusaders slaughtered Jews (whom they incorrectly labeled "Christ-killers"), regardless of whether they were men, women, or children, all in the name of the Prince of Peace. The Crusaders looked upon both Moslems and Jews as inferior peoples as well as enemies.

In the following passage, Brewton Berry offers several other examples of ethnocentric thinking in past times:

> Some writers have attributed the superiority of their people to favorable geographical influences, but others incline to a biological explanation. The Roman, Vitruvius, maintained that those who live in southern climates have the keener intelligence, due to the rarity of the atmosphere, whereas "northern nations, being enveloped in a dense atmosphere, and chilled by moisture from the obstructing air, have but a sluggish intelligence." A certain Ibn Khaldun argued that the Arabians were the superior people, because their country, although in a warm zone, was surrounded by water, which exerted a cooling effect. Bodin, in the sixteenth century, found an astrological explanation for ethnic group differences. The planets, he thought, exerted their combined and best influence upon that section of the globe occupied by France, and the French, accordingly, were destined by nature to be the masters of the world. Needless to say, Ibn Khaldun was an Arab, and Bodin a Frenchman. The Italian, Sergi, regarded the Mediterranean peoples as the true bearers of civilization and insisted that Germans and Asiatics only destroy what the Mediterraneans create. In like manner, the superiority of Nordics, Alpines, Teutons, Aryans, and others has been asserted by those who were members of each of these groups, or thought they were.[10]

Anthropologists, in examining the cultures of other peoples, have identified countless instances of ethnocentric attitudes. One frequent practice has been in geographic reference and map making. There have, for example, been commercially prepared Australian world maps that depicted that continent in the center in relation to the rest of the world.

> There is nothing unusual about this type of thinking: the Chinese, who called their country the Middle Kingdom, were convinced that China was the center of the world, and similar beliefs were held by other nations — and are still held. The British drew the Prime Meridian of longitude to run through Greenwich, near London. Europeans drew maps of the world with Europe at the center, Americans with the New World at the center.[11]

Ethnocentrism is more than just a group-centered approach to living. It is also of utmost significance in understanding motivation, attitudes, and behavior when members of racially or ethnically distinct groups interact.

BEHAVIOR

Contrary to popular belief, most forms of social behavior are not "natural." We learn how to do things through the socialization process, which propagates cultural values, attitudes, customs, and beliefs. We even satisfy our hunger and sexual needs in culturally determined ways.

Certain American Indian tribes consider dog stew a fine delicacy to serve honored guests, although someone from a different culture may not find the prospect of such a meal very appetizing. Many Americans eat beef and pork, much to the chagrin of Hindus and Orthodox Jews, respectively. Westerners may find distasteful the Chinese fondness for aged, foul-smelling eggs, but the Chinese may find equally repugnant the Westerners' fondness for aged, foul-smelling milk, better known as cheese. Others enjoy eating raw fish, cooked squid, eel, snake, or insects, to the clear disgust of still others.

Incest has not been an acceptable practice in most societies, but certain cultures have considered it critically important, as, for example, did the pharaohs of ancient Egypt. During the Eighteenth Dynasty, the daughter inherited the throne, and the son acquired title to the throne by marrying his sister.[12] Many Americans do not condone extramarital affairs, although they occur in our society, and many resent women being treated as sex objects. However, among the central Eskimo peoples of Alaska and the Bahimas of East Africa, a man would be branded a poor host if he did not share his wife (or wives) with his overnight guest.

Therefore, what we consider "proper" behavior, or "pleasurable," or "right," or "wrong," does not necessarily correspond to what others believe. What we consider to be "natural" is more likely to be culturally prescribed. Yet our ethnocentric judgment of behavior different from our own, including such basic areas as eating and sex, often results in our branding the behavior with such labels as "strange," "inferior," "disgusting," or "immoral." Although some of the behavior one would regard as most exotic is practiced by peoples who are rather isolated from the rest of the world, the United States itself, as the greatest receiving nation of immigrants, has always comprised many diverse types of people who have had varying orientations to living.

The diversity of culturally learned behavior patterns is interesting in itself, but what happens when different groups interact? Sociologists are interested in why prejudicial attitudes and discriminatory actions may or may not arise when groups whose actions or appearances differ come into contact with one another. What factors influence attitudes, expectations, and behavior toward the other group? Numerous theories and findings about such matters exist, and these will be examined in this book.

OBJECTIVITY

When discussing people, usually those who are different from ourselves, it is not unusual for us to offer our own assumptions and opinions more readily than in some other area such as statistics or biology. But if we are to undertake a sociological study of ethnicity, we must question our assumptions and opinions — everything we have always believed without question. How can we scientifically investigate a problem if we have already reached a conclusion?

Sociologists attempt to examine group relationships objectively, but it is impossible to exclude their own subjectivity altogether. All human beings have values, which influence their orientations, actions, reactions, and interpretations. For example, selecting intergroup relations as an area of interest and concern, emphasizing the sociological perspective of this subject, and the thematic organization of the material in this book all represent value judgments regarding priorities.

Although neutrality of values may be impossible to attain (and many would even argue that it is undesirable), it is nevertheless most important that the reader exercise a conscientious effort to maintain an open mind in order to examine this subject as objectively as is humanly possible. You must be aware of your own strong feelings about these matters and be willing to examine new concepts, even if they challenge previously held beliefs. To study this subject properly, you should try to be a stranger in your familiar world. Look at everything as if you were seeing it for the first time, trying to understand how and why it is, rather than just taking it for granted.

Trying to be objective about race and ethnic relations presents a strong challenge. People tend to use selective perception, accepting only information that agrees with their values or interpreting information so that it remains consistent with their attitudes about other groups. Many variables in life influence people's subjectivity about minority relations. Some views may be based upon personal or emotional considerations, or even upon false premises. However, sometimes quite reasonable and responsible people disagree on the matter in an unemotional way. Whatever the situation, the study of minority-group relations poses a challenge for objective examination.

The subject of race and ethnic relations is a very complex one, and it touches our lives in many ways. All who are reading this book must face the realization that they are in fact coming to this subject with preconceived notions. Because many individuals have a strong tendency to "tune out" disagreeable information, the reader must make a continual, conscientious effort to remain open-minded and receptive to new data.

A SOCIOLOGICAL PERSPECTIVE

Sociology is the study of human relationships and patterns of behavior. Through scientific investigation, sociologists seek to determine the social forces that influence behavior, as well as the recurring patterns through which they can better understand that behavior.

When two different groups of people come into contact with one another, many possible forms of interaction can occur, ranging from open conflict to close cooperation. The initial relationship, whatever it is, may later change or become even more solidly entrenched. For instance, the two groups may adopt some of each other's culture and intermarry. In contrast, they may live separately in the same area, with one group dominant over the other and with continuing prejudice and hostility toward one another. These examples do not exhaust the possibilities, of course, but they do illustrate various behavior patterns and indicate that behavior might change over a period of time.

Using historical documents, reports, surveys, ethnographies, journalistic materials, and direct observation, the sociologist systematically gathers empirical evidence about such intergroup relations. The sociologist then analyzes these data in an effort to discover and describe the causes, functions, relationships, meanings, and consequences of intergroup harmony or tension. Ascertaining reasons for the beginning, continuance, intensification, or alleviation of readily observable patterns of behavior among different peoples is a complex and difficult matter, and not all sociologists concur in interpreting the data. Different theories, ideas, concepts, and even ideologies and prejudices may also influence a sociologist's conclusions.

Disagreement among sociologists about the best means of explaining a particular phenomenon is not unusual. Conflicting theories to explain known facts arise for several reasons, including judgmental or philosophical differences. A *judgmental difference* refers to several people viewing the same thing differently, much like an argument in sports over a close call. A *philosophical difference* suggests that the different observers may approach data interpretation with their own predetermined orientation. The latter possibility again illustrates how people's frames of reference may influence their views, whether the people are students or sociologists.

Recently, two major and opposing schools of thought — the functionalist and the conflict schools — have influenced attempts to explain human behavior. Proponents of the *functionalist* school believe that a stable, cooperative social system is the basis of a society, and that conflict is either dysfunctional for it or else a temporary maladjustment to an otherwise interdependent, relatively harmonious society. Without denying the existence of problems or conflicts, they believe that the members of a society stick together to function effectively. The *conflict* school, on the other hand, sees society as constantly in a series of clashes, with peaceful cooperation only a temporary interlude. Influenced by the Hegelian dialectical process (the theory that change occurs through the meeting of opposing forces of any kind) and by Marxian dialectical materialism (the theory that class conflict between property owners and workers eventually leads to socialism), this sociological approach views conflict as the process through which social change occurs. Some sociologists do not see any dichotomy between the order and the conflict theories of society, for each must also explain the times when the other is present.

A third approach, the *interactionist* perspective, does not focus on the larger social institutions and societal processes of stability and change. Instead, it concentrates on fundamental social processes and the more minute, personal aspects of everyday life. *Symbolic interaction*, the use of signs, gestures, shared rules, and language in human interaction, is studied to understand how people create and interpret the situations they experience. Although the interactionist perspective concerns itself only with the microsocial world of interpersonal relations, it does offer meaningful insight into the dynamics of intergroup relations.

In this text, the student can utilize each of these perspectives to come to an understanding of the experiences of various racial and ethnic groups in the United States.

MINORITY GROUPS

Although the term *group* is commonly used to refer collectively to a racial or ethnic people, it is a very problematic word. *Group*, in its sociological usage, usually connotes a small, closely interacting set of persons. The term *minorities* sometimes refers to aggregates of millions of persons, clearly a size even larger than a *secondary* group, people who interact on an impersonal or limited emotional basis for some practical or specific purpose. Nonetheless, *group* is a familiar term to most readers, and with the above caveat in mind, I shall use that term throughout this book in referring to racial and ethnic groupings.

Sociologists use the term *minority* to designate not a group's numerical representation, but rather its relative power and status in a society. The term was first used in the World War I peace treaties to protect approximately 22 million out of 110 million people in East Central Europe, but it was most frequently used as a description of biological features or national traits. Donald Young in 1932 thus observed that Americans make distinctions among people according to race and national origin.[13]

Louis Wirth expanded Young's original conception of minority groups to include the consequences of those distinctions: group consciousness and differential treatment.[14] The significance of Wirth's contribution was that it marked two important turning points in sociological inquiry. First, by broadening the definition to include any physical or cultural trait instead of just race or national origin, he enlarged the range of variables to include also the aged, handicapped, members of various religions or sects, and groups with unconventional life styles. Second, his emphasis upon the social consequences of minority status leads to a focus on prejudice, discrimination, and oppression. Not everyone agrees with this approach. Richard Schermerhorn, for example, notes that this "victimological" approach does not adequately explain the similarities and differences among groups or analyze relationships between majority and minority groups.[15]

A third attempt to define minority groups rests upon examining relationships between groups in terms of each group's position in the social hierarchy.[16] This approach stresses a group's social power, which may vary from one country to another, as, for example, does that of the Jews in the Soviet Union and in Israel. The emphasis upon stratification instead of population size explains situations in which a small-sized group subjugates a larger number of people (for example, the European colonization of African and Asian populations). A variation on this viewpoint is represented by Schermerhorn. He also viewed social power as an important variable in the determination of a group's position in the hierarchy, but he believed that other factors were equally important. Size (a minority group must be less than one-half the population), ethnicity (as defined by Wirth's physical and cultural traits), and group consciousness also help to define a minority group.[17]

In this book, I shall use the concepts of social power and group distinction when referring to minority groups to understand better the relations between superordinate and subordinate groups as well as the ways in which various groups are similar to or different from one another. *Minority groups*, then, are groups of people lacking social power and varying from the dominant group in their physical or cultural traits, or both.

ETHNIC GROUPS

The meanings of the terms *ethnic group* and *race* have often been confused. The distinction, however, is clear enough: a *race* is a biologically similar group; an *ethnic group* has the same cultural heritage. Ethnic groups have a sense of peoplehood based upon national origin as well as upon language, religion, and other cultural attributes. Although *race* and *ethnic group* are different in meaning, they are not mutually exclusive. Sometimes a race consists of several ethnic groups and, similarly, an ethnic group may embrace one or more races.

The word *race* is often incorrectly used as a social rather than a biological concept. Thus, the British and Japanese are often classified as races, as are Hindus, Latins, Aryans, Gypsies, Arabs, American Indians, Basques, and Jews.[18] Many people, even sociologists, anthropologists, and psychologists, use *race* as the general rubric to include both racial and ethnic groups, thereby giving the term both a biological and a social meaning. Recently, *ethnic group* has been used more frequently as the general rubric to include the three elements of race, religion, and national origin.[19] Needless to say, the misuse and reuse of these terms result in endless confusion.

In this book, the word *race* will refer to biological distinctions such as skin color, hair texture, eye shape, and so on. If a sociologist has used this term but actually means both racial and ethnic groups, I will bring that point to the reader's attention. Similarly, the term *ethnic* group will refer only to social groupings that the superordinate group considers unique because of religious, linguistic, or cultural characteristics. If a sociologist has used this word but means to include racial groups also, I will make this clear. Both terms will be used when discussing groups with an overlapping of racial and ethnic characteristics.

THE DYNAMICS OF INTERGROUP RELATIONS

The study of intergroup relations is both fascinating and challenging because they are continually changing. The patterns of relating may change for many reasons: industrialization, urbanization, shifts in migration patterns, social movements, upward or downward economic trends, and so on. However, sometimes the changing relationships also reflect changing attitudes, as, for example, the interaction between the whites and the American Indians. There was a continually changing emphasis: exploitation, extermination, isolation, segregation, paternalism, forced assimilation, and, more recently, tolerance for pluralism and restoration of certain, but not all, Indian ways. Similarly, blacks, Asians, Jews, Catholics, and other minority groups have all had varying relations with the host society.

Some recent world events also illustrate changing orientations toward minority groups. After years of relatively harmonious relations, Ugandan leader Idi Amin became hostile to his country's Asian population and expelled it. After England experienced a large influx of dark-skinned West-Indian people, the resulting numerous racial incidents and economic reversals led to restrictions on the immigration of this group. Internal and external pressures forced Rhodesia and South Africa to reassess their treatment of blacks as these oppressed people became more militant. After years of paternalism in those two countries, a previously static situation grew tense and uncertain, with blacks in Rhodesia gaining political power. Christians and Moslems in Lebanon, Arabs and Jews in the Middle East, and Protestants and Catholics in Northern Ireland all go through varying periods of stability and instability in their dealings with one another. Another vivid example of world events influencing one group's orientation toward another is the Americans' hostility against Iranians in the United States following the seizing of American hostages at the U.S. Embassy in Iran in November 1979.

The field of race and ethnic relations is alive with theoreticians and investigators. Each year a vast outpouring of information from papers presented at meetings and from articles, books, and other sources adds to our knowledge. New insights, new concepts, and new interpretations of old knowledge inundate the interested observer. What both the sociologist and the student must attempt to understand, therefore, is not a fixed and static phenomenon, but rather a dynamic, ever changing one, about which more is still being learned.

QUESTIONS FOR DISCUSSION

1. What is the difference between a race and an ethnic group? between a minority group and an ethnic group?
2. What is ethnocentrism and why is it important in relations between dominant and minority groups?
3. Why is the objective study of racial and ethnic minorities a difficult matter?

NOTES

1. See C. Bowman, "Must the Social Sciences Foster Moral Skepticism?" *American Sociological Review*, 10 (December 1945), 709–715; Dan W. Dodson, "The Creative Role of Conflict Reexamined," *The Journal of Intergroup Relations*, 1 (Winter 1959–1960), 5; Robert Friedricks, *A Sociology of Sociology*, Macmillan, New York, 1970; Larry Reynolds (ed.), *The Sociology of Sociology*, McKay, New York, 1970.
2. Lyn H. Lofland, *A World of Strangers*, Basic Books, New York, 1973, p. 16.
3. Georg Simmel, "The Stranger," in *The Sociology of Georg Simmel*, ed. Kurt H. Wolff, Free Press, New York, 1950.
4. Alfred Schutz, "The Stranger," *American Sociological Review*, 69 (May 1944), 449–507.

5. William Graham Sumner, *Folkways*, Ginn, Boston, 1906, p. 13.
6. See Marc J. Schwartz, "Negative Ethnocentrism," *Journal of Conflict Resolution*, 5 (March 1961), 75–81.
7. Robin M. Williams, Jr., *Strangers Next Door*, Prentice-Hall, Englewood Cliffs, N.J., 1964, p. 23.
8. Robert A. Levine and Donald T. Campbell, *Ethnocentrism: Theories of Conflict, Ethnic Attitudes, and Group Behavior*, Wiley, New York, 1972, pp. 68, 202.
9. Kenneth E. Boulding, *Conflict and Defense: A General Theory*, Harper, New York, 1962, pp. 162–163; Lewis A. Coser, *Sociological Theory: A Book of Readings*, Macmillan, New York, 1957, pp. 87–110; P. C. Rosenblatt, "Origins and Effects of Group Ethnocentrism and Nationalism," *Journal of Conflict Resolution*, 8 (1964), 131–146; M. Sherif and C. W. Sherif, *Groups in Harmony and Tension*, Harper, New York, 1953, p. 196.
10. Brewton Berry, *Race and Ethnic Relations*, 3rd ed., Houghton Mifflin, Boston, 1965, p. 55.
11. Morton Klass and Hal Hellman, *The Kinds of Mankind*, Lippincott, New York, 1971, p. 61.
12. Immanuel Velikovsky, *Oedipus and Akhnaton*, Doubleday, New York, 1960, p. 96.
13. Donald Young, *American Minority Peoples*, Harper and Row, New York, 1932, p. viii.
14. Louis Wirth, "The Problem of Minority Groups," in *The Science of Man in the World Crisis*, ed. Ralph Linton, Columbia University Press, New York, 1945.
15. Richard Schermerhorn, *Comparative Ethnic Relations*, Random House, New York, 1970, p. 8.
16. Tamotsu Shibutani and Kian M. Kwan, *Ethnic Stratification*, Macmillan, New York, 1965.
17. Schermerhorn, *Comparative Ethnic Relations*, p. 12.
18. Brewton Berry and Henry L. Tischler, *Race and Ethnic Relations*, 4th ed., Houghton Mifflin, Boston, 1978, pp. 30–32.
19. Milton Gordon, *Assimilation in American Life*, Oxford University Press, New York, 1964, p. 27; Shibutani and Kwan, *Ethnic Stratification*, p. 47; Jerry D. Rose, *Peoples: The Ethnic Dimension in Human Relations*, Rand McNally, Chicago, 1976, pp. 8–12.

TWO

MAJORITY-MINORITY RELATIONS

⚞When strangers from different groups come into contact with one another, their interrelationships may take several forms. The nature of their social interaction depends upon many variables. This book stresses particularly (1) the values and attitudes prevailing among members of both the majority and minority groups; (2) the degree of physical, cultural, and social-class differences between the groups; and (3) the structural conditions within the society, particularly the distribution of resources and power. This chapter examines the various patterns of behavior that may emerge when prejudice and discrimination become the basis of interaction.

PREJUDICE

The word *prejudice* is derived from the Latin word *praejudicium* and originally meant prejudgment. Thus some scholars defined a prejudiced person as one who hastily reached a conclusion before examining the facts.[1] However, this definition proved inadequate because social scientists discovered that prejudice often arose *after* groups came into contact and had at least some knowledge of one another. For that reason, Louis Wirth described prejudice as "an attitude with an emotional bias."[2]

Because feelings shape our attitudes, they reduce our receptivity to additional information that may alter those attitudes. Ralph Rosnow had this fact in mind when he broadened the definition of prejudice to encompass "any unreasonable attitude that is unusually resistant to rational influence."[3] In fact, a deeply prejudiced person is one who is almost totally immune to information. Gordon Allport offers a classic example of such an individual in the following dialogue:

Mr. X: The trouble with the Jews is that they only take care of their own group.

Mr. Y: But the record of the Community Chest campaign shows that they gave more generously, in proportion to their numbers, to the general charities of the community, than did non-Jews.

Mr. X: That shows they are always trying to buy favor and intrude into Christian affairs. They think of nothing but money; that is why there are so many Jewish bankers.

Mr. Y: But a recent study shows that the percentage of Jews in the banking business is negligible, far smaller than the percentage of non-Jews.

Mr. X: That's just it; they don't go in for respectable business; they are only in the movie business or run night clubs.[*]

---

*Gordon W. Allport, *The Nature of Prejudice*, 1954, Addison–Wesley, Reading, Mass., pp. 13–14.

It is almost as if Mr. X is saying, "My mind is made up; don't confuse me with the facts." He does not refute the argument; rather, he ignores the new and contradictory information, and moves on to a new area in which he distorts other facts to support his prejudice against Jews.

Prejudicial attitudes may be either positive or negative; however, negative prejudice is of primary concern to the sociologist studying minorities because only negative attitudes can lead to turbulent social relations between dominant and minority groups. Numerous writers, therefore, have defined prejudice as an attitudinal "system of negative beliefs, feelings, and action-orientations regarding a certain group or groups of people."[4] The status of the strangers is an important factor in the development of a negative attitude. Prejudicial attitudes exist among members of both the dominant and minority groups. In seeking to understand the nature of relations between dominant and minority groups, it is important to realize that the antipathy felt between groups is quite often prevalent on both sides.

LEVELS OF PREJUDICE

Bernard Kramer suggests that prejudice exists on three levels: cognitive, emotional, and action-orientation.[5]

COGNITIVE LEVEL The *cognitive level* refers to a person's beliefs and perceptions of a group as threatening or nonthreatening, inferior or equal (for example, in terms of intellect, status, or biological composition), seclusive or intrusive, impulse-gratifying, acquisitive, or possessing other positive or negative characteristics. Mr. X's cognitive beliefs are that Jews are intrusive and acquisitive. Other illustrations of cognitive beliefs are that the Irish are heavy drinkers and fighters, blacks are musical and lazy, and the Polish are thick-headed and unintelligent. Generalizations shape both ethnocentric and prejudicial attitudes, but there is a difference. *Ethnocentrism* is a generalized rejection of all outgroups based on an ingroup focus, whereas *prejudice* is a rejection of certain people based solely upon their membership in a particular group or groups.

In many societies, majority-group members often believe that a particular low-status minority group is "dirty," "immoral," "violent," or "law-breaking." In the United States, the Irish, Italians, blacks, Mexicans, Chinese, Puerto Ricans, and others have at one time or another been labeled with most, if not all, of the above adjectives. In most European countries and the United States, the group that was lowest on the socioeconomic ladder has often been depicted in caricature as also lowest on the evolutionary ladder. The Irish and blacks in the United

States, peasants and ethnic groups in Europe, have each been pictured at one time as apelike in cruel jokes and cartoons.

> The Victorian images of the Irish as "white Negro" and simian Celt, or a combination of the two, derived much of its force and inspiration from physiognomical beliefs . . . [but] every country in Europe had its equivalent of "white Negroes" and simianized men, whether or not they happened to be stereotypes of criminals, assassins, political radicals, revolutionaries, Slavs, gypsies, Jews or peasants.[6]

EMOTIONAL LEVEL   The *emotional level* refers to the feelings that a minority group arouses in an individual. Although these feelings may be based upon stereotypes from the cognitive level, they represent a more intense stage of personal involvement. The emotional attitudes may be negative or positive, such as fear, distrust, trust, disgust, sympathy, nonsympathy, contempt, admiration, envy, or anger. These feelings, based upon beliefs about the group or groups, may come about through social interaction or the possibility of interaction. For example, whites might react with fear or anger to the integration of their schools or neighborhoods, or Protestants might be jealous of the life style of a highly successful Catholic business executive.

ACTION-ORIENTATION LEVEL   An *action-orientation* is the positive or negative predisposition to engage in discriminatory behavior. If someone harbors strong feelings about members of a certain racial or ethnic group, that individual may have a tendency to act for or against them — being aggressive or nonaggressive, offering assistance or withholding it. Such individuals would also be likely to want to exclude or include members of that group both in their close, personal social relations and in their peripheral social relations. For example, some people would want to exclude members of the disliked group from doing business with them or living in their neighborhood. Another manifestation of the action-orientation level of prejudice is the desire to change or maintain the status differential or inequality between the two groups, whether the area be economic, political, educational, social, or a combination. Note that an action-orientation refers to a predisposition to act, not the action itself.

STEREOTYPING

One of the most common reactions to strangers is broad categorization of them. Prejudice at the cognitive level is often the result of false perceptions of others, which are enhanced by stereotypes, either cultural or

FIGURE 2.1

"MUTUAL: BOTH ARE GLAD THERE ARE BARS BETWEEN 'EM!"

This visual stereotype of an apelike Irishman reinforced prevailing beliefs that the Irish were emotionally unstable and morally primitive. Cartoon appeared in *Judge*, November 7, 1891. (The Distorted Image, Anti-Defamation League. John and Selma Appel Collection)

racial. A *stereotype* is an oversimplified generalization by which we attribute certain traits or characteristics to any person in a group without regard to individual differences. Most cultural stereotypes emphasize variance from societal norms. Racial stereotypes suggest that there are peculiarities about certain traits or characteristics that are hereditary and will thus continue, regardless of what society does. Both forms of stereotypes are doubly abusive. Not only do they deny an individual the right to be judged and treated on the basis of merit, but by being applied to the image of the entire group, they become a justification for discriminatory behavior.

Negative stereotypes also serve as important reference points in people's evaluations of what they observe in everyday life. Following is an excellent illustration of how we attribute motives and causes that are consistent with our stereotypes to other people's behavior:

> Prejudiced people see the world in ways that are consistent with their prejudice. If Mr. Bigot sees a well-dressed, white, Anglo-Saxon Protestant sitting on a park bench sunning himself at three o'clock on a Wednesday afternoon, he thinks nothing of it. If he sees a well-dressed black man doing the same thing, he is liable to leap to the conclusion that the person is unemployed — and he becomes infuriated, because he assumes that his hard-earned taxes are paying that shiftless good-for-nothing enough in welfare subsidies to keep him in good clothes. If Mr. Bigot passes Mr. Anglo's house and notices that a trash can is overturned and some garbage is strewn about, he is apt to conclude that a stray dog has been searching for food. If he passes Mr. Garcia's house and notices the same thing, he is inclined to become annoyed, and to assert that "those people live like pigs." Not only does prejudice influence his conclusions, his erroneous conclusions justify and intensify his negative feelings.[7]

In 1932, David Katz and Kenneth Braly conducted one of the earliest studies of the prevalence of ethnic stereotypes.[8] From a list of eighty-five characteristics, they asked some Princeton undergraduates to select five that were most representative of different racial and ethnic groups. The high level of agreement in selecting group characteristics, sometimes exceeding 50 percent, indicated the existence of pervasive generalizations about various peoples. Some of the most common stereotypes were as follows:

1. Americans are industrious (48%), intelligent (47%), and materialistic (33%)

2. Blacks are superstitious (84%), lazy (75%), and happy-go-lucky (38%)

3. Chinese are superstitious (74%), sly (29%), and conservative (29%)

4. Germans are scientifically minded (78%), industrious (65%), and stolid (44%)

5. Irish are pugnacious (45%), quick-tempered (39%), and witty (38%)

6. Italians are artistic (53%), impulsive (44%), and passionate (37%)

7. Japanese are intelligent (45%), industrious (43%), and progressive (24%)

8. Jews are shrewd (79%), mercenary (49%), and industrious (48%)

Once established, stereotypes are difficult to eradicate, even among succeeding generations when structural conditions may have changed. G. M. Gilbert tested a new generation of Princeton undergraduates in 1951 and reported similar findings, except that several stereotyped characteristics appeared to be fading in their pervasiveness.[9] When Marvin Karlins, Thomas L. Coffman, and Gary Walters conducted a third study of Princeton undergraduates in 1967, they found that although many students were reluctant to make such generalizations, considerable agreement still existed about the characteristics.[10] Those characteristics that Gilbert thought to be less pervasive had now either increased in the frequency chosen or been replaced by other similar characteristics. Additionally, students still showed a tendency to agree on the same generalizations others had chosen in previous studies. Here are some of the most common stereotypes from the 1967 study:

1. Americans are materialistic (67%), ambitious (42%), pleasure-loving (28%), and industrious (23%)

2. Blacks are musical (47%), happy-go-lucky (27%), pleasure-loving (26%), and lazy (26%)

3. Chinese are loyal to family ties (50%), tradition-loving (32%), industrious (23%), and quiet (23%)

4. Germans are industrious (59%), scientifically minded (47%), efficient (46%), and extremely nationalistic (43%)

5. Irish are quick-tempered (43%), extremely nationalistic (41%), very religious (27%), and tradition-loving (25%)

6. Italians are passionate (44%), pleasure-loving (33%), artistic (30%), and impulsive (28%)

7. Japanese are industrious (57%), ambitious (33%), efficient (27%), and loyal to family ties (23%)

8. Jews are ambitious (48%), materialistic (46%), intelligent (37%), and industrious (33%)

These studies have demonstrated that a substantial number of people share generalized beliefs about other groups and that these beliefs tend to remain relatively persistent through the years. Many of the characteristics checked most frequently in 1932 were essentially the same as those checked in 1951 and 1967. New adjectives may have replaced some old ones, but the similarity remains. Positive stereotypes regarding work achievement continue for Americans, Germans, Japanese, and Jews. Emotional stereotypes for Irish and Italians are repeated, blacks maintain a carefree image, and Chinese still appear committed to the past, family, and status quo.

ETHNOPHAULISMS An *ethnophaulism* is a derogatory word or expression used to describe a racial or ethnic group. This is the language of prejudice, the verbal picture of a negative stereotype. Howard J. Ehrlich believes that ethnophaulisms can be of three types: (1) disparaging nicknames (chink, dago, polack, jungle bunny, honky); (2) explicit group devaluations ("jew him down" for trying to get something for a lower price, "luck of the Irish" suggesting undeserved good fortune, "to be in Dutch" meaning to be in trouble); (3) irrelevant ethnic names used as a mild disparagement ("jewbird" for black cuckoos having prominent beaks, "Irish confetti" for bricks thrown in a fight).[11]

Although ethnophaulisms are good indications of intergroup relations and of the relationship between attitudes and actions, they have not received much scientific study. Erdman Palmore, however, did such a study and concluded that all racial and ethnic groups use ethnophaulisms. He also observed that a correlation exists between the number of them used and the degree of group prejudice, and that they express and support negative stereotypes about the most visible racial or cultural differences.[12]

Sometimes members of a racial or ethnic minority group will use an ethnophaulism directed against themselves in their conversations with one another. On occasion they may use the term as a reprimand to one of their own kind for acting out the stereotype, but more often they mean it as a humorous expression of friendship and endearment. However, when an outsider uses that same term, they resent it because of its prejudicial derision.

Through most of the 1970s the long-running television program "All in the Family" featured Archie Bunker, a confirmed bigot who continually used ethnophaulisms against a great many classifications of people. As the show popularized racial and ethnic epithets not so generally known, arguments swirled concerning whether the show encouraged or deflated bigotry. Archie mellowed somewhat as the years passed, but studies indicated that most people — particularly those groups who were Archie's targets — were, in general, favorably inclined toward the show even at its beginning.[13] This was probably because the depicted minority-group members typically bested Archie as he learned a lesson from them.

STEREOTYPES AND THE MEDIA In an era when the mass media play such an important part in so many people's lives, the images presented can either greatly prolong or help eliminate stereotypes. Aside from the obviousness of "All in the Family," or even "The Jeffersons" and "Charlie's Angels," observers have long found the media guilty of many stereotypical portrayals.[14]

In 1946, Bernard Berelson and Patricia Salter called attention to the profusion of minority stereotypes in popular magazine fiction.[15] Since that time, other studies have reported that American minorities are constantly stereotyped in the movies,[16] comic strips,[17] magazine pictures,[18] and textbooks.[19]

In August 1977, on the basis of a six-year study, the U.S. Civil Rights Commission released a highly critical report, "Window Dressing: Women and Minorities in Television." The report charged the television industry with perpetuating racial and sexual stereotypes in programming and news. Aside from the almost exclusively negative racial portrayals on police shows, the report attacked the television world for portraying "a social structure in which males are very much in control of their lives . . . older, more serious, more independent, and more likely to hold prestigious jobs. Women, on the other hand, were younger, often unemployed, more 'family bound,' and often found in comic roles. Those women who were employed were in stereotyped and sometimes subservient occupations."

CAUSES OF PREJUDICE

There appears to be no single cause of prejudice, but rather, many causes that are frequently interrelated. Because fear and suspicion of outgroups are so widespread, scholars and scientists once believed that prejudice was a natural or biological human attribute. Today, because of increased knowledge about the growth of prejudices in children and about the varying patterns of interaction throughout world history, behavioral scientists realize that prejudices are socially determined. A great many theories exist concerning exactly how we become prejudiced (Figure 2.2).

SOCIALIZATION In the socialization process, individuals acquire the values, attitudes, beliefs, and perceptions of their culture or subculture, including religion, nationality, and social class. Generally, the child conforms to the parents' expectations in acquiring an understanding of the world and its people. Being young and therefore impressionable, and knowing of no alternative conceptions of the world, the child usually accepts these concepts without questioning. We thus learn the prejudices of our parents and others, and they subtly become a part of our values and beliefs. Even if they are based on false stereotypes, prejudices shape our perceptions of various peoples and influence our attitudes

FIGURE 2.2

Self-justification

Frustration

Socialization

Social norms

Authoritarian personality

Competition

CAUSES OF PREJUDICE

and actions toward particular groups. For example, if we develop negative attitudes about Jews because we are taught that they are shrewd, acquisitive, and clannish — all-too-familiar stereotypes — as adults we may refrain from business or social relationships with them. We may not even realize the reason for such avoidance, so subtle has been the prejudice instilled within us.

People may learn certain prejudices because of their pervasiveness. The cultural screen that we develop and through which we view the world around us is not always accurate, but it does reflect shared values and attitudes, which are reinforced by others. Prejudice, like cultural values, is taught and learned through the socialization process. The prevailing prejudicial attitudes and actions are often deeply embedded in custom or law (for example, Jim Crow laws), and the new generation may accept them as proper, maintaining them in their adult lives.

Although socialization explains how prejudicial attitudes may be transmitted from one generation to the next, it does not explain their origin nor why they intensify or diminish over the years. These aspects of prejudice must be explained in another way.

Herbert Blumer suggests that prejudice always involves the notion of group position in society.[20] Prejudiced people believe that one group is inferior to another, and they place each group in a hierarchical position in society. This perception of group position is an outgrowth of the individual's experiences and understanding of them. The group stereotypes are socially approved images held by members of one group about another.[21]

SELF-JUSTIFICATION Through self-justification, we denigrate a person or group to justify our maltreatment of them. In this situation, self-justification leads to prejudice and discrimination against another's group.

Some philosophers argue that we are not so much rational creatures as we are rationalizing creatures. We require reassurance that the things we do and the lives we live are proper, that good reasons for our actions exist. If we are able to convince ourselves that another group is inferior, immoral, or dangerous, then we can feel justified in discriminating against them, enslaving them, or even killing them.

History is replete with examples of people who thought their maltreatment of others was just and necessary: As defenders of the true faith, the Crusaders killed "Christ-killers" (Jews) and "infidels" (Moslems). Participants in the Spanish Inquisition imprisoned, tortured, and executed "heretics," "the disciples of the Devil." The Puritans burned witches, whose refusal to confess "proved" they were evil. Indians were "heathen savages," blacks were "an inferior species," and thus both could be mistreated, enslaved, or killed. The civilians in the Vietnamese village of My Lai were probably aiding the Vietcong, so the soldiers felt justified in slaughtering the old men, women, and children they found there.

Some sociologists believe that self-justification works the other way around.[22] That is, instead of self-justification serving as a basis for subjugation of a people, the subjugation occurs first and the self-justification follows, resulting in prejudice and continued discrimination. The evolvement of racism as a concept after the establishment of the African slave trade would seem to support this idea. Philip Mason offers an insight into this view:

A specialized society is likely to defeat a simpler society and provide a lower tier still of enslaved and conquered peoples. The rulers and organizers sought security for themselves and their children; to perpetuate the power, the esteem, and the comfort they had achieved, it was necessary not only that the artisans and labourers should work contentedly but that the rulers should sleep without bad dreams. No one can say with certainty how the myths originated, but it is surely relevant that when one of the founders of Western thought set himself to frame an ideal state that would embody social justice, he — like the earliest city dwellers — not only devised a society stratified in tiers but believed it would be necessary to persuade the traders and work-people that, by divine decree, they were made from brass and iron, while the warriors were made of silver and the rulers of gold.[23]

Another example of self-justification serving as a cause of prejudice is the dominant group's assumption of an attitude of superiority over other groups. In this respect, establishing a prestige hierarchy — ranking the status of various ethnic groups — results in differential association. To enhance or maintain one's own self-esteem, one may avoid social contact with groups deemed inferior and associate only with those identified as being of high status. Through such behavior, self-justification may come to intensify the social distance between groups. *Social distance* refers to the degree to which ingroup members do not engage in social or primary relationships with members of various outgroups.

PERSONALITY In 1950, T. W. Adorno and his colleagues reported a correlation between individuals' early childhood experiences of harsh parental discipline and their development of authoritarian personalities as adults.[24] If parents assume an excessively domineering posture in their relations with a child, exercising stern measures and threatening the withdrawal of love if the child does not respond with weakness and submission, then the child tends to be very insecure, nurturing much latent hostility against the parents. When such children become adults, they may demonstrate *displaced aggression*, directing their hostility against a powerless group as compensation for feelings of insecurity and fear. Highly prejudiced individuals tend to come from families that emphasize obedience.

The authors identified authoritarianism by the use of a measuring instrument called an F scale (the *F* standing for potential fascism). Other tests included the A-S (anti-Semitism) and E (ethnocentrism) scales, the latter measuring attitudes toward various minorities. One of their major findings was that people who scored high on authoritarianism also consistently showed a high degree of prejudice against all minority groups. These highly prejudiced persons were characterized by rigidity of viewpoint, dislike for ambiguity, strict obedience to leaders, and intolerance of weakness in themselves or others.

No sooner did *The Authoritarian Personality* appear than controversy began. H. H. Hyman and P. B. Sheatsley challenged the methodology and analysis.[25] Solomon Asch questioned the assumptions that the F-scale responses represented a belief system and that structural variables, such as ideologies, stratification, mobility, and other social factors, do not play a role in shaping personality.[26] E. A. Shils argued that because of the leftist politics of the authors, they were only interested in measuring authoritarianism of the political right while ignoring such tendencies in those at the other end of the political spectrum.[27] Other investigators sought alternative explanations for the authoritarian personality. D. Stewart and T. Hoult extended the framework beyond family childhood experiences to include other social factors.[28] H. C. Kelman and Janet Barclay demonstrated that substantial evidence exists showing that lower intelligence and less education also correlate with high authoritarianism scores on the F scale.[29]

Despite the critical attacks, many of which were accurate, the underlying conceptions of *The Authoritarian Personality* were important, and research on personality as a factor in prejudice has continued. Subsequent investigators have refined and modified the original study. Correcting scores for response bias, they have conducted cross-cultural studies. Respondents in Germany and Near East countries, where a more authoritarian social structure exists, scored higher on authoritarianism. In Japan, Germany, and the United States, authoritarianism and social distance were moderately related. Others frequently have shown that an inverse relationship exists between social class and F-scale scores.[30]

Although the authoritarian-personality studies have been helpful in the understanding of some aspects of prejudice, they have not provided a causal explanation. Most of the findings in this area show a correlation, but the findings do not prove, for example, that harsh discipline of children *causes* them to become prejudiced adults. Perhaps the strict parents were themselves prejudiced, and the child learned those attitudes from them. Or, as George Simpson and J. Milton Yinger say,

> One must be careful not to assume too quickly that a certain tendency — rigidity of mind, for example — that is correlated with prejudice necessarily causes that prejudice. . . . The sequence may be the other way around. . . . It is more likely that both are related to more basic factors.[31]

For some people, prejudice may indeed be rooted in subconscious childhood tensions, but we simply do not know whether these tensions directly cause a high degree of prejudice in the adult or whether other powerful social forces are the determinants. Whatever the explanation, authoritarianism is a significant phenomenon and worthy of continued investigation. Recent research, however, has stressed social and situational factors, rather than personality, as important causes of prejudice and discrimination.[32]

FRUSTRATION Frustration is the result of relative deprivation in which expectations remain unsatisfied. *Relative deprivation* refers to a lack of resources, or rewards, in one's standard of living in comparison with others in the society. A number of investigators have suggested that frustrations tend to increase aggression toward others.[33] Frustrated people may easily strike out against the perceived cause of their frustration. However, this reaction is not always possible because the true source of the frustration is often too nebulous to be identified or too powerful to act against. In such instances, the result may be a displaced or free-floating aggression; in this situation, the frustrated individual or group usually redirects the aggressiveness against a more visible, vulnerable, and socially sanctioned target, one unable to strike back. Minorities meet these criteria and are thus frequently the recipients of displaced aggression by the dominant group.

Placing blame on others for something that is not their fault is known as *scapegoating*. The term comes from the ancient Hebrew custom of using a goat during the Day of Atonement as a symbol of the sins of the people. In an annual ceremony, a priest placed his hands upon the head of a goat and listed the people's sins in a symbolic transference of guilt; he then chased the goat out of the community, thereby freeing the people of sin.[34] Since those times, the powerful group has usually punished the scapegoat group rather than allowing it to escape.

There have been many instances throughout world history of minority groups serving as scapegoats, including the Christians in ancient Rome, the French Huguenots, the Jews, the Chinese, the Irish, the Japanese, the Quakers, and many more. Gordon Allport suggests that certain characteristics are necessary for a group to become a suitable scapegoat.[35] The group must be (1) highly visible in physical appearance or observable customs and actions; (2) not strong enough to strike back; (3) situated within easy access of the dominant group or, ideally, concentrated in one area; (4) a past target of hostility, for whom latent hostility still exists; and (5) the symbol of an unpopular concept.

Some groups fit this typology better than others, but racial and ethnic groups have continually been a favorite choice. Irish, Italians, Catholics, Jews, Quakers, Mormons, Chinese, Japanese, blacks, Puerto Ricans, and Chicanos have all been, at one time or another, the scapegoat in the United States. Especially in times of economic hardship, there seems to be a tendency to blame some group for the general conditions, often leading to aggressive action against the group as an expression of frustration. For example, a study by Carl Hovland and Robert Sears found that between 1882 and 1930, a definite correlation existed between a decline in the price of cotton and an increase in the number of lynchings of blacks.[36]

In several controlled experiments, sociologists have attempted to measure the validity of the scapegoat theory. Neal Miller and Richard Bugelski tested a group of young men about their feelings toward various minority groups.[37] They were re-examined about these feelings after experiencing frustration by being obliged to take a long, difficult test and denied an opportunity to see a film at a local theater. This group showed some evidence of increased prejudicial feelings, whereas a control group, which did not experience any frustration, showed no change in prejudicial attitudes.

Donald Weatherley conducted an experiment with a group of college students to measure the relationship between frustration and aggression against a specific disliked group.[38] After identifying students who were or were not highly anti-Semitic and subjecting them to a strong frustrating experience, he asked the students to write stories about pictures shown to them. Some of the students were shown pictures of people who had been given Jewish names; other students were presented with pictures of unnamed people. When the pictures were unidentified, no difference appeared between the stories of the anti-Semitic students and those of other students. However, when the pictures were identified, the anti-Semitic students wrote stories reflecting much more aggression against the Jews in the pictures than did the other students. Frustration had led to aggression against an identifiable group, predetermined to have been disliked beforehand, but frustration did not increase aggression against any specific group when it had not been identified.

Talcott Parsons suggests that the family and the occupational system are both likely to produce anxieties and insecurities that create frustration.[39] According to this view, the growing-up process (gaining parental affection and approval, identifying with and imitating sexual role

FIGURE 2.3

Bandits' roost, 39½ Mulberry Street, circa 1888. (Photograph by Jacob A.
Riis, Jacob A. Riis Collection, Museum of the City of New York)

models, competing with others in adulthood) may involve severe emotional strain. The result is an adult personality with a large reservoir of repressed aggression that becomes *free-floating* — susceptible to redirection against convenient scapegoats. Similarly, the occupational system is a source of frustration: its emphasis on competitiveness and individual achievement, its function of conferring status, its requirement that people inhibit their natural impulses at work, and its relationship to the state of the economy are but a few of the factors that generate emotional anxieties. Parsons pessimistically concludes that minorities fulfill a functional "need" as targets for displaced aggression and will therefore remain targets.[40]

The scapegoat is not always the weakest target. Sometimes the scapegoat is similar to the actual source of frustration and is thus perceived as an acceptable substitute. In other situations, a more powerful person or group is falsely identified as the root cause of the problem. Some presumed flaw of that scapegoat (a negative stereotype) is then used as solace by those who are frustrated: "Things may be bad, but at least I'm not deceitful like them," or "I'm not greedy," and so on.

Although the frustration-aggression theory is helpful in understanding the dynamics of prejudice, it does not explain why one group rather than another becomes the object of aggression. Most of the studies reported in this section, for example, have measured responses among people already identified as having biases, but they have not shown a causal relation between frustration and prejudice.

COMPETITION People tend to be more hostile toward others when they feel their security is threatened; thus, many social scientists conclude that economic competition and conflict breed prejudice. Certainly a great amount of evidence shows that negative stereotyping, prejudice, and discrimination increase strongly whenever competition for a limited number of jobs increases.

An excellent illustration concerns the Chinese sojourners in the nineteenth century. Prior to the 1870s, the transcontinental railroad was being built, and the Chinese filled many of the jobs made available by this project in the sparsely populated West. Although they were expelled from the gold mines and schools, having no redress of grievances in the courts, they managed to convey to some whites an image of a clean, hard-working, law-abiding people. The completion of the railroad, the flood of former Civil War soldiers into the job market, and the economic depression of 1873 worsened their situation. The Chinese were even more frequently the victims of open discrimination and hostility. Their positive stereotype among some whites became more commonly a negative one: they were now "conniving," "crafty," "criminal," "the yellow menace." Only after they retreated into Chinatowns and entered specialty occupations not in competition with whites did the intense hostility abate.

One of the early pioneers in the scientific study of prejudice, John Dollard, demonstrated how prejudice against the Germans, which had been virtually nonexistent, came about in a small American industrial town when times got bad.

> Local whites largely drawn from the surrounding farms manifested considerable direct aggression toward the newcomers. Scornful and derogatory opinions were expressed about the Germans, and the native whites had a satisfying sense of superiority toward them. . . . The chief element in the permission to be aggressive against the Germans was rivalry for jobs and status in the local woodenware plants. The native whites felt definitely crowded for their jobs by the entering German groups and in case of bad times had a chance to blame the Germans who by their presence provided more competitors for the scarcer jobs. There seemed to be no traditional pattern of prejudice against Germans unless the skeletal suspicion of all out-groupers (always present) be invoked in this place.[41]

Both experimental studies and historical analyses have added credence to the economic-competition theory. Muzafer Sherif has directed several experiments showing how intergroup competition at a boys' camp leads to conflict and escalating hostility.[42] Donald Young has shown that, throughout American history, in times with high unemployment and thus intense job competition, strong nativist movements against minorities have existed.[43] This pattern has held true regionally — with the Asians on the West Coast, the Italians in Louisiana, and the French Canadians in New England — and nationally, with the antiforeign movements always peaking during periods of depression. So it was with the Native American Party in the 1830s, the Know-Nothing Party in the 1850s, the American Protective Association in the 1890s, and the Ku Klux Klan after World War I. More recently, Andrew Greeley and Paul Sheatsley have reported that most antiblack prejudice occurs in groups that are just slightly above the blacks socioeconomically.[44] The group that applies the pressure of job competition most directly upon another group will be the target of the strongest prejudicial attitudes.

Once again, a theory offers some excellent insights into prejudice — there *is* a correlation between economic conditions and hostility toward minorities — but also has some serious shortcomings. Not all groups who have been objects of hostility have been economic competitors (for example, Quakers and Mormons). Moreover, why is there greater hostility against some groups than against others? Why do the negative feelings in some communities run against groups whose numbers are so small that they cannot possibly be an economic threat? It would appear that other values, besides economic ones, cause people to be antagonistic to a group perceived as an actual or potential threat.

SOCIAL NORMS Some sociologists have suggested that a relationship exists between prejudice and a person's tendency to conform to societal expectations.[45] *Social norms* — the norms of one's culture — provide the generally shared rules of what is and is not proper behavior; by learning and automatically accepting the prevailing prejudices, the individual is simply conforming to those norms. This theory says that there is a direct relationship between degree of conformity and degree of prejudice. If this is true, then people's prejudices would decrease or increase significantly when they move into areas where the prejudicial norm is either lesser or greater. Evidence supports this view. Thomas Pettigrew found that Southerners became less prejudiced against blacks when they interacted with them in the army, where the social norms were less prejudicial.[46] In another study, Jeanne Watson found that people moving into an anti-Semitic neighborhood in New York City became more anti-Semitic.[47]

In 1937, John Dollard published his major study, *Caste and Class in a Southern Town*, providing an in-depth look into the emotional adjustment of whites and blacks to rigid social norms.[48] In his study of the processes, functions, and maintenance of accommodation, Dollard shows how the "carrot-and-stick" method is employed. Intimidation, or sometimes even severe reprisals for going against social norms, ensures compliance. However, such actions are usually unnecessary. The advantages whites and blacks gain in psychological, economic, or behavioral terms serve to perpetuate the caste order. These gains in personal security and stability set in motion a vicious circle. They encourage a way of life that reinforces the rationale of the social system in this community.

The problem with the social-norms theory is that although it explains prevailing attitudes, it explains neither their origins nor the reasons for the development of new prejudices when other groups move into an area. In addition, the theory does not explain why prejudicial attitudes against a particular group continue to rise and fall in cyclical fashion over the years.

Although many social scientists have attempted to identify the causes of prejudice, no single factor has proven to be an adequate explanation. Prejudice is a complex phenomenon, and it is most likely to be the product of more than one causal agent. Sociologists now tend either to emphasize multiple-causation explanations or else to stress social forces at work in specific and similar situations, such as economic conditions, stratification, or hostility toward an outgroup.

CAN PREJUDICE BE REDUCED?

A great many organizations and movements whose prime objective was to reduce prejudice have existed over the years. Though they have varied in their orientation and focal point of activity, their techniques have basically been two: (1) to promote greater interaction between dominant and minority groups in all aspects of living, by either voluntary or compulsory means; and (2) to dispense information that will destroy stereotypes and expose rationalizations (self-justifications). Neither approach has been successful in all instances, probably because the inequalities that encourage such attitudes still exist.

CONTACT Contact between people of different racial and ethnic backgrounds does not necessarily lead to friendlier attitudes. In fact, the situation may worsen, as has happened frequently when schools and neighborhoods experienced the influx of a different group of people. However, many instances show that interaction reduces prejudice.[49] It would appear that a great many other variables determine the effect of contact, including the frequency and duration of contacts, the relative status of the two parties and their backgrounds, whether their meeting is voluntary or compulsory, competitive or cooperative, and whether they meet in a political, religious, occupational, residential, or recreational situation.[50]

INFORMATION Many people have long cherished the hope that education would reduce prejudice. Some studies, such as that by Gertrude Selznick and Stephen Steinberg, have found a definite correlation between level of education and degree of tolerance,[51] but other studies have not.[52] Charles Stember's research led him to conclude that more highly educated persons were not more tolerant — they were simply more sophisticated in recognizing measures of bias and more subtle in expressing their prejudices.[53] In sum, it appears that formal education is far from a perfect means of reducing prejudice. One reason for this failure is that people tend to use *selective perception*; that is, they learn information that accords with their own beliefs and rationalize away that which does not. Another reason is the almost quantum leap from the classroom to real-life situations. Dealing with prejudice from a detached perspective is one thing, but dealing with it in actuality quite another, as emotions, social pressures, and many other factors are all involved.

Despite these criticisms, courses in race and ethnic relations certainly have value in that they raise the students' level of consciousness about intergroup dynamics. However, a significant reduction or elimination of prejudice is more likely to occur by changing the structural conditions of inequality, which promote and maintain prejudicial attitudes. As

Herbert Blumer suggests, the sense of group position dissolves and racial prejudice declines when major shifts in the social order overtake the current definition of a group's characteristics.[54] So long as the dominant group does not react with fear, instituting a countermovement, the improvement of a minority's social position changes the power relations and reduces the negative stereotypes. Therefore, continued efforts at public enlightenment and extension of constitutional rights and equal opportunities to all Americans, regardless of race, religion, or national origin, appear to be the most hopeful means of attaining a prejudice-free society.

DISCRIMINATION

Prejudice is an attitude. *Discrimination* is behavior — the practice of differential and unequal treatment of other groups of people, usually along racial, religious, or ethnic lines.

Prejudice can lead to discrimination and, conversely, discrimination can lead to prejudice. Depending upon the situation, either discrimination or prejudice may cause the other, but no certainty exists that one will follow the other. Although our attitudes and our overt behavior are closely interrelated, they are not identical. We may harbor hostile feelings toward certain groups without ever making them known through word or deed. Similarly, through our overt behavior we may effectively conceal our real attitudes.

It is true that prejudiced people are more likely than others to practice discrimination; discrimination is thus quite often the overt expression of prejudice. However, it is wrong to assume that discrimination is always the acting out of prejudice. It may be instead the result of a policy decision protecting the interests of the majority group, such as the curtailment of immigration for economic reasons. It may be due to social conformity, such as when people submit to outside pressures despite their personal views.[55] Discriminators may explain their actions with reasons other than prejudice toward a particular group, and those reasons may be valid to the discriminators.

RELATIONSHIP BETWEEN PREJUDICE AND DISCRIMINATION

Robert Merton formulated a model showing the possible relationships between prejudice and discrimination. Merton demonstrates that, quite conceivably, a nonprejudiced person will discriminate and a prejudiced person will not. In his paradigm, Merton classifies four types of people according to how they accept or reject the American Creed, "the right of equitable access to justice, freedom and opportunity, irrespective of race or religion, or ethnic origin."[56]

THE NONPREJUDICED NONDISCRIMINATOR OR ALL-WEATHER LIBERAL All-weather liberals are consistent. They are neither prejudiced nor practicers of discrimination. Accordingly, they are properly motivated to illuminate others and to fight against all forms of discrimination. However, says Merton, they have their shortcomings in that they confuse discussion with action. They talk chiefly to others sharing their viewpoint, and so they deceive themselves into thinking that they represent the consensus of the community. Further, because their "own spiritual house is in order," they feel no pangs of conscience pressing them to work collectively on the problem. A counterargument would be that some all-weather liberals are activists and do speak to others with different viewpoints, thereby transforming discussion into action.

THE NONPREJUDICED DISCRIMINATOR OR FAIR-WEATHER LIBERAL Expediency is the byword for those in this category, for their actions often conflict with their personal beliefs. They may, for example, be free of racial prejudice, but they will keep silent when bigots speak out, they will not condemn acts of discrimination, and they will join in efforts to keep blacks out of their neighborhood for fear of its deterioration. These people frequently feel guilt and shame because they are acting against their beliefs.

THE PREJUDICED NONDISCRIMINATOR OR FAIR-WEATHER ILLIBERAL Merton's term "timid bigots" best describes fair-weather illiberals. They believe in many of the stereotypes about minorities and definitely feel hostility toward these groups. However, they keep silent in the presence of those who are more tolerant; they conform because they must. If there were no law or pressure to be unbiased in certain actions, they would discriminate.

THE PREJUDICED DISCRIMINATOR OR ALL-WEATHER ILLIBERAL Without doubt, such folks as the all-weather illiberals are active bigots. They have no conflict between attitudes and behavior. Not only do they openly express their beliefs, practice discrimination, and defy the law, if necessary, but they also believe that it is their duty to do so.

SUMMARY Merton's first category, the nonprejudiced nondiscriminator, is an ideal type to be understood in relation to the other categories, because everyone is prejudiced to some degree. The second and third categories, the nonprejudiced discriminator and the prejudiced nondiscriminator, are the most helpful classifications: they show that social-situational variables sometimes determine whether or not discriminatory behavior occurs; the individuals act in a manner inconsistent with their beliefs because of the pressure of group norms.

OTHER ASPECTS OF DISCRIMINATION

Discriminatory practices are frequent in the areas of employment and residence, although such actions are often covert and denied. Another dimension of discrimination, often unrealized, is *social discrimination*, or the creation of a "social distance" between groups. Simply stated, in their intimate primary relationships, people tend to associate with those of a similar ethnic background and socioeconomic level; the dominant-group members thus usually exclude minority-group members from close relations with them.

Hubert Blalock, developing an earlier idea of Robert Park, argues that extreme discrimination will usually result when the dominant group feels that its self-interests — such as primacy and the preservation of cherished values — are threatened. Blalock believes that the dominant group will not hesitate to employ discriminatory action if it thinks that this will be an effective means of undercutting the minority group as a social competitor. Also, the dominant group will aggressively discriminate if it interprets minority variation from cultural norms as a form of social deviance threatening society's sacred traditions (for example, the large influx of Catholic immigrants in nineteenth-century America, or the appearance of "dishonest" Gypsies among "decent, hard-working" people). Discrimination, then, can be described as "a technique designed to neutralize minority group efforts."[58]

REVERSE DISCRIMINATION

At what point do efforts to secure justice and equal opportunities in life for one group infringe upon the rights of other groups? Is justice a utilitarian concept — the greatest happiness for the greatest number — or is it a moral concept — a sense of good that all people share? Is the proper role of government to provide a climate in which there is equal opportunity to participate in a competitive system, or is it government's responsibility to ensure equal results in any competition? These issues have engaged moral and political philosophers for centuries, and they go to the core of the affirmative-action controversy.

Over 2,300 years ago, Plato wrote in the *Republic* that justice must be relative to the needs of the people who are served, not to the desires of those who serve them. For example, physicians are obliged to make the patients' health their primary concern if they are to be just. In the modern classic *A Theory of Justice,* John Rawls interprets justice as fairness, which maximizes equal liberty for all.[59] Society must eliminate social and economic inequalities in order to provide the greatest benefit to the least advantaged, placing disadvantaged persons in offices and positions that are open to all under conditions of fair equality of opportunity. Both men see the ideal society as well ordered and strongly pluralistic: each of the component elements performs functionally differentiated roles in working harmony; society must arrange its practices to make this so.

Anticipating the emergence of the equal-protection-under-the-law clause of the Fourteenth Amendment as a major force for social change, Joseph Tussman and Jacobus tenBroek examined the problems of the doctrine of equality five years before the 1954 Supreme Court desegregation ruling.[60] Americans, they argued, have always been more concerned with liberty than with equality, identifying liberty with the absence of governmental interference.

> What happens, then, when government becomes more ubiquitous? Whenever an area of activity is brought within the control or regulation of government to that extent equality supplants liberty as the dominant ideal and constitutional demand.[61]

Tussman and tenBroek note that those who insist upon constitutional rights for all are not so much demanding the removal of governmental restraints as they are asking for positive governmental action to provide equal treatment for "minority groups, parties, or organizations whose rights are too easily sacrificed or ignored in periods of popular hysteria."[62] Responsibility for promoting individual rights is increasingly being placed upon public authority.

In the past twenty-five years, the three branches of the federal government have acted to promote minority rights in judicial decisions, legislative programs, and executive actions. As their impact was felt at state and local levels; in college and graduate school admissions; in hiring, training, and promotion policies; and in other facets of life, many whites reacted with anger, feeling that their own rights were now being denied. They argued that they were being penalized for past societal wrongs and were thus victims of reverse discrimination.

The issue was partially resolved with the *Bakke* decision in July 1978. In what one observer termed a "Solomonic" compromise, the Supreme Court ruled 5–4 that it is illegal for a university to use racial or ethnic quotas in its admissions program, but also that race may be considered as one factor in the admissions policy. The principle of affirmative action, designed to improve educational and job opportunities for racial minorities and women, was thus upheld, though in refined form. The ruling was not a definitive one, however. Other cases pending before the Supreme Court will further clarify the matter in areas other than university admissions. In the same week as the *Bakke* decision, for example, the Court ruled that the use of racial quotas at AT&T (American Telephone and Telegraph) was justified because of long-standing discriminatory practices in this corporation that required corrective action.

Two of the majority opinions from the *Bakke* decision seem to best summarize the Court's assessment of this extremely complex matter. Justice Lewis F. Powell stated: "The guarantee of equal protection cannot mean one thing when applied to one individual and something else when applied to a person of another color. If both are not accorded the same protection, then it is not equal." Justice Harry A. Blackmun pointed out the other part of the problem: "In order to get beyond racism, we must first take account of race. There is no other way. And in order to treat some persons equally, we must treat them differently. We cannot — we dare not — let the Equal Protection Clause perpetuate racial superiority."

Another important case involved the United Steelworkers of America and Kaiser Aluminum & Chemical Corporation, which reserved half of the positions in its skilled-craft training programs for minorities and women. Brian Weber, a white Louisiana factory worker, filed a class action suit when two blacks with less seniority were picked ahead of him for this program. When the U.S. Supreme Court handled the case of *Weber v. Kaiser* in July 1979, it further upheld affirmative action in ruling that private employers may voluntarily adopt quotas to remedy past discrimination, even if blameless themselves. Considered by some analysts a potentially more significant decision than the *Bakke* case, the Court considered the spirit and intent of the law, the serious racial imbalance among craft employees, and the fact that the temporary plan did not deny promotions to, or cause firings of, whites.

The matter is far from closed. Further actions, decisions, challenges, and compliance will keep the reverse discrimination issue before us for some time to come.

MINORITY-GROUP RESPONSES TO PREJUDICE AND DISCRIMINATION

Although personality characteristics play a large role in determining how individuals respond to unfavorable situations, certain patterns of group behavior have recurred among various groups of people during different historical periods. Sometimes more than one pattern may be discerned for a particular group. The minority group's perception of its *power resources* — its power to change established relationships with the dominant group in a significant way — will, to a large extent, determine which response it will be more likely to make.[63]

AVOIDANCE

One way of dealing with discriminatory practices is to avoid encountering them, if possible. Throughout history, minority groups — from the ancient Hebrews to the Pilgrims to the Soviet Jews today — have attempted to solve their problems by leaving them behind. One motivation for migration, then, is avoidance of discrimination. If leaving is not possible, minorities may turn inward to their own group for their social and economic activities. This approach serves to insulate minority groups against the antagonistic actions of the dominant group, but it also promotes charges of "clannishness" and "nonassimilation." However, lacking adequate economic, legal, or political power, avoidance may be the only choice open to the minority group.

By clustering together in small subcommunities, minority peoples not only recreated a miniature version of their familiar world in the strange land, they also established a safe place in which they could live, relax, and interact with others like themselves who could understand their needs and interests. For some minority groups, seeking such shelter from the prejudices of others was probably a secondary motivation, following a primary choice to live amongst their own kind.

Asian immigrants, for example, followed this pattern. When the Chinese first came to this country, they worked in many occupations in which workers were needed, frequently clustering together in neighborhoods close to their jobs. Prejudicial attitudes had always existed against the Chinese, but in the post–Civil War period, they became even more the targets of bitter hatred and discrimination, for economic and other reasons. Evicted from their jobs by race-baiting union strikes and limited in residential choice by restrictive housing covenants, many had no choice but to live in Chinatowns within the larger cities. They entered occupations not competitive with whites (curio shops, laundries, restaurants, and so on), and followed their tradition of settling their disputes among themselves, rather than subjecting themselves to public law adjudication.

DEVIANCE

When a group is continually rejected and discriminated against, some of the members find it difficult to identify with the dominant society and to accept its norms. People at the bottom of the socioeconomic ladder, particularly members of victimized racial and ethnic groups, may respond to the pressures of everyday life in ways they consider reasonable but others view as deviant. In particular, this situation occurs when laws represent an attempt to impose the moral standards of the dominant group on the behavior of other groups. Many minority groups in the United States — Irish, Germans, Chinese, Italians, blacks, Native Americans, Hispanics — have been, at one time or another, arrested and punished in disproportionate numbers for so-called crimes of personal disorganization. Included among the outrages to the morality of the dominant group have been public drunkenness, drug abuse, gambling, and sexual "misconduct." It is a matter of dispute whether this is a function of the frequency of misconduct or of selective arrests.

Part of the problem regarding law enforcement is its subjective nature and the discretionary handling of violations. Many people have criticized the American criminal justice system for its disparities in according fair and equal treatment to the poor and minority group members as compared with the middle and upper classes.[64] The complaints have included (1) the tendency of police to arrest suspects from minority groups more than those from the majority group when discretionary judgment is possible; (2) the overrepresentation of certain dominant social, ethnic, and racial groups on juries; (3) the difficulty for the poor in affording bail; (4) the poor quality of free legal defense; and (5) the disparities in sentences for dominant and minority groups. Because social background constitutes one of the factors that the police and courts consider, those who belong to a racial or ethnic group with a negative stereotype are at a severe disadvantage.

Often when a particular racial or ethnic group commits a noticeable number of deviant offenses, such as delinquency, crime, drunkenness, or some public-nuisance problem, the public may extend a negative image to all members of that group. Some common associations, for example, are Italians and gangsters, Irish and heavy drinking and fighting, Chinese and opium, blacks and street crimes such as mugging and purse snatching, and Puerto Ricans and knife fighting. Even though a very small percentage of a group actually engages in such behavior, sometimes the entire group becomes negatively stereotyped. A number of factors — including values, behavior patterns, and structural conditions in both the native and adopted lands — help explain the various kinds of deviance among different minority groups. The best means of stopping the deviance is a debatable issue between proponents of corrective versus preventative measures.

Deviant behavior among minority groups occurs not because of race or ethnicity, as prejudiced people would claim, but partly because of poverty and lack of opportunity. Clifford Shaw and Henry McKay, in a classic study of juvenile delinquency in Chicago, suggested that structural conditions, not membership in a particular minority group, determine crime and delinquency rates.[65] They found that the highest juvenile-delinquency rates occurred in areas with poor housing, few job opportunities, and the widespread incidence of prostitution, gambling, and drug use. The delinquency rate was consistently high over a thirty-year period, even though five different ethnic groups had moved in and out of those areas during that period of time. Nationality was unimportant; the unchanged conditions brought unchanged results. Other studies have also demonstrated a correlation between higher rates of either juvenile or adult crime and income level and place of residence.[66]

Because many minority groups are heavily represented among low-income populations, studies emphasizing social-class variables provide insight into the minority experience. For example, Albert Cohen found that a lack of opportunities encourages delinquency by lower-class males.[67] Social aspirations may be similar in all levels of society, but opportunities are not. Belonging to a gang may give a youth a sense of power and help overcome feelings of inadequacy; hoodlumism becomes an expression of resentment against a society whose norms seem impossible to follow.[68] The large majority of racial and ethnic-group members do not join gangs or engage in criminally deviant behavior. Nevertheless, because some minority groups are represented disproportionately in such activities, despite the small percentage of the total group involved, the public image of the group as a whole suffers. Some social factors, particularly parental attitudes about education and social ascent, appear to be related to delinquency rates. For example, parental emphasis on academic achievement may partially explain the low juvenile-delinquency rate among second-generation Jews compared with the high juvenile-delinquency rate among second-generation Italians, whose parents often viewed formal education as a frill. [69]

DEFIANCE

If a minority group is sufficiently cohesive and conscious of its growing economic or political power, its members may act openly to challenge and eliminate discriminatory practices. In defying discrimination, the minority group is taking a strong stance regarding its position in the society. Prior to this time, certain individuals of that group may have been in the vanguard (for example, by challenging laws in court).

Sometimes the defiance is violent and appears to be spontaneous, although it is usually the outgrowth of long-standing conditions. One example is the Irish draft riot in New York in 1863 during the Civil War. When its volunteer armies proved insufficient, the Union utilized a military draft to secure the needed troops. In those days, if a male were well-to-do, he could legally buy the military services of a substitute. Because the Irish were mostly poor and concentrated in urban areas, many

FIGURE 2.4

Mexican-American demonstrators throw wooden barricades onto two burning motorcycles during violent 1973 protest in downtown Dallas. (United Press International)

of them were drafted. Their defiance of what they considered an unfair practice became a riot, in which the blacks became the scapegoats, with lives lost and property destroyed or damaged.

A militant action, such as the takeover of a symbolic site, is a moderately aggressive act of defiance. The late 1960s witnessed many building takeovers by blacks and other disaffected, angry, alienated students on college campuses. In many instances the purpose of the action was to call public attention to what the group considered indifference or discrimination accorded their people. Similar actions occurred in this period to protest the war in Vietnam. A small group of American Indians took this approach in the 1970s to protest their living conditions; they seized Alcatraz Island in California, the Bureau of Indian Affairs in Washington, D.C., and the village of Wounded Knee in South Dakota. The influence of the media helped to validate and spread the idea of using militant actions to obtain one's ends.

Any peaceful action that challenges the status quo is less aggressive but is defiant, nonetheless; parades, marches, picket lines, mass meetings, boycotts, and demonstrations are examples. Another form of peaceful protest is to deliberately break discriminatory laws to challenge their constitutionality or to break a discriminatory tradition. The civil rights actions of the 1960s — sit-ins, lie-ins, and freedom rides — challenged Jim Crow laws that restricted access by blacks to public establishments in the South. Shop-ins at stores that had previously catered to an exclusively white clientele illustrated deliberate efforts to break traditional store practices.

ACCEPTANCE

Many minority people, to the frequent consternation of their leaders and sympathizers, accept the situation in which they find themselves. Some do so stoically, even justifying it by subtle rationalizations. Others are resentful but accept the situation for reasons of personal security or economic necessity. Although this approach maintains the superior position in society of the dominant group and the subordinate position of minority groups, it does ease the open tensions and conflicts between the two groups.

Conforming to prevailing patterns of interaction between dominant and minority groups can also be a subconscious action, the end result of social conditioning. Just as socialization can serve as a cause of prejudice, so too it can cause minority-group members to disregard or be unaware of alternative status possibilities. How much acceptance of lower status is of this nature and how much is characterized by resentful submission is a question that has not been completely answered.

However, some sociologists believe that instances of conscious but disliked role-playing by minority peoples in order to survive are quite common.[70] Brewton Berry and Henry Tischler state: "It is not uncommon for one to conform externally while rejecting the system mentally and emotionally."[71]

Blacks, Chicanos, and American Indians have experienced a multigenerational subordinate position in the United States. Until the 1960s, a combination of structural discrimination, racial stratification, and a sense of powerlessness and the futility of trying to change things caused many to accommodate to the situation imposed upon them. Similarly, Japanese-Americans had little choice when, following the bombing of Pearl Harbor and the subsequent rise in anti-Japanese sentiment in the United States, the government in 1942 uprooted and imprisoned 110,000 of them in "temporary relocation centers."

Acceptance as a minority response is not as common in the United States as it once was. More aware of the alternative ways of living that are presented on television and in the movies, minorities are hopeful of sharing in them. No longer are they receptive to the status quo, which denies them the comfortable living and leisure pursuits others have. Society — as evidenced by court decisions, legislation, new social services, and other efforts — has created a more favorable climate for improvement of the status of minority groups. Perhaps televised news features and behavioral science courses have helped to heighten the public's social awareness.

NEGATIVE SELF-IMAGE

The apathy that militant leaders find among their own people often results from a negative self-image, a rather common consequence of prejudice and discrimination. Continual treatment as an inferior encourages a loss of self-confidence. If everything about a person's position and experiences — jobs with low pay, substandard housing, the hostility of others, the need for assistance from governmental agencies — works to destroy pride and hope, that person may become apathetic. To remain optimistic and determined in the face of constant negative experiences from all directions is almost impossible.

Over thirty years ago Kurt Lewin observed that among minority-group members, development of a negative self-image was a fairly general tendency.[72] According to this view, the pervasiveness of dominant-group values and attitudes, which include negative stereotypes of the minority group, may cause the minority-group member to accept them. A person's self-image includes race, religion, and nationality; thus, individuals may feel embarrassed and inferior if they are aware that any of these attributes are held in low esteem within the society. In effect, minority-group members begin to perceive themselves as negatively as the dominant group originally perceived them.

This negative self-image, or self-hatred, manifests itself in many ways. People may try to "pass" as members of the dominant group and deny membership in a disparaged group. They may fully agree with the dominant group's prejudices and accept their state. They may also engage in ego defense by blaming others within the group for their low status.

> Some Jews refer to other Jews as "kikes" — blaming them exclusively for the anti-Semitism from which all alike suffer. Class distinctions within groups is often a result of trying to free oneself from responsibility for the handicap from which the group as a whole suffers. "Lace curtain" Irish look down on "shanty" Irish. Wealthy Spanish and Portuguese Jews have long regarded themselves as the top of the pyramid of Hebraic peoples. But Jews of German origin, having a rich culture, view themselves as the aristocrats, often looking down on Austrian, Hungarian, and Balkan Jews, and regarding Polish and Russian Jews at the very bottom. *

Negative self-image, then, can cause people to accept their fate passively. It can also cause a sense of personal shame for possessing undesired qualities or can create antipathy toward other members of the group for possessing them. Minority-group members frequently attempt to overcome their negative self-image by changing their name or religion, having cosmetic surgery, or moving into a locale where the stereotype is not as prevalent.

Portraying negative self-image as a fairly general tendency among minority-group members, as Lewin does, may be too broad a generalization. For example, members of tightly cohesive religious groups could draw emotional support from their faith and from one another. The insulation of living in an ethnic community, strong ingroup loyalty, or the determination to maintain their cultural heritage may also prevent minority-group members from developing a negative self-image.

THE VICIOUS CIRCLE

Sometimes the relationship between prejudice and discrimination is circular. Gunnar Myrdal refers to this pattern as *cumulative causation*, a vicious circle wherein prejudice and discrimination each cause the other.[73] The dynamics of the relations between dominant and minority

*Gordon W. Allport, *The Nature of Prejudice*, 1954, Addison-Wesley, Reading, Mass., pp. 152–153.

groups set in motion an almost perpetual sequence of reciprocal stimuli and responses. For example, a discriminatory action in jobs leads to a minority reaction, poverty, which in turn reinforces the dominant-group attitude that the minority group is inferior, which leads to still more discrimination, and so on.

Myrdal points out that this pattern may be desirable or undesirable. The expectations held about the newcomers are the key to the nature of the pattern that develops.[74] If the dominant group makes the newcomers welcome, they in turn are likely to react in a positive manner, which reinforces their friendly reception. If the new group is ignored and made to feel unwelcome, the members may react negatively, which also reaffirms original attitudes and actions. As Allport says, "If we foresee evil in our fellow man, we tend to provoke it; if good, we elicit it."[75] In other words, negative expectations engender negative reactions. The reactions encourage greater prejudicial opinions, broaden the social distance between the groups, and cause the vicious circle to continue.

When the Jews were denied access to many vacation resorts in the nineteenth century, their reaction served to reinforce their negative stereotype in the minds of some, thus reinforcing the discrimination. Some Jews demanded the right of equal access, showing the resort operators that Jews were "pushy." As the Jews, because of this discriminatory policy, began going to their own resorts in the Catskill Mountains, they were then labeled "clannish." Similarly, the Irish encountered severe job discrimination in the mid-nineteenth century, and because of the poverty that resulted, many of them lived in urban slums and had trouble with the law. With this evidence of their "inferiority" and "undesirability," their job opportunities became even more limited. In the same way, white discrimination against blacks, based partly on their low standard of living, furthers the problems of poverty, thus fueling even more any white antipathy for blacks.

MARGINALITY

Minority-group members sometimes find themselves caught in a conflict between their own identity and values and the necessity to behave in a certain way in order to be accepted by the dominant group. This situation is usually found when a member of a minority group is undergoing a transitional period. In an attempt to enter the mainstream of society, the *marginal* person internalizes the dominant group's cultural patterns but has not yet gained full acceptance. Such individuals are in an ill-defined role, no longer at ease within their own group but not yet fully a part of the *reference group*, the one to which they refer when evaluating themselves and their behavior.[76]

Over the years, sociologists have differed in their interpretation of the effects of marginality. Robert E. Park, who gave this social phenomenon its name, believed it caused the individual a great deal of strain and difficulty. Such a person, he observed, is one "whom fate has condemned to live in two societies and in two not merely different but antagonistic cultures."[77]

According to Park's thesis, this situation can cause the marginal person to suffer anxiety over a conflict of values and loyalties. This inner conflict can occur among both adults and children. The adults leave the security of their cultural group, thereby risking being labeled renegades by their own people. They seek sustained social contacts with the dominant group, which may view them as outsiders. No longer comfortable with the old ways, but influenced by them and identified with them nonetheless, the adults often experience feelings of frustration, hypersensitivity, and self-consciousness.

The children of immigrants also find themselves caught between two worlds. At home their parents attempt to raise them in their social heritage, according to the established ways of the old country. The children, through school and other outside experiences, become exposed to the American culture, and want to be like the other children. Moreover, they quickly learn that the dominant group views the ways of their parents as inferior and that they too are socially rejected because of their background. Consequently, many young people may develop emotional problems and be embarrassed to bring classmates home.

Marginality, according to this view, is an example of cultural conflict, primarily due to the clash of values within the individual. However, many sociologists now believe that the reaction to marginal status depends in large measure upon whether or not the individual receives reassurances of self-worth from the community. Thus, defining the situation and adjusting to it are contingent upon the individual's sense of security within the community.[78] In addition, ethnic subcommunities and institutions and a sense of solidarity among members of the ethnic group contribute to that sense of well-being. These observations have led some sociologists to emphasize stable individuals in a marginal culture rather than marginal persons in a dominant culture.[79] In other words, individuals in a marginal culture share their cultural duality with many others in primary-group relationships, institutional activities, and interaction with members of the dominant society, without encountering any dichotomy between their desires and actuality.

Whether this phase of the assimilation process represents an emotionally stressful experience or an insulated one, minority-group members nonetheless pass through a transitional period during which they are not fully a part of either world. An immigrant group may move into the mainstream of American society within the lifetimes of the first-generation members, or they may choose not to do so or simply be unable to. Usually, marginality is a one- or two-generational phenomenon. After that, members of the minority group have either assimilated or formed a distinctive subculture. No matter which route they take, they are no longer caught between two cultural worlds.

DOMINANT-GROUP RESPONSES TO MINORITY GROUPS

Members of a dominant group frequently react to minority peoples with tolerance and compassion, although they may sometimes be condescending in their attitudes. This type of favorable response usually occurs when the minority is small in number, not perceived as a threat, or both. As the minority group increases in population, threatening the natives' monopoly on jobs and other claims to privileged cultural resources, the dominant group's attitude is likely to become suspicious or fearful. If the fear becomes great enough, the dominant group may take some form of action against the minority group (Figure 2.5).

LEGISLATIVE CONTROLS

If the influx of racial and ethnic groups appears too great for a country to absorb, or if prejudicial fears prevail, that nation may act to regulate and restrict their entry. Australia, Canada, and the United States — the three greatest receiving countries in international migration — once had discriminatory immigration laws that either excluded or curtailed the number of immigrants from countries other than those in northern and western Europe. Following similar patterns of policy change, Canada (in 1962), the United States (in 1965), and Australia (in 1973) began to permit entry from all parts of the world.

To maintain a paternalistic social system, the dominant group frequently restricts the educational opportunities and voting of the subordinate group. This denial assures the dominant group of maintaining its system of control, whether over internal minorities such as the blacks in the Old South and the various ethnic minorities in the Soviet Union, or over colonized peoples such as those ruled by the Belgians, British, Dutch, French, Japanese, and Portuguese. Colonial powers have usually committed themselves to stability, trade, and tapping the natural resources of a country rather than to its development and self-governance. Token local leadership without real power in important matters, limited educational opportunities, and restricted political participation have been the usual experience of native populations under colonial rule. Other means of denying political power have been disenfranchising voters through high property qualifications (British West Indies), high income qualifications (Trinidad), and poll taxes (United States), although

FIGURE 2.5

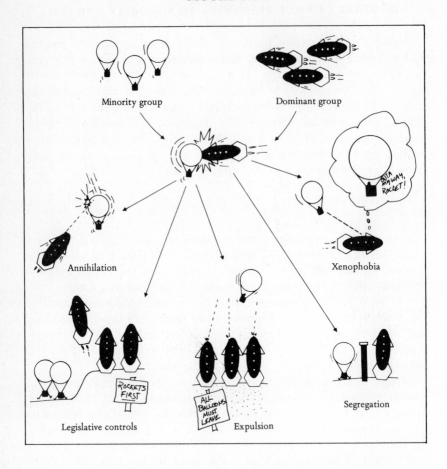

RESPONSES OF DOMINANT GROUP TO MINORITY GROUP

none of these practices exist today in those areas. The most conspicuous recent example of rigid social control is in South Africa, where a legislated apartheid society denies not only equal education and the ballot to blacks, but almost every other privilege as well.

SEGREGATION

Through a policy of containment, by avoiding social interaction with members of a minority group as much as possible and keeping them "in their place," the dominant group can effectively create both spatial and social segregation.

Spatial segregation refers to the physical separation of a minority people from the rest of society. This most commonly occurs in residential patterns but also takes place in education, in the use of public facilities, and in the occupational area. The majority group may institutionalize this form of segregation by law (de jure segregation) or establish it as an ongoing practice through norms (de facto segregation).

Physical segregation of minorities has been quite common for a long time. Since the days of the preindustrial city with its heterogeneous populations, the dominant group has relegated racial and ethnic minorities to special sections of the city, often the least desirable areas.[80] In Europe, this medieval ecological pattern resulted in minority groups being situated on the city outskirts nearest the encircling wall. Because this pattern remains in much of Europe today, Europeans, unlike Americans, consider it a sign of high prestige to live near the center of the city.[81]

The dominant group may use covert or overt means to achieve spatial segregation of a minority group. Some examples of covert actions are restrictive covenants, "gentlemen's" agreements, and collusion between the community and real estate agents to steer "undesirable" minorities only into certain neighborhoods.[82] Overt actions may include restrictive zoning, segregation laws, or intimidation. Both covert and overt segregation actions have been targets of U.S. court rulings over the past twenty-five years.

An important dimension of spatial segregation is that the dominant group can also achieve it through avoidance, or residential mobility. Usually referred to as the *invasion-succession ecological pattern*, this process has been a common one, involving different religions and nationalities as well as different races. The most recognized example in the United States is previously all-white neighborhoods becoming black, but any study of most urban neighborhoods would reveal the same pattern as successive waves of immigrants came here over the years. Residents of a neighborhood may attempt to resist the influx of a minority

FIGURE 2.6

"WHERE THE BLAME LIES"

"JUDGE (to Uncle Sam) — 'If Immigration was properly Restricted you would no longer be troubled with Anarchy, Socialism, the Mafia and such kindred evils!' " Cartoon appeared in *Judge*, 1891. (The Bettmann Archive)

group, eventually abandoning the area when their efforts are not successful. This pattern results in neighborhoods with a concentration of a new racial or ethnic group, a new segregated area.

Social segregation involves confining participation in social, service, political, and other types of activities to members of the ingroup. The dominant group excludes the outgroup from any involvement both in meaningful primary-group activities and in secondary-group activities. Organizations have screening procedures to keep out unwanted types, and informal groups also act to preserve their composition.

Segregation, whether spatial or social, can be either involuntary or voluntary. Minority-group members may choose not to live among the dominant group but by themselves instead; such a course of action is an avoidance response, discussed previously. On the other hand, minority-group members may have no choice at all about where they live because of economic or residential discrimination.

Whether by choice or against their will, minority groups form ethnic subcommunities, whose existence in turn promotes and maintains the social distance between the minority groups and the rest of society. Not only are minority-group members physically congregated in one area and thus spatially segregated, but they are also not engaging in any social interaction with others outside of their own group.

Frequent interaction usually lessens prejudice, but when interaction is severely limited, the acculturation process is slowed considerably. Instead, a reinforcement of values occurs concerning what is regarded as normal or different, paving the way for stereotyping, social comparisons, and prestige ranking.

EXPULSION

When other methods of dealing with a minority group fail, an intolerant dominant group may persecute or expel the minority group from the territory in which it resides. Henry VIII banished the Gypsies from England in the sixteenth century, Spanish rulers drove out the Moors in the early seventeenth century, and the British expelled the Acadians from Nova Scotia in the mid-eighteenth century. A more recent example is Idi Amin, the former authoritarian ruler of Uganda, who decreed in 1972 that all Asians must leave his country.

The United States also has its examples of mass expulsion. In colonial times, the Puritans forced Roger Williams and his followers out of Massachusetts for their nonconformity, and they settled in what became Rhode Island. The forcible removal of the Cherokee from rich Georgia land and the subsequent "Trail of Tears," in which four thousand perished along the thousand-mile forced march, is another illustration.

FIGURE 2.7

In 1923, anti-Japanese signs like these were prominent throughout the Hollywood community as part of a campaign to prevent the Japanese from settling there. (United Press International)

Mass expulsion reflects an effort to remove a group that is seen as a social problem rather than attempting to resolve the problem. This policy often takes form after other methods, such as assimilation or extermination, have failed. Whether a dominant group chooses to remove a minority group by extermination or by the somewhat more humane method of expulsion depends in part on how sensitive the country is to world opinion. Sensitivity to world opinion is often related to the country's economic dependency on other nations.

XENOPHOBIA

If the dominant group's suspicions and fears of the minority group become greatly heightened, they sometimes result in volatile, irrational feelings and actions. This overreaction is known as *xenophobia*, the undue fear of or contempt for strangers or foreigners. This almost hysterical response — reflected in print, in speeches and sermons, in legislation, and in violent actions — begins with ethnocentric views. Ethnocentrism encourages the creation of negative stereotypes, which in turn can lead to prejudice and discrimination, and which can escalate through some catalyst into a highly emotional reaction.

The Federalists, fearful of "wild Irishmen" and "French radicals" and anxious to eliminate what they saw as a foreign threat to the country's stability, succeeded in passing the Alien and Sedition Acts in 1798. When a bomb exploded at an anarchist gathering at Chicago's Haymarket Square in 1886, many Americans thereafter linked foreigners with radicals. The Bolshevik Revolution in 1917 led to the Palmer raids, in which Russian-Americans were illegally rounded up and incarcerated, and some even deported. Similarly, in 1942 the placement in concentration camps of 110,000 Japanese-Americans, many of them second- and third-generation Americans, was an irrational overreaction. All of these are examples of a xenophobic reaction to people and events.

ANNIHILATION

The Nazi extermination of over 6 million Jews brought the term *genocide* into the English language, but the practice of killing all the men, women, and children of a particular group goes back to ancient times. In warfare among the ancient Hebrews, Assyrians, Babylonians, Egyptians, and others, the usual practice was for the victor in battle to slay all the enemy, partly to prevent their children from seeking revenge. For example, preserved in Deuteronomy are these words of Moses:

> when Sehon offered battle at Jasa, coming out to meet us with all his forces. . . . We made an end of him and of his sons and of all his people, took all his cities there and then, putting all that dwelt there, men, women, and children, to the sword, and spared nothing except the beasts we drove off for our use, and such plunder as captured cities yield.
>
> . . . Og, that was king of Basan, came out to meet us with all his forces, and offered battle at Edrai. . . . So the Lord our God gave us a fresh victory over Og, king of Basan, and all his people, and we exterminated them, there and then laying waste all his cities. . . . We made an end of them as we had made an end of Sehon, that reigned in Hesebon, destroying all the inhabitants of their cities, men, women, and children, plundering their cattle and all the plunder their cities yielded.[83]

In modern times various countries have used extermination as a means of solving a so-called race problem. Arnold Toynbee once said that the "English method of settlement" followed this pattern.[84] The British, through extermination and close confinement of survivors, succeeded in annihilating the entire Tasmanian race between 1803 and 1876.[85] The Dutch considered South African Bushmen less than human and attempted to obliterate them.[86] When the Indians of Brazil resisted the settlement of Portuguese in their land, the whites solved the problem by systematically killing them. One of their favored means of doing so was to place the clothing of recent smallpox victims in their villages and allow the contagion to decimate the native population.[87] In the 1890s and again in 1915, the Turks massacred hundreds of thousands of Armenians, events still solemnly remembered each year by Armenian-Americans. One classic example in the United States was the massacre at Little Big Horn in 1890, when the Seventh Cavalry killed about two hundred Indian men, women, and children.

Lynchings are not a form of annihilation, for the intent is not to exterminate an entire group but to set an example through selective and drastic punishment. Nonetheless, the victims are usually minority-group members, and often that fact is the reason they were hanged instead of receiving some other punishment. Although lynchings have occurred in the United States throughout its history, only since 1882 have reasonably reliable statistics been kept (Figure 2.10). Sources such as the *Chicago Tribune* and Tuskegee Institute, which have kept data on this subject, reveal that five thousand lynchings have occurred since 1882. They have happened in every state except the New England states, with the Deep South (including Texas) claiming the most victims. In fact, 90

FIGURE 2.8

"THE MASSACRE OF THE CHINESE AT ROCK SPRINGS, WYOMING"
Engraving by T. de Thulstrup, 1885, from photographs by Lieutenant C. A.
Booth, Seventh United States Infantry. (The Bettmann Archive)

FIGURE 2.9

Black man lynched for assumed rape of white woman. Photograph circa 1880, Beekly, West Virginia. (The Bettmann Archive)

percent of the lynchings in this period have occurred in the Southern states; blacks have accounted for 80 percent of the victims and other minority-group members the remainder. The statistics do not, however, include lynchings during the nation's first hundred years, including those in the western frontier, which would increase the total number of victims, many of them white majority-group members.

Annihilation is sometimes unintended, as when whites inadvertently spread their sicknesses to the American and Canadian Indians, Eskimos, and Polynesians. With such ailments as measles, mumps, chicken pox, and smallpox unknown to them, the native populations had little resistance and thus often succumbed to these contagious diseases. Other forms of annihilation, usually intentional, occur during times of mob violence, overzealous police actions, and quiet, calculated small-group actions.[88]

RETROSPECT

Members of an ingroup perceive all outgroup members as strangers, whether they be immigrants or native-born Americans, and the degree of differences between groups will influence the nature of the intergroup relations. Different patterns may emerge, including one based on prejudice and discrimination. Prejudicial attitudes may exist at three levels: cognitive, emotional, and action-orientation. Two illustrations of prejudicial attitudes are negative stereotypes, or generalizations, and ethnophaulisms, derogatory language used to describe a group.

No single cause can account for all instances of prejudice; each theory has its limits and exceptions. Among the explanations social scientists offer are childhood socialization, self-justification, personality factors, frustration, competition, and social norms. Each of these factors explains some cases of prejudice, and sometimes various combinations of them explain other cases. Social-situational variables, such as economic conditions, stratification, and hostility toward the outgroup, also are important in understanding the existence of prejudice.

Discrimination is the unequal treatment of outgroup members, whether in job opportunities, housing, social interaction, or other areas. However, discrimination is not necessarily an acting out of prejudice. Social pressures may oblige nonprejudiced individuals to discriminate or prevent prejudiced people from discriminating.

Minority-group responses to prejudice and discrimination may be acceptance, avoidance, deviance, or defiance, depending in large measure upon the group's perception of its power to change the status quo. After continual treatment as an inferior, a negative self-image may result.

FIGURE 2.10

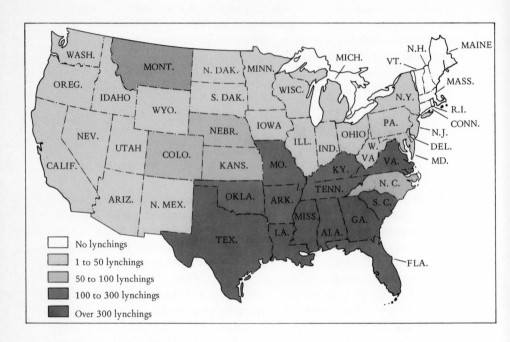

LYNCHINGS IN THE UNITED STATES, 1882–1963

Marginality is a social phenomenon that occurs during the transitional period of assimilation.

Dominant-group actions toward the minority group may also take various forms, including favorable or indifferent responses. When the reaction is a negative one, the group in power may place restraints upon the minority group (for example, legislative controls, segregation, or suppression). If the reaction becomes more emotional or even xenophobic, expulsion or annihilation may occur. Sensitivity to world opinion and economic dependency on other nations may curtail such drastic actions. When the dominant group reacts more favorably to the minority group, intergroup tensions may be resolved through genuine or token reform.

QUESTIONS FOR DISCUSSION

1. What is prejudice? What are some of its manifestations?
2. What are some of the possible causes of prejudice? Can it be eliminated?
3. What is the relationship between prejudice and discrimination?
4. What are some common minority-group responses to prejudice and discrimination?
5. What are some common dominant-group responses to minorities?

SUGGESTED READINGS

Allport, Gordon. The Nature of prejudice. Addison-Wesley, Reading, Mass., 1954.

Blumer, Herbert. "Race Prejudice as a Sense of Group Position," Pacific Sociological Review, 1 (1958), 3–7.

Ehrlich, Howard J. The Social Psychology of Prejudice. Wiley, New York, 1973.

Francis, E. K. Interethnic Relations. Elsevier, New York, 1976.

Greeley, Andrew M. Why Can't They Be Like Us? Institute of Human Relations Press, New York, 1969.

Mason, Philip. Patterns of Dominance. Oxford University Press, New York, 1970.

Simpson, George E., and J. Milton Yinger. Racial and Cultural Minorities: An Analysis of Prejudice and Discrimination, 3rd ed. Harper & Row, New York, 1965.

NOTES

1. See Hortense Powdermaker, Probing Our Prejudices, Harper & Row, New York, 1941, p. 1.

2. Louis Wirth, "Race and Public Policy," The Scientific Monthly, 58 (March 1944), 303.

3. Ralph L. Rosnow, "Poultry and prejudice," *Psychology Today*, March 1972, p. 53.

4. Reported by Daniel Wilner, Rosabelle Price Walkley, and Stuart W. Cook, "Residential Proximity and Intergroup Relations in Public Housing Projects," *Journal of Social Issues*, 8, No. 1 (1952), 45. See also James W. Vander Zanden, *American Minority Relations*, 3rd ed., Ronald Press, New York, 1972, p. 21.

5. Bernard M. Kramer, "Dimensions of Prejudice," *Journal of Psychology*, 27 (April 1949), 389–451.

6. L. Perry Curtis, Jr., *Apes and Angels: The Irishman in Victorian Caricature*, Smithsonian Press, Washington, D.C., 1971.

7. Eliot Aronson, *The Social Animal* Freeman, San Francisco, 1972, p. 174.

8. David Katz and Kenneth Braly, "Racial Stereotypes of One Hundred College Students," *Journal of Abnormal and Social Psychology*, 28 (October–December 1933), 280–290.

9. G. M. Gilbert, "Stereotype Persistence and Change Among College Students," *Journal of Abnormal and Social Psychology*, 46 (1951), 245–254.

10. Marvin Karlins, Thomas L. Coffman, and Gary Walters, "On the Fading of Social Stereotypes: Studies in Three Generations of College Students," *Journal of Personality and Social Psychology*, 13 (1969), 1–16.

11. Howard J. Ehrlich, *The Social Psychology of Prejudice*, Wiley, New York, 1973, p. 22.

12. Erdman Palmore, "Ethnophaulisms and Ethnocentrism," *American Journal of Sociology*, 67 (January 1962), 442–445.

13. See Peter I. Rose, *They and We*, 2nd ed., Random House, New York, 1974, p. 134. Some research was done by Joseph T. Klapper, Director of the Office of Social Research, CBS. Some of his findings were reported at the annual meeting of the Society for the Study of Social Problems, August 29, 1971.

14. See Dallas W. Smythe, "Reality as Presented by Television," *Public Opinion Quarterly*, 18 (1954), 143–156.

15. Bernard Berelson and Patricia Salter, "Majority and Minority Americans: An Analysis of Magazine Fiction," *Public Opinion Quarterly*, 10 (1946), 168–190.

16. J. T. McManus and Louis Kronenberger, "Motion Pictures, the Theater, and Race Relations," *Annals of the American Academy of Political and Social Science*, March 1946, pp. 152–157.

17. M. Spiegalman, C. Terwilliger, and F. Fearing, "The Content of Comics: Goals and Means to Goals of Comic Strip Characters," *Journal of Social Psychology*, 37 (1953), 189–203.

18. Audrey M. Shuey, "Stereotyping of Negroes and Whites: An Analysis of Magazine Pictures," *Public Opinion Quarterly*, 17 (1953), 281–292.

19. Stewart G. Cole and Mildred Wiese, *Minorities and the American Promise*, Harper & Row, New York, 1954.

20. Herbert Blumer, "Race Prejudice as a Sense of Group Position," *Pacific Sociological Review*, 1 (1958), 3–7.

21. William M. Newman, *American Pluralism*, Harper & Row, New York, 1973, p. 197.

22. See Marvin B. Scott and Stanford M. Lyman, "Accounts," *American Sociological Review*, 33 (February 1968), 40–62.

23. Philip Mason, *Patterns of Dominance*, Oxford University Press, New York, 1970, p. 7. Also, Philip Mason, *Race Relations*, Oxford University Press, New York, 1970, pp. 17–29.

24. T. W. Adorno, Else Frankel-Brunswik, Daniel J. Levinson, and R. Nevitt Sanford, *The Authoritarian Personality*, Harper & Row, New York, 1950.

25. H. H. Hyman and P. B. Sheatsley, "The Authoritarian Personality: A Methodological Critique," in *Studies*

in the Scope and Method of "The Authoritarian Personality," ed. R. Christie and M. Jahoda, Free Press, Glencoe, Ill., 1954.

26. Solomon E. Asch, Social Psychology, Prentice-Hall, Englewood Cliffs, N.J., 1952, p. 545.

27. E. A. Shils, "Authoritarianism: Right and Left," in Studies in the Scope and Method of "The Authoritarian Personality."

28. D. Stewart and T. Hoult, "A Social-Psychological Theory of 'The Authoritarian Personality,'" American Journal of Sociology, 65 (1959), 274.

29. H. C. Kelman and Janet Barclay, "The F Scale as a Measure of Breadth of Perspective," Journal of Abnormal and Social Psychology, 67 (1963), 608–615.

30. For an excellent summary of authoritarian studies and literature, see John P. Kirscht and Ronald C. Dillehay, Dimensions of Authoritarianism: A Review of Research and Theory, University of Kentucky Press, Lexington, 1967.

31. George E. Simpson and J. Milton Yinger, Racial and Cultural Minorities: An Analysis of Prejudice and Discrimination, Harper & Row, New York, 1953, p. 91.

32. Ibid., pp. 62–79.

33. John Dollard, Leonard W. Doob, Neal E. Miller, O. H. Mowrer, and Robert P. Sears, Frustration and Aggression, Yale University Press, New Haven, 1939; A. F. Henry and J. F. Short, Jr., Suicide and Homicide, Free Press, New York, 1954; Neal Miller and Richard Bugelski, "Minor Studies in Aggression: The Influence of Frustration Imposed by the In-group on Attitudes Expressed Toward Out-groups," Journal of Psychology, 25 (1948), 437–442; Stuart Palmer, The Psychology of Murder, T. Y. Crowell, New York, 1960; Brenden C. Rule and Elizabeth Percival, "The Effects of Frustration and Attack on Physical Aggression," Journal of Experimental Research on

Personality, 5 (1971), 111–188.

34. Leviticus 16:5–22.

35. Gordon W. Allport, "The ABC's of Scapegoating," 5th rev. ed., Anti-Defamation League pamphlet, New York.

36. Carl I. Hovland and Robert R. Sears, "Minor Studies of Aggression: Correlation of Lynchings with Economic Indices," Journal of Psychology, 9 (Winter 1940), 301–310.

37. Miller and Bugelski, "Minor Studies of Aggression," pp. 437–442.

38. Donald Weatherley, "Anti-Semitism and the Expression of Fantasy Aggression," Journal of Abnormal and Social Psychology, 62 (1961), 454–457.

39. Talcott Parsons, "Certain Primary Sources and Patterns of Aggression in the Social Structure of the Western World," Essays in Sociological Theory, Free Press, New York, 1964, pp. 298–322.

40. For an excellent review of Parsonian theory in this area, see Stanford M. Lyman, The Black American in Sociological Thought: A Failure of Perspective, Putnam, New York, 1972, pp. 145–169.

41. John Dollard, "Hostility and Fear in Social Life," Social Forces, 17 (1938), 15–26.

42. Muzafer Sherif, O. J. Harvey, B. Jack White, William Hood, and Carolyn Sherif, Intergroup Conflict and Cooperation: The Robbers Cave Experiment, University of Oklahoma Institute of Intergroup Relations, Norman, Okla., 1961. See also M. Sherif, "Experiments in Group Conflict," Scientific American, 195 (1956), 54–58.

43. Donald Young, Research Memorandum on Minority Peoples in the Depression, Social Science Research Council, New York, 1937, pp. 133–141.

44. Andrew Greeley and Paul Sheatsley, "The Acceptance of Desegregation Continues to Advance," Scientific American, 210 (1971), 13–19.

45. See Harry H. L. Kitano, "Passive Discrimination in the Normal Person," *Journal of Social Psychology*, 70 (1966), 23–31.

46. Thomas Pettigrew, "Regional Differences in Anti-Negro Prejudice," *Journal of Abnormal and Social Psychology*, 59 (1959), 28–36.

47. Jeanne Watson, "Some Social and Psychological Situations Related to Change in Attitude," *Human Relations*, 3 (1950), 15–56.

48. John Dollard, *Caste and Class in a Southern Town*, 3rd ed., Doubleday Anchor Books, Garden City, N.Y., 1957.

49. See Gordon W. Allport, *The Nature of Prejudice*, Addison-Wesley, Reading, Mass., 1954, p. 261 ff.; Robin M. Williams, Jr., *Strangers Next Door*, Prentice-Hall, Englewood Cliffs, N.J., 1964, p. 150 ff.; James W. Vander Zanden, *American Minority Relations*, 3rd ed., Ronald Press, New York, 1972, pp. 460–469.

50. Brewton Berry and Henry L. Tischler, *Race and Ethnic Relations*, 4th ed., Houghton Mifflin, Boston, 1978, p. 250.

51. Gertrude J. Selznick and Stephen Steinberg, *The Tenacity of Prejudice*, Harper & Row, New York, 1969.

52. For evidence of both findings, see Robin M. Williams, Jr., *The Reduction of Intergroup Tensions*, Social Science Research Council, Washington, D.C., 1947, p. 27 ff.; Gordon W. Allport, *The Nature of Prejudice*, p. 483 ff.

53. Charles H. Stember, *Education and Attitude Change*, Institute of Human Relations Press, New York, 1961.

54. Blumer, "Race Prejudice as a Sense of Group Position," pp. 3–7.

55. Williams, *Strangers Next Door*, pp. 124–125.

56. Robert K. Merton, "Discrimination and the American Creed," in *Discrimination and National Welfare*, ed. Robert M. MacIver, Harper & Row, New York, 1949, pp. 99–126.

57. Hubert M. Blalock, Jr., *Toward a Theory of Minority Group Relationships*, Capricorn Books, New York, 1970, pp. 204–207. For insight into the origin of this argument, see Stanford M. Lyman, "Cherished Values and Civil Rights," *The Crisis*, 71 (December 1964), 645–654, 695.

58. William M. Newman, *American Pluralism*, Harper & Row, New York, 1973, p. 231.

59. John Rawls, *A Theory of Justice*, The Belknap Press of Harvard University, Cambridge, Mass., 1971.

60. Joseph Tussman and Jacobus ten-Broek, "The Equal Protection of the Laws," *California Law Review*, 37 (September 1949), 341–381.

61. *Ibid.*, p. 380.

62. *Ibid.*, p. 381.

63. See Williams, *The Reduction of Intergroup Tensions*, p. 61; William J. Wilson, *Power, Racism, and Privilege*, Free Press, New York, 1973, pp. 47–68.

64. President's Commission on Law Enforcement and Administration of Justice, *Task Force Report: The Courts*, U.S. Government Printing Office, Washington, D.C., 1967; Lee Silverstein, *Defense of the Poor in Criminal Cases in American State Courts*, I, American Bar Association, New York, 1965; Caleb Foote, "The Bail System and Equal Justice," *Federal Probation*, 23 (September 1959), 45–47; Rita M. James, "Status and Competence of Jurors," *American Journal of Sociology*, 64 (May 1959), 565–566.

65. Clifford R. Shaw and Henry D. McKay, *Juvenile Delinquency and Urban Areas*, University of Chicago Press, Chicago, 1942.

66. John P. Clark and Eugene P. Wenninger, "Socio-economic Class and Area as Correlates of Illegal Behavior Among Juveniles," *American Sociological Review*, 27 (December 1962), 826–843; Karl Schnessler, "Components of Variation in City Crime Rates," *Social Problems*, 9 (1962), 314–323.

67. Albert K. Cohen, *Delinquent Boys*, Free Press, New York, 1955.

68. For a study of Chinese gangs, see Stanford M. Lyman, "Red Guard on Grant Avenue: The Rise of Youthful Rebellion in Chinatown," *The Asian in North America*, A-B-C Clio Press, Santa Barbara, Calif., 1977, pp. 177–200. The classic study on Italian gangs is William F. Whyte, *Street Corner Society*, University of Chicago Press, Chicago, 1943.

69. Jackson Toby, "Hoodlum or Business Man: An American Dilemma," in *The Jews*, ed. Marshall Sklare, Free Press, New York, 1958, pp. 544–549.

70. See Charles S. Johnson, *Patterns of Segregation*, Harper & Row, New York, 1943, pp. 244–266; *Minority Responses: Comparative Views of Reactions to Subordination*, ed. Minako Kurokawa, Random House, New York, 1970, pp. 187–227.

71. Berry and Tischler, *Race and Ethnic Relations*, p. 389.

72. Kurt Lewin, *Resolving Social Conflicts*, Harper & Row, New York, 1948, pp. 186–200.

73. Gunnar Myrdal, *An American Dilemma*, McGraw-Hill, New York, 1964, pp. 25–28; originally published by Harper & Row, 1944.

74. Gordon W. Allport, "The Role of Expectancy," in *Tensions that Cause Wars*, ed. H. Cantril, University of Illinois Press, Urbana, 1950, chap. 2.

75. Allport, *The Nature of Prejudice*, p. 160.

76. Robert K. Merton, *Social Theory and Social Structure*, Free Press, Glencoe, Ill., 1957, pp. 290–291.

77. Robert E. Park, "Human Migration and the Marginal Man," *American Journal of Sociology*, 33 (May 1928), 891; see also Everett V. Stonequist, *The Marginal Man*, Scribner, New York, 1937.

78. George E. Simpson and J. Milton Yinger, *Racial and Cultural Minorities: An Analysis of Prejudice and Discrimination*, 4th ed., Harper & Row, New York, 1972, p. 186.

79. Milton M. Goldberg, "A Qualification of the Marginal Man Theory," *American Sociological Review*, 6 (February 1941), 52–58.

80. See Gideon Sjoberg, "The Preindustrial City," *American Journal of Sociology*, 60 (March 1955), 438–445; Claude S. Fischer, *The Urban Experience*, Harcourt Brace Jovanovich, New York, 1976, p. 13; Lyn H. Lofland, *A World of Strangers*, Basic Books, New York, 1973, p. 50.

81. See Noel P. Gist and Sylvia F. Fava, *Urban Society*, 6th ed., Thomas Y. Crowell, New York, 1974, p. 204.

82. See Allport, *The Nature of Prejudice*, pp. 53–54.

83. Deuteronomy 2:32–35; 3:1 3–4, 6–7.

84. Arnold J. Toynbee, *A Study of History*, Oxford University Press, London, 1934, p. 465.

85. G. P. Murdock, *Our Primitive Contemporaries*, Macmillan, New York, 1934, pp. 16–18.

86. See I. D. MacCrone, *Race Attitudes in South Africa*, Oxford University Press, London, 1937, pp. 89–136.

87. Donald Pierson, *Negroes in Brazil*, University of Chicago Press, Chicago, 1942, p. 6.

88. See Gunnar Myrdal, *An American Dilemma*, Harper & Row, New York, 1944, pp. 566, 1350.

THREE

CULTURE AND SOCIAL STRUCTURE

⚔ To understand the minority experience in a dominant society, we must consider what happens when people of different cultures — strangers — interact. Differences in cultures may result from the unequal distribution of power in the social structure or from variations in ethnic background. Differing cultural orientations attained through socialization and conformity[1] will also shape expectations concerning how a minority group should fit into the society. Accordingly, in this chapter we shall examine the role of cultural and structural differentiation as a basis for conflict. We shall also examine the major theories regarding minority integration.

THE CONCEPT OF CULTURE

Most sociologists emphasize the impact of culture in shaping behavior.[2] Through language and other forms of symbolic interaction, the members of a society learn the thought and behavior patterns that constitute their commonality as a people.[3] In this sense culture is the social cement that binds a society together. *Culture,* then, consists of the values, attitudes, customs, beliefs, and habits that are shared by members of a society; anything contrary to this "normal" state is seen as negative or deviant. Minority groups often change their distinctive cultural traits to those of the host society, and this process is called *acculturation.*

Shared cultural norms encourage solidarity and orient the behavior of members of the ingroup. *Norms* are a culture's rules of conduct — internalized by the members — embodying the fundamental expectations of society. Through norms, ingroup members (majority or minority) know how to react toward the acts of outgroup members that surprise, shock, or annoy them, or in any way go against their shared expectations. When minority-group members "act uppity" or "don't know their place," majority-group members often get upset, and sometimes act out their anger. Violations of norms usually result in strong reactions because they appear to threaten the social fabric of a community or society.

THE REALITY CONSTRUCT

Our perception of reality is related to our culture; that is to say, through our culture we learn how to perceive the world about us. Cultural definitions help us to interpret the sensory stimuli from our environment and tell us how to respond to them. Thus, "culture is something that intervenes between the human organism and its environment to produce actions."[4] It is the screen through which we "see" (Figure 3.1).

FIGURE 3.1

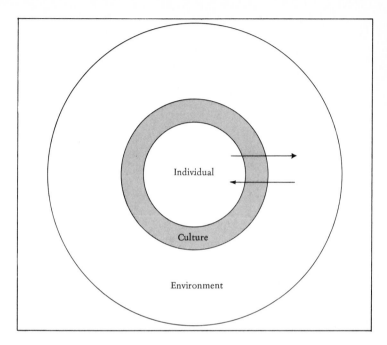

CULTURAL REALITY

INDIVIDUAL
   observes the world through
SENSE PERCEPTIONS;
   which are evaluated in terms of
CULTURE:
   values, attitudes, customs, and beliefs.

LANGUAGE AND OTHER SYMBOLS   Culture is learned behavior, acquired chiefly through verbal communication or language. A word is nothing more than a symbol — something that stands for something else. Whether it be tangible (*chair*) or intangible (*honesty*), the word represents a mental concept that is based on empirical reality. However, words reflect the culture, and one word may have different meanings in different cultures. If you have a *flat* in England, you have an apartment, not a deflated tire; if you could use a *lift*, you want an elevator, not a ride or a boost to your spirits. Because words symbolically interpret the world to us, language may connote both intended and unintended prejudicial meanings. For example, the word *black* sometimes suggests

(71)

dirty or *evil,* and *white* sometimes suggests *clean* or *good,* and these meanings may be subtly transferred to black and white people.

Walter Lippmann, a prominent political columnist, once remarked, "First we look, then we name, and only then do we see." What he meant was that until we learn the symbols of our world, we cannot understand the world. A popular pastime in the early 1950s called "Droodles" illustrates Lippmann's point. The object was to interpret drawings such as those in Figure 3.2. Many people were unable to see the meaning of the drawings until it was explained. They looked but did not see until they knew the "names."[5] (See "Notes" for answers.)

Interpreting symbols is not just an amusing game; it is extremely significant in real life. Human beings do not respond to stimuli, but to their definitions of those stimuli, as mediated by their culture.[6] The definition of beauty is one example. Beyond the realm of personal taste, definitions of beauty have cultural variations. For instance, in different times and places a woman's beauty has been based upon her having distended lips, scar markings, tattoos, or beauty marks, or upon how plump or thin she was.

Nonverbal communication, or body language, is highly important too. Body movements, gestures, physical proximity, facial expressions (there are between 100 and 136 facial expressions, each of which conveys a distinct meaning![7]), and *paralinguistic signals* (sounds but not words) all convey information to the observer-listener. Body language is important in intergroup relations, whether in conversation, interaction, or perception. Body language may support or belie one's words; it may suggest friendliness, or aloofness, or deference.

Although some body language is fairly universal (for example, most facial expressions), many cultural variations exist in body language itself and in the interpretation of its meanings. Body movements such as posture, bearing, or gait vary from culture to culture. The degree of formality in a person's environment (both past and present) and other cultural factors have an influence on such forms of nonverbal communication. Consider the different meanings one could attach to a student's being unwilling to look directly into the eyes of a teacher. The teacher may consider this to reflect embarrassment, guilt, shyness, inattention, or even disrespect. Yet if the student were Hispanic, such an action would be a mark of respect. The symbol's definition, in this case the teacher's interpretation of what the student's action meant, determines the response.

A person who is foreign to a culture must learn both its language and the rest of its symbol system. Certain gestures may be signs of friendliness in one culture but obscene or vengeful symbols in another. For example, in America, placing thumb and forefinger in a circle with the other fingers upraised indicates that everything is fine, but in Japan this sign refers to money, and in Greece it is an insulting anal expression.[8] Kisses, tears, dances, emblems, silence, open display of emotions, and thousands of other symbols can, and often do, have very different meanings in different cultures. Symbols, including language, help construct a reality for an ingroup that may be unknown to or altogether different for an outgroup. Members of one group may then select, reject, ignore, or distort their sensory input regarding the other group because of cultural definitions.

FIGURE 3.2

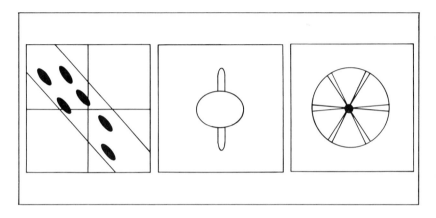

"DROODLES"

THE THOMAS THEOREM Many years ago, William I. Thomas made an oft-repeated observation that if people define situations as real, those situations become real in their consequences.[9] His statement is further testimony to the truth of reality constructs: human beings respond to their definitions of stimuli rather than to the stimuli themselves. People behave according to the meaning they assign to the situation, and the consequences of their behavior serve to reaffirm the meaning; the definition becomes a self-fulfilling prophecy. For example, when whites define blacks as inferior and then offer them fewer opportunities because of that alleged inferiority, the result is that blacks are disadvantaged, which in turn supports the initial definition.

Several variables determine the initial definition, but culture is a very important one. Culture establishes the framework through which an individual perceives others, classifies them into groups, and assigns them certain general characteristics. Because ethnocentrism leads people to consider their way of life as the best and most natural, their culturally defined perceptions of others often lead to suspicion and differential treatment of other groups. In effect, each group constructs myths about other groups and supports those myths through ingroup solidarity and outgroup hostility. As each group's attitudes and actions toward other groups continue, the *vicious-circle phenomenon* is at work.[10] In such instances, people create a culturally determined world of reality, and their actions reinforce their beliefs. Social interaction or social change may counteract such situations, leading to their redefinition.

Gregory Razran conducted a well-known study illustrating how cultural definitions can influence perception.[11] Twice within a two-month interval, he showed the same set of thirty pictures of unknown young women to the same group of one hundred male college students and fifty noncollege men. Using a five-point scale, the subjects rated each woman's beauty, character, intelligence, ambition, and general likableness. At the first presentation, the pictures had no ethnic identification, but at the second presentation, they had Irish, Italian, Jewish, and old American (English) surnames. All women were rated equally on the first presentation, but when the names were given, the ratings changed. The "Jewish" women received higher ratings in ambition and intelligence. Both "Jewish" and "Italian" women suffered a large decline in general likableness and a slight decline in beauty and character evaluations. This study illustrates how cultural definitions affect judgments about others.

Through *cultural transmission*, each generation passes on its culture to the next generation, which learns those cultural definitions at an early age. This fact is dramatically expressed in the Rodgers and Hammerstein musical *South Pacific*. The tragic subplot is the touching romance between Lieutenant Cable and Liat. Although he and the Tonkinese girl are sincerely in love, his friends remind him that the couple's life would not be the same in America. Their differences in race and culture would work against a happy marriage for them, as would his own acceptance in Philadelphia high society. Miserable because of the choice his cultural values force him to make, he sings "Carefully Taught," a poignant song about how prejudice is taught to children.

> You've got to be taught to hate and fear,
> You've got to be taught from year to year.
> It's got to be drummed in your dear little ear,
> You've got to be carefully taught.

> You've got to be taught to be afraid,
> Of people whose eyes are oddly made,
> Of people whose skin is a different shade.
> You've got to be carefully taught.

THE CONCEPT OF CULTURE

> You've got to be taught before it's too late,
> Before you are six or seven or eight,
> To hate all the people your relatives hate.
> You've got to be carefully taught.
> You've got to be carefully taught.[12]

Peter Berger and Thomas Luckmann have pointed out how reality is socially constructed through a three-stage process of social interaction.[13] Individuals create a background against which to understand their separate actions and their interactions with others. When a social situation is a continuing one, the participants' interactions during the course of their shared history result in reciprocal typifications. Taken-for-granted routines emerge, based upon shared expectations. This socially constructed world of reality is seen as legitimate by all participants by virtue of its "objective" existence. When problems arise, specific "universe-maintenance" procedures become necessary to preserve stability within society. Such conceptual machineries as mythology, theology, philosophy, or science may be used. In short, people create cultural products: material artifacts, social institutions, ideas, and so on (*externalization*); they lose awareness that they have created their own social and cultural environment (*objectification*); and then they learn these supposedly objective facts of reality through the socialization process (*internalization*).

CULTURAL CHANGE

Culture refers to the prevailing values, attitudes, customs, and beliefs of a society, all of which can change. Natural disasters, innovations from within society, and influences of other cultures can have a profound effect upon how people think and act.

CULTURAL DIFFUSION A striking paradox is that although the members of a dominant culture wish to keep their society untainted by the influence of foreign elements, all cultures are inevitably influenced by other cultures. Ideas, inventions, and practices spread from one culture to another, though the rate of diffusion varies considerably. Negative attitudes and a large distance between groups can be effective barriers, and sometimes cultural diffusion occurs only under the right conditions. Also, sometimes ideas are modified or reinterpreted before being accepted, such as the Latin American Indians' fondness for automobile tires: they use them to make sandals, for they neither own nor drive cars.[14]

The prominent American anthropologist Ralph Linton calculated that any given culture contains about 90 percent borrowed elements. To demonstrate both the enormity and the subtlety of cultural diffusion, he offered a classic portrait of the "100 per cent American."

Our solid American citizen awakens in a bed built on a pattern which originated in the Near East but which was modified in Northern Europe before it was transmitted to America. He throws back covers made from cotton, domesticated in India, or linen, domesticated in the Near East, or wool, from sheep, also domesticated in the Near East, or silk, the use of which was discovered in China. All of these materials have been spun or woven by processes invented in the Near East. He slips into his moccasins, invented by the Indians of the Eastern woodlands, and goes to the bathroom, whose fixtures are a mixture of European and American inventions, both of recent date. He takes off his pajamas, a garment invented in India, and washes with soap invented by the ancient Gauls. He then shaves, a masochistic rite which seems to have been derived from either Sumer or ancient Egypt.

Returning to the bedroom, he removes his clothes from a chair of southern European type and proceeds to dress. He puts on garments whose form originally derived from the skin clothing of the nomads of the Asiatic steppes, puts on shoes made from skins tanned by a process invented in ancient Egypt and cut to a pattern derived from the classical civilizations of the Mediterranean, and ties around his neck a strip of bright-colored cloth which is a vestigial survival of the shoulder shawls worn by the seventeenth-century Croatians. Before going out for breakfast he glances through the window, made of glass invented in Egypt, and if it is raining puts on overshoes made of rubber discovered by the Central American Indians and takes an umbrella, invented in southeastern Asia. Upon his head he puts a hat made of felt, a material invented in the Asiatic steppes.

On his way to breakfast he stops to buy a paper, paying for it with coins, an ancient Lydian invention. At the restaurant a whole new series of borrowed elements confronts him. His plate is made of a form of pottery invented in China. His knife is of steel, an alloy first made in southern India, his fork a medieval Italian invention, and his spoon a derivative of a Roman original. He begins breakfast with an orange, from the eastern Mediterranean, a cantaloupe from Persia, or perhaps a piece of African watermelon. With this he has coffee, an Abyssinian plant, with cream and sugar. Both the domestication of cows and the idea of milking them originated in the Near East, while sugar was first made in India. After his fruit and first coffee, he goes on to waffles, cakes made by a Scandinavian technique from wheat domesticated in Asia Minor. Over these he pours maple syrup, invented by the Indians of the Eastern woodlands. As a side dish he may have the egg of a species of bird domesticated in

Indo-China, or thin strips of the flesh of an animal domesticated in Eastern Asia which have been salted and smoked by a process developed in northern Europe.

When our friend has finished eating he settles back to smoke, an American Indian habit, consuming a plant domesticated in Brazil in either a pipe, derived from the Indians of Virginia, or a cigarette, derived from Mexico. If he is hardy enough he may even attempt a cigar, transmitted to us from the Antilles by way of Spain. While smoking he reads the news of the day, imprinted in characters invented by the ancient Semites upon a material invented in China by a process invented in Germany. As he absorbs the accounts of foreign troubles he will, if he is a good conservative citizen, thank a Hebrew deity in an Indo-European language that he is 100 per cent American.*

CULTURE CONTACT Another way in which culture can undergo change is through people of different cultures coming into contact with one another. Because people tend to take their own culture for granted, it operates at a subconscious level in forming their expectations. When people's assumptions are jolted through contact with another culture with different expectations, they often experience *culture shock*, which is characterized by feelings of disorientation and anxiety and a sense of being threatened.

Culture shock does not always occur. When people of two different cultures interact, many possible patterns can emerge. The two groups may live in peaceful coexistence with a gradual cultural diffusion occurring. History offers some excellent examples of connections between migrations and innovations, wherein geographical conditions and native attitudes have determined the extent to which a group has resisted cultural innovations, despite invasions, settlements, or missionary work. The persistent pastoralism of Bedouin tribes and the long-sustained resistance to industrialization of the American Indians are but two examples.[15] Stanley Lieberson, however, suggests that power alone determines the outcome, causing one group to become dominant and the other subservient.[16] If the subordinate group was not the migratory group, the changes to their social organization can be particularly devastating. No longer possessing the flexibility and autonomy they once enjoyed, they may suffer material deprivation and find their institutions undermined. If the migratory group finds itself in the subordinate position, it must adapt to its new environment to survive. Most commonly, the minority group draws from its familiar world as it attempts to cope with the different conditions. Group members form a subculture in

*Ralph Linton. *The Study of Man*, © 1936, pp. 326–327. Reprinted by permission of Prentice-Hall, Inc., Englewood Cliffs, New Jersey.

which their behavior and interests are unique to themselves, not shared with others in the larger society. In doing so, they create a modified version of the culture of the old country that also reflects the influence of the new country. For example, both Catholicism and Judaism have undergone changes in form and expression since taking root in America. Each of the ethnic subcultures has represented a blend of native and American cultures, as group members have acclimated to their new environment.

SUBCULTURES

Most large societies — especially complex, industrial ones — contain various subgroupings of people. Quite commonly, people share some characteristics of the society at large, but they have other characteristics unique to their own group. Such groups are called *subcultures,* which can be regional, age-related, occupational, racial, ethnic, and so on.

As ethnic subcultures among immigrants in the United States evolved in response to conditions within the host society, the immigrants sometimes developed a group consciousness unknown in their old countries. Many first-generation Americans possessed a village orientation toward their homeland rather than a national identity. They spoke different dialects, feuded with other regions, and had different values. However, their common experience in the United States caused them to coalesce into a national grouping. One example is the Italian-Americans, who at first identified with their cities of origin: Calabria, Palermo, Naples, Genoa, Salerno, and so on. Within a generation, many came to view themselves as Italians, partly because the host society classified them as such.

CONVERGENT SUBCULTURES   Most ethnic subcultures are *convergent;* that is, they tend toward assimilation with the dominant society. Although recognizable by residential clustering and adherence to the language, dress, and cultural norms of their native land, these ethnic groups are nonetheless becoming assimilated. As the years pass — possibly several generations — the distinctions between the dominant culture and the convergent subculture gradually lessen. Eventually this form of subculture becomes completely integrated into the dominant culture.

Because this subculture is undergoing change, its members may experience the problems of marginality.[17] The older generation may seek to preserve its traditions and heritage, but the younger generation may be impatient to be fully accepted within the dominant society. Because the impetus is to assimilate, time obviously favors the younger generation. Some examples of once prevalent ethnic subcultures are the Irish,

Germans, and Dutch, in order of decreasing visibility today. These nationality groups still exhibit ethnic pride in many ways, but, for the most part, they are no longer set apart by place of residence or subcultural behavior. Based upon their multigenerational length of residence, these nationality groups are less likely to live in clustered housing arrangements or to display particular behavior patterns such as conflict, deviance, or endogamy, to any greater degree than the rest of the majority group.

PERSISTENT SUBCULTURES   Not all subcultures assimilate, and some do not even desire to do so. Some steadfastly adhere to their own way of life as much as possible, resisting absorption into the dominant culture. Two relatively isolated religious groups, the Amish and the Hutterites, have long insisted upon maintaining a way of life different from that of the "ungodly" majority and may represent the purest form of a *persistent* subculture in American society. Other ethnic groups adopt a few aspects of the dominant culture but remain adamant about preserving their own way of life; examples are most Indians who live on reservations and many Spanish-Americans in the Southwest. Chinatowns also manifest in many ways the preservation of the Chinese way of life.

A minority group's insistence upon the right to be different has not usually been very well received among dominant-group members. This clash of wills has the potential for conflict; at the very least, it is the breeding ground for stereotyping and prejudice on both sides.

Just as convergent subcultures illustrate assimilation, persistent subcultures illustrate pluralism. We shall discuss these two forms of minority integration shortly.

STRUCTURAL CONDITIONS

Relationships between majority and minority groups are influenced as much by structural conditions as by differences in culture. The nature of those conditions influences not only the distribution of power resources (economic, political, social) but also the accessibility of those resources to groups who are seeking upward mobility. An expanding economy and an open social system allow for increased opportunities for minority-group members, thereby reducing the possibility of frustrations and tensions arising. A stagnant or contracting economy thwarts many efforts to improve status and antagonizes those who feel most threatened by another group's competition for scarce resources. Such a situation may breed conflicts among minority groups even more than between majority and minority groups, because the group next highest on the socioeconomic ladder may perceive a threat more quickly and react negatively.

The state of the economy is just one of the important structural factors influencing the opportunities for upward mobility. Another factor is the degree of change between a minority group's old society and the new one. A traditional or agrarian society will have a much more stable social structure than a society undergoing a transformation through industrialization. The latter society will offer dramatic changes in opportunities and life styles, not all of them for the better. For a minority group migrating to another country, its compatibility with the social structure of the new land will be contingent upon the degree of similarity with structural conditions in its homeland. A person who leaves an agrarian society for an industrial one is poorly prepared to do anything but enter the lowest stratum in a low-paying position. Opportunities for upward mobility, however, may exist if the economy is growing rapidly. In this sense, the structural conditions of 1880 to 1920 were better for the unskilled immigrant than are conditions today. Low-skill jobs are not as plentiful today as they once were, and an unskilled worker's desire to support a family through hard work and sweat may not be matched by the opportunity to do so.

Another change in structural conditions has been the advancement in technology, which has made for a smaller world. Rapid transportation and communications (radio, television, telephone, telegraph, satellites, air mail) make it possible for ties to other parts of the world to remain stronger than in the past.[18] Accessibility to one's homeland, friends, or relatives may make one less interested in becoming fully assimilated in a new land. Befriending strangers in the new country becomes less necessary. Additionally, people's greater knowledge of the world, the rising social consciousness of a society, and structural opportunities for mobility all help to create a more hospitable environment for minority-group members.

STRATIFICATION

Social stratification is the hierarchical classification of the members of society based upon the unequal distribution of resources, power, and prestige. *Resources* refer to such factors as income, property, and borrowing capacity. *Power*, usually reflected by the stratified layers, concerns the ability to influence or control others. *Prestige* relates to status, either *ascribed* — based on age, sex, race, or family background — or *achieved* — based on individual accomplishments.

The process of stratification may serve to moderate or exacerbate any strains or conflicts between groups, depending upon the form that the

FIGURE 3.3

Street urchins in area of Mulberry Street, circa 1889. Homeless children, fending for themselves, were not uncommon in the immigrant communities. (Photograph by Jacob A. Riis, Jacob A. Riis Collection, Museum of the City of New York)

stratification takes. The form can range from rigid to flexible and subtle, from slavery, caste, and forced labor to class distinctions and discrimination based on race or ethnic group. Whether racial and ethnic groups face insurmountable barriers or minor obstacles in achieving upward mobility is determined by the form of stratification. The more rigid the stratification, the more likely racial, religious, or other ideologies justifying the existing arrangement are to arise.

The form of stratification affects how groups within the various strata of society view one another. Some people confuse structural differentiation with cultural differentiation. For example, they may believe a group's low socioeconomic status is the result of its values and attitudes rather than the result of such structural conditions as racism, economic stagnation, or high urban unemployment. The form of stratification is an important determinant of the potential for intergroup conflict. In the United States, both the possibility of upward mobility and structural obstacles to that possibility have existed. When the disparity between the perception of the American Dream and the reality of the difficulty of achieving it grows too great, the possibility of conflict increases.

CULTURE OF POVERTY

Beginning in 1932 with E. Franklin Frazier's conception of a disorganized and pathological lower-class culture,[19] a controversial school of thought has existed that has become known as the culture-of-poverty theory. The culmination of this idea came in 1965 with the release of a U.S. Department of Labor document known as the "Moynihan Report."[20] The report actually contained nothing new, relying heavily on Frazier's observations. However, this time it came from a federal government agency, at a time when the civil rights movement was at its height. The report angered a great many people, including blacks, civil rights workers, and social workers.

In examining the problems of high unemployment, welfare dependency, illegitimacy, low achievement, juvenile delinquency, and adult crime, Moynihan argued that family deterioration was a major factor.

> At the heart of the deterioration of the fabric of Negro society is the deterioration of the Negro family. It is the fundamental source of weakness of the Negro community at the present time. . . . The white family has achieved a high degree of stability and is maintaining that stability. By contrast, the family structure of the lower class Negroes is highly unstable, and in many urban centers is approaching complete breakdown.[21]

Moynihan described black males as occupying an unstable place in the economy, which prevents their being strong fathers and husbands.

This environment serves as a breeding ground for a continuing vicious cycle: the women often not only raise the children, but also earn the family income. Consequently, the children grow up in a poorly supervised, unstable environment; they often do not do well or stay in school; they can secure only low-paying jobs — and so the cycle begins anew.[22]

> At the center of the tangle of pathology is the weakness of the family structure. Once or twice removed, it will be found to be the principal source of most of the aberrant, inadequate, or anti-social behavior that did not establish but now serves to perpetuate the cycle of poverty and deprivation. . . .
>
> What then is the problem? We feel that the answer is clear enough. Three centuries of injustice have brought about deep-seated structural distortions in the life of the Negro American. At this point, the present tangle of pathology is capable of perpetuating. itself without assistance from the white world. The cycle can be broken only if these distortions are set right.[23]

The crux of the culture-of-poverty thesis, and its most controversial point, was the contention that distinctive lower-class values were transmitted from one generation to the next. Oscar Lewis gave perhaps the most persuasive commentary for the culture-of-poverty school in his introduction to his classic case study of a Puerto Rican family.[24]

> The culture of poverty, however, is not only an adaptation to a set of objective conditions of the larger society. Once it comes into existence it tends to perpetuate itself from generation to generation because of its effect on the children. By the time slum children are age six or seven they have usually absorbed the basic values and attitudes of their subculture and are not psychologically geared to take full advantage of changing conditions or increased opportunities which may occur in their lifetime.[25]

This proposition — that poverty continues because of subcultural patterns — has had important implications. Those who hold this view often believe that federal efforts to eliminate poverty would be more successful if they turned to a more direct, sociopsychological approach. Edward Banfield, for example, felt that this was the best solution to the poverty problem. He argued that good jobs, good housing, tripled welfare payments, new schools, quality education, and armies of police officers would not stop the problem. He continued:

> If, however, the lower classes were to disappear — if, say, its members were overnight to acquire the attitudes, motivations, and habits of the working class — the most serious and intractable problems of the city would all disappear with it. . . . The lower-class forms of all problems are at bottom a single problem: the existence of an outlook and style of life which is radically present-oriented and which

FIGURE 3.4

A Spanish boy, one of eight children abandoned by their father, sleeps in his mother's rented house in Brooklyn, New York. The mother could speak no English and knew nothing about welfare. (Bob Combs, Photo Researchers)

therefore attaches no value to work, sacrifice, self-improvement, or service to family, friends, or community.[26]

William Ryan criticized Banfield for failing to realize that the present-time orientation of the poor is a function of the hopelessness of their situation.[27]

Racial and ethnic minorities are disproportionately represented among the poor.[28] Therefore, the elimination of poverty would assist many minority-group members. Although few argued over this goal, not everyone agreed that the cause of the problem lay in a self-perpetuating, distinct social ethos. A 1972 study, however, indicated that the majority of Americans felt that the poor were responsible for their poverty.[29] In a national cross section of adults, 53 percent said that the poor were at fault for their dilemma and 22 percent felt that the social structure was at fault. However, many social scientists have decried this view. Critics of the culture-of-poverty school have argued that fatalism, apathy, low aspiration, and other similar orientations are situational responses within each generation and are not passed down. In 1963, Michael Harrington's *The Other America* helped spark the federal government's "War on Poverty" program. He maintained that society was to blame for poverty.

> The real explanation of why the poor are where they are is that they made the mistake of being born to the wrong parents, in the wrong section of the country, in the wrong industry, or in the wrong racial or ethnic group.[30]

Charles Valentine stated that the distinctive patterns of life among the poor result from structural conditions in the larger society that are beyond the control of low-income people, not from socialization to different cultural values.[31] Others argued that all people would desire the same things and cherish the same values if they were in an economic position to do so. Because they are not, they adopt an alternative set of values in order to survive.[32] Eliot Liebow, in a participant-observer study of lower-class black males, concluded that they try to achieve many of the goals of the larger society, but fail for many of the same reasons as their fathers did: discrimination, unpreparedness, lack of job skills, and self-doubt.[33] The similarities between generations are due not to cultural transmission, but to the sons' independent experience of the same failures. What appears to be a self-sustaining cultural process is in reality a secondary adaptation to an adult inability to overcome structural constraints.

The debate between those who argue that ghetto culture is the product of *economic determinism* (structural differentiation) and those who believe it is caused by *cultural determinism* (a culture of poverty) continues. A person's attitudes toward welfare, toward the urban poor, who are mostly racial and ethnic minorities, and toward different orientations to life all reflect the individual's beliefs about this issue. About the only common ground shared by the two schools of thought is their mutual support of increased employment and educational opportunities.

SOCIAL CLASS

Social class is one categorization by which sociologists designate people's place in the stratification hierarchy; people in a particular social class have similar income, amount of property, degree of power, status, and life style. Many factors help to determine a person's social class, including that individual's membership in particular racial, religious, and status groups. Although no clearly defined boundaries exist between class groupings in the United States, people have a tendency to cluster together according to certain socioeconomic similarities. Classes result from sociopsychological distinctions people make about one another based, for example, on where they live and what they own, as well as on the types of interactions that occur because of those distinctions.

Social class becomes important in intergroup relations because it serves as a basis for expectations. As Alan Kerckhoff states, social class provides a particular setting for the interplay between the formative experiences of a child, others' expectations of the child, and what kind of adult the child becomes.[34] First as a significant determiner and later as a point of reference in others' responses and in a person's self-view, social class helps to shape an individual's world of reality and influences group interactions. This view is in some ways similar to the culture-of-poverty hypothesis, but it does not negate a person's receptivity to change given increased opportunities. Social class *is* an important determiner of attitudes and behavior, but that does not necessarily mean they are immutable.

In the 1930s, W. Lloyd Warner headed a classic study of social-class differentiation.[35] Using the *reputational method* — asking people how others compared to them — Warner found a well-formulated class system in existence. In Newburyport, Massachusetts, a small town of about seventeen thousand which he called "Yankee City," Warner identified six classes: upper-upper, lower-upper, upper-middle, lower-middle, upper-lower, and lower-lower. When he and his associates examined the distribution of ethnic groups among the various classes, certain factors emerged. First, a significant relationship existed between an ethnic group's length of residence and class status; the more recent arrivals tended to be in the lower classes. Other factors were also found to have an important influence on class status. An ethnic group tended to be less assimilated and less upwardly mobile if its population in the community was relatively large, if its homeland was close (such as in the case of the French-Canadians), if its members had a sojourner rather than a permanent-settler orientation, and if limited opportunities for advancement existed in the community.[36]

CLASS CONSCIOUSNESS   Just how important are the ethnic factors that Warner and others have reported in shaping an awareness of social class? The answer is that the significance of ethnic factors depends on a great many variables; some of these variables are economic conditions, mobility patterns, and prevailing attitudes. John Leggett found that class consciousness depends on the ethnic factor: the lower a group's ethnic status in the society, the higher the level of class consciousness.[37] Other studies have shown that working-class ethnic groups tend to view their class as hostile to, and under the political control of, the higher classes.[38]

Because ethnic minorities are disproportionately represented among the lower classes, and because middle-class values dominate in the United States, a reasonable assumption is that at least some of the attitudes of each group result from people's value judgments about social class. That is to say, the dominant group's criticism and stereotyping of the minority group probably rests in part on class distinctions.

ETHNICITY AND SOCIAL CLASS   Social-class status plays an important role in determining a minority group's adjustment to and acceptance by society. For example, because the Cuban and Vietnamese refugees arrived possessing the education and occupational experience of the middle class, they succeeded in overcoming early native concerns and did not encounter the same degree of negativism as had earlier groups. On the other hand, when unskilled and often illiterate peasants have entered the lower-class positions in American society, many Americans have belittled, avoided, and discriminated against them because of their supposedly inferior ways. Frequently, these attitudes and actions have represented an awareness of class differences as well as cultural differences. Since the dominant group usually represents a higher stratum in the social-class hierarchy, the differing social-class values and life styles provide a source of friction in addition to the ethnic cultural differences.

Social class and ethnic group membership are closely intertwined, but, according to Colin Greer, many social observers have placed too much emphasis on ethnic-centered analyses and ignored the larger question of class.

This kind of ethnic reductionism forces us to accept as predetermined what society defines as truth. Only through ethnicity can identity be securely achieved. The result is that ethnic questions which could, in fact, further our understanding of the relationship of individuals to social structures are always raised in a way that serves to reconcile us to a common heritage of miserable inequities. Instead of realizing that the lack of a well-defined stratification structure, linked to a legitimated aristocratic tradition, led Americans to employ the language of ethnic pluralism in exchange for direct divisions by social class, we continue to ignore the real factors of class in our society. . . . What we must ultimately talk about is class. The cues of felt ethnicity turn out to be the recognizable characteristics of class position in this society: to feel black, Irish, Italian, Jewish has meant to learn to live in accommodation with that part of your heritage that is compatible with the needs and opportunities in America upon arrival and soon thereafter.[39]

In 1964, ten years before Greer's observations, Milton Gordon had suggested that dominant-minority relations be examined within the larger context of the social structure.[40] This proposition marked an important turning point in racial and ethnic studies.[41] Although he believed that all groups would eventually become assimilated, Gordon offered an explanation of the present pluralistic society. His central thesis was that four factors or social categories play a part in forming subsocieties within the nation: ethnicity (by which Gordon also meant race), social class, rural or urban residence, and regionalism.[42] These factors unite in various combinations to create a number of *ethclasses*. These subsocieties result from the intersection of the stratifications of race and ethnic group with the stratifications of social class. Additional determinants are the rural or urban setting and the particular region of the country in which a group lives. Examples of ethclasses are lower-middle-class white Catholics in a northeastern city, lower-class black Baptists in the rural South, and upper-class white Jews in a western urban area.

Numerous studies have supported the concept that race and ethnicity, together with social class, are important in social structures and intergroup conflicts.[43] Not only do ethclass groupings exist, but people tend to interact mostly within them for their intimate primary relationships. To the extent that this is true, multiple allegiances and conflicts will occur. According to this view, both cultural and structural pluralism currently exist. Even those whose families have been here for several generations are affiliated with, and participate in, subsocieties. Gordon does, however, view assimilation as a linear process in which eventual assimilation, including structural, will occur.

INTERGROUP CONFLICT

Conflict does not necessarily occur when different peoples make contact. Brazil and Hawaii are just two examples of places where peaceful and harmonious interactions have existed among different peoples. In many other instances of intergroup relations, however, some form of stress, tension, or conflict does occur. In this chapter we have presented the major factors that may set the stage for such conflict: cultural and structural differentiation. Those factors may be applied to an understanding of conflict between dominant and minority groups.

CULTURAL DIFFERENTIATION

When similarities between the minority group and the indigenous group exist, the probability is greater that the relationship will be relatively harmonious and that assimilation will eventually occur.[44] The greater and more visible the cultural differences, the greater the likelihood that conflict will occur. When large numbers of German and Irish Catholics came to this country in the mid-nineteenth century, Protestant America grew uneasy. As priests and nuns also arrived, and as the Catholics built churches, convents, and schools, Protestant America became alarmed at what it considered a papal conspiracy to gain control of the country. Emotions ran high, and the result was unrest and violence.

Religion is often a basis for cultural conflict, as demonstrated by the examples of the Mormons, Jews, and Quakers, who have all suffered discrimination in this country. Yet many other aspects of cultural visibility can also serve as sources of contention. Cultural differences might range from clothing (for example, Sikh turbans and saris) to leisure activities (for example, Hispanic cockfights). Americans once condemned the Chinese as opium smokers, even though the British had introduced opium smoking into China and promoted it among the lower-class Chinese population.

Cultural differences do not necessarily cause intergroup conflict. To understand the reason for the variance in relations between culturally distinct groups, we must look elsewhere for the catalyst. The nature of the structural conditions and their possible evolution help to determine whether or not conflict occurs.

STRUCTURAL DIFFERENTIATION

Sometimes economic and technological conditions facilitate minority integration. When the economy is healthy and jobs are plentiful, newcomers find it easier to get established and work their way up the socioeconomic ladder. In present-day America, however, technological progress has reduced the number of low-status blue-collar jobs and increased the number of high-status white-collar jobs, which require more highly skilled and educated workers. The result is that fewer jobs are available for unskilled, foreign, marginal, and unassimilated people.

Perhaps because of the importance of one's job as a source of economic security and status, *occupational mobility* — the ability to improve one's job position — seems to be an important factor in determining whether prejudice will increase or decrease. A number of studies have shown that downward social mobility increases ethnic hostility.[45] Bruno Bettelheim and Morris Janowitz report from seven studies that persons moving downward in status are not only more prejudiced than the group they left but also more prejudiced than the lower-status group they enter. Additionally, upwardly mobile people are generally more tolerant than nonmobile individuals.[46] It would appear that loss of status and prestige increases hostility toward outgroups, whereas upward gains enable people to be more magnanimous toward others.

If one group becomes dominant and another subservient, obviously one group has more power than the other. Social-class status partly reflects this unequal distribution of power, which may also fall along racial or ethnic lines. For ethnicity to become a basis for stratification, it appears that several factors must be present.

> Ethnic stratification will emerge when distinct ethnic groups are brought into sustained contact *only* if the groups are characterized by a high degree of ethnocentrism, competition, *and* differential power. Competition provides the motivation for stratification; ethnocentrism channels the competition along ethnic lines; and the power differential determines whether either group will be able to subordinate the other.[47]

This power differential is of enormous importance in race and ethnic relations. If the stratification system is rigid, as in a slave or caste system, with no hope or means of improving status, then intergroup relations may be stable though perhaps far from mutually satisfactory. Dominant power, whether expressed in legalized ways or through structural discrimination, intimidation, or coercion, maintains the social system. Even if the stratification system allows for upward mobility, some members of the dominant group may believe that the lower-class racial and ethnic groups are challenging the social order as they strive for their share of the "good life." If the dominant group does not feel threatened, the change will be peaceful. If the minority group meets resistance but retains hope and a sense of belonging to the larger society, the struggle for more power will be within the system (for example, by means of demonstrations, boycotts, voter-registration drives, or lobbying) rather than through violence.[48]

As a minority group struggles for a larger share of economic and political power, another group — either a majority group or another minority group — may resist, especially if it views the situation as threatening to its own power resources. Intergroup competition for scarce resources is a breeding ground for racial and ethnic hostilities. Most regional antiforeign flare-ups — such as the late-nineteenth-century race-baiting riots on the West Coast against Chinese and Japanese workers or the 1919 Chicago race riots against blacks entering the meat-packing industry — have occurred as a reaction to minority-group strivings for greater power resources.

Social-class antagonisms also influence people's perceptions of racial and ethnic groups.[49] Some social scientists maintain that the problem of black-white relations is more a problem of social class than of racism. Illustrative of this view is James M. O'Kane:

> The gap exists between the classes, not the races; it is between the white and black middle classes on the one hand, and the white and black lower classes on the other. Skin color and the history of servitude do little to explain the present polarization of the classes. . . . Class differentials, not racial differentials, explain the presence and persistence of poverty in the ranks of the urban Negro.[50]

O'Kane suggests several parallels between Irish, Italian, and Polish immigrants and Southern blacks who migrated to Northern cities (the Chinese, some of the Japanese, and others could also be included). All came from agrarian poverty to industrial slums. Encountering prejudice and discrimination, some sought alternative routes of upward mobility: crime, ethnic politics, stable but unskilled employment.[51] Other social scientists argue that the black experience does not equate with that of European immigrants. They hold, as did the Kerner Commission investigating the urban riots of the late 1960s, that the dominant society's colonization of blacks deprived them of the strong social organizations that other groups had. Moreover, today's labor market offers fewer unskilled jobs for blacks than it once offered for other immigrant groups, thereby depriving blacks of a means to begin moving upward.[52]

Conflict theorists such as Ralf Dahrendorf suggest that social class is an important variable affecting conflict. Dahrendorf maintains that a correlation exists between a group's economic position and the intensity of its conflict with the dominant society. The greater the deprivation in economic resources, social status, and social power, the more probable it is that the weaker group will resort to intense and violent conflict to achieve gains in any of these three areas. As the social-class position of a group increases, intergroup conflict will be less intense and less violent.[53]

Years earlier, Max Weber argued that when economic resources become more evenly distributed among classes, relative status will become the issue of conflict, if conflict occurs at all.[54] Conflict occurs not only because a lower-class group seeks an end to deprivation, but also because the group next higher on the socioeconomic ladder feels most

FIGURE 3.5

In 1962, militant Catholics picket in front of the residence of the New Orleans archbishop to protest his order desegregating the parochial schools.
(United Press International)

threatened.[55] Quite often the working-class group displays the most prejudice and most frequently engages in violence against the upward-striving minority group. Other factors may also be at work, but status competition is significant in causing conflict.

THEORIES OF MINORITY INTEGRATION

Over 50 million immigrants have come to the United States since its founding as a nation. During this vast ethnic experience, three different theories have emerged concerning how these ethnically different peoples either should or did fit into American society. These schools of thought have been (1) *assimilation*, or the majority-conformity theory; (2) *amalgamation*, or the "melting pot" theory; and (3) *accommodation*, or the pluralistic theory.

The type of interaction between minority peoples and those of the dominant culture has been partly dependent upon which of these ideologies was then accepted by those already established in the community. People formulate attitudes and expectations based upon the values they hold. If those values include a clear image of how an "American" should look, talk, and act, then people who are different from that model will find their adjustment and acceptance by others a more difficult matter. Conversely, if those values allow for diversity, then a greater possibility exists that harmonious relationships will evolve (Figure 3.6).

ASSIMILATION

Generally speaking, *assimilation* means the functioning of racial or ethnic minority-group members within a society without any marked cultural, social, or personal differences from the people of the majority group. Physical or racial differences may persist, but they do not serve as the basis for group prejudice or discrimination. In effect, the minority groups no longer appear to be strangers.

Because the majority of the people living in the United States during the eighteenth century were of English descent, English influence upon the new nation's culture was enormous — in language, institutional forms, values, and attitudes. By the first quarter of the nineteenth century, a distinct national consciousness had emerged, and many wanted to de-emphasize their English origins and influences. However, when migration patterns changed the composition of the American population in the 1880s, the Yankees re-established the Anglo-Saxon as the superior

FIGURE 3.6

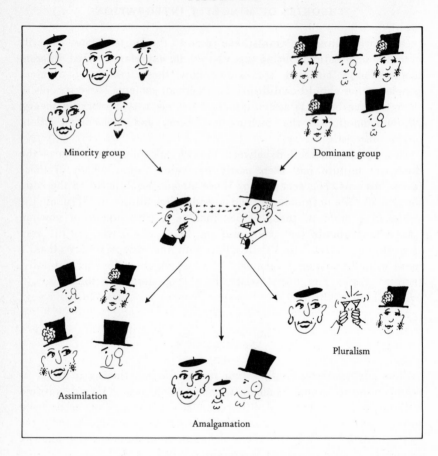

Minority group

Dominant group

Assimilation

Amalgamation

Pluralism

THEORIES OF MINORITY INTEGRATION

archetype.[56] Anglo-Saxonism remained dominant well into the twentieth century as the mold into which any newcomers must fit.

In order to preserve their Anglo-Saxon heritage, Americans often attempted, sometimes with success, to curtail the large numbers of non-Anglo-Saxon immigrants. For those who did come, social pressures demanded that they shed their native culture and attachments as quickly as possible and be remade into Americans along cherished Anglo-Saxon lines. The schools served as an important socialization agent in promoting the shedding of cultural differences.

Sometimes insistence upon assimilation reached feverish heights, as evidenced by the Americanization movement during World War I. United States participation in a European conflict caused questions to be raised about those who were not "100 percent American." Governmental agencies at all levels, together with many private organizations, acted to implement more immediately foreigners' adoption of American practices: citizenship, reverence for American institutions, and use of the English language.[57] Because this policy required that all minority groups divest themselves of their distinctive ethnic characteristics and adopt those of the dominant group, George R. Stewart suggested that it be called the "transmuting pot" theory.[58]

Other assimilation efforts have not been very successful — for example, with people whose ancestral history in an area predates the nation's expansion into that territory. Most Indian tribes throughout the country as well as the Mexican-Americans of the Southwest have resisted this cultural hegemony. In fact, some critics argue that assimilation has not yet occurred for most racial and ethnic groups. Milton Gordon offered an important insight into this matter with his analysis that assimilation has several aspects or subprocesses.[59] The degree of assimilation can be partly measured by the extent of a group's identification as American and its intermarriage with members of the dominant culture, and by the absence of prejudice, discrimination, and intergroup conflict about power and values. Most importantly, *cultural assimilation* (acculturation) and *structural assimilation* (large-scale entrance into the cliques, clubs, and institutions of the host society on a primary-group level) best reveal the extent of acceptance of minority groups in the larger society. Gordon states that "Once structural assimilation has occurred, either simultaneously with or subsequent to acculturation, all other types of assimilation will naturally follow."[60] Other sociologists disagree with Gordon, claiming that cultural assimilation does not necessarily result from structural assimilation. Some studies have shown that structural assimilation has not yet occurred to any significant degree.[61]

Many sociologists, including Robert E. Park and Louis Wirth, have viewed assimilation as an ongoing process. Park suggested a deterministic race-relations cycle, in which a universal pattern of contact, competition, accommodation, and eventual assimilation occur in a progressive

FIGURE 3.7

Saluting the flag in the Mott Street Industrial School, circa 1889–1890. The
schools served as a major means of acculturation. (Photograph by Jacob A.
Riis, Jacob A. Riis Collection, Museum of the City of New York)

and irreversible pattern.[62] The inflexibility of this model and its exceptions made it less than satisfactory as an explanation.[63] Influenced by Park, Wirth maintained that situational variables are important in the assimilation of minority groups.[64] Wirth distinguished among pluralism, assimilation, secession, and militancy as successive minority responses to majority-group prejudice and discrimination. As groups begin to gain some power, they generally attempt to gain social tolerance of the group's differences (*pluralism*), then go beyond this and become absorbed by the dominant society (*assimilation*). Those groups who are prevented from assimilating withdraw (*secession*), but if conflict then ensues, they seek more extreme remedies (*militancy*).

Assimilation may be both a majority-group and a minority-group goal, but it is also possible that one or both may view assimilation as undesirable. Accordingly, the preceding typologies are not always helpful in examining majority-minority relationships. Gordon shows the complexity of the assimilation process; Park offers a general model of how the process evolves. Wirth suggests that the dynamics of the situation shape the evolvement of majority-minority relations throughout the assimilation process. The larger question, whether the assimilation process is linear, remains in all cases. Not all groups seek assimilation, nor do all groups who seek assimilation attain it. Varying goals, social arrangements, and historical conditions may also affect majority-minority patterns.

Assimilation — as a belief, goal, or pattern — helps explain many aspects of majority-minority relations, particularly acceptance and adjustment. For many members of the dominant society, assimilation of minorities has meant their absorption into the mold, reflecting what Barbara Solomon calls "the Anglo Saxon complex."[65] For physically or culturally distinct groups (for example, blacks, Indians, Asians, or Moslems), such a concept has raised an often insurmountable barrier. Even without the Anglo-Saxon role model, assimilation has been preceded by a transitional period in which the newcomer has gradually blended in with majority-group members. In doing so, the individual has acquired a new behavioral identity, perhaps at some personal cost.

THE MELTING-POT THEORY

The democratic experiment in the new land of America fired many an imagination. Here a new society was being shaped, peopled by immigrants from different European nations and not slavishly dependent upon the customs and traditions of the past. This set of circumstances generated a romantic notion of America as a melting pot. The *melting-pot theory*, or the theory of *amalgamation*, states that all the diverse peoples blend their biological and cultural differences into an altogether new breed — the American.

J. Hector St. John de Crèvecoeur, a French settler in New York, popularized this concept in 1782 with his description of an American. That Crèvecoeur included only white Europeans partly explains the weakness of this approach to minority integration.

> He is either a European, or the descendant of a European; hence that strange mixture of blood which you will find in no other country. I could point out to you a man whose grandfather was an Englishman, whose wife was Dutch, whose son married a French woman, and whose present four sons have now four wives of different nations. He is an American, who, leaving behind him all his ancient prejudices and manners, receives new ones from the new mode of life he has embraced, the new government he obeys and the new rank he holds. . . . Here individuals of all nations are melted into a new race of men, whose labors and posterity will one day cause great changes in the world.[66]

This idealistic concept found many advocates over the years. In 1893, Frederick Jackson Turner updated it with his frontier thesis, a notion that greatly influenced historical scholarship for more than forty years. Turner believed that the challenge of frontier life was the catalyst that fused the immigrants into a composite new national stock within an evolving social order.

> Thus the Middle West was teaching the lesson of national cross-fertilization instead of national enmities, the possibility of a newer and richer civilization, not by preserving unmodified or isolated the old component elements, but by breaking down the line-fences, by merging the individual life in the common product — a new product, which held the promise of world brotherhood.[67]

In the early twentieth century, many believed that the large influx of minority peoples would enter an urban melting pot, as dramatized in Israel Zangwill's extraordinarily popular play in the early 1900s, appropriately called *The Melting Pot*. However, beginning in the 1930s, that concept and Turner's frontier melting-pot hypothesis both came under heavy criticism. Today few social scientists accept this explanation of minority integration into society.

Over several generations, intermarriages frequently have occurred between people of different nationalities and, to a lesser degree, of different religions and, to a still lesser degree, of different races. One could thus argue that a biological merging of previously distinct ethnic stocks, although not so much of different races, has taken place.[68] However, the melting-pot theory spoke not only of intermarriages among the different groups but also of a distinct new national culture evolving from elements of all other cultures. Here the theory has proven unrealistic. This country, from its founding, has been dominated by an Anglo-Saxon population and thus by the English language and Anglo-Saxon institutional forms. Rather than a melting of various cultural patterns into a new American culture, what actually has occurred is a metamorphosis of elements of minority cultures into the Anglo-Saxon mold.

Although the United States Constitution guaranteed freedom of religion from the outset, for the first eighty years the country was almost exclusively Protestant. Gordon suggests that only in the institution of religion have minority groups altered the national culture; the United States is now a land of three major faiths: Protestant, Catholic, and Jewish.[69] In other areas, the entry of many diverse minority groups into American society has not resulted in new social structures or institutional forms in the larger society. Instead, subcultural social structures and institutions have evolved to meet group needs, and the dominant culture has benefited from the labors and certain cultural aspects of minority groups within the already existing dominant culture. For example, minority influences are found in word usage, names of places, cuisine, architecture, art, and recreational activities. To use a biological analogy, an organism consumes food and is in some way affected (nourished) by it, but the food is assimilated in the sense that it becomes an integral part of the organism, retaining none of its original characteristics.[70] In a similar manner, American culture has remained basically unchanged, though strengthened, despite the influx of many minority groups.

Some social observers have viewed the emergence of three major faiths as evidence that America was actually a "triple melting pot." Based on her studies in New Haven in 1944 and 1952, Ruby Jo Reeves Kennedy concluded that intermarriage was occurring between various nationalities, but only within the three major religious groupings.[71] A few years later, Will Herberg echoed this analysis, arguing that ethnic differences were disappearing as religious groupings became the primary foci of identity and interaction.[72] Subsequent studies have offered conflicting evidence of assimilation versus pluralism based on religion, national origin, social class, and residence. We shall examine some of these findings shortly.

Most sociologists (including the author) believe that the melting-pot theory is a myth and always has been. Its idealistic rhetoric has attracted many followers and still does. In reality, the melting meant Anglo-conformity, being remade according to the idealized Anglo-Saxon mold. Herberg offered some observations on the theory of Anglo-conformity as opposed to the idea of the melting pot.

But it would be a mistake to infer from this that the American's image of himself — and that means the ethnic group member's image of himself as he becomes American — is a composite or synthesis of the ethnic elements that have gone into the making of the American. It is nothing of the kind; the American's image of himself is still the Anglo-American ideal it was at the beginning of our independent existence. The "national type" as ideal has always been, and remains, pretty well fixed. It is the *Mayflower*, John Smith, Davy Crockett, George Washington, and Abraham Lincoln that define the American's self-image, and this is true whether the American in question is a descendent of the Pilgrims or the grandson of an immigrant from southeastern Europe.[73]

The rejection of the melting-pot theory by many people, coupled with an ethnic consciousness, spawned the third ideology, cultural pluralism.

PLURALISM

Pluralism recognizes the persistence of racial and ethnic diversity. Pluralist theorists argue that minorities can maintain their distinctive subcultures and simultaneously interact with relative equality in the larger society. In countries such as Switzerland and the United States, this combination of diversity and togetherness is possible in varying degrees because the people agree on certain basic values (for example, the American Creed in the United States). At the same time, minorities may interact mostly among themselves, live within well-defined communities, have their own forms of organizations, work in similar occupations, and marry within their own group.

Horace Kallen is generally recognized as the first exponent of cultural pluralism. In 1915, he published "Democracy Versus the Melting Pot," in which he rejected the assimilation and amalgamation theories.[74] Not only did each group tend to preserve its own language, institutions, and cultural heritage, he maintained, but the very nature of democracy gave them the right to do so. To be sure, minority groups learned the English language and participated in American institutions, but what the United States really had become was a "cooperation of cultural diversities." Seeing Americanization movements as a threat to minority groups and the melting-pot notion as unrealistic, Kallen believed that cultural pluralism could be the basis for a great democratic commonwealth. A philosopher, not a sociologist, Kallen nonetheless directed scholarly attention to a practice that many Americans had long followed.

A continual pattern throughout American history has been that of immigrants settling in clusters with their compatriots. Germans and Scandinavians in the Midwest, and Irish, Italians, Jews, and others in the cities all illustrate how a group attempts to ease adjustment in a strange land by re-creating in miniature much of the cultural world left

FIGURE 3.8

"UNCLE SAM'S TROUBLESOME BEDFELLOWS"

This cartoon pictures Uncle Sam annoyed by groups who were seen as unassimilable. Both racial differences (blacks, Chinese, and Indians) and religious differences (Irish Catholics and Mormons) were cause for being kicked out of the symbolic bed. Cartoon appeared in San Francisco illustrated weekly, *The Wasp*, February 8, 1879. (The Distorted Image, Anti-Defamation League. John and Selma Appel Collection)

behind. Gordon was prompted to comment: "Thus cultural pluralism was a fact in American society before it became a theory — at least a theory with explicit relevance for the nation as a whole and articulated and discussed in the general English-speaking circles of American intellectual life."[75]

In essence, those who believe in cultural pluralism hold that various ethnic groups tend to interact in primary-group relationships mostly with others like themselves. Immigrants who adopt a new land as their home do not necessarily reject all of their past. The comfort of familiarity and security, the identification with and pride in their heritage, especially when reinforced by compatriots, may encourage the immigrants to retain their culture and to have face-to-face contacts with understanding ingroup members, while still becoming a part of the new society.

RETROSPECT

Culture provides the definitions by which members of a society perceive the world about them. Language and other forms of symbolic interaction provide the means through which this knowledge is perceived and transmitted. Becoming acculturated requires learning both the language and the symbol system of the society. Unless it is isolated from the rest of the world, a society undergoes change through culture contact and the diffusion of ideas, inventions, and practices. Within large societies, subcultures usually exist. They may be gradually assimilated (convergent subcultures) or they may remain distinct (persistent subcultures).

Structural conditions also influence people's perceptions of the world, whether they live in an industrialized or agrarian society, a closed or open social system, a growing or contracting economy, a friendly or unfriendly environment, or whether or not their homeland, friends, and relatives are accessible. Distribution of power resources and compatibility with the existing social structure will greatly determine majority-minority relations as well.

The interplay between the variables of race, ethnic group, and social class are important for understanding how some problems and conflicts arise. What often gets mistaken for an attribute of race or ethnic group may be a broader aspect of social class. Because many attitudes and values are situational responses to socioeconomic status, a change in status or opportunities will also bring about a change in those attitudes and values.

Three theories of minority integration have evolved since the nation's beginning. The romantic notion of a melting pot, in which a new breed of people with a distinct culture would emerge, proved unrealistic. Assimilation, or majority-conformity, became a goal of many, both native-born and foreign-born; yet not all sought this goal or were able to achieve it. Finally, pluralism emerged as a school of thought in recognition of the persistence of ethnic diversity in a society with a commonly shared core culture.

QUESTIONS FOR DISCUSSION

1. What is the relationship between culture, reality, and intergroup relations?

2. What are subcultures? What forms do they take? What significance do these forms have for intergroup relations?

3. What is the relationship between a society's structural conditions and intergroup relations?

4. Why must stratification be considered in any discussion of racial or ethnic groups?

5. What factors contribute to the likelihood of intergroup conflict? Why?

6. Discuss the major theories of minority integration.

SUGGESTED READINGS

Bettelheim, Bruno, and Morris Janowitz. *Social Change and Prejudice.* Free Press, New York, 1964.

Blalock, Hubert M., Jr. *Toward a Theory of Minority-Group Relations.* Wiley, New York, 1967.

Feldstein, Stanley, and Lawrence Costello (eds.). *The Ordeal of Assimilation.* Doubleday Anchor Press, New York, 1974.

Gordon, Milton M. *Assimilation in American Life.* Oxford University Press, New York, 1964.

Hartmann, Edward G. *The Movement to Americanize the Immigrant.* Columbia University Press, New York, 1948.

Newman, William M. *American Pluralism.* Harper & Row, New York, 1973.

Park, Robert E. *Race and Culture.* Free Press, Glencoe, Ill., 1950.

Shibutani, Tamotsu, and Kian M. Kwan. *Ethnic Stratification.* Macmillan, New York, 1970.

NOTES

1. See the discussion on pp. 25–26, 35.

2. Louis Schneider and Charles Bonjean (eds.), *The Idea of Culture in the Social Sciences,* Cambridge University Press, Cambridge, England, 1973.

3. The importance of symbols to social

interaction has drawn much attention in sociology. See Benjamin L. Whorf, *Language, Thought and Reality*, Wiley, New York, 1956; Gertrude Jaeger and Philip Selznick, "A Normative Theory of Culture," *American Sociological Review*, 29 (October 1964), 653–659; Herbert Blumer, *Symbolic Interaction: Perspective and Method*, Prentice-Hall, Englewood Cliffs, N.J., 1969.

4. Harry C. Bredemeier and Richard M. Stephenson, *The Analysis of Social Systems*, Holt, New York, 1962, p. 3.

5. Giraffe going by a second-story window. Hot dog on a hamburger roll. Spider doing pushups on a mirror.

6. This connection between Lippmann's comments, the Droodles, and human response to definitions of stimuli was originally made by Harry C. Bredemeier and Richard M. Stephenson, *The Analysis of Social Systems*, pp. 2–3.

7. Edward O. Wilson, *Sociobiology*, The Belknap Press of Harvard University Press, Cambridge, Mass., 1975, p. 550.

8. Desmond Morris, *Manwatching: A Field Guide to Human Behavior*, Abrams, New York, 1977.

9. William I. Thomas, "The Relation of Research to the Social Process," in *Essays on Research in the Social Sciences*, The Brookings Institution, Washington, D.C., 1931, p. 189.

10. See the discussion on pp. 48–49.

11. Gregory Razran, "Ethnic Dislike and Stereotypes: A Laboratory Study," *Journal of Abnormal and Social Psychology*, 45 (1950), 7–27.

12. Copyright © 1949 by Richard Rodgers and Oscar Hammerstein II. Copyright renewed. Williamson Music, Inc., owner of publication and allied rights for the Western Hemisphere and Japan. International copyright secured. All rights reserved. Used by permission.

13. Peter L. Berger and Thomas Luckmann, *The Social Construction of Reality*, Doubleday, New York, 1963.

14. John Gillis, *The Ways of Men*, Appleton-Century-Crofts, New York, 1948, p. 556.

15. For a case study of England from 1000 to 1899, see Margaret T. Hodgen, *Change and History*, Wenner-Gren Foundation for Anthropological Research, New York, 1952.

16. Stanley Lieberson, "A Societal Theory of Race and Ethnic Relations," *American Sociological Review*, 26 (December 1961), 902–910.

17. See the discussion on pp. 49–51.

18. Mary C. Sengstock, "Social Change in the Country of Origin as a Factor in Immigrant Conceptions of Nationality," *Ethnicity*, 4 (March 1977), 54–69.

19. E. Franklin Frazier, *The Negro Family in Chicago*, University of Chicago Press, Chicago, 1932; see also *The Negro Family in the United States*, rev. ed., University of Chicago Press, Chicago, 1966.

20. Daniel P. Moynihan, *The Negro Family: The Case for National Action*, U.S. Department of Labor, Washington, D.C., 1965.

21. *Ibid.*, p. 5.

22. *Ibid.*, p. 6.

23. *Ibid.*, pp. 30, 47.

24. Oscar Lewis, *La Vida*, Vintage, New York, 1966, pp. xlii–lii.

25. *Ibid.*, p. xlv.

26. Edward C. Banfield, *The Unheavenly City: The Nature and Future of Our Urban Crisis*, Little, Brown, Boston, 1970, pp. 210–211.

27. William Ryan, "Is Banfield Serious?" *Social Policy*, 1 (November–December 1970), 74–76.

28. Charles A. Valentine, *Culture and Poverty*, University of Chicago Press, Chicago, 1968, p. 122.

29. Joe R. Feagin, "Poverty: We Still Believe that God Helps Those Who Help Themselves," *Psychology Today*, 6 (November 1972), 101–110, 129.

30. Michael Harrington, *The Other America: Poverty in the United States*, Penguin, Baltimore, 1963, p. 21.

31. Valentine, *Culture and Poverty*, p. 129.

32. Lola M. Irelan, Oliver C. Moles, and Robert M. O'Shea, "Ethnicity, Poverty, and Selected Attitudes: A Test of the 'Culture of Poverty' Hypothesis," *Social Forces*, 47 (1969), 405–413.

33. Eliot Liebow, *Tally's Corner: A Study of Negro Streetcorner Men*, Little, Brown, Boston, 1967, pp. 222–223. See also Ulf Hannerz, *Soulside: Inquiries into Ghetto Culture and Community*, Columbia University Press, New York, 1969.

34. Alan C. Kerckhoff, *Socialization and Social Class*, Prentice-Hall, Englewood Cliffs, N.J., 1972, pp. 126–128.

35. W. Lloyd Warner and Paul S. Lunt, *The Social Life of a Modern Community*, Yankee City Series, Vol. 1, Yale University Press, New Haven, Conn., 1941.

36. W. Lloyd Warner and Leo Srole, *The Social System of American Ethnic Groups*, Yankee City Series, Vol. 3, Yale University Press, New Haven, Conn., 1945.

37. John C. Leggett, "Working Class Consciousness in an Industrial Community," unpublished Ph.D. thesis, University of Michigan, 1962, reported in Bruno Bettelheim and Morris Janowitz, *Social Change and Prejudice*, Free Press, New York, 1964, p. 33.

38. Richard Centers, *The Psychology of Social Classes: A Study of Class Consciousness*, Princeton University Press, Princeton, 1949; Oscar Glantz, "Class Consciousness and Political Solidarity," *American Sociological Review*, 23 (August 1958), 375–382; Robert W. Hodge and Donald J. Treiman, "Class Identification in the U.S.," *American Journal of Sociology*, 73 (March 1968), 535–547; Werner S. Landecker, "Class Crystal-lization and Class Consciousness," *American Sociological Review*, 28 (April 1963), 219–229; Robert T. Morris and Raymond J. Murphy, "A Paradigm for the Study of Class Consciousness," *Sociology and Social Research*, 50 (April 1966), 298–313.

39. Colin Greer (ed.), *Divided Society*, Basic Books, New York, 1974, p. 34.

40. Milton M. Gordon, *Assimilation in American Life*, Oxford University Press, New York, 1964.

41. William M. Newman, *American Pluralism*, Harper & Row, New York, 1973, p. 84.

42. Gordon, *Assimilation in American Life*, p. 47.

43. See August B. Hollingshead, "Trends in Social Stratification: A Case Study," *American Sociological Review*, 17 (December 1952), 685–686; Raymond Mack (ed.), *Race, Class and Power*, 2nd ed., Van Nostrand Reinhold, New York, 1963; John Leggett, *Class, Race and Labor*, Oxford University Press, New York, 1968.

44. Warner and Srole, *Social Systems of the American Ethnic Groups*, pp. 285–286.

45. See Fred B. Silberstein and Melvin Seeman, "Social Mobility and Prejudice," *American Journal of Sociology*, 60 (November 1959), 258–264; Joseph Greenblum and Leonard J. Pearlin, "Vertical Mobility and Prejudice: A Socio-Psychological Analysis," in *Class, Status and Power*, ed. Richard Bendix and S. M. Lipset, Free Press, Glencoe, Ill., 1953, pp. 483–491.

46. Bettelheim and Janowitz, *Social Change and Prejudice*, pp. 29–34.

47. Donald L. Noel, "A Theory of the Origin of Ethnic Stratification," *Social Problems*, 16 (Fall 1968), 157–172.

48. Lewis A. Coser, "Conflict: Social Aspects," in *International Encyclopedia of the Social Sciences*, ed. David Sills, Macmillan, New York, 1968, pp. 234–235.

49. See Hubert M. Blalock, Jr., *Toward a Theory of Minority-Group Relations*, Wiley, New York, 1967, pp. 199–203.

50. James M. O'Kane, "Ethnic Mobility and the Lower-Income Negro: A Socio-Historical Perspective," *Social Problems*, 16 (1969), 309–311; see also Leonard Reissman and Michael N. Halstead, "The Subject Is Class," *Sociology and Social Research*, 54 (1970), 301–304.

51. *Ibid.*, pp. 303–311.

52. See Robert Blauner, "Internal Colonialism and Ghetto Revolt," *Social Problems*, 16 (1969), 397; Stuart L. Hills, "Negroes and Immigrants in America," *Sociological Focus*, 3 (Summer 1970), 85–96; Nathan Glazer, "Blacks and Ethnic Groups," *Social Problems*, 18 (1971), 444–461.

53. Ralf Dahrendorf, *Class and Class Conflict in Industrial Society*, Stanford University Press, Stanford, Calif., 1959, pp. 215–218.

54. Max Weber, "Class, Status, Party," 1922, in *From Max Weber*, trans. and ed. Hans Gerth and C. Wright Mills, Oxford University Press, New York, 1946, pp. 193–194.

55. See the discussion on pp. 33–35.

56. Barbara Solomon, *Ancestors and Immigrants*, University of Chicago Press, Chicago, 1956, pp. 59–61.

57. John Higham, *Strangers in the Land*, Rutgers University Press, New Brunswick, N.J., 1955, p. 247.

58. George R. Stewart, *American Ways of Life*, Doubleday, New York, 1954, pp. 23, 28.

59. Gordon, *Assimilation in American Life*, pp. 70–71.

60. *Ibid.*, p. 81.

61. See Gerhard Lenski, *The Religious Factor*, Doubleday, New York, 1961, pp. 326–330; Will Herberg, *Protestant-Catholic-Jew*, Doubleday, New York, 1955; William M. Dobriner, *Class in Suburbia*, Prentice-Hall, Englewood Cliffs, N.J., 1963; Bennett M. Berger, *Working Class Suburbs*, 2nd ed., University of California Press, Berkeley, 1960.

62. Robert E. Park, *Race and Culture*, Free Press, Glencoe, Ill., 1950, p. 150.

63. See the discussion in Chapter 11.

64. Louis Wirth, "The Problem of Minority Groups," in *The Science of Man in the World Crisis*, ed. Ralph Linton, Columbia University Press, New York, 1945.

65. Solomon, *Ancestors and Immigrants*, pp. 59–81.

66. J. Hector St. John de Crèvecoeur, *Letters from an American Farmer*, Albert and Charles Boni, New York, 1925, pp. 54–55. Reprinted from the original edition, London, 1782.

67. Frederick Jackson Turner, *The Frontier in American History*, Henry Holt, New York, 1920, p. 351.

68. Actually, any student of western civilizations would point out that centuries of invasions, conquests, boundary changes, etc., had often resulted in cross-breeding and that truly distinct or pure ethnic types were virtually nonexistent long before the eighteenth century.

69. Gordon, *Assimilation in American Life*, pp. 109–110.

70. Henry Pratt Fairchild, *Immigration*, Macmillan, New York, 1925, p. 396 ff.

71. Ruby Jo Reeves Kennedy, "Single or Triple Melting Pot? Intermarriage Trends in New Haven, 1870–1940," *American Journal of Sociology*, 49 (January 1944), 331–339; see also her follow-up study in *American Journal of Sociology*, 58 (July 1952), 56–59.

72. See Will Herberg, *Protestant-Catholic-Jew*, Doubleday, New York, 1955.

73. *Ibid.*, pp. 33–34.

74. Horace M. Kallen, "Democracy Versus the Melting Pot," *The Nation*, Feb. 18, 1915, pp. 190–194; Feb. 25, 1915, pp. 217–220.

75. Gordon, *Assimilation in American Life*, p. 135.

FOUR

THE "OLD" IMMIGRANTS:

NORTHERN AND WESTERN EUROPEANS

⚔ A trickle of immigrants from almost all parts of the world arrived during the early history of the United States. The story of the colonial period and the first one hundred years as an independent nation, however, is predominantly the experience of immigrants from the British Isles, France, Holland, Scandinavia, and Germany, and their descendants.

HISTORICAL AND SOCIOLOGICAL PERSPECTIVES

At first, all Europeans were strangers to these shores, and they responded with wonder and excitement in their journals and reports about the vastness, resources, and promise of the New World. In those early years, all shared in the adventure of creating a new society. First the necessity to survive, then pro- or anti-British sentiments dominated relations among diverse peoples. As life stabilized and a common culture evolved, many newcomers not only found themselves in strange surroundings, but were more quickly perceived as strangers in a society in which homogeneity had come to be taken for granted. Thus, many Irish and Germans, with their cultural, religious, and social-class differences from the natives, often experienced open hostility upon their arrival.

Before examining the connection between theory and the actual experience of any group, note that a pitfall is inherent in considering ethnic groups only within a limited historical framework. A tendency to do so results from the fact that immigration patterns have varied among countries and have peaked at different times. The word *peak* provides a clue to how the experiences of each racial or ethnic group should be viewed. Although each minority group usually has had a significant period of migration, thus providing a focal point for examination, each country has sent a continual flow of immigrants over the years. It follows, then, that the immigrants' experiences have varied with changing conditions and that each nationality has usually had a first-generation American grouping at any given time.

THE COLONIAL PERIOD

Members of each ethnic group came to the New World for economic, political, or religious reasons, or sometimes for the adventure of beginning a new life in a new land. As strangers, most encountered yet another ethnic group — the American Indians — who at a much earlier time may have been immigrants to this land as well. Although limited social interaction between the European settlers and the natives occurred, their cultural differences frequently resulted in a xenophobic reaction from both sides. The story of Indian-white relations is usually one of misunderstanding, fear, suspicion, exploitation, hostility, and violence. Coming from vastly different cultural worlds, they quickly came into conflict with one another.

CULTURAL DIVERSITY   From the moment the first Europeans settled in America, cultural differences existed throughout the land. The settlements were culturally distinct from one another in nationality or religion, like, for example, the Puritans in Massachusetts and the Congregationalists in Connecticut. Some settlements, even in their very early stages, were composed of a mixture of ethnic groups. To strengthen his Pennsylvania colony, the English Quaker William Penn recruited several hundred Dutch and many more German settlers. In fact, the "Pennsylvania Dutch" are actually Germans, the word *Dutch* being a corruption of *Deutsch,* which means German. The settlement of New Amsterdam in the colony of New Netherland was also a pluralistic community, reflecting the home country's positive attitude toward minorities and refugees within its borders.

In 1660, William Kieft, the Dutch governor of New Netherland, remarked to the French Jesuit Issac Jogues that there were eighteen languages spoken at or near Fort Amsterdam at the tip of Manhattan Island. . . . The first shipload of settlers sent out by the Dutch was made up largely of French-speaking Protestants. British, Germans, Finns, Jews, Swedes, Africans, Italians, Irish [quickly] followed, beginning a stream that has never yet stopped.[1]

Religious differences caused social problems more frequently than did nationality during this period. Many people who first crossed the Atlantic as immigrants had been religious dissenters in their native land and were seeking a utopia in the new land — a place with religious harmony. Unfortunately, they brought with them their own religious prejudices. Although they themselves came seeking religious freedom, they were intolerant of others with different religious beliefs. When the Colonies were mostly Protestant, there was antagonism among the various denominations and sects. Later, when Catholic immigrants arrived, the old hostilities that had existed in Europe generations earlier manifested themselves once again in the United States.

EXPULSION AND AVOIDANCE   Mass *expulsion*, the forced removal of an entire group of people, is sometimes a dominant group's intolerant solution to a minority "problem." Thus, involuntary migration by a minority group occurs; this is somewhat different from voluntary migration, in which a minority group, in an avoidance response, chooses to move elsewhere. In both cases, however, prejudice and discrimination cause a minority group to change its locale.

The most frequently cited example of expulsion during the colonial period is that of the Puritans driving out the "heretic" Roger Williams and his followers, who settled in Rhode Island. Of course, the settlers also displaced the Indians, often forcibly. Many of the early settlers — for example, the Pilgrims, the French Huguenots, and the Sephardic Jews — had themselves been driven from their native lands in Europe.

With ample land available in the seventeenth and eighteenth centuries, religious, national, or racial groups experiencing prejudice and discrimination could move elsewhere if they wished. As long as there was open land, many did so, forming new societies or living in isolation in small family groups. Driven from New York State at gunpoint in the early nineteenth century, the Mormons exemplify both expulsion and avoidance. As they journeyed westward, they frequently encountered intense hostility and violence because of their religious beliefs and their practice of polygamy. They crossed the country seeking a place of refuge until they were able to make their home in the still unsettled regions of Utah, Nevada, and California.

SPATIAL SEGREGATION The early settlements of the seventeenth century — Jamestown (Virginia), Plymouth (Massachusetts), New Sweden (Delaware and New Jersey), New Amsterdam (New York), Philadelphia (Pennsylvania) — were actually small ethnic enclaves. Immigrants from different countries and with differing religious beliefs settled among their own kind. Even in the pluralistic settlements in Philadelphia and New Amsterdam, members of the various ethnic groups sought to live near their own people. Each of these instances of residential clustering in a recognizable ethnic community was a voluntary act of spatial segregation. In the years to follow, other minority groups would also congregate within well-defined communities, either by choice or because of societal demands.

England eventually dominated the 13 Colonies. English influence upon the Colonies — and, later, the United States — was extensive, including not only language and common law but also Anglo-Saxon chauvinism, imbuing within many a pride in their cultural heritage. In the eighteenth century, New England and the Tidewater areas were the only sections that actually contained a large proportion of people of English descent, but these families were long established and now powerful.

During the colonial period these Americans welcomed the newer immigrants as buffers along the frontier, but it was a "welcome tinged with misgivings."[2] The immigrants' good character and ability to support themselves were considered more important than their nationality; nevertheless, the Germans, French, and Scotch-Irish did encounter hostility from time to time.

The immigrants originally lived in scattered ethnic settlements. As the English came to dominate, they inhabited primarily the Eastern Seaboard. Some minority peoples settled in ethnic pockets in this region, while others settled on the edge of the frontier. Most of this spatial segregation was voluntary, as virgin land was available to all who wished to strike out on their own. The immigrants had come to the new land to start a new life, and found their own land to do so.

THE EARLY NATIONAL PERIOD

Larger conflicts often curtail or absorb smaller conflicts. With growing dissension within the Colonies, the newcomers, regardless of their national origins, were thrust into positions either as loyalists or as revolutionaries. The success of the Revolutionary War united the diverse elements behind a leadership of second- or third-generation Americans, predominantly of English descent.

The new nation's Constitution was a compromise among various factions. It guaranteed in its First Amendment that there would be no state religion, no governmental interference in religion, no religious requirements of any kind. However, it is impossible to legislate attitudes. Strong religious faith often encourages divisiveness. If one believes his or her faith to be the right one, by implication all others are not only different but inferior. Consequently, religious minorities in America — Quakers, Mormons, Catholics, Jews — have all encountered prejudice, discrimination, persecution, and, on occasion, violence.

PREJUDICE One might think that in a new nation with an abundance of land, people would be receptive to immigrants. Although this attitude did exist, many voiced a concern as to the type and quantity of immigrants who should be allowed to come. All three levels of prejudice — cognitive, emotional, and action-orientation — existed among many Americans at that time.

Many new immigrants arrived during the immediate post-Revolution period, and an antiforeign attitude, sporadic and localized until then, asserted itself. Both political factions feared that their opponents would benefit from the newcomers. The Jeffersonians were alarmed at the arrival of so many refugees, particularly the French, from the collapsing European aristocracies. The Federalists, the conservatives of their day, feared that the ranks of the anti-Federalists would grow, since poor immigrants, particularly the Irish, had no commitment to preserving a strong central government.

Whatever their motives, the dominant English-Americans' beliefs about and actions toward the newly arriving northern and western European immigrants followed a familiar pattern in dominant-minority relations. Suspicious of those different from themselves, the members of the dominant culture felt threatened.

In a letter to John Adams in 1798, George Washington indicated his reservations about newcomers, especially when they settled in their own little communities. His words are similar to others to be uttered in the nineteenth and twentieth centuries.

> My opinion, with respect to immigration, is that except of useful mechanics and some particular descriptions of men or professions, there is no need of encouragement, while the policy or advantage of its taking place in a body (I mean the settling of them in a body) may be much questioned; for, by so doing, they retain the language, habits and principles (good or bad) which they bring with them.[3]

XENOPHOBIA   Many Federalists, in fact, believed that the large foreign-born population was the root of all the evil in the United States. In letters, speeches, and newspapers they expressed the fear that

> coming from "a quarter of the world so full of disorder and corruption" as Europe, it was to be feared that immigrants would "contaminate the purity and simplicity of the American character"; warned "their principles spread like the leaven of unrighteousness; the weak, the ignorant and the needy are thrown into a ferment, and corruption threatens the whole mass." True some immigrants were industrious, peaceable, and voted the Federalist ticket — but for one such "good" European, lamented Noah Webster, "we receive three or four discontented, factious men — the convicts, fugitives of justice, hirelings of France, and disaffected offscourings of other nations." "Generally speaking," said a Federalist, "none but the most vile and worthless, none but the idle and discontented, the disorderly and the wicked, have inundated upon us from Europe." Clearly, the property and the virtue of the United States would not be secure until foreign immigration had been reduced to a mere trickle of hand-picked newcomers of approved political sympathies.[4]

LEGISLATIVE ACTION   The Federalists attempted to limit all office holding to the native-born and to extend the period for naturalization from five to fourteen years. Although they succeeded in having the longer periods enacted, the states — faced with the problems of establishing a new nation — successfully evaded this legislation.

In 1798, with a volatile situation in Europe and a distinct possibility of war with France, the Federalists succeeded in passing a series of laws known collectively as the Alien and Sedition Acts. Many factors contributed to the successful passage of this notorious legislation. One factor was the presence of a large foreign-born population, perceived as a threat to the stability of the country. Significantly, the legislation passed because of sectional block voting, with New England almost unanimously in favor of the bills. Few foreigners resided in New England, and hence little contact had occurred; nonetheless, widespread negative stereotyping existed in that region. Jefferson's election to the presidency in 1800 ended this xenophobia, and the acts were abrogated.

POPULATION COMPOSITION At this stage in history, the young nation possessed several distinct ethnic groups, differing in heritage, language, customs, and religion. Within the several states admitted to the Union lived the northern and western Europeans, dominated by the English Protestants. The French lived in the New Orleans region and gave the country its only ethnic flavor truly distinct from the English and the various Indian tribes. In the territories awaiting conquest and statehood were other Indian tribes and the Spanish. Of course, many other ethnic groups were present — though relatively small in numbers — and contributed to the growth and development of the young nation.

THE PRE—CIVIL WAR PERIOD

Not until 1820 did the national census include a person's country of origin as part of its data, and new regulations required shipmasters to submit passenger lists to customs officials. This census (which excluded the Indians) listed approximately 9.6 million Americans, of whom 20 percent were blacks and most of the remainder white Protestants from northern and western Europe. Between 1820 and 1860, over 5 million immigrants — more than half the U.S. population in 1820 and more than the entire population in 1790 — would cross the Atlantic and Pacific oceans to disembark on American shores.

In these forty years preceding the Civil War, the first great wave of immigrants produced still more arrivals from England and Scandinavia. Ireland and Germany, however, supplied the greatest numbers. In fact, so great was the Irish immigration that they accounted for 44 percent of all immigration in the 1830s and 49 percent of all immigration in the 1840s. Consequently, they accounted for 7 percent of the total population by the end of the Civil War. Not only was the arrival of so many foreigners overwhelming, but many of the newcomers were Catholic — a religion to which many Protestant groups were openly hostile.

STRUCTURAL CONDITIONS The land the immigrants came to in the first half of the nineteenth century was quite different from that of past centuries. From rudimentary beginnings a nation had evolved, bursting with exuberance and confidence. A common culture now prevailed, marked by strong beliefs in Protestantism, individual enterprise, and political democracy. The institutions of society were strongly linked to an Anglo-Saxon heritage. Americans admired and emulated English

FIGURE 4.1

The Battery, New York, 1855, where European immigrants disembarked. Castle Garden, the predecessor of Ellis Island as the processing center, is on the left. Painting by Samuel B. Waugh. (Museum of the City of New York)

writers. In a new country filled with nationalistic fervor, England was still the model for a civilization.

Improvements in sailing vessels made the rest of the world less remote than it once had been. Farming, manufacturing, and trade were the major occupations, with a growing interdependency among the three. The land east of the Mississippi River was becoming more and more populated. New communities continued to spring up, and older ones grew in size and complexity.

Along the East Coast and in the large cities west of the Appalachian Mountains, life was stable and established. Although regional variations as well as differences in religion and social status existed, the prevailing cultural norms were relatively homogeneous.

Urban living conditions, particularly for the poor Irish immigrants, were very substandard, even for those days. The poverty-stricken newcomers, forced to live in a squalid environment, suffered high disease and mortality rates, as well as the condemnation of the dominant society for living the way they did. Like so many others in the generations that followed, such critics did not realize that their own attitudes and actions might well have helped to create the situation in the first place.

> Typical of overcrowded cellars was a house in Pike Street which contained a cellar ten feet square and seven feet high, with one small window and an old-fashioned inclined cellar door; here lived two families consisting of ten persons of all ages. The occupants of these basements led miserable lives as troglodytes amid darkness, dampness, and poor ventilation. Rain water leaked through cracks in the walls and floors and frequently flooded the cellars; refuse filtered down from the upper stories and mingled with the seepage from outdoor privies. From such an abode emerged the "whitened and cadaverous countenance" of the cellar dweller.[5]

XENOPHOBIA Americans perceived the large influx of immigrants between 1820 and 1860 as a threat to their institutions and their social order. Not only were many of the newcomers Catholic, but they were also from countries embroiled in political turmoil. Anxiety mounted over the imagined radical threat as well as the Catholic threat.

In the 1830s, antiforeign organizations, calling themselves "Native" Americans, originated in many cities. They frequently raised up "mobs to burn Catholic convents, churches and homes, assault nuns, and murder Irishmen, Germans, and Negroes."[6] These sporadic outbursts gradually coalesced into the powerful Know-Nothing movement of the 1850s. They unleashed a vicious hate campaign, frequently accompanied by brutal violence, particularly in the large cities where many immigrants lived. Surprisingly successful, the Know-Nothings "became the magnet

FIGURE 4.2

This man slept here for four years, circa 1890 Many poverty-stricken newcomers lived in such cold, dirt-floor cellars. Others spent the night in
flophouses or free lodging rooms in police stations. (Photograph by Jacob A.
Riis, Jacob A. Riis Collection, Museum of the City of New York)

for all dazed elements in the political whirlpool; they fed on pathological fears and fanned to white heat all the petty animosities that had
bored into the public mind."[7]

A Whig presidential candidate, General Winfield Scott, waged an
anti-Catholic, antiforeign campaign with Know-Nothing support, but
lost badly to Democrat Franklin Pierce in 1852. By 1854 the Know-
Nothing Party was strong enough to elect 75 congressmen and many
city, county, and state officials.[8] In 1855 the party elected six governors,
and many contemporaries believed that this reactionary movement
would capture the White House in the 1856 election.[9] A strong candidate, former President Millard Fillmore, sought to return to office on the
Know-Nothing ticket. The conservative Whig party endorsed Fillmore,
but a serious split within its ranks, with defections to Republican candidate John C. Fremont, enabled Democrat James Buchanan to win the
three-way race. The bitter sectional rivalry of the Civil War period effectively ended this ethnocentric-turned-xenophobic movement.

Not all voices were raised against the European expatriates. In defense
of the newcomers, Harriet Martineau (*Society in America*, 1837) answered some of the criticisms:

> It would certainly be better that the immigrants should be well-
> clothed, educated, respectable people (except that, in that case, they
> would probably never arrive). But the blame of their bad condition
> rests elsewhere, while their arrival is, generally speaking, a pure
> benefit. . . . Every American can acknowledge that few or no canals
> or railroads would be in existence now in the United States, but for
> the Irish labor by which they have been completed; and the best
> cultivation that is to be seen in the land is owing to the Dutch and
> Germans it contains.[10]

Ralph Waldo Emerson, a profound thinker and articulate literary figure of the times, was also a popular speaker on the lyceum lecture circuit. In those days many communities had a *lyceum*, or association, for
discussion and popular instruction by lectures or other means. In his
lectures, Emerson tried to convince his listeners through an eloquent
expression of deeply felt ideas. One of his journal entries in 1845 shows
how he tried to combat the nativism movement by stressing the "smelting-pot" concept.

> I hate the narrowness of the Native American Party. It is the dog in
> the manger. It is precisely opposite to true wisdom. . . . Well, as in
> the old burning of the Temple at Corinth, by the melting and inter-
> mixture of silver and gold and other metals, a new compound more
> precious than any, called Corinthian brass, was formed; so in this
> continent, — asylum of all nations, — the energy of Irish, Swedes,
> Poles, and Cossacks, and all the European tribes, — of the Africans,

and of the Polynesians, will construct a new race, a new religion, a new state, a new literature, which will be as vigorous as the new Europe which came out of the smelting-pot of the Dark Ages, or that which earlier emerged from the Pelasgic and Etruscan barbarism.[11]

Currents and countercurrents occurred then, as now. Not all members of the same ethnic group encountered problems, nor did all native-born Americans react so negatively to the newcomers. Yet patterns of harmony or conflict did exist, and they very often depended upon the degree of cultural and structural differentiation that existed in each region.

THE ENGLISH

Despite earlier explorations by other countries, the English were the first white ethnic group to establish permanent settlements in the New World. The first two successful ones were Jamestown and Plimmoth (Plymouth) Plantation (the word *plantation* was first used in the North).

These two settlements were culturally quite different from one another; they offer an excellent example of cultural diversity among the same nationality as opposed to a stereotyped concept of a people. Jamestown served as the seed from which the Southern aristocracy and slavery would grow. Plymouth was the forerunner of town meetings (participatory democracy), the abolition movement, and "Yankee ingenuity" (capitalistic enterprise). Many factors, such as the different purposes of the settlements, and different religions, climates, and terrains, played a role in determining the unfolding of events and life styles.

The writings of William Bradford, the first governor of the Plymouth colony, provide evidence that the English were an ethnically conscious people. More than 350 years have passed since the time of the Pilgrims, but Bradford's words regarding their experiences could apply to many other immigrant groups — past, present, and future.

THE DEPARTURE

Leaving one's native land for another country known only by reputation can be an awesome experience. For many it is a time of joy and sorrow, anticipation and trepidation. People know what they are leaving behind, but they are not certain what they will find. The Pilgrims first fled England for Holland, which opened its doors to all refugees, and later journeyed to the United States. In the following passages, Bradford is speaking about the Pilgrims' journey to Holland, but the locale is only incidental to the expression of the immigrant's typical sensations.

Being thus constrained to leave their native soil and country, their lands and livings, and all their friends and familiar acquaintances, it was much, and thought marvelous by many. But to go into a country they knew not but by hearsay, where they must learn a new language and get their livings they knew not how, it being a dear place and subject to the miseries of war, it was by many thought an adventure almost desperate; a case intolerable and a misery worse than death.[12]

CULTURE SHOCK

Arrival at one's destination brings with it culture contact. One's world of reality, that familiar way of life one accepts subconsciously, is jolted to some degree as the group encounters a different civilization. Bradford continues:

Being now come into the Low Countries, they saw many goodly and fortified cities, strongly walled and guarded with troops of armed men. Also, they heard a strange and uncouth language, and beheld the different manners and customs of the people, with their strange fashions and attires, all so far differing from that of their plain country villages (where they were bred and had so long lived) as it seemed they were come into a new world.[13]

RESISTING ASSIMILATION Not all immigrants desire to be full, participating citizens in the country to which they move. Many, in fact, do not become naturalized citizens. Although they are starting a new life, they do not necessarily intend to forsake their cultural heritage. More often, they seek to preserve that heritage as a familiar world in a strange land, and to pass it on to their children. Often the children become assimilated into the new ways despite their parents' efforts. The Pilgrims feared that their children would be assimilated into the Dutch culture, and viewed such an outcome as an evil to be avoided.

But that which was more lamentable, and of all sorrows most heavy to be borne, was that many of their children, by these occasions and the great licentiousness of youth in that country, and the manifold temptations of the place, were drawn away by evil examples into extravagant and dangerous courses, getting the reins off their necks and departing from their parents. . . . So that they saw their posterity would be in danger to degenerate and be corrupted.[14]

ENGLISH INFLUENCE The English immigrants' major impact on American culture occurred during the colonial period. Settling in the 13 original Colonies, they so established themselves that succeeding generations were culturally and numerically dominant by the time of the American Revolution. In 1790, about 90 percent of the population could claim nationality or descent from the British Isles. This large majority of English-speaking citizens made an indelible imprint upon American culture in language, law, customs, and values. The wars of 1776 and 1812 notwithstanding, the descendants of English immigrants still prided themselves on their heritage, as indicated in their writings at that time. For example, in his *Sketchbook*, Washington Irving encouraged Americans to pattern themselves after the English nation rather than any other.

After 1825, when the British Parliament repealed the ban on the emigration of artisans, many English, Scottish, and Irish mill hands came to southern Massachusetts and Philadelphia. There they found work in the textile factories, often at twice or more the salary they had been earning at home. As experienced mill operatives, the English continued to come throughout the nineteenth century, especially to the Massachusetts towns of Fall River and New Bedford. When the American silk industry clustered in Paterson, New Jersey, in the 1840s, many British immigrants moved there, several of them starting their own factories. British immigrants formed a solid base for the rising American textile industry, and many became managers and proprietors.[15]

Many British coal miners also came, but by the latter part of the nineteenth century they were being replaced by Slavic and Italian workers. Those who remained in the coal industry were usually supervisors and foremen. Some British farmers also emigrated to the United States, scattering throughout the Midwest. British immigrants of all occupations seldom concentrated in any one area, going instead wherever the job market led them.

As foreigners with the same language and cultural heritage as the dominant society, British immigrants seldom experienced prejudice or discrimination in the United States. Rowland Berthoff cites numerous studies and reports indicating that the English were rarely ridiculed on the vaudeville stage except as titled fops (an inaccurate representation). Ethnophaulisms did not exist, except for such inoffensive nicknames as "John Bull" or "limey," and even these were not widely used.[16]

England was the source of a great many immigrants over the years; between 1820 and 1977, a total of 3,160,595 people came to the United States from England.[17] It ranks seventh in the list of nations that have supplied immigrants to the United States since 1820. Even though England has been one of the four largest European suppliers of immigrants throughout much of the 1970s, these immigrants are not a very visible ethnic group because they are not readily detected as strangers.

The British were usually accepted by the natives more easily than other immigrants because of their commonality of language and culture with the Americans and because of their dispersed settlement patterns. However, the British themselves were not always comfortable in the new land. Ilja M. Dijour found similar results among immigrants to other countries and reported, "the return of British from Australia, South Africa, and Canada or of Portuguese from Brazil, or Spaniards and Italians from the rest of Latin America is incomparably higher than the re-emigration of say Japanese from Brazil, Slavic people from Australia or Canada, or others." Dijour explained that a major cause of these findings was that the first group had the exaggerated expectation of finding no differences in the new country, whereas the second group was psychologically prepared to find everything different in the new country.[18] Those not expecting to be strangers were unprepared when they realized that they actually were strangers.

During the first hundred years after American independence, many British immigrants found the new country less inviting than England. Comparing the criticisms of 75 returnees prior to 1865, Wilbur Shepperson found some common themes reflecting a failure of the new land to live up to their expectations.

The Republic was peopled by men of action who cared little for the deeper meaning of life, who were blind to the beauties of their natural environment, and who were hostile to refinement and sensitivity. The blot of slavery and its deleterious effects on society, the false message of community-makers, the massive imprint of the wilderness, and the buffoonery, brutality, and uncertainty provided the theme for the novels as well as for much of the literature of return.

. . . Rather than vigorous, they found America boring; rather than questioning and vital, republican communities were suspicious and moribund. Although they were often unemployed, Americans boasted of their economic opportunities; although they condemned politicians, they defended the political system; although they advocated freedom, they enforced conformity. . . .

The absence of European papers, the need for intellectual interplay, and the lack of artistic controversy left America without challenge, without variety, without eccentrics, and without freedom to choose. . . .

Knowledge of the language allowed for rapid assimilation of English immigrants, but at the same time it permitted them to compare critically American authors, newspapers, and theaters with those at home. Acquaintance with English government and legal traditions provided easy understanding of American law, but it sometimes provoked censure of political methods and frontier justice. Nearness to markets, cheap labor, and advanced technological methods in Britain often led immigrants of the entrepreneur class to despair of the New World's inefficient agricultural methods and unorthodox business practices. British workers once associated with the trade union or Chartist movements found American labor groups lacking in organization, leadership, and purpose.[19]

In the post–Civil War period, some degree of Anglophobia still prevailed, and British immigrants discovered that they had to exercise self-restraint to be accepted as Americans. An ethnic consciousness led many British to resent this necessity and to dislike the ways of the new country. Between 1881 and 1889, a total of 370,697 British and Irish aliens left the United States for their native land.[20]

Englishmen were disconcerted, of course, to find that in Yankee breasts a family grudge rankled against the old mother country. "The instant they find you are English they immediately drop all other topics of conversation to refer to the time 'we licked you badly,' or to discuss the degeneracy of the House of Lords, or some other topic they think will be of interest to you." . . . American Anglophobia had many sources: old wars against redcoats, the Irish bias of the press, manufacturers' dread of free trade, free-silverites' fear of London bankers, and behind all a lingering sense of colonial inferiority. . . .

In fact, in all things but money and quick promotion, British-Americans thought the United States a debased copy of their homeland. Many seemingly familiar customs and institutions had lost their British essence. "The Land of Slipshod," one immigrant in 1885 called the country, its language not English but a "silly idiotic jargon — a mere jumble of German idioms and popular solecisms, savored by a few Irish blunders," the enforcement of its basically English legal code "totally farcical," and its children half-educated, spoiled, and unruly. . . . Many returned home discontented with "the manners and habits of the people."

. . . Although as the years passed the immigrants' personal ties came to be in America rather than in Britain, their fondness for and pride in the old country waxed. British travelers found them everywhere, "British in heart and memory, . . . always with a touch of the exile, eager to see an English face and to hear an English voice!"[21]

Despite certain similarities, enough differences and ethnic consciousness remained to restrain British immigrants from merging in a totally smooth fashion. Second-generation British-Americans, however, had no such problem and identified with the United States as their country.

THE DUTCH

In recent years Dutch immigration has been low, 1,000 or less per year in the 1970s; however, the total immigration from the Netherlands in the 1820–1977 period was 358,171, placing it among the 25 nations supplying the largest number of immigrants.[22] Curiously, almost 50 percent of the Dutch immigration occurred from 1880 to 1920, when immigrants from southern, central, and· eastern Europe dominated among the incoming nationalities. Despite these statistics, the major impact of Dutch influence upon American society, which is quite significant, comes from a much earlier period.

During the Age of Exploration, sea captains for the Dutch East India Company sailed into the uncharted waters of the New World. From their explorations, they provided important information that encouraged the organization of a trading center, Fort Nassau, on an island in the Hudson just south of Albany. Some of these sea captains became famous — for example, Henrik Hudson and Adriaen Block, for whom, respectively, a river and an island are named.

In 1624 thirty Dutch families settled in Beverwyck, later called Albany, and in 1625 the Dutch built a moat and fort on Manhattan Island and called it New Amsterdam. A year later Governor Peter Minuit concluded his famous deal and bought the whole island from the Indians for 60 guilders — 24 dollars — worth of merchandise.

Pearl Street in present-day New York City marks the limit of dry land in the days of New Amsterdam, where palisades had been erected against Indian raiders. In Dutch, these were called *de wal,* and thus the northern boundary gave its name to the Wall Street of today. Breukelen (later Brooklyn) became a town in 1646. Peter Stuyvesant's farm or *bouwerij* in Manhattan, where he lived after the English takeover in 1664 until his death in 1672, gave its name to the Bowery, a well-known street in New York.

Other Dutch settlements sprang up in the Bronx, on Staten Island, in New Jersey at Bergen (named after a town in Holland, and later known as Jersey City), at Ridgewood, at Hackensack, in the Raritan and Ramapo valleys, and in South Carolina at St. James Island. So widespread were the Dutch settlements and so strong was the Dutch imprint that Dutch remained a major language in American society for quite some time.

STRUCTURAL CONDITIONS

During the colonial period, few Dutch were willing to exchange the security at home for the hardships of the New World. With their stable economy and a harmonious society, the Dutch had little inducement to venture forth in great numbers as other ethnic groups had. Urban areas in Holland had heterogeneous populations because the Dutch had offered shelter to many refugees from other countries. In seeking to establish trading settlements in the New World, the Dutch therefore sought other minority-group members willing to journey to the New World. As a result, immigrant Dutch settlements became as heterogeneous as their counterparts in Holland.

The spirit of seventeenth-century Holland resulted in a cosmopolitan and tolerant atmosphere in New Amsterdam that outlasted Holland's rule. This is perhaps the most important contribution of Dutch colonization to the future character of the United States, and the influence was especially marked on New York City.

Although a severe Calvinist, Governor Stuyvesant was ordered by his company to prevent discrimination and to accept the settling of Lutherans, Quakers, and Jews. In 1654 the "Jewish Mayflower" — the French ship *Sainte Catherine* — brought the first group of Jewish settlers to New Amsterdam.

The somewhat more relaxed atmosphere of New Amsterdam contrasted with that of the English colonies to the north, restricted by their rigid blue laws. New York City, with its large number of places to eat, drink, and dance, seems to have inherited this New Amsterdam characteristic. Sports were popular too. The colonists loved boat and carriage races, and from Holland they imported the game of *kolf*, which later became golf.

To the north of New Amsterdam, the Dutch introduced a feudalistic anachronism. By shipping 50 colonists to America at his own expense, a man was entitled to buy a stretch of land along the Hudson River 12 miles wide and as far inland as he wished. He would have complete jurisdiction over his domain, as well as extensive trading privileges, in perpetuity for himself and his heirs. The most successful of the *patroons* was Kiliaen van Rensselaer, whose name is preserved today in Rensselaer Polytechnic Institute in Troy, New York.

The English takeover of New Amsterdam in 1664 caused no hardship for the Dutch settlers. They enjoyed a basically favorable social environment during the time of the American Colonies, in the post–Revolutionary War period, and thereafter. A relatively tolerant people in an intolerant age, similar in physical appearance and religious beliefs to other Americans, the Dutch were generally accepted, though sometimes they were the butt of gentle humor as illustrated in the writings of Washington Irving.

Holland's early support of the American Revolution and its status as the second country to give formal recognition to the United States further strengthened positive American attitudes toward the Dutch. In 1782, John Adams succeeded in securing the first loan for Congress from three Amsterdam banking houses; the loan was for 5 million guilders, or 2 million dollars — a very substantial amount in those days. By 1794 the total amount loaned by Holland had risen to 30 million guilders, or 12 million dollars. This amount comprised most of the foreign debt incurred by the United States.

In 1846 a group of religious separatists settled in what became Holland, Michigan. Spurred by religious and economic motives, a new wave of Dutch immigrants followed suit, settling mostly in Michigan, Iowa, Wisconsin, and Illinois because of their favorable soil and climate conditions. The social bond proved to be religion rather than nationality, and schisms ensued, resulting in the Dutch Reformed Church, the Christian Reformed Church, and the Netherland Reformed Church. The success of the first group's efforts to propagate the faith and achieve higher social standing rested partly upon Hope College in Holland, Michigan. Their success encouraged the Christian Reformed Church, a more conservative group, to establish Calvin College in Grand Rapids to achieve the same objectives for their people.

PLURALISM

The Dutch immigrants who came here, whether during the colonial period or the nineteenth century, found their liberal attitude toward other groups was usually reciprocated. They were a distinct ethnic group — in language as well as in other ways — but they generally found a friendly atmosphere wherever they went. Nonetheless, like many other nationalities yet to come, some of whom would not find such openness, they formed their own enclaves and tried to preserve their language and traditions through their own churches, schools, and associations.

Dutch culture and influence persisted for many generations despite the Anglo-Saxon cultural dominance, for several reasons. The Dutch were self-sufficient and enjoyed high social standing in the society. Their church, rather than American ways, formed the basis of their social life; the more orthodox they were, the more they resisted assimilation. A steady migration into concentrated residential communities reinforced the old ways. Finally, a friendly atmosphere enabled the Dutch to coexist in a pluralistic society.

The following passage gives some insight into the extensive use of the Dutch language and the resistance to the English language. Note, for example, that not until 1774 were the children taught English, more than one hundred years after New York became an English colony.

In 1764 Dr. Archibald Laidlie preached the first English sermon to the Dutch Reformed congregation in New York City. Ten years later English was introduced in the schools. In Kingston, Dutch was used

FIGURE 4.3

"DEPARTURE FROM HOME"

Engraving from *Harper's Weekly*, June 26, 1858. (Museum of the City of New York)

in church as late as 1808. A few years before, a traveler had reported that "on Long Island, in New York, along the North River, at
Albany, how Dutch was in general still the common language of
most of the old people." Francis Adrian van der Kemp, who had
come to this country as a refugee in 1788, wrote that his wife was
able to converse in Dutch with the wives of Alexander Hamilton
and General George Clinton. Much later, in 1847, immigrants from
Holland were upon their arrival welcomed in Dutch by the Rever-
end Isaac Wyckoff of New York, a descendant of one of the first
settlers in Rensselaerwyck, who only in school had learned to speak
English; and until very recently many communities in New Jersey
adhered to the tradition of a monthly church service in Dutch. As
late as 1905 Dutch was still heard among the old people in the
Ramapo Valley of that state.[23]

Although most of the Dutch immigrants have come to the United
States during the same period as the southern, central, and eastern
Europeans, they have not encountered ethnic antagonism and they have
assimilated more easily. Their physical features, their religion, their
comparatively small numbers, and their more urbanized background
have enabled them to both adapt to and gain approval from the dominant society more easily than other groups.

THE FRENCH

Except for the depression decade of 1931–1940, France has been the
most consistent of the European countries in its immigration pattern.
Since 1820, it has sent a large, continual flow of immigrants. French-
Americans fall into three population segments: migrants from France,
migrants from French Canada (who have settled primarily in New England), and French Louisianans brought under U.S. jurisdiction. (The
French Louisianans, also known as "Cajuns," were expelled from
Acadia, French Canada, by the British in 1755, and by 1790 about 4,000
of them had resettled in Louisiana.) Each group's experiences have been
somewhat different, illustrating different patterns in dominant-minority
relations.

MARGINALITY AND ASSIMILATION

In the seventeenth century, the Huguenots fled either to Holland or to
the United States to escape religious persecution. It is often thought that
because of their Protestantism, their willingness to work hard, their

conversion to the Anglican Church, and their rapid adoption of the English language, the Huguenots assimilated easily into colonial society. However, the transition was not altogether a smooth one, and the second generation apparently agonized over their marginal status in the same way as other groups did.

> By 1706, sufficient time had elapsed since the Revocation [in 1685 Louis XIV formally eliminated religious liberty, causing the renewal of persecution and extermination of the Huguenots] to give rise to a younger generation unsatisfied with the adherence to old French forms, a generation adverse to a language not in general use in the province, clamoring for the new and the popular. . . . The children of many of the refugees were even ashamed to bear French names. The idea of remaining foreigners in a land in which they were born and reared was alien to their thought.[24]

Encountering distrust and some violence from the dominant society, partly explained by the frequent hostilities between England and France, the Huguenots tried to Anglicize themselves as quickly as possible to avoid further unpleasantness. They changed their names and their customs, learned to speak English, and soon succeeded in assimilating completely into American society. For them, assimilation and loss of ethnic identity was the desired goal. Not all Americans or ethnic groups agree with such a goal; many prefer instead a pluralistic society.

With time, attitudes changed. The Revolutionary War period made England an enemy and France an ally. The Marquis de Lafayette was a war hero, and such popular figures as Benjamin Franklin and Thomas Jefferson openly admired the French and their culture. The French architect Pierre Charles L'Enfant was commissioned to design the new federal capital of the United States.

AMALGAMATION AND NATIVISM

A French agriculturist, diplomat, and author, J. Hector St. John de Crèvecoeur, first popularized the idea of a melting pot. Envisioning the United States as more than just a land of opportunity, de Crèvecoeur in 1782 spoke of a new breed of humanity coming forth from the new society.

> In this great American asylum the poor of Europe have by some means met together, and in consequence of various causes. . . . Urged by a variety of motives, here they came. Everything has tended to regenerate them: new laws, a new mode of living, a new social system. Here they are men. In Europe they were so many useless plants, wanting vegetative mold and refreshing showers. They withered; and were mowed down by want, hunger, and war. But

now, by the power of transplantation, like all other plants, they have taken root and flourished! Formerly they were not numbered in any civil lists of their country, except in those of the poor; here they rank as citizens. . . .

What attachment can a poor European emigrant have for a country where he had nothing? . . . Here individuals of all nations are melted together into a new race of men, whose labors and posterity will one day cause great changes in the world.[25]

Others were not so enthusiastic as de Crèvecoeur about the poor of Europe coming to the United States. William Smith Shaw, the young nephew of President John Adams, wrote to the First Lady in 1798, "The grand cause of all our present difficulties may be traced . . . to so many hordes of Foreigners imigrating [sic] to America. . . . Let us no longer pray that America may become an asylum to all nations."[26]

The French Revolution brought thousands of French aristocrats fleeing to the United States. A proud people, many were contemptuous of Americans. They kept to themselves, avoided any social interaction with Americans, and gave no thought to assimilation or U.S. citizenship. They returned home after the fall of Napoleon, having made little impact upon American society.

FRANCOPHOBIA

When the French Revolution was still in its moderately liberal stage, the Jeffersonians were French sympathizers and the Federalists vehemently anti-French. Then came the celebrated XYZ Affair, in which French officials demanded bribes before permitting U.S. diplomats to secure desired conferences or agreements. This inflamed public opinion against the French and their sympathizers. The lives of French immigrants during those passionate times were at best uncomfortable, and at worst filled with trouble and turmoil.

The fear and detestation in which American "Jacobins" were held were no less powerful than the abhorrence felt for the French revolutionists themselves. "Medusa's Snakes are not more venomous," declared a Federalist, "than the wretches who are seeking to bend us to the views of France." "The open enemies of our country," declared the Albany Centinel, "have never taken half the pains to render our Government and our rulers infamous and contemptible in the eyes of the world, than those wretches who call themselves Americans, Patriots and Republicans." This "Gallic faction" was believed to be in close communication with Paris, "the immense reservoir, and native spring of all immorality, corruption, wickedness and methodized duplicity."

... In the eyes of the Federalists, however, every Frenchman was a potential enemy: whether royalists or revolutionists, they were eager to extend French influence over the United States, and, actuated by national pride, they might join a French army of invasion. Moreover, their notoriously loose morals and irreligion threatened to infect Americans.[27]

By 1801 the Republicans effectively ended the Federalists' political dominance. President Thomas Jefferson purchased the Louisiana Territory from France in 1803, and with it the French city of New Orleans, which retains much of its ethnic flavor to this day, including the famed Mardi Gras celebration.

PLURALISM

The persistence of a French subculture in southern Louisiana is interesting in that not only has it grown stronger over the years, but it has succeeded in absorbing other ethnic groups in that area.

The French assimilated the Germans while both were under Spanish rule and both subject to strenuous programs designed to stamp them with a Spanish cultural heritage. But the virile French culture was not content with this, and even made a beginning at swallowing the politically dominant Spaniards themselves, a beginning which has been practically consummated during the American period while both were enveloped in the so-called melting pot which was heralded as bringing about Americanization. Under American rule the Louisiana French have, to the present time, perpetuated their language and culture and, at the same time, have absorbed most of the diverse Anglo-Saxon elements which have settled among them.[28]

T. Lynn Smith and Vernon Parenton attribute this social phenomenon to the intermarriage of Louisiana-French women with outgroup men, high fertility rates, and the dominance of the French mother in the socialization process. The strong influence and control of the French Catholic priest and the appeal of the French way of life to outgroup members are other factors.[29]

French is rapidly declining as the principal language spoken in the home. In 1940, the Census Bureau estimated that 1,412,060 persons spoke French primarily, of whom 300,000 lived in Louisiana. In 1976, the Census Bureau gave 300,000 as the total number of French-speaking people in the United States, with about one-fifth of them in Louisiana. Although language usage has weakened, a distinctive ethnic subculture is still in evidence.

Today, urbanizing influences are permeating the entire section. These include improved communication, mechanization of agriculture (with its concomitant social implications) and, particularly, mass media of education (radio, movies, and newspapers) as well as increased contacts outside French-speaking Louisiana. Nevertheless, the system of common values which was generated by language, national origin, settlement pattern, as well as familial, kinship, and religious ties, has thus far retained its societal integrative forces in this period of rapid and far-reaching technological changes now operative among these people.[30]

In addition to the nineteenth-century French aristocrats and the present-day Louisiana French, the French-Canadians living in New England offer a third example of a persistent subculture. The Industrial Revolution brought rapid expansion to the New England factories, and the owners actively recruited labor in French Canada. Many French-Canadians flocked from Quebec to the mill towns, competing with the Irish and others for jobs. The heaviest migration occurred in the forty years following the Civil War. By 1873, approximately 400,000 French-Canadians were living in the United States, half of them in New England and most of the remainder in the Midwest, primarily Illinois and Michigan.[31]

As in Louisiana, the family and the church have served as strong cohesive units in retaining language and culture. French parochial schools have also had a unifying effect upon the community. The French-Canadians still remain a distinct ethnic group, and their loyalties to their institutions and to their original home, Quebec, suggest that they will continue to remain a strong subculture in the foreseeable future.

THE GERMANS

Germany has supplied the greatest number of immigrants to the United States: 6,968,216 people between 1820 and 1977. In the colonial period and the nineteenth century, the influx of large numbers of German immigrants raised fears among the native-born. The rapid assimilation of German-Americans makes today's average citizen unaware of them as a distinct ethnic group even though the number of newcomers remains high.

EARLY REACTIONS

William Penn was so successful in recruiting German immigrants to his Pennsylvania colony that by the outbreak of the Revolutionary War, they numbered over 100,000 — one-third of the colony's total population. England's deployment of Hessian (German) mercenary troops in this area may have been done in part to secure sympathetic German colonial assistance in such areas as supplies, intelligence reports, and so on.

The Germans' situation provides a good example of a dominant culture reacting to a perceived threat from a distinct minority group. They were different in language, customs, and religion (being primarily Lutherans), as were other groups, but their high visibility due to their numbers and settlement patterns brought them to public attention.

Many Germans also had the additional disadvantage of having been placed in a subservient position at the outset. A very popular system, particularly in Pennsylvania, was the use of indentured servants or "redemptioners." Through this plan, persons unable to pay their passage would serve from three to seven years as laborers, artisans, domestics, or tutors. Upon their arrival in the harbor, such persons were advertised for sale in the newspapers, and the ship became a market as the ship captain or entrepreneur was paid for advancing the passage money. Occasionally families were separated. Such a situation could not help but encourage ethnocentric feelings of superiority among native-born Americans over such "poor foreigners."[32] Some English immigrants also came to the New England colonies as indentured servants, but in Pennsylvania the Germans represented a different ethnic group as well.

By 1750 the influx of German immigrants had become so great that Benjamin Franklin became quite disturbed and asked:

Why [should] the Pennsylvanians . . . allow the Palatine Germans to swarm into our settlements, and by herding together to establish their Language and Manners to the exclusion of ours? Why should Pennsylvania, founded by the English, become a colony of Aliens, who will shortly be so numerous as to Germanize us instead of our Anglifying them?[33]

These expressed fears were to be repeated by others at a later time, with respect to different immigrant groups. Franklin's worries about the duality of language display a marked similarity to some twentieth-century concerns regarding the Spanish-speaking populace and bilingual education. Franklin particularly opposed the Mennonites, fearing that members of this religious sect were pacifists. Maurice Davie reports that Franklin had misgivings about the Germans also because of their clannishness, their meager knowledge of English, their separate German press, and their increasing need for interpreters. Speaking of the latter, Franklin said, "I suppose in a few years they will also be necessary in the Assembly, to tell one-half of our legislators what the other half say."[34] Franklin was not arguing for restrictions on immigration, but rather for rapid assimilation (Anglo-conformity).

THE SECOND WAVE: SEGREGATION AND PLURALISM

The German immigrants of the eighteenth century settled first in Pennsylvania and then in other mid-Atlantic states, but the nineteenth-century immigrants went to the Midwest. So many migrated to the Ohio, Mississippi, and Missouri river valleys that by the middle of the nineteenth century they were looked upon as a factor to be reckoned with. They became homesteaders, preserving their heritage through their schools, churches, newspapers, language, mutual-aid societies, and recreational activities.

The failure of the liberal German revolution brought many political refugees to the United States in 1848. Known as "Forty-eighters," these Germans settled in the large cities of the East and Midwest. Most settled in Baltimore, New York, St. Louis, Milwaukee, and Minneapolis. Having been political activists in their homeland, the Forty-eighters quickly became active in American politics. Many Germans even gave serious thought to an all-German state within the union with German as the official language; some considered creating a separate German nation, believing that the slavery issue would cause the dissolution of the Union.

Brewton Berry and Henry Tischler report an anecdote relating to the large German-American population and political participation:

> So important was the Teutonic element in Illinois before the Civil War that Abraham Lincoln, astute politician that he was, tried to master the German tongue, and for a time was the owner of a German-language newspaper. A great influx of British settlers, however, was sufficient to tip the scales.[35]

Lincoln had made a wise investment in that German newspaper. The Forty-eighters, who had adopted the Republican party, persuaded thousands of their compatriots to do the same. They exerted considerable influence in 1860 to secure the nomination for Lincoln and to elect him to the presidency.

The subcommunities of Germans in the cities were similar to the separate German communities in the agrarian regions. In both situations, the Germans were physically and socially segregated, mostly by their own choice. In a city like Milwaukee, Germans at one time were in the absolute majority; the 1850 census showed six thousand Germans and four thousand native-born Americans. Today the Germantown sections of most of these cities still retain some vestige of their ethnic identity.

Many German Jewish immigrants also came to the United States during the nineteenth century. The first of these immigrants were mostly impoverished and poorly educated. By mid-century, the German Jewish immigrants were more prosperous and educated, bringing with them university-trained rabbis who had played a role in the Judaic reform movement. This Jewish migration was the first mass migration —

FIGURE 4.4

FROM THE OLD TO THE NEW WORLD

German emigrants for New York embark on a Hamburg steamer. From
Harper's Weekly, November 7, 1874. (Museum of the City of New York)

groups of entire families from a single locality or community. From an 1840 Jewish population of 15,000, Jewish Americans increased in number to 50,000 in 1850, 150,000 in 1860, and 250,000 in 1880. "By 1880 the American Jewish community was almost entirely a German community."[36] These German Jewish immigrants, as well as those who later fled Nazi Germany, will be discussed in Chapter 5 in a special section on Jewish immigrants.

SOCIETAL RESPONSES

Tensions were increased by the large numbers of Germans, most of them Catholics and Jews, and by the mid-nineteenth century, many violent confrontations occurred with native-born Americans. During the height of the Know-Nothing movement in the 1850s, the Germans were often victims of verbal abuse, open discrimination, and even mob violence. On August 5, 1855, a day long remembered in Louisville, Kentucky, as Bloody Monday, a mob of Know-Nothings — incited by fiery articles in the Louisville *Journal* — stormed into the German section of the city. When the riot was over, 22 men had been killed, several hundred were wounded, and 16 houses had been burned.[37]

German immigrants assimilated fairly rapidly, but because of the large, continual flow of newcomers, a significant ethnic subculture was always in evidence. Some 230 years after the arrival of the first German settlers, this continuing subculture came under xenophobic attack. Becoming embroiled for the first time in 1917 in a European war so traumatized Americans that a strong wave of anti-German feeling prevailed for several years. Patriotic hysteria brought intense pressure upon the Germans to eliminate their cultural manifestations. This Americanization movement, which was sometimes brutal, did succeed in eliminating distinct "Little Germany" subsocieties. This was one instance where forced assimilation succeeded, because the Germans wanted to identify with the land of their children, not the land of their forebears.

CULTURAL IMPACT

American speech, eating, and drinking reflect German influence. Frankfurters, sauerkraut, sauerbraten, hamburgers, wiener schnitzel, pumpernickel bread, liverwurst, pretzels, zwieback, and lager beer were introduced by German immigrants. The words *stein* and *rathskeller* are also of German origin, as are the concepts of the kindergarten and the university. Germans almost exclusively dominated the brewing industry, founding Anheuser-Busch, Schaefer, Schlitz, Schmidt's, Pabst, Ruppert, and many others.

Some leading German industrialists were George Westinghouse, electrical engineering; Frederick Weyerhaeuser, lumber; John Jacob Astor, fur trade; Bausch and Lomb, optical instruments; Chrysler, Studebaker, and Kaiser, car manufacturers; Steinway and Wurlitzer, piano makers; and Heinz, food canning. A German immigrant, Thomas Nast, was America's first great caricaturist and political cartoonist, and he created the Democratic donkey, the Republican elephant, and the "I want you" Uncle Sam recruiting poster of World War I vintage.

The Germans no longer predominate as a distinct ethnic minority, even though some remain unassimilated. Their earlier experiences, particularly those of mid-nineteenth-century German Catholics and of German-Americans during World War I, were a forerunner of the types of conflict certain other minority groups also would encounter.

THE IRISH

Their religion, their peasant culture, and their rebelliousness against England not only marked the Irish as strangers to the Americans, but also set the stage for the most overt discrimination and hostility any ethnic group had thus far encountered. Almost all theoretical considerations discussed in the earlier chapters can be applied to the history of the Irish in the United States.

Originally made unwelcome in the New England settlements, most of the early Irish immigrants settled in Pennsylvania or in Maryland, which had been founded as an English Catholic colony in 1634 but which had become Protestant-controlled by the mid-eighteenth century. By 1790 the Irish accounted for almost 2 percent of the total population of 3,172,444. Their numbers became a source of increasing concern to the Federalists, especially during the presidency of John Adams. Fearing that the "wild Irish" rebels would attempt to turn the United States against England, and also that they would join the Republican party, the Federalists were strongly against the incoming "hordes of wild Irishmen." Rufus King, American minister in London, was one of the foremost opponents of Irish emigration to the United States. He expressed to Secretary of State Timothy Pickering his fear that the disaffected Irish would "disfigure our true national character," which was purest in untainted New England. Massachusetts-born John Quincy Adams agreed that the United States had "too many of these people already."[38]

After 1830, emigration to America became increasingly essential to the Irish, whose oppression under British rule prevented their becoming successful in their native land. The successive failures of the potato crop and the resulting famine in the late 1840s accelerated the exodus.

Approximately 1.2 million people emigrated between 1847 and 1854, the peak year being 1851, when almost a quarter of a million Irish came to the United States.

CULTURAL DIFFERENTIATION

The Irish attracted attention because of their sheer numbers, and also because they were Catholic and had strong anti-British feelings. Both factors weighed heavily against them in Anglo-Saxon Protestant America. In addition, they were a poverty-stricken rural people who settled in groups mainly in the slum areas of cities on the East Coast. Because they could find only unskilled jobs, they began life in America with a lower-class status, bearing that stigma at a time when America was becoming increasingly class conscious.

The Irish were the first ethnic group to come to the United States in large numbers as a minority very different from the dominant culture of the country. They were to be the harbingers of the "new" immigrants yet to come. As Charles Marden and Gladys Meyer point out:

> This was America's first confrontation with a peasant culture. The English, Scandinavians, or Germans who came to America in the nineteenth century came from towns or from freehold farming patterns. The Irish had been long exploited by the English landholding system. The unchallenged position of the Catholic church cemented bonds of identity. A history of famine, a family and inheritance system that led to late marriage and many unmarried men and women, the ambivalent situation of being English-speaking but not part of English-derived institutions, and migration in large numbers put the Irish in a peculiar relationship to dominants. Some welcomed them as a necessary working-class contingent; others engaged in flagrant discrimination.[39]

Even when they were welcomed as people who would fill the working-class jobs, it was with an ethnocentric attitude of superiority over a lowly breed of people, typified by these comments of a Massachusetts senator in 1852:

> That inefficiency of the pure Celtic race furnishes the answer to the question: How much use are the Irish to us in America? The Native American answer is, "none at all." And the Native American policy is to keep them away.
>
> A profound mistake, I believe. . . . We are here, well organized and well trained, masters of the soil, the very race before which they have yielded everywhere besides. It must be, that when they come in among us, they come to lift us up. As sure as water and oil each finds its level they will find theirs. So far as they are mere

hand-workers, they must sustain the head-workers, or those who have any element of intellectual ability. Their inferiority as a race compels them to go to the bottom; and the consequence is that we are, all of us, the higher lifted because they are here.[40]

SOCIETAL REACTION

The Native American movement, which had briefly been evident in the immediate post–Revolutionary War period, now swept across the land in a shameful display of bigotry and intolerance. The growth of anti-Irish feeling was strongly linked to anti-Catholic feeling. Fears of "Popery" arose, strengthened by the influx of priests to minister to the needs of the Irish Catholics. The Irish were brutalized by this movement far more than the Germans were by Know-Nothing violence; destruction of property, beatings, and loss of life occurred in the Irish sections of many cities. In addition to frequent street brawls, the mob violence sometimes resulted in the burning of churches and convents. In an ironic twist of fate, the Irish later tended to dominate some urban police forces, and they would be the ones to either control or arrest unruly Know-Nothing mobs, thus maintaining the American way of life that the Irish had once been accused of destroying.

Antagonism toward the Irish was manifested most strongly in social and job discrimination. For a long time, job advertisements in Boston and elsewhere included the line "No Irish need apply."

Indeed, they suffered severe discrimination in the new land and most often found employment only in the lowest-paying and hardest-working jobs: as ditchdiggers, or dockers, or "terriers" working on the railroads and in the canal beds. In some respects (clearly not in all), the urban experience for blacks in the twentieth century — in terms of the attitudes of others and in terms of occupations — has its parallel in the Irish experience in the middle of the previous century.[41]

CULTURAL IMPACT

Irish labor played a key role in the industrial expansion of the United States, particularly in building the great systems of canals, waterways, and railroads. As Roman Catholicism evolved into a major faith in a Protestant country, through increased membership and the power of the church hierarchy, Irish-Americans exerted a great moral force upon the nation. As the Irish began to assimilate, they often served as a "middleman minority," aiding new European immigrant groups in work,

FIGURE 4.5

"THE AMERICAN RIVER GANGES"

Many consider this the most vicious anti-Catholic, anti-Irish cartoon ever printed in a mass-circulation magazine. It illustrates the belief that the Irish Catholics were endangering public education (symbolized by the upside-down American flag). Note the Irish Harp and Papal Tiara flying above Tammany Hall, the teachers being executed, and children being thrown to the river bank by Democratic politicians. One Protestant teacher (Bible in pocket) is protecting children from the crocodiles, which represent Catholic bishops. Their jaws are mitres, their scales are vestments, and their faces are Irish stereotypes. Cartoon by Thomas Nast, *Harper's Weekly*, September 30, 1871. (The Distorted Image, Anti-Defamation League. John and Selma Appel Collection)

church, school, and city life.[42] The Irish were not so hospitable to the Chinese, however, often clashing with them in the cities and in railway labor disputes.

MINORITY RESPONSE

The Irish experience was the prototype for the experiences of later immigrants, not only in their hostile reception by the dominant culture, but also in their reaction to the prejudice and discrimination that they frequently encountered. One should not underestimate the hardship involved in leaving one's native land — alone or with family — journeying far to another country, feeling both anxieties and hopes, and then finding oneself an unwanted stranger in a strange land. Irish responses were both retreatist and aggressive, as demonstrated through their social behavior and their involvement in the labor movement and in the urban political machine. Because these activities frequently offended American norms of behavior, they reaffirmed the suspicions of native-born Americans, thereby reinforcing the stereotypes of the Irish and prolonging the vicious circle.

Just as the pioneers, having no quick escape route or outside help, would put their wagons in a circle as a defense against Indian attack, so the Irish erected a "circle of wagons" for their survival. Their circles of wagons, however, were usually in slum subcommunities within densely populated cities. The Irish were socially isolated, and their occupational escape route was effectively blocked. Whatever sense of group consciousness they had brought with them became more pronounced as they relied on one another for their social and emotional welfare.

> Unable to participate in the normal associational affairs of the community, the Irish felt obliged to erect a society within a society, to act together in their own way. In every contact therefore the group, acting apart from other sections of the community, became intensely aware of its peculiar and exclusive identity.[43]

The small degree of intermarriage both reflected and buttressed the distinction between the Irish and other Americans. Among the Irish, religious and social considerations encouraged a tendency to mate with their own kind. As Catholics, they were repeatedly warned that union with Protestants was tantamount to loss of faith, and the great majority of non-Irish in the city considered marriage with them degrading. As a result, the percentage of Irish intermarriage was extremely low.

As the colonial forces had once usurped "Yankee Doodle," the British satirical song about them, the Irish now seized upon their group identity as a rallying point for pride and camaraderie. That ebullience still manifests itself across the country each Saint Patrick's Day. In the

"The nicest thing I ever experienced was seeing the Statue of Liberty. It meant we were here and we were all right."

"Like many more immigrants like myself, I came to this country to seek a living because living over there was very, very poor. Work was scarce and hard. I decided that I ought to try the United States to make a living.

"I left my home in Ireland on a Friday morning. I went to a place then called Queenstown in County Cork. I was there for the greater part of Friday and Saturday because you had to go through quite a number of tests and screening to be allowed to board ship. On Sunday morning around eight o'clock I boarded the ship.

"We arrived in the United States a week from that Monday, around two o'clock in the afternoon in the harbor of New York. The nicest thing I saw after being so seasick — and I might say I was very, very seasick — the nicest thing I ever experienced was seeing the Statue of Liberty. It meant we were here and we were all right. We had landed and we were safe. Then, of course, I had to go through customs and things like that.

"I had heard a great deal about the United States, that it was a good country, and I might very well say that it was a good country, although at that time I was disappointed because I wasn't the one to find the gold in the streets. I really had to go out and look for a job. I worked for awhile in a doctor's office and from there I went to work for a chemical company. There was disappointment. There were loans from my family and my friends. It's something you wonder if you can make it. Thank God I did."

Irish immigrant who came to the United States in 1920 at age 18

nineteenth century, the Irish community was united through family, church, and school, as well as through their social and recreational activities. Such "clannishness" only added fuel to the fires of resentment among the American assimilationists, even though the Anglo-Saxon community had helped to cause the situation. Jewish immigrants would later experience similar problems when their community was subject to charges of clannishness.

Quite often, some members of a low-status minority group are arrested more frequently than members of other groups for certain crimes, particularly those of personal disorganization. The Irish, for example, were disproportionately represented in arrests and convictions for brawling, drunkenness, disturbing the peace, and more serious crimes during the nineteenth century. These occurrences reinforced the dominant society's stereotyped attitudes toward them. The greatest notoriety surrounded the violence and murders committed by the Molly Maguires, a secret terrorist group that aided the Irish miners in their struggle with the mine owners. Following infiltration of their group by a secret agent for the Pinkerton Detective Agency and a highly questionable court proceeding, the Molly Maguire movement ended in the hanging of 20 men, the largest mass execution in the nation's history.

Irish labor was diversified, but it was concentrated in low-status unskilled or semiskilled occupations. The Irish worked at the hard, physical jobs in the cities, in the mines of Appalachia, or in railroad construction from the Alleghenies to the Rockies. With their knowledge of the English language, the Irish provided strong, articulate membership and leadership in such early labor movements as the Knights of Labor. A central characteristic of these unions was hostility to Asian workers. As the Asians began to demand a voice in the unions, the Irish majority reacted with anger; they felt that they had worked hard to gain a higher job status, and the "aliens" had no right to challenge their authority.

UPWARD MOBILITY

A combination of factors — living only in certain sections of the cities, knowledge of the English language, and a strong group consciousness — enabled the Irish to build an urban political machine. The rise of ward leaders and the implementation of a spoils system of a far greater magnitude than anything native-born Americans had devised helped the Irish establish a power base in American society. Their entrance into public service — police, fire, postal, and civil services — brought them greater respectability in the eyes of the dominant society.

Their upward climb was, nevertheless, a slow one, as antipathy continued toward their "insurgent" activities that seemed to threaten the democratic process. A common fear was that the Catholic clergy would come to exercise control over the local political machine. The passage of time and the arrival of the "new" immigrants, visibly different from the "old," greatly reduced prejudice and discrimination against the Irish as a minority group. Later Irish immigrants would seldom encounter difficulty in gaining acceptance in American society.

THE SCANDINAVIANS

Norwegians, Swedes, and Danes have come to the United States from lands with different governments, different traditions, and different

FIGURE 4.6

"UNCLE SAM'S LODGING-HOUSE"

"UNCLE SAM (to the Irishman) — 'Look here, you, everybody else is quiet and peaceable, and you're all the time a-kicking up a row!'" Cartoon by J. Keppler, *Puck*, circa 1855. (The Bettmann Archive)

spoken languages, although the Norwegian and Danish written language is the same. Because of the physical similarities among the three groups and because they frequently settled together in the new land, use of the term *Scandinavian* to designate all three groups became common throughout American society.

> The common use of the term *Scandinavian* to describe Swedes, Norwegians, and Danes in a broad and general way is one of the products of the commingling of these three peoples on the American side of the Atlantic. The word really fits even more loosely than does the word *British* to indicate the English, Welsh, and Scotch. It was applied early in the history of the settlements in Wisconsin and Illinois, to groups which comprised both Norwegians and Danes on the one hand, or Norwegians and Swedes on the other hand, when no one of the three nationalities were strong enough to maintain itself separately, and when the members of one were inclined . . . to resent being called by one of the other names; for example, when a Norwegian objected to being taken for a Swede. The Scandinavian Synod of the Evangelical Lutheran Church, organized in 1860, included both Norwegians and Danes.
>
> . . . The use and acceptability of the word steadily grew; the great daily paper in Chicago took the name *Skandinaven*; in 1889, the editor of *The North* declared: "the term has become a household word . . . universally understood in the sense in which we here use it to designate the three nationalities . . ."[44]

Some Swedes and Finns came to what is now the United States as early as 1638, making their landfall at the mouth of the Delaware River. They established a colony, New Sweden, a land of promise encompassing parts of modern-day Delaware, Pennsylvania, and New Jersey. Combating the Dutch and the English as well as the heat and the mosquitoes, these settlers constructed the first log cabin in the New World.

Although small numbers of Norwegians, Swedes, and Danes continued to emigrate to the United States, they did not come here in substantial numbers until after 1865. Thereafter, motivated by religious dissension, voting disenfranchisement, crop failures, and other economic factors, the Scandinavians emigrated in large numbers. The Swedes hit their peak year of immigration in 1913, and the Norwegians in 1924. The total number of Scandinavians who have emigrated to the United States is now approximately 2.5 million.

A great many of these immigrants settled in the northern region of the Midwest, in rural communities where the soil was highly fertile and where they could enjoy social and political equality and yet retain their ethnicity.

Their settlements in the farmlands of the northern Middle West became strongholds of church-centered Norwegian and Swedish traditions. Isolation from the dominant drift of American social patterns permitted their widespread and long-lived retention of indigenous lifeways, which continue, in some measure, to this day.[45]

Ole Rolvaag presented an eloquent and poignant saga of late-nineteenth-century Norwegian pioneers in the Dakota Territory in *Giants in the Earth*, a vivid social-psychological portrait of pioneer life. Capturing the exuberant hopes, fears, despair, struggles, and interactions of the immigrants in the heartland of America, this monumental work offers vivid testimony to the human quest of a dream.

And it was as if nothing affected people in those days. They threw themselves blindly into the Impossible, and accomplished the Unbelievable. If anyone succumbed in the struggle — and that happened often — another would come and take his place. Youth was in the race; the unknown, the untried, the unheard-of, was in the air; people caught it, were intoxicated by it, threw themselves away, and laughed at the cost. Of course it was possible — everything was possible out here. There was no such thing as the Impossible any more. The human race had not known such faith and such self-confidence since history began. . . . And so had been the Spirit since the day the first settlers landed on the eastern shores; it would rise and fall at intervals, would swell and surge on again with every new wave of settlers that rolled westward into the unbroken solitude.[46]

In addition to farming, the Scandinavians primarily worked as lumberjacks, sailors, dock workers, and craftsmen in the building and machine trades. Since they came from countries with compulsory education, their literacy rate was very high, and a large percentage of them acquired U.S. citizenship. Danes tended to spread out more and to downplay the role of church and fraternal organizations, in comparison to Norwegians and Swedes. For that reason, the Danes assimilated more quickly, although all groups succeeded in blending into the American social fabric fairly easily.

THE SCOTS

The first wave of Scottish migration occurred during the colonial period; by 1790 they were second in number only to the English, totaling 221,562, or 7 percent of the population, compared with the

2,605,699 English, who made up 82 percent. Consequently, Scottish-Americans played a prominent role during the formative years of the new nation. As an illustration, 11 of the 56 signers of the Declaration of Independence were Scottish-Americans. Almost 80 percent of all Scottish emigrants came to America later, however; between 1871 and 1930, more than 640,000 Scots arrived. This group was primarily from the working class, and they entered various semiskilled occupations.

The Scots should not be confused with the Scotch-Irish, who were mostly Lowland Scots who came from the Irish city of Ulster. Before the Revolution, 50,000 of them had settled on the southern frontier and in the central Appalachians. They were concentrated primarily in North Carolina and Pennsylvania.

Although the Scotch-Irish actively supported the rebel cause, the Scots from the Highlands of Scotland were loyalists throughout the Revolutionary War. They settled in established areas rather than along the frontier and insisted upon maintaining their ethnic identity even though they were easily assimilated almost from the outset.

The rigid discipline of Scottish church life — either Presbyterian or Episcopalian — was reflected in their life style. Deeply religious, they adhered to a strict moral code; the Protestant Ethic of hard work, frugality, and honesty was as evident among them as among Calvinist New Englanders. Like many other communities, they also sought to preserve their culture and to duplicate the way of life from the old country.

Scottish emigration did not maintain its magnitude after 1936. Lack of new Scottish immigrants in sizable numbers reduced their proportional representation in the total population, and the assimilation process mostly removed their visibility. Maintaining their ethnic identity was a losing battle. The Scots did continue, however, to wear disguises on Halloween (a practice now followed by many children in the United States on this holiday) and to regularly celebrate the January 25 birthday of Robert Burns, the Scottish poet.

THE WELSH

Though frequently lumped together with the English, the Welsh were a distinct ethnic minority in the United States; there were sufficient numbers during the pre–Civil War period to warrant the printing of newspapers and some books in Welsh.

Welsh immigrants came here with the early colonists, settling together to a much greater degree than the English. They were very active during the Revolution, and five Welsh-Americans — William Floyd, Button Gwinnett, Thomas Jefferson, Francis Lewis, and Lewis Morris — were signers of the Declaration of Independence.

FIGURE 4.7

Scene in Castle Garden, New York City, on the arrival of Mormon converts from Europe. From Frank Leslie's *Illustrated Newspaper*, November 23, 1878. (Museum of the City of New York)

As with other immigrants, economic and religious motives lured the Welsh to the United States. They were of different Protestant denominations; Baptists and Quakers came first, followed later by Anglicans and Presbyterians. Primarily farmers and miners, many settled in Cambria County, Pennsylvania, where they exerted a strong social and political influence; others settled in Oneida County, New York, a region in which "Welsh butter" became famous. By the late nineteenth century, many Welsh miners — like their English counterparts — had become superintendents and foremen of coal mines in many states, including Ohio, Illinois, and Washington.

RETROSPECT

Structural and cultural differentiation played important roles in determining the nature of intergroup relations among northern and western Europeans in the United States. Generally, as long as the social structure was in its formative period and thus very fluid, the ethnic groups did not experience discrimination or low status for long. Relative isolation from European influences and sharing the commonality of forging a new life in the wilderness helped reduce any nationalistic biases. Although sporadic flare-ups occurred due to nationalistic rivalries, the different ethnic groups were usually hospitable to one another, welcoming strangers coming to settle because they themselves would benefit from the community's growth.

As life became more settled, residential patterns more densely clustered, and the social structure more solidified, recently arrived strangers became more conspicuous. Their cultural differences were often accentuated by their less fortunate economic circumstances. German and Irish immigrants of the nineteenth century, for example, encountered hostility not only because of their religion and culture but also because of their lack of power. Many settled in already established areas and thus started a new life in a region already dominated by others who looked upon them with scorn. Those who kept to themselves by settling in rural areas — the Scandinavians, the French, and some of the German immigrants — fared better than those who tried to settle in already urbanized areas.

Prevailing attitudes were of critical importance to a minority group's experience. The Dutch and Quakers, tolerant of those who were different, encouraged religious and cultural diversity within their settlements. Cultural diffusion and assimilation were least likely among the religiously orthodox. This was true not only for a dominant group such as the New Englanders, who expelled or denied welcome to dissenters, Quakers, Catholics, and Jews. It was also true for minority groups who resisted intermarriage and assimilation, such as the nineteenth-century Dutch, Scandinavians, and Irish.

Cultural diversity was a reality from the outset. Each settlement was an ethnic enclave, in which people of similar beliefs and values clustered together and helped one another to adjust in a new land. As the settlements became more populated, growing into towns and cities, the ethnic enclaves formed by the newer immigrants were actually subcommunities within a larger society. Although they were not as physically isolated as earlier ethnic groups, they were, nonetheless, socially and spatially segregated, often voluntarily, from those unlike themselves.

All immigrants, in varying degrees, faced hardships in adjusting to the strangeness of a new land and people. To ease that adjustment, they tried to re-create the familiar old world here in the new, through their churches, schools, newspapers, and fraternal and mutual-aid societies. Their efforts to preserve their language and culture helped to bring them a measure of security, but the attempts also often led to suspicion, dissension, and hostility between the dominant and minority cultures.

Discrimination and xenophobia occur especially when the superordinate group views the size and influence of the subordinate group as a threat to the stability of the job market, the community, or the nation itself. The nativist movements against the French and the Irish during John Adams' presidency, and against the Germans and the Irish in the mid-nineteenth century, testify to that pattern. Through legislative efforts and violent actions, the dominant-group members sought to justify their discriminatory behavior as appropriate to preserve the American character.

For the "old" immigrants, the Civil War brought to an end the difficulties they had encountered because of their background, for they were now comrades-in-arms for a common cause. Then too, a new threat loomed on the horizon as "new" immigrants — shorter, swarthier, with unfamiliar dress, foods, and customs — began the second great wave of migration to the United States. These new immigrants seemed to be totally unlike all that Americans were or should be. People found a new target for their fears, distrust, prejudices, and discrimination in these "undesirable" aliens.

QUESTIONS FOR DISCUSSION

1. What are some examples of cultural pluralism among the Dutch, French, German, Irish, and Scandinavian peoples in nineteenth-century United States?

2. What significance did the dominance of northern and western Europeans in early America have for later immigrant groups?

3. What groups suffered from xenophobic reactions? Why? In what ways?

4. In what ways did the patterns of settlement and adjustment among the "old" immigrants parallel those of later immigrants? How did they differ?

5. How were structural conditions, as well as cultural, class, and power differentials, conducive or detrimental to adjustment and acceptance of the minority groups discussed in this chapter?

SUGGESTED READINGS

Anderson, Charles H. White Protestant Americans. Prentice-Hall, Englewood Cliffs, N.J., 1970.

Baltzell, Digby. The Protestant Establishment: Aristocracy and Caste in America. Random House, New York, 1964.

Beals, Carleton. Brass Knuckle Crusade, rev. ed. Hastings House, New York, 1960.

Billigmeier, Robert H. Americans from Germany: A Study in Cultural Diversity. Wadsworth, Belmont, Calif., 1974.

Dolan, Jay P. The Immigrant Church: New York Irish and German Catholics, 1815–1865. Johns Hopkins, Baltimore, 1975.

Duff, John B. The Irish in the United States. Wadsworth, Belmont, Calif., 1971.

Glazer, Nathan, and Daniel P. Moynihan. Beyond the Melting Pot, 2nd ed. M.I.T. Press, Cambridge, Mass., 1970.

Handlin, Oscar. Boston's Immigrants, rev. ed. Harvard University Press, Cambridge, Mass., 1959.

Higham, John. Strangers in the Land. Atheneum, New York, 1973.

McCague, James. The Second Rebellion: The Story of the New York City Draft Riots of 1863. Dial Press, New York, 1968.

McKiernan, Joan, and Robert St. Cyr (eds.). "Mick!" — Anti-Irish Prejudice in America. World Publishing, New York, 1972.

Miller, John C. Crisis in Freedom. Little, Brown, Boston, 1951.

Rolvaag, Ole E. Giants in the Earth. Harper & Row, New York, 1927.

Shannon, William V. The American Irish. Macmillan, New York, 1963.

Smith, James M. Freedom's Fetters. Cornell University Press, Ithaca, N.Y., 1956.

Wittke, Carl. The Irish in America. Louisiana State University Press, Baton Rouge, 1956.

———. We Who Built America, rev. ed. The Press of Case Western Reserve University, Cleveland, 1967.

NOTES

1. Nathan Glazer and Daniel P. Moynihan, Beyond the Melting Pot, 2nd ed., M.I.T. Press, Cambridge, Mass., 1970, p. 1.

2. Maldwyn Allen Jones, American Immigration, University of Chicago Press, Chicago, 1960, p. 40.

3. American Observer, 50 (Nov. 29, 1971), 4.

4. Quotations and commentary taken from John C. Miller, Crisis in Freedom, Little, Brown, Boston, 1951, pp. 41–42.

5. R. Ernst, "The Living Conditions of

the Immigrant," in *The Urbanization of America*, ed. A. M. Wakestein, Houghton Mifflin, Boston, 1949, p. 266.

6. Carleton Beals, *Brass Knuckle Crusade*, Hastings House, New York 1960, p. 5.

7. *Ibid.*

8. Ray Allen Billington, *The Protestant Crusade, 1800–1860*, Macmillan, New York, 1938, p. 388.

9. John Higham, *Strangers in the Land*, Atheneum, New York, 1973, p. 7.

10. Harriet Martineau, *Society in America*, 1837, quoted in *American Observer*, 50 (Nov. 29, 1971), 4.

11. *The Journals and Miscellaneous Notebooks of Ralph Waldo Emerson*, eds. Ralph H. Orth and Alfred K. Ferguson, The Belknap Press of Harvard University Press, Cambridge, Mass., 1971, IX, 299–300.

12. William Bradford, *Of Plymouth Plantation*, ed. Harvey Wish, Capricorn Books, New York, 1962, p. 29.

13. *Ibid.*, p. 33.

14. *Ibid.*, pp. 16–17, 184.

15. Rowland Berthoff, *British Immigrants in Industrial America, 1790–1950*, Harvard University Press, Cambridge, Mass., 1953, pp. 30–56.

16. *Ibid.*, pp. 125–131.

17. U.S. Immigration and Naturalization Service, *Annual Report: 1976*, Washington, D.C., 1976, Table 13, p. 88.

18. Ilja M. Dijour. "A Seminar on the Integration of Immigrants," 1960, p. 6, quoted in Wilbur S. Shepperson, *Emigration and Disenchantment: Portraits of Englishmen Repatriated from the United States*, Univ. of Oklahoma Press, Norman, 1965, p. 182.

19. Wilbur S. Shepperson, *Emigration and Disenchantment: Portraits of Englishmen Repatriated from the United States*, University of Oklahoma Press, Norman, 1965, pp. 16–17, 184.

20. A Report of the Commissioner of Immigration upon the Causes Which Incite Immigration to the U.S., 52nd Congress, 1st session (1891–1892), *House Executive Document 235*, Part I, pp. 260, 282.

21. Berthoff, *British Immigrants in Industrial America, 1790–1950*, pp. 103–104.

22. U.S. Immigration and Naturalization Service, *Annual Report: 1976*, Washington, D.C., 1976, Table 13, p. 64.

23. Hans Koningsberger, *Holland and the United States*, Netherlands Information Service, New York, 1968, p. 20.

24. Arthur Henry Hirsch, *The Huguenots of Colonial South Carolina*, Shoe String Press, Hamden, Conn., 1962, p. 95.

25. J. Hector St. John de Crèvecoeur, *Letters from an American Farmer*, London, 1782, reprinted by Albert and Charles Boni, New York, 1925, pp. 54–55.

26. W. S. Shaw to Abigail Adams, Cambridge, Mass., May 20, 1798, *Adams Papers*, Vol. 8, No. 48, Massachusetts Historical Society.

27. Miller, *Crisis in Freedom*, pp. 13, 42–43.

28. T. Lynn Smith and Vernon J. Parenton, "Acculturation Among the Louisiana French," *American Journal of Sociology*, 44 (November 1938), 357.

29. *Ibid.*, p. 364.

30. Vernon J. Parenton, "Socio-Psychological Integration in a Rural French-Speaking Section of Louisiana," *The Southwestern Social Science Quarterly*, 30 (December 1949), 195.

31. Marcus L. Hansen and J. B. Prebner, *The Mingling of the Canadian and American Peoples*, Yale University Press, New Haven, Conn., 1940, pp. 123–168.

32. Albert B. Faust, *The German Element in the United States*, Arno Press, New York, 1969, I, 66–72.

33. Quoted in W. C. Smith, *Americans in the Making*, Appleton-Century, New York, 1939, p. 394.

34. Maurice R. Davie, *World Immigration*, Macmillan, New York, 1936, p. 36.

35. Brewton Berry and Henry L. Tischler, *Race and Ethnic Relations*, 4th ed., Houghton Mifflin, Boston, 1978, p. 186.

36. Nathan Glazer, *American Judaism*, 2nd ed., University of Chicago Press, Chicago, 1972, pp. 23, 31.

37. Beals, *Brass Knuckle Crusade*, p. 168.

38. Quoted in James M. Smith, *Freedom's Fetters*, Cornell University Press, Ithaca, N.Y., 1956, p. 25.

39. Charles F. Marden and Gladys Meyer, *Minorities in American Society*, 5th ed., Van Nostrand Reinhold, New York, 1978, p. 77.

40. Edward Everett, "Letters on Irish Emigration," in *Historical Aspects of the Immigration Problem, Select Documents*, ed. Edith Abbott, University of Chicago Press, Chicago, 1926, pp. 462–463.

41. Peter I. Rose, *They and We*, 2nd ed., Random House, New York, 1974, p. 39.

42. For information about middleman minorities, see Hubert M. Blalock, Jr., *Toward a Theory of Minority Group Relations*, Wiley, New York, 1967, pp. 79–84; Edna Bonacich, "A Theory of Middleman Minorities," *American Sociological Review*, 38 (October 1973), 583–594.

43. Oscar Handlin, *Boston's Immigrants*, rev. ed., Harvard University Press, Cambridge, Mass., 1959, p. 176.

44. Kendric C. Babcock, *The Scandinavian Element in the United States*, 1914, reprint edition, Arno Press and The New York Times, New York, 1969, pp. 15–16.

45. Rose, *They and We*, p. 68.

46. Ole E. Rolvaag, *Giants in the Earth*, Copyright, 1927, by Harper & Brothers, p. 425.

FIVE

THE ''NEW'' IMMIGRANTS: SOUTHERN, CENTRAL, AND EASTERN EUROPEANS

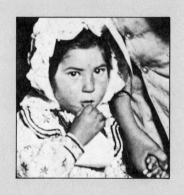

⫹During its colonial period, immigrants came to the United States from southern, central, and eastern Europe. Many, in fact, played important roles in the Revolutionary War and during the early years of the new nation. Not until the late nineteenth century, however, would immigrants come from this part of the world in any significant numbers.

HISTORICAL AND SOCIOLOGICAL PERSPECTIVES

In the late nineteenth century, a noticeable shift occurred in the kind of immigrant coming to America. By 1896 the turning point was reached: the number of immigrants from northern and western Europe was surpassed by the number of immigrants from the rest of Europe. Their physical and cultural differences made the newcomers easier to identify as strangers, and they were often broadly categorized as being alike, despite their many intrinsic differences as individuals and as separate ethnic groups. They arrived in large enough numbers to be able to preserve their culture and social boundaries within an urban subcultural setting, but this also increased the probability of prejudice and discrimination because of their visibility, clannishness, differentness, and low socioeconomic status. Consequently, structural and cultural differentiation made possible intergroup conflict and the various dominant-minority response patterns previously discussed.

THE PUSH-PULL FACTORS

A number of reasons accounted for the great wave of immigration from 1880 to 1920 (Figure 5.1). During that time American industry was growing rapidly, requiring ever larger numbers of workers. Improved transportation — quicker, sturdier steamships with their highly competitive rates for steerage dropping to ten dollars or less — encouraged an ocean crossing.

Peasant life was especially harsh in Europe. The ruling classes and local landed estate farmers exploited the common people. They crushed most peasant revolts and protests instead of reforming the basic agricultural economy. Peasants saw their sons drafted into the army for periods of 12 to 31 years. Trying to eke out an existence amid poverty, unemployment, sickness, and tyranny, some of Europe's poor looked elsewhere for a better life.

Letters from friends or relatives already in America were eagerly read and circulated among villagers. Newspapers, books, pamphlets, and transportation and labor recruiting agents all stimulated what contemporaries came to call "America fever." Following a familiar minority

FIGURE 5.1

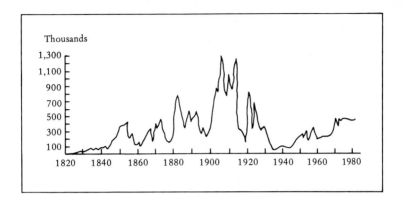

PATTERNS OF IMMIGRATION TO THE UNITED STATES, 1820–1976
Source: Based on data from U.S. Immigration and Naturalization Service,
1976 Annual Report, Table 1.

pattern of avoidance, Europe's poor and persecuted peoples fled their homelands for the promise of "Golden America."

Political and economic unrest in Europe also encouraged the exodus. Governments faced the pressures of overpopulation, chronic poverty, the decline of feudalism, dissident factions, and a changing agrarian economy. For them, large-scale emigration to America was an expedient solution to many problems, so they sponsored emigration drives that served as an additional impetus.

And so they came — Italians, Portuguese, Greeks, and Armenians from the southern part of the continent; Hungarians, Poles, Czechs, Slovaks, and others from the plains of Central Europe; Byelorussians, Ukrainians, Ruthenians, and others from the western regions of Czarist Russia; Jewish emigrants, whose religion and Yiddish culture had frequently made them targets of discrimination and persecution, from all parts of eastern and Central Europe, particularly Russia. All of these different peoples came, leaving behind their familiar world and seeking a new destiny.

STRUCTURAL CONDITIONS

The America the immigrants came to was far different from what earlier immigrants had found. The frontier was rapidly disappearing; industrialization and urbanization were changing the life style of the na-

(155)

tion. The immigrants, mostly illiterate, unskilled, rural peasants, were plunged into a new cultural and social environment.

Since they had virtually no resources, many of these immigrants settled in the cities that had been their ports of entry or in the inland cities along railroad lines, such as Chicago. At the turn of the century, living conditions in the cities were far worse than they are today. Overcrowding, disease, high mortality rates, crime, filth, and congestion were commonplace. Crowded into poorly ventilated tenements and cellars, the immigrants often lived in squalor.

Settling in the oldest city sections, the immigrants formed ethnic sub-communities, re-creating the nationality quilt of Europe. Although these groups were neighbors because of necessity, intermarriage or joint organizational activities were rare. In an effort to find security in a strange land, they repeated the adjustment patterns of the "old" immigrants. They sought and interacted with their own people, establishing their own churches, schools, and organizations to preserve their traditions and culture.

As unskilled workers, most found employment in the low-status, manual labor jobs in the factories, mines, needle trades, and construction. At that time the worker had no voice in working conditions, for labor unions had not yet become effective. The fourteen-hour day, six-day week for low wages was common. There were no vacations, sick pay, or pension plans. Child labor was the norm, and entire families often worked to provide family income. Lighting, ventilation, and heating were poor; in the factories, moving pieces of machinery were dangerously exposed. There was no worker's compensation if, as was likely, someone was injured on the job. A worker who objected was likely to be fired and blacklisted. Exploited by the captains of industry, the immigrants became deeply involved with the labor union movement, so much so that to tell the story of one without the other is virtually impossible. It is also difficult to apply simplistic, all-encompassing models of immigrant behavior because of the particular cultural attitudes the immigrants brought with them.

New studies suggest that each group, using the values of its old world heritage, developed its own strategy to cope with new demands upon its work habits and attitudes. These strategies took many forms. It is true that many immigrants embraced the industrial ethos and found fulfillment in it. But many could not adjust to the new work discipline required of them and drifted from job to job; a good percentage returned to the Old Country, defeated and disillusioned. Some tried and failed to find work for which their skills and previous experience equipped them. Others turned to collective action — temperance societies, workers' educational associations, fraternal benefit societies, cooperatives, and unions — either

FIGURE 5.2

"HERE AND THERE; OR, EMIGRATION A REMEDY"

Woodcut, circa 1848, illustrating emigration from England to the United States. (The Bettmann Archive)

BOX 5.1

"It was so hot in the shop, the sweat was running from the body and from the hand. . . . Big people used to faint."

"Working conditions were terrible, terrible. If you have to sit two-three hours overtime for ten cents, what can I explain you? It don't get worse. But these ten cents I need. Whenever it was overtime, I was the first one to raise my hand.

"The boss watches you. You shouldn't talk to one another. He watches you between lunch and supper, you know. So you want something, you have something in your drawer like candy. He watches. No, no, no, nothing. You can't eat while you're working. So, you watch, you put the candy in your mouth.

"It was so hot in the shop, the sweat was running from the body and from the hand and the material got stained. The boss didn't care, the foreman didn't care. Once two policemen came in. They stopped the power. They said we couldn't work in such a heat. You haven't even got a fan here to have a little coolness. Nothing! People used to faint. Big people used to faint.

"In winter — it was such a hard winter. When I opened the door in the morning to go to work, I couldn't take away my hand from the knob — the frost. Terrible, terrible. At work in the big shop in the middle was a stove. It kept us a little warm. But, you know, young people, young blood — we put on a sweater. Yeah, the conditions was terrible. Can't be worse. Can't be worse. It was terrible. And the boss had a fresh mouth always for the workers."

Austrian Jewish immigrant who came to the United States in
1914 at age 17

to protect themselves from a system that was often pitiless, or to try in a small way to change the social and economic environment in which they found themselves. Still others resorted to radical and "direct" action to forcibly change a system which did not yield what they had crossed the Atlantic to find.[1]

Despite the adverse conditions, many immigrants worked hard and made sacrifices. Things were still better than what they had left behind. More importantly, America gave them hope and a promise of better things — if not for themselves, then surely for their children.

FIGURE 5.3

Immigrants on the deck of the *Kroonland* arrive at Ellis Island, September 1920. (United Press International)

SOCIETAL REACTIONS

Although the immigrant groups kept themselves socially segregated from one another, outsiders mostly saw them as un-American strangers and tended to lump them all together. Italians and Jews stood out from the others because of their large numbers, clustering, religion, language, appearance, and cultural practices. Although many people viewed all "new" immigrants as both undesirable and nonassimilable, American society directed the greatest antagonism against the more visible Italians and Jews.

RACISM A negative reaction to incoming minority groups had occurred many times before. This time, however, it developed a new dimension — actions based on physical features.

The arrival on American shores of these darker swarms of migrants — the so-called "new immigration" — was countered by the development of a new note in American nativism: the racist claim of ineluctable biological superiority for those with lighter skins, fairer hair, and earlier debarkation dates. Together with the older nativist themes of anti-Catholicism, fear of "foreign radicalism," and general xenophobia, this newer development in collective hatred, along with an awakening anti-Semitism, combined to produce the onslaught on the immigrant's culture, social organization, and self-regard known as the Americanization movement — a development which as we have seen before, was brought to its highest pitch by the events of World War I and the immediate post-war period.[2]

Although necessary to the country's growth, the low-status jobs that the newcomers took served to reinforce dominant attitudes about their inferiority. Many viewed the immigrants in the construction gangs, for example, as working at jobs "no self-respecting white man would take." Such attitudes set the new immigrants apart in biological terms as well as in social status levels.

Probably the most significant blending of the nativist and racist thinking of this period came from Madison Grant's influential book, The Passing of the Great Race, which appeared in 1916. Relying upon what he considered scientific truth, Grant used race as the key factor determining culture and behavior. He argued that racial hybridism can only lead to a reversion to the "lower type." As his pessimistic title suggests, Grant saw the vastly superior Old American stock as disappearing ("racial suicide") as a result of lower birth rates because they chose not to contaminate their racial purity.

FIGURE 5.4

The faces of these immigrants reflect the anxiety of being processed and examined at Ellis Island. Photograph taken in 1920. (The Bettmann Archive)

FIGURE 5.5

New York's Lower East Side at Broadway and 15th Street, 1896. Pushcart peddlers and crowded tenements were commonplace at that time. (United Press International)

[Native Americans of colonial stock] will not bring children into the world to compete in the labor market with the Slovak, the Italian, the Syrian and the Jew. The native American is too proud to mix socially with them and is gradually withdrawing from the scene, abandoning to these aliens the land which he conquered and developed. The man of the old stock is being crowded out of many country districts by these foreigners just as he is today being literally driven off the streets of New York City by the swarms of Polish Jews. These immigrants adopt the language of the native American, they wear his clothes, they steal his name and they are beginning to take his women, but they seldom adopt his religion or understand his ideals; and while he is being elbowed out of his own home, the American looks calmly abroad and urges on others the suicidal ethics which are exterminating his own race.[3]

Grant's book was highly influential with other writers and congressional leaders. Popular magazines, such as the *Saturday Evening Post,* quoted and praised Grant. Scholars offered eugenic explanations to show a correlation between racial physique and culture.

Previously vague and romantic notions of Anglo-Saxon peoplehood were combined with general ethnocentrism, rudimentary wisps of genetics, selected tidbits of evolutionary theory, and naive assumptions from an early and crude imported anthropology (later, other social sciences, at a similar stage of scientific development added their contributions) to produce the doctrine that the English, Germans, and others of the "old immigration" constituted a superior race of tall, blonde, blue-eyed "Nordics" or "Aryans." Whereas the peoples of Eastern and Southern Europe made up the darker Alpines or Mediterraneans — both inferior breeds whose presence in America threatened, either by intermixture or supplementation, the traditional American stock and culture.[4]

Ronald M. Pavalko maintains that racism was the fundamental basis for the negative response to the "new" immigrants, and that any economic argument for immigration restrictions was a smokescreen.[5] He cites economist Isaac A. Hourwich, who reported that in reality unemployment rates tended to be lowest in years of *high* immigration and highest during years of *low* immigration.[6] However, "specific economic and political events — industrial conflict, World War I, and the Russian Revolution — contributed to [a] redefinition" of these groups in nonracial terms.[7] As the emphasis shifted to national loyalty and stability, the Americanization movement marked a "crucial turning point."

The transformation of the new immigrants from a stigmatized racial entity to a threat to economic and political order represents a shift in the definition of them as *unassimilable* to one emphasizing the

FIGURE 5.6

"AN INTERESTING QUESTION"

"How long will it be before the rats own the garden and the man gets out?"
This cartoon shows Uncle Sam relaxing in his garden, while foreign rats in-
vade it. The rat faces are stereotyped depictions of Jews, Russians, Italians,
and other immigrants from southern and eastern Europe. Cartoon by E. M.
Ashe, *Life*, June 22, 1893. (The Distorted Image, Anti-Defamation League.
John and Selma Appel Collection)

point that they *must be assimilated.* We can only speculate on whether the new immigrants would have continued to be the focus of a racist ideology if this redefinition had not occurred. It does seem clear that the conscious and explicit emphasis on "Americanization" did not represent a rejection of racist assumptions about them as much as the substitution of economic and political concerns as more pressing.[8]

AMERICANIZATION Without any assistance from governmental agencies, and with little or no knowledge of the language or customs, the immigrants were expected to "fit" into the society quickly. Moreover, Americans expected them to speak only English, strip away their old culture, and avoid any ethnic institutions or organizations. These demands often led to ethnic self-hatred or a negative self-image because of the newcomers' ambivalence, or their inability or slowness to assimilate.[9]

To preserve the stability of the country, many people attempted to hasten the assimilation of the new immigrants already here. They looked upon the schools as agents of socialization, one of the key forces in effecting Anglo-conformity. The following quotation, by an educator of the early twentieth century, is representative of the prevailing dominant-group attitudes of that period.

These southern and eastern Europeans are of a very different type from the north Europeans who preceded them. Illiterate, docile, lacking in self-reliance and initiative, and not possessing the Anglo-Teutonic conceptions of law, order, and government, their coming has served to dilute tremendously our national stock, and to corrupt our civic life. The great bulk of these people have settled in the cities of the North Atlantic and North Central states and living, moral and sanitary conditions, honest and decent government, and proper education have everywhere been made more difficult by their presence. Everywhere these people tend to settle in groups or settlements, and to set up here their national manners, customs, and observances. Our task is to break up these groups or settlements, to assimilate and amalgamate these people as a part of our American race, and to implant in their children, so far as can be done, the Anglo-Saxon conception of righteousness, law and order, and popular government, and to awaken in them a reverence for our democratic institutions and for those things in our national life which we as a people hold to be of abiding worth.[10]

The children of the immigrants felt the conflicts between majority-group expectations and their minority perspective more keenly than did their parents. They were truly marginal people, caught between two worlds. The schools were promoting the shedding of cultural differences, and the children were growing up in a society contemptuous of foreigners. Because the land they knew was America and because they wanted to be accepted, the children began to be self-conscious about themselves. Many, for example, were embarrassed to bring friends to their homes, where a foreign language, foreign cooking, and a different atmosphere prevailed.

XENOPHOBIA Historians often cite the Haymarket Affair as the single most important factor in causing a xenophobic reaction against all immigrants. In Chicago, in May 1886, at the height of a general strike for an eight-hour workday, the anarchist organizers — almost all of them immigrants — held a rally in Haymarket Square. As nervous police approached the peaceful gathering, someone threw a bomb at the police. It exploded in their midst, killing one officer and wounding 70. The bomb thrower's identity was never discovered, but the courts sentenced six immigrants and one native-born American to death; another immigrant received a long prison term. Newspapers fostered a negative stereotype of the immigrant and attacked immigrants on this basis. National hysteria and fear of anarchy built up, particularly in the large cities of the Northeast and Midwest. This defensive outlook marked the initial phase of racial nativism.[11]

The current social scene presented a troubling contrast to the image of America that Anglo-Saxon intellectuals cherished. The tradition of racial nationalism had always proclaimed orderly self-government as the chief glory of the Anglo-Saxons — an inherited capacity so unique that the future of human freedom surely rested in their hands. But now the disorders of the mid-eighties cast doubt on the survival of a free society. The more anxious of the Anglo-Saxon apostles knew that the fault must lie with all the other races swarming to America. Did they not, one and all, lack the Anglo-Saxon's self-control, almost by definition? So, behind the popular image of unruly foreigners, a few caught sight of unruly races; and Anglo-Saxon nativism emerged as a corollary to anti-radical nativism — as a way of explaining why incendiary immigrants threatened the stability of the republic. *

John Higham's commentary provides insight into the combination of ethnocentric thinking and group stereotyping that influenced majority attitudes toward minorities. A few examples from that period not only illustrate his analysis but also remind us of similar comments that have

*John Higham, *Strangers in the Land: Patterns of American Nativism, 1860–1925*, Rutgers University Press, New Brunswick, N.J., 1955, pp. 137–138.

FIGURE 5.7

"THE PROPOSED EMIGRANT DUMPING SITE"

"STATUE OF LIBERTY — 'Mr. Windom, if you are going to make this island a
garbage heap, I am going back to France.' " (The Bettmann Archive)

been made in recent years about other "different" groups. One editorial writer said:

> These people are not Americans, but the very scum and offal of Europe ... long-haired, wild-eyed, bad-smelling, atheistic — reckless foreign wretches, who never did an honest hour's work in their lives ... crush such snakes ... before they have time to bite.[12]

A magazine writer warned Americans that anarchy was a "blood disease" unknown to the Anglo-Saxons but common to the "darker swarms" from Europe:

> I am no race worshipper but ... if the master race of this continent is subordinated to or overrun with the communistic and revolutionary races, it will be in grave danger of social disaster.[13]

For a long time after the Haymarket Affair, *foreign* and *radical* were linked together in American culture. Negative stereotyping and nativistic movements increased. Calls for restrictions on immigration mounted and continued until the Immigration Law of 1921 was passed.

LEGISLATIVE ACTION   In 1907, in response to public pressure, Congress established a joint Senate-House commission to investigate the entire immigration situation. Chaired by Senator William P. Dillingham of Vermont, the commission issued a voluminous report in 1911. This report was the first to use the concept of "old" versus "new" immigration. The Dillingham Commission reported that the "new" immigrants tended to congregate, slowing the assimilation process, unlike the "old" immigrants, who had dispersed. Also, "new" immigrants were less skilled and less educated, had greater criminal tendencies, and were more willing to accept lower wages and a lower standard of living. As a solution, the commission suggested that either a literacy test be required of immigrants or immigration be restricted based upon a percentage of the immigrants from a given country already here.

Although it supposedly used social science statistics, the commission made several major errors. First, by using two simplistic categories, it failed to take into consideration vast differences in ability, opportunity, and social organization among the various ethnic groups. Second, it overlooked the longer period of time the "old" immigrants had had to achieve economic stability. The previous chapter discussed the differing structural conditions and the problems of adjustment and acceptance that many earlier groups had actually faced. Released during a time of economic recession, the report further encouraged calls for restrictions on immigration.

Congress' first response, in 1913, was to pass a literacy bill requiring all immigrants over 16 to be able to read some language. President Taft vetoed the bill, however, just as President Cleveland had vetoed a similar proposal in 1896. Finally, in 1917, Congress overrode President Wilson's veto of a new literacy bill similar in content to the earlier bills that had been vetoed. This law did little to stem the tide of immigrants, however, for it exempted those fleeing religious persecution, of whom there were a great many. Also, the literacy rate in Europe had risen, and so the literacy test was not a serious obstacle for many people. Because of the continual flow of immigrants from war-ravaged Europe, the fear that such political upheavals as the Bolshevik revolution would spread to the United States, and the general mood of isolationism that swept over postwar America, pressures for immigration restrictions mounted.

Although outgoing President Wilson vetoed the congressional bill dealing with immigration, it became law after it was reintroduced in a special session of Congress and signed by President Harding. The National Origins Quota Act of 1921, adopting a proposal that the Dillingham Commission had made ten years earlier, limited the numbers of immigrants. It imposed, for three years, a quota system under which the number of new immigrants allowed was only 3 percent of the number of people of that nationality already in the United States in 1910. The effect of this legislation was to reduce the number of southern, central, and eastern European immigrants from the 780,000 annual average in 1910–1914 to about 155,000 annually.

When the act expired, it was replaced by the even tougher Johnson-Reed Act of 1924, which reduced each country's annual quota to 2 percent of its emigrants already in the United States in 1890. This legislation discriminated even more strongly against the "newer" immigrant countries.

Henry Pratt Fairchild, a sociologist, summed up the ethnocentric attitudes of his time when he said:

> The highest service of America to mankind is to point the way, to demonstrate the possibilities, to lead onward to the goal of human happiness. Any force that tends to impair our capacity for leadership is a menace to mankind and a flagrant violation to the spirit of liberalism.
>
> Unrestricted immigration was such a force. It was slowly, insidiously, irresistibly eating away at the very heart of the United States. What was being melted in the great Melting Pot, losing all form and symmetry, all beauty and character, all nobility and usefulness, was the American nationality itself.[14]

Although an exception was made to receive approximately 400,000 Displaced Persons following World War II, the 1924 legislation remained in effect until the McCarran-Walter Act of 1952 was passed. This new law, passed over President Truman's veto, still reflected

FIGURE 5.8

"LOOKING BACKWARD"

"They desire to ban the newest arrivals at the bridge over which they and theirs arrived." Five wealthy men — from left to right, an Englishman, a German Jew, and Irishman, a German, and a Scandinavian — prevent the new immigrant from coming ashore and enjoying the same privileges that they now enjoy. The shadows of the five wealthy men are representations of their social status before immigration: the Englishman's shadow is a stable man, the German Jew's is a notions peddler, and the Irishman's is a farm worker. Cartoon by Joseph Keppler, *Puck*, January 11, 1893. (The Distorted Image, Anti-Defamation League. John and Selma Appel Collection)

nativist biases. It simplified the quota formula to one-sixth of one percent of the foreign-born population from each country in the 1920 census.

The Immigration Act of 1965 ended the quota system (except that no more than 10 percent of the total number admitted could be from any one country). Instead of a national origins quota system, the new law attempted to eliminate partiality toward any one part of the world by establishing a different preferential system. Today, those who have close relatives in the United States already or occupational skills needed in the United States can come, up to a yearly maximum of 120,000 from the Western Hemisphere and 170,000 from the rest of the world.

Critics of the current immigration policy argue that the occupational preference contributes to a "brain drain" from other countries, depriving them of qualified people who could help them raise their standard of living. Importing alien professionals, some say, reduces the opportunities for upward mobility available to minority people already in the United States. This fallacious argument ignores the additional positions required by a growing population and also ignores such programs as affirmative action that are specifically designed to help minorities. Further, this policy makes it easier for immigrants to adjust to the American economy; since they enter with marketable skills, they are likely to have fewer social problems than would less skilled immigrants in this technological nation.

Another argument is that the current law excludes the poor, who once came in such numbers as to inspire Emma Lazarus to write her sonnet "The New Colossus" (1883), inscribed on the pedestal of the Statue of Liberty, the final lines being:

> Give me your tired, your poor,
> Your huddled masses yearning to breathe free,
> The wretched refuse of your teeming shore.
> Send these, the homeless, tempest-tossed to me.
> I lift my lamp beside the golden door!

THE SLAVIC PEOPLES

Often included under the general classification "Slavic peoples" are the Poles, Russians, Ukrainians, Ruthenians, Bulgarians, Rumanians, Czechs, Serbs, Croatians, Slovaks, and Slovenians. The first four groups came to the United States in much greater numbers during the 1880–1920 mass migration period. Since these were more visible minorities, more information is available about their experiences, allowing separate discussions. However, American public opinion during the 1880–1920 period usually made no distinctions among these groups, and as a result their experiences in this country were frequently similar.

Slavic people had been in the New World since colonial times. New Amsterdam and New Sweden, for example, received Protestant refugees from this region in the seventeenth century, and Moravians fled to the Quaker colony of Pennsylvania in the eighteenth century. In the mid-nineteenth century many political refugees came to America, and almost all of them remained. In the post–Civil War period, however, Slavic people began to come in steadily increasing numbers, and this influx continued until the Immigration Act of 1921 sharply curtailed it.

These "new" immigrants scattered throughout the country, although a good many tended to concentrate in the mining and industrial areas in Pennsylvania and the Midwest. Beginning as unskilled workers, they formed the large majority of the workers in the coal fields, the iron and steel factories, and the slaughterhouses of Chicago. By 1917 they outnumbered all other ethnic groups in those places of occupation. The normal pattern was for the males to come first and their families later, if at all. Like many Greeks and Italians, many Slavic males merely came as sojourners to earn money for land, dowries, or just a better life, returning to their native land after a year or two. These various nationalities were the majority of the more than 2 million aliens who returned to Europe between 1908 and 1914.

In his book *The Slavic Community on Strike*, Victor R. Greene offers many vivid pictures of the immigrant experience in the mining industry. In the following excerpt he portrays the anxiety and arrival of a newcomer to the Pennsylvania coal region:

The typical greenhorn would have alighted from the immigrant train in the Pennsylvania hard-coal region undoubtedly apprehensive if he had not yet met his correspondent. With luck, one or both had a photograph to aid in recognizing the other. Otherwise, the weary traveler at the depot asked or shouted the name of his sponsor. One can imagine the tears of joy on both sides when to the immigrant's call his countryman responded, and their relief was expressed in a demonstrative embrace. . . .

The sponsor then led his charge to a group of shacks usually at the edge of town. This ghetto was separated from the rest of the populace, just as in other places in America where the East Europeans lived. Here in the coal country inhabitants term the foreign nest the Slavic mining "patch." If he arrived at night, the bundle-laden traveler would have to grope through the darkness, as no street illumination, paved roads or signs (even if he could have read them) facilitated this last, short trip.[15]

Here we can visualize the social segregation and the resulting ethnic enclave so common to all the immigrant groups. Although their languages and customs varied, the Slavic peoples commonly experienced economic hardship. Children were often put to work to help the family survive, instead of being sent to school. This not only deprived these immigrant children of a "normal" childhood but also delayed upward mobility by at least a generation.

> The sight of so many children employed in mining along with their fathers appalled many Americans. The Slav would give a ready answer when accused of practising child labor — economic necessity. Popular American abhorrence of the evil forced through minimum age laws, but to little avail, as parents and employers violated them with rare penalty. Some child labor reformers announced that they had found boys as young as six working at the mines; nine or ten was probably the actual minimum. A leading reformer sympathized with the East European youngster as the "helpless victim of the frugality, ignorance, and industrial instincts of his parents." The value placed by Americans on educating the young little interested the Slav, for the valuable child was the working one. Above a minimum education was useless, and the pressing need for income forced sons into the pits at or before their teens. . . . All of the workers here, men and boys, labored the normal ten-hour, six-day week, when at full time.[16]

The Slavic immigrants' need to use their children is not unlike the situation facing migrant workers today. Many of the field workers who harvest the nation's fruits and vegetables must use their children to help the family. They are paid only for what they harvest, and their income is so meager that everyone in a family must work when the crops are ready. As a result, the children's education suffers badly. Few of them finish high school, if they ever attend, and many end up in the fields as adults.[17] This is yet another instance of patterns repeating themselves. The values attributed to a group may often be situational responses rather than cultural tenets.

In the case of the Slavic immigrants, a combination of factors — their peasant background, economic deprivation, child labor and little education — slowed their rise up the socioeconomic ladder. A high proportion of second- and third-generation Slavic-Americans, for example, have lower income and educational levels than the Greek- and Jewish-Americans.[18] Among the reasons for these differences was the fact that the latter groups often came from more urbanized areas and were able to establish effective community organizations in the United States more quickly. Many Slavic-Americans today are blue collar workers whose income and standard of living have been improving as a result of the bargaining power of their unions.

THE POLES

Included among other Slavic groups until 1899, when they began to be counted separately, the Poles constituted the third largest ethnic group of the "new" immigration. With their homeland under the divided control of Germany, Russia, and Austria-Hungary, 1 million Poles came here between 1899 and 1914, fleeing poverty and seeking economic opportunity. In fact, the desire for economic improvement was so common to almost all the new immigrants that the expression to be "after bread" is found in the vocabularies of most central and eastern Europeans.

A 30-year-old Polish, Nobel prize-winning writer, Henryk Sienkiewicz, visiting the United States from 1876 to 1878, illustrates this last point in his classic observation of the difficulties his people first encountered here. Note also the traces of ethnocentrism in his observation of Americans.

> Their lot is a severe and terrifying one and whoever would depict it accurately would create an epic of human misery. . . . Is there anyone whose hand is not against them? Their early history is a tale of misery, loneliness, painful despair and humiliation. . . . They are primarily peasants and workers who have come in quest of bread. Thus you will easily understand that in a country inhabited by a people who are not at all sentimental, but rather energetic, industrious, and whose competition it is difficult to survive, the fate of these newcomers, poorly educated, unfamiliar with American conditions, ignorant of the language, uncertain how to proceed, must be truly lamentable.[19]

Although Sienkiewicz recorded his observations before the large influx of Polish immigrants, which peaked in 1907, he found a great many Polish immigrants in the United States. At that time there were Polish communities at Radom, Illinois; Krakow, Missouri; Polonia, Wisconsin; and Panna Maris, Texas.[20] Buffalo, Detroit, Milwaukee, and Chicago — the chief Polish center — all had a very sizable Polish population also.

CULTURE SHOCK

The effects of culture shock — bewilderment and disorganization, particularly in family life — can be seen in many immigrants' writings and in the records of courts and social service agencies. This initial immigrant reaction has received considerable attention from sociologists. One of the early sociological classics, *The Polish Peasant in Europe and America*, by William I. Thomas and Florian Znaniecki, explored this theme, and the framework they used has dominated other studies of Polish-American life.[21]

Leaving behind a *Gemeinschaft* society, where behavior was regulated by custom and habit, the Polish immigrants found themselves isolated, surrounded by unsympathetic and even hostile people whose language and customs they did not comprehend. Thomas and Znaniecki maintained that even if active demoralization and antisocial behavior did not occur, those who made the transition suffered a "partial or general weakening of social interests, a growing narrowness or shallowness of the individual's social life." The authors showed how many immigrant families found the adjustment too difficult, and how crime, delinquency, divorce, desertion, prostitution, and economic dependency were often the by-product of family disorganization. Such tendencies could often be found in immigrant communities caught in a web of economic and social instability.

COMMUNITY ORGANIZATION

The values and forms of village life in rural Poland were reintegrated, though not completely, in the parish structure of the urban American Roman Catholic Church.[22] For example, St. Stanislaus Kostka Church in Chicago in 1899 became the world's largest parish. The church blended staunch Roman Catholicism, Polish culture, and a full range of social services to help the immigrants become Americanized.

Not all Poles wanted to become Americanized, however, and many wanted the church to reflect Polish culture. Many were also frustrated by vain attempts to have Polish priests elevated in a church hierarchy dominated by the Irish and Germans. Consequently, representatives from various "independent" parishes formed the Polish National Catholic Church; Lithuanians formed a similar movement. Both church groups used their native languages in the Mass rather than Latin. They also added other elements of their culture (patriotic songs, patron saint feast days) to their church activities.

The peasants of pre–World War I Poland had negative attitudes toward education. Summarizing the numerous scholarly references to this point, Helena Znaniecki Lopata reported:

The attitudes of the Polish peasants toward education — which defined it as a waste of time at best, and as a dangerous thing undermining the traditional way of life at worst — were transplanted to the American soil. Ideally, the children of Polonia began working at an early age to help the family in its endless struggle for money. The United States Immigration Commission, which undertook an intensive study of immigrants in 17 American cities in 1911, found the children of Poles following this typical educational career: parochial school from the ages of 8 to 12, first communion, public school for two years, and then work.[23]

At that time all the Polish immigrant wanted education to do was to provide children with a strict moral upbringing in a well-disciplined atmosphere. Lopata reports that there has been a dramatic change in educational achievement among newer generations of Polish-Americans, but the median is still low because of first- and second-generation immigrants.[24]

POLONIA TODAY

The Polish community did not fall into complete family disorganization and demoralization, as reported by Thomas and Znaniecki. Lopata reports that today these ethnic communities are stable and integrated, sources of prestige and status competition. The reason for this appears to be that the peasant culture was not a rigid set of norms subject to collapse from constant attack.

The history of Polonia over the years, locally or as a superterritorial community, indicates that its cultural fabric was much more flexible and viable, based on the social structure and gradually changing, bending, and modifying as new norms were introduced purposely or through unconscious diffusion by its members.[25]

Several studies have shown the rate of Polish upward mobility to have been below that of other ethnic groups.[26] While this was true of the first two generations, recent studies show a change. The older Polish-Americans are at the top of the blue collar world, and most of their offspring are entering the professions and the white collar world.[27]

Examining the Polish-American community in Los Angeles, Neil C. Sandberg found a lessening in cultural ethnicity among the third- and fourth-generation members.[28] Since successive generations had experienced upward mobility, he found an inverse correlation between social class and ethnicity.[29] In other words, greater individualism and less group cohesiveness accompanied social mobility. Lopata also suggests that the Polish communities could dissolve through continued assimilation, but that a Polish national cultural base could conceivably replace the organizational and institutional base of the immigrants.[30]

THE HUNGARIANS

In the nineteenth century the Hungarians, or Magyars, were a minority in control of the Kingdom of Hungary. They began a campaign of

"Magyarization" — imposing the Magyar language and culture — on all peoples living within their boundaries. As emigration to the United States increased, the Hungarian government financed both Catholic and Protestant churches and various immigrant societies in an effort to maintain its influence over Hungarians living in America. The government was not successful, as many of the immigrants sought their own identity and attempted to preserve their own languages and culture.

Like others before and after them, the Hungarians congregated in their own ethnic clusters. Most settled in New Jersey, New York, Ohio, Pennsylvania, Illinois, Indiana, and West Virginia. Cleveland and New York City attracted the greatest concentration of immigrants. With over 76,000 Hungarians living in New York City in 1920, it was the "third largest Hungarian city in the world."[31]

In each such ethnic community the Hungarians established their own institutions and organizations, embodying the same religious division among Catholics, Protestants, and Jews as in their homeland. They established their own social and fraternal organizations to provide sick benefits and to pay for funerals. They also founded their own newspapers and nationalistic cultural groups.

LABOR CONDITIONS

America was seeking industrial workers, and so the Hungarians forsook farming and worked instead in the mines, steel factories, and other heavy industries. The labor agitation of the late nineteenth century often included Hungarian as well as Lithuanian and Slavic workers. These confrontations were frequently violent and bloody.

> The most violent episode occurred outside of Hazelton, Pennsylvania in 1897. A posse, headed by a sheriff who was a former mine foreman, fired several vollies into an unarmed group of 150 strikers, mostly Hungarian, who were marching to a nearby town to urge other miners to join the strike. Twenty-one immigrants were killed and another forty wounded. There was general agreement among other mine foremen that there would have been no bloodshed if the strikers had not been foreign-born.[32]

It may have been because of the prominence of Hungarians in the labor unrest that the ethnophaulisms "hunky" (for Hungarian) and "bohunk" (for Bohemian) were applied to all Central Europeans except the Jews, for whom there were special epithets. Some believe that the former term evolved into "honky" as a black reference to a white.[33]

The number of Hungarians in America at this time is somewhat difficult to determine exactly, since the U.S. government did not distinguish Hungarians from Austrians until 1905, and even the Poles living in that country were included with the Hungarians until 1919. However, based upon immigration records and the research of Emil Lengyel, it is estimated more than 2 million Hungarians came to the United States between 1871 and 1920, many from the middle Danube region. As many as half may have returned to their homeland once they had saved enough money to buy their own farms or for some other purpose.

POLITICAL REFUGEES

More recently, an entirely different group of Hungarians has come to America for political rather than economic reasons. When the Soviet Union crushed the Hungarian rebellion in 1956, Congress passed special legislation to circumvent the restrictive national quotas of the McCarran-Walter Bill of 1952. The United States airlifted the refugees — families, minors unaccompanied by parents, and students — and gave them temporary shelter at Camp Kilmer, New Jersey. Many voluntary agencies and Hungarian-Americans assisted the 30,000 newcomers, who, after the initial shock of displacement, quickly adjusted to America and began to rebuild their lives.

THE GYPSIES

Gypsies are perhaps America's most elusive minority. Although more than 5,000 books have been written about them, many of these are fictional and few are based on close observation. Although Gypsies number somewhere between 250,000 and a million or more in the United States,[34] they have been studied less than some American Indian tribes just one-hundredth their size. Several reasons account for this: census and immigration authorities have never kept official statistics on them; Gypsies actively discourage any form of "snooping"; and they are frequently on the move.

Who are the Gypsies? Because they are nomads and without territorial confinement, their major distinguishing characteristics are language and culture. They speak Romany, a form of Sanskrit, which has enabled researchers to trace their origins to northern India.[35] There are the *roms* (Gypsies) and the *gadje* (others). Words that distinguish between the ingroup and the outgroup in this way are quite common in tribal societies. When individual Gypsies assimilate into the dominant culture, they are no longer considered to be Gypsies. Thus we must view the Gypsies as a persistent subculture, maintaining a unique cultural system.

Throughout the second half of the seventeenth century, Gypsies from Scotland came to work the Virginia plantations. Records indicate that Gypsies also settled among the French in Louisiana, the Germans in Pennsylvania, and the Dutch in New Amsterdam.[36] In the 1840s, because of repressive actions against them in England, Gypsies began migrating to the United States in substantial numbers.[37] What with the Nazis having exterminated somewhere between 300,000 and 500,000 Gypsies, and their being generally unwelcome throughout Europe, many legal and illegal Gypsy immigrants undoubtedly came to the United States during the postwar period. Our only evidence for this, however, is their increased visibility at that time.

The most important social structure is the family, and second most important, the tribe. The family is strongly patriarchal, with the men working at a variety of trades for short spans of time. Women are important sources of income, primarily from fortune telling, flim-flam activities, begging, and stealing. A central social function is setting the bride-price and arranging marriages; this has usually been completed by the time a girl is 12. Her earning potential, not her looks or wishes, determines the price, which may be as high as $10,000 in the United States. It is rare for a Gypsy family to have fewer than two women, and those with more (usually in several generations) will invariably be the wealthiest because of the women's dowries and their foraging activities. Since women are a basis for wealth, an extended family arrangement is quite common. The combination of parents, siblings, cousins, godchildren, and in-laws provides a larger female contingent. Thus, for a Gypsy male and his wife and children to remain in a patrilocal family situation rather than forming a separate household is economically advantageous.[38]

Most Gypsies cannot read or write. Their values and life style encourage nonliteracy, for they are constantly on the move and they distrust all formal organizations.

No gypsy likes to be pinned down on anything. Real birth certificates, for example, are anathema to him. If he needs a passport or otherwise requires proof of date and place of birth, he will obtain an affidavit for this purpose supplied and sworn to by other gypsies, or he will get a "delayed" certificate of birth one way or another from a cooperative doctor or midwife. The main thing is to be flexible about such matters, since he never knows what kind of potential bureaucratic booby trap lies in wait for him, and he always operates on the theory that it is best to expect the worst. . . .

In thwarting the great computer numbers game that pigeonholes the rest of us, any self-respecting gypsy carries at least three social security cards, a handful of driver's licenses and a revolving collection of credit cards in a variety of names.[39]

Because they are illiterate, they find the telephone a crucial means of communication; it is one of the first possessions they obtain when they establish a new residence.[40] Since they view the regulations and formalities of the external host society as an impediment to their way of life, the outgroup becomes fair game. Depending on chance and opportunity, they make individuals or companies targets for swindles, fraud, or theft. Illiterate Gypsies are especially adept at using bureaucratic procedures to outsmart business people and credit agencies.

> He got a phone listing for a fake roofing company. Then he applied for various charge accounts, presenting himself as an employee of the firm currently earning two hundred and fifty dollars a week. The fact that he could not write and had to have the credit forms completed for him only added to his credibility. As he told me, "They just sit there putting down what I tell them, and they're thinking, well, what do you expect, the guy's just a roofer, but he's holding down a regular job," and in the next few days he sat back taking calls from credit agencies as well as individual stores, solemnly verifying all the information that he himself had supplied.[41]

Gypsy sexual mores concerning intimacy are very strict; this is an outgrowth of their normally confined living arrangements and their social structure. Gypsy women will rarely resort to prostitution, although they might solicit in order to pick a man's pocket. Women are a valuable commodity as brides, foragers, and mothers. Birth control and abortions are rare, and as a result the birth rate is very high. Since Gypsies do not officially record these births, our only information on the birth rate comes from case studies. Peter Maas, for example, reports on one couple that has 14 children and 76 grandchildren, most under 30 years of age; these have already produced 183 children, with more likely to come.[42]

The safety valve within the social organization is the *kris*, or Gypsy court. Through an effective grapevine, Gypsies send word to the different tribes of the time and place of the *kris*. Much like Indian chieftains at a powwow, the tribal leaders confer, settle disputes, and place restraints upon more powerful members. The most potent social sanction is shunning, no longer acknowledging someone as a *rom*. The *kris* operates with ceremonial dignity; it forms the social cement that binds Gypsy society together. Once it is over, the convention becomes an occasion for general feasting, renewal of friendships, bartering, and bride-buying, since such large gatherings are not very frequent.

The Gypsies have kept their tribal codes and morals virtually unchanged in an urbanized and industrialized society by remaining outside the educational institutions and being passively antagonistic to the larger society. Although they are highly conscious of ritual, Gypsies survive through adaptation to their environment. Despite enormous pressure from every society in which Gypsies have lived, they have retained their identity and resisted assimilation.

THE UKRAINIANS AND RUTHENIANS

Ukrainians and Ruthenians speak a common language and are quite alike culturally, except for their religious beliefs. The Ukrainians, who sometimes call themselves Carpatho-Russians or Little Russians, are mostly Greek Orthodox; the Ruthenians, on the other hand, are usually Roman Catholic. For both peoples religion is a very important part of life, and it serves as the strongest cultural bond in a new land.

From the Middle Ages to the close of the First World War, both peoples were at various times part of the Russian, Polish, or Austro-Hungarian Empires. Though they tried to distinguish themselves from the Russians through their language and culture, other Americans usually thought of them as Russians. Immigration authorities did not treat them as separate groups until 1896; because of this, their actual number in this country is only an estimate. Based on census data, church records, and immigration reports, historians believe that about 700,000 Ukrainians and several hundred thousand Ruthenians had emigrated to the United States by 1914.

CONTACT AND CONFLICT

Although a few Ukrainians settled in the western United States and Canada and became farmers, most settled in the urban industrial centers of the Northeast and Midwest, working in the factories and coal mines. Wasyl Halich offers a good example of one Ukrainian group's early contacts with Americans and their fights with Irish miners who saw them as a serious economic threat.

> The experience of the first Ukrainian group in America contains some of the basic elements of that of other pioneers on this continent. When they landed in New York, they did not understand a word of English; their colorful attire attracted much attention, and they were regarded as a curiosity. Being unable to get lodgings, they had to leave the city. They walked to Philadelphia, being forced to sleep outdoors because people were afraid to give shelter to such curious strangers. . . .
>
> This group of immigrants arrived in the mining communities during a labor strike. Not understanding the conditions, or probably because of necessity, they went to work as strike-breakers; consequently they brought upon themselves the hatred of old miners,

BOX 5.2

"During our first six months stay in Maryland, our home must have been the first case of integration in the South and we were not even aware of it."

"Finally in 1949 we were given permission to come to the United States as Displaced Persons, to be taken by sponsors who were to provide for us in America, where food and clothing were plentiful and freedom was everyone's right. The D.P. families boarded a huge ship where the men stayed in one part and the women and children remained in another. There were no separate compartments, but one large barrack filled with beds. Because the passengers were not used to the ocean, most of them spent their trip in sick bay or on deck trying to survive the voyage.

"On July 7, 1949, our ship landed in Baltimore, Maryland, where we were greeted by the Red Cross. We were taken to a depot and given blankets which were to be placed on the cement floor for the purpose of sleeping. At that time food and old clothes were distributed while we waited for the arrival of our sponsors. An American man bought me a Coca Cola from a vending machine. I had never tasted anything so delicious before and to this day I can still recall the incident so vividly that I can actually taste that first Coke although all others lack that particular flavor.

". . . My sister and I were sent to a public school in the local town. This experience was devastating to me since I did not know one word of English. The teacher, who seemed like a friendly person, must have tried with much frustration to communicate with me, but I was frustrated too, and so did what most children do under those circumstances — I turned her off and did what my imagination led me to do. I colored, cut, played imaginary games and had an all-around good time till I finally started to put some of the sounds together and began to realize the meaning of a few English words.

". . . Because we lived in Maryland, race prejudice was the first unpleasant and embarrassing situation which my family had to encounter. My father was the only white man to work in the fields. During the lunch break he was allowed to come into the farmhouse to eat while the others ate their lunch outside. Soon my father learned that dark-skinned men were not allowed to eat with fair-skinned men. I heard my parents discussing this problem. Since they did not know American history and did not speak English, they had to figure that for some reason the dark people were not liked in this country. We did not even know what they were called except that the farmer sometimes called them 'niggas', which later I learned was niggers.

"One day the farmer became very angry because he learned that we were entertaining the other farm hands in our home. My mother, being a good neighbor, invited the other workers to our house for supper. We had pirogis and the men drank corn liquor. The Negro families reciprocated and we were invited to their homes. It seemed a very natural thing to do and we could not understand why the farmer became so excited. During our first six months stay in Maryland, our home must have been the first case of integration in the South and we were not even aware of it.

"Although I was only seven years old at the time, my observations of the treatment which the whites inflicted on the blacks had a lasting effect on me. While riding in the all-white school bus, I was shown the shabby school for the 'niggas.' I could not understand why two schools were needed in the first place. While shopping for food in the town, I saw only whites were served in most stores. No matter where I went, the blacks were excluded. . . . Looking back, I guess that my education in Maryland did not take place in the segregated public school but on the farm, where I learned more about human behavior than any college course could ever offer."

Ukrainian refugee who came to the United States in 1949
at age 7

---

mostly Irishmen. There were frequent assaults on the strike-breakers which ended in riots. The influx of fresh immigrants tended to keep the wages low, and this prolonged the racial and labor antagonism between the Ukrainian and Irish groups. In connection with this racial animosity not infrequently the newcomer became a victim of "accidental" injury in the mine, or even death.[43]

Like the Ukrainians and other nationality groups, the Ruthenians settled mostly in large industrial cities, taking whatever industrial jobs they could find. Their experiences paralleled those of other immigrant groups, as shown by this excerpt from Jerome Davis' *Russians and Ruthenians in America* concerning their spatial and social segregation and their first taste of America at Ellis Island.

The majority of Russians and Ruthenians are almost as completely isolated from the American people as if they were in the heart of giant Russia. They have no points of contact with the sound elements of American life. The dream of the Russian as he leaves his native shore is that everything is beautiful in America. It is the land of liberty and equality but he begins to feel that perhaps he has been hoodwinked almost as soon as he reaches Ellis Island. The Russians claim that the coarse and brutal treatment they received at the immigrant stations is far worse than that in the Russia of the Tsars. Certainly, the wholesale tagging of the immigrant, the physical inspection, the turning back of the eyelids, rushed through with machine-like regularity resembles more the inspection of cattle than of thousands of human souls.[44]

LATER IMMIGRANTS

After World War II, there were thousands of Ukrainian Displaced Persons in Europe. In 1948 Congress passed the Displaced Persons Act, allowing homeless people from war-ravaged Europe to enter, in addition to the annual quota under existing immigration laws. Under this special legislation and with the assistance of many Ukrainian-Americans, about 60,000 Ukrainian refugees came to America. The new arrivals were better educated, more politically oriented, and better able to adapt to American life than the older immigrants; they were refugees, not "economic" immigrants, and, significantly, structural conditions in their homeland had changed.

THE RUSSIANS

Of the more than 3 million Russian immigrants who came to the United States between 1881 and 1920, approximately 43 percent were Jewish.[45] Because many Jewish immigrants also came from other countries and all Jewish immigrants are often grouped together, and because the majority of Russian immigrants were not Jewish, we shall discuss the two groups separately.

Included among the peoples of Russia who came to the United States were the Ukrainians and Ruthenians previously mentioned, the Jews, the "Great Russians" from the medieval Duchy of Muscovy, the Byelorussians or White Russians from the western region, and to a lesser extent the Finns, Estonians, Latvians, and Lithuanians. In its efforts to "Russianize" its empire and to solve its problems with political dissidents and poverty, the Czarist government openly encouraged its ethnic minorities to leave.

CULTURAL DIFFERENTIATION

The great majority of Russian-Americans are members of the Russian Orthodox Church, but in other respects they differ from one another. In addition to ethnic distinctions based on regional residence in eastern Europe, the emigrants also came from all levels of society.

The first wave of Russian immigrants were Mennonites, who were actually of German origin and had maintained the German language and German customs within the Russian borders for a century. As they became targets of forced assimilation, military conscription, and persecution in the 1870s, they began to emigrate to the Great Plains of the United States. Though there were never a substantial number — only thirty to forty thousand in total by 1900 — they made a significant contribution to American agriculture by introducing Turkish wheat, a hard winter wheat that had become the leading first-class wheat product by the turn of the century.

The peak Russian migration occurred between 1881 and 1914, with poor, illiterate peasants emigrating for economic reasons and others seeking political or religious freedom. In America they had to make the transformation from a rural to an industrial environment. They settled in the industrialized regions, joining other immigrants in the grueling labor in the mines and factories of America. They were heavily exploited and often complained about the harshness of their work situation. Not at all passive, they were active in the labor movement and sought to improve their working conditions.

Following the Bolshevik revolution, a new type of Russian immigrant sought asylum in the United States. Czarist army officers, landowners, professional people, and political activists all fled from the new regime. Thereafter Soviet restrictions sharply curtailed Russian emigration, except for those Russians who succeeded in coming to the United States as Displaced Persons.

LIFE IN AMERICA

During the boom immigration period, the Russian peasants were at the bottom of the socioeconomic ladder in their newly adopted country. Two excerpts, although they refer to Russian immigrants, are excellent illustrations of the recurring pattern of the minority experience. They could just as easily be applied to other groups who live or have lived in the urban slums. In the first, a religious-newspaper editor tells of the toll exacted by the long working hours under wretched conditions in 1916:

> Each working day shortens the worker's life for a few months, saps the living juice out of him, dries out the heart, dampens the noblest aspirations of the soul; transforms a living man into a sort of machine, embitters the whole life. The ragged soul and body of the worker bring forth to the world half-sick children, paralytic, idiotic — therefore the factory's poison kills not merely the unfortunate workers, but also whole generations.[46]

Closely related to working conditions are poor living conditions because of low wages. This timeless commentary by a social worker of that period analyzes the effects of the squalor and apathy in the urban ghettoes upon the Russian immigrants:

> Parental neglect, congestion of population, dirty milk, indigestible food, uncleaned streets, with the resulting contaminated atmosphere, the prevalence of infectious diseases, multiplied temptations to break the law. . . . Add a twelve-hour day, and a seven-day week, irregular, casual employment, sub-standard wages, speeding processes which have no regard to human capacities or nervous strains for which the system is unprepared, indecent housing, unsanitary conditions both in home and factory, and we have an explanation amply adequate to account for sub-normal wage earners.[47]

XENOPHOBIA

Many Russian-Americans who had worked hard to achieve some economic security in America found themselves jobless and unable to find work after the Bolshevik Revolution in 1917. Employers, fearful of any threat to capitalism in the United States, removed all Russian workers from their labor force lest they be Bolsheviks. Most Russian peasant immigrants were probably ignorant of the ideology of Bolshevism or, in the case of second-generation Americans, more attuned to American values and attitudes, but they were identified as "Bolsheviks" because of their nationality alone. Some may have been sympathetic to the Bolshevik regime, but only because it had overthrown the hated Czarist government. The thought of spreading that revolution to the United States, where the political, labor, and social conditions were very different, appears to have been in the minds of only a very small percentage.[48]

Nevertheless, labor unrest and radical agitation during that period caused a strong xenophobic reaction against many foreigners. A. Mitchell Palmer, a new attorney general, stepped into the federal power vacuum caused by the incapacity of President Wilson. His first target was the Union of Russian Workers, and his men raided 11 of their meeting places in various cities. About a month later 249 immigrants were deported, many forced to leave their wives and children behind in most dire circumstances. The Palmer raids continued with a vast dragnet of East Europeans, primarily Russians.

> Officers burst into homes, meeting places, and pool rooms, as often as not seizing everyone in sight. The victims were loaded into trucks, or sometimes marched through the streets handcuffed and chained to one another, and massed by the hundreds at concentration points, usually police stations. . . . Many remained in federal

FIGURE 5.9

Victims of the 1917 Palmer raids, these immigrants are rounded up for possible deportation. A xenophobic reaction to the Bolshevik revolution, these actions were later ruled illegal. (United Press International)

BOX 5.3

"I thought we came into a palace and I used to correspond with my girlfriends overseas and I told them what beautiful things we have."

"The closer we came to the United States the better we felt after being so dizzy and nauseous. The trip took us ten days and we landed in Ellis Island in 1924. We saw a big, big building. It was like an armory and, yes, we went through inspection. Before we went on the boat we went through inspection and the physical, and when we came to Ellis Island it was the same thing. They inspected all the clothing of ours and the physical too. Everything was all right with us. Some people didn't pass the inspection and they had to go back, with their health and all.

"All the immigrants were holding their bundles, the baggage, by them. Also we ate by huge tables and most of the food they served was herring. There were some young immigrant boys and they played the mandolin and I was dancing and I didn't think about anything. We were laughing and dancing. I didn't understand what they were saying but we had a lot of fun. We stayed in Ellis Island three days because we came in on a Friday and on the weekend they didn't let anyone out. So we stayed there three days.

"When my father came in — they told me it's my father, of course, but I didn't know him because I hadn't seen him in ten years — I was thrilled to see him. And, of course, as a young girl, I was very happy and I was giggling a lot and that worried my father because he heard a lot of girls came here in this country and they got in trouble. He asked me, 'My dear daughter, why are you giggling so much?' I didn't have an answer for him then. I never saw my father and yet I saw him worry for me and giving me orders what to do, what not to do. It was very strange to me, but we were all very happy to see him and finally he took us on a subway. The subway was very new to me. This I didn't see in Europe.

"When we came to America I was not of age yet to go to work, so from the Board of Education they came and they told me I must go to day school, and so my brother and I did. When I went into the school all the children spoke English and the teacher — whatever she said to me — I didn't understand. When it came to arithmetic I was tops but as far as language, she couldn't teach me much because she was busy with all the children.

"But I saw my father was struggling very much and he didn't make too good of a living here, so I went on my own and I took out working papers and I found a job. I was working in a silk mill and I went to night school.

"All the immigrants who came here were there and the teacher was teaching us, 'Open the door,' 'Close the door,' and so everyone had these advantages to learn how to speak.

"Now I see it wasn't such a big palace my father took us in. It was four rooms but everything looked so nice. It was a piece of carpet on the floor with a victrola with the letters, chairs, and a little sofa, and I thought we came into a palace and I used to correspond with my girlfriends overseas and I told them what beautiful things we have. But now when I look back it wasn't really so beautiful.

"It was a nice experience but I wouldn't like to go through with it again. I like this country. I'm very happy that we came to this country. After I got married, we had two children and we brought them up in a free country and that make me very happy by this day that we are here."

Russian immigrant who came to the United States in 1923
at age 15

custody for a few hours only; some lay in crowded cells for several weeks without a preliminary hearing. For several days in Detroit eight hundred men were held incommunicado in a windowless corridor, sleeping on the bare stone floor, subsisting on food which their families brought in, and limited to the use of a single drinking fountain and single toilet. Altogether, about three thousand aliens were held for deportation, almost all of them eastern Europeans.*

Opposition to these brazen and illegal actions arose, and many of the immigrants were freed. Yet more than five hundred of them actually were deported. Expulsion was still an effective weapon of the government in America. Eventually the growing strength of the CIO (Congress of Industrial Organizations) within the labor movement would bring these people a measure of economic security and domestic tranquility.

THE JEWS

The Jewish people are a unique minority, since no general agreement exists as to whether they are a racial, ethnic, religious, or nationality grouping.[49] In the biological sense, the Jews are not a race. Despite popular stereotypes about certain physical characteristics, the fact re-

*John Higham, Strangers in the Land: Patterns of American Nativism, 1860–1925, Rutgers University Press, New Brunswick, N.J., 1955, pp. 230–231. See also Frederick R. Barkley, "Jailing Radicals in Detroit," Nation, 110 (1920), 136.

mains that Jews vary greatly in physical appearance. Because Jewish people live in so many different countries and are culturally distinct from one another because of their country of origin, to consider all Jews as an ethnic grouping becomes rather difficult.

Nor can all Jews be classified as a religious group, since atheists and agnostics have long existed among them. Although religion has been an important bond among the Jews, it is no longer the cohesive force it once was.

Thinking of the Jews as a nation is also unsatisfactory. They once were a nation, and now there is the state of Israel. But many Israelis are Arabs, Christians, and Moslems, and millions of Jews throughout the world call another country their homeland. Perhaps Brewton Berry and Henry L. Tischler offer the best criterion for this minority group when they suggest that the grouping is a cognitive one resting solely upon the concept of "Jewishness."

> Perhaps it is *the consciousness of being a Jew* that is crucial. How-ever unsatisfactory this concept may be as a definition, it ap-proaches the reality of the situation to say that Jews are people who think of themselves as Jews and are treated by others as being Jewish, regardless of their physical features, language, or nationality.[50]

IMMIGRATION PRIOR TO 1880

The first group of Jewish immigrants — four men, six women, and thirteen younger people — arrived in New Amsterdam in 1654 as refugees from the Portuguese takeover of Dutch-ruled Brazil. Later, many Jewish refugees from the Spanish Inquisition came to the American Colonies. Nathan Glazer esti-mates that there were between two and three thousand Jews living in America by the end of the eighteenth century.[51] Jewish participation in the Revo-lutionary War was proportionately high. Several Jewish military officers dis-tinguished themselves, particularly Colonel Isaac Franks, on Washington's staff, and Major Benjamin Nonez, who fought with Lafayette, and they sel-dom had difficulty relating to the mainly Protestant troops.

The experience of the Jews during the colonial and early Federal periods illustrates the difference between prejudice and discrimination. Although anti-Jewish biases, part of the European influence, did exist in America, to be Jewish then was usually not a handicap. An act of the British Parliament in 1740 had allowed Jews to obtain British citizen-ship, and they did participate in politics to some degree. The United States Constitution, in providing for separation of church and state, had thereby guaranteed rights for all religions. A few unsuccessful attempts were made to restrict Jewish rights in early America, but the institutions of the new society did not reinforce those prejudices. Some states, how-ever, such as Maryland and New Hampshire, initially denied Jews the right to vote or hold elected office. Business restrictions on Jews, arising either directly, from discrimination and prejudice, or indirectly, from enforcement of the Christian Sabbath and other holiday laws, began in the colonial era and still continue — although with lesser effect — in the present time.

Some of the older families were gradually assimilated into American society through intermarriage. Most of the Jews who came during colonial times were Sephardic, of Spanish and Portuguese origin, victims of the Inquisition, who came by way of Holland, the West Indies, or South America. By the mid-nineteenth century the second influx, from several German provinces, settled in some of the towns and cities of an expanding America. The Jewish population grew from two or three thousand in 1790 to 15,000 in 1840, and 250,000 by 1880. In fact, by the mid-nineteenth century, scarcely a town of any substantial size was without a modest Jewish congregation.

NEWCOMERS AND TENSION

The third wave was the most significant — in numbers, cultural influence, work contributions, and dominant-group reaction. From 250,000 in 1880, the Jewish population rose to almost 3 million before generally restrictive immigration laws were enacted in the 1920s. The initial impetus for this massive migration was the pogroms that followed the assassination of Czar Alexander II (1881). Though no Jews were involved in the regicide, the Czarist government used them as a scapegoat to divert people's attention from long-festering social, political, and economic grievances. This marked the beginning of a long series of pogroms, with many attacks, loss of lives, and extensive property damage in Jewish communities throughout the Russian Empire's Pale of Settlement. In addition to the need to escape government-incited violence, there were powerful economic incentives for emigration. Some people came to escape from destitution. Others fled from economic instability that resulted from government efforts to industrialize Russia.

Considerable cultural tensions developed among Jews from the different areas of Europe. Some Sephardic Jews, the first to be transplanted to America, considered themselves superior to German Jewish newcomers (Ashkenazic), who later looked with disdain on newcomers from eastern Europe. Although a few Jewish immigrants from central and eastern Europe had arrived as early as the eighteenth century, for some Jewish ethnics the distinctions based on place of origin and time of arrival in America persisted well into the mid-1940s, as this report indicates:

The earlier arrivals scarred the later ones as crude, superstitious, and economically indigent, and the latter despised the former as snobs and religious renegades. As recently as 1925, one student of immigrant groups asserted that "intermarriage between a Sephardic Jew and a Russian Jew, for instance, is as rare, if not rarer, than intermarriage between Jew and Gentile." Even within each of these divisions of Jews there was at first aversion to marriage with some of the subdivisions. Bavarian Jews hesitated to marry with those German Jews who came from the area near the Polish border, derisively labelled "Pollacks." The Russian Jew looked down on the Polish and Galician Jews and refused to marry them or permit his children to do so. Although these intra-Jewish barriers to marriage have largely disappeared in recent times, first generation Jewish parents may still go through the motions of embarrassment when their children marry the sons and daughters of a ridiculed sub-group.[52]

Thus ethnic prejudices as well as cultural and class differences led to strain between the "old" Jewish population and the "new" Jewish arrivals. Some German Jews, who had by this time supplanted the Sephardic Jews as an ethnic elite, were embarrassed by their lowly coreligionists with their strange appearance, Yiddish language, and orthodox religious practices. At first, many rejected the new arrivals, partly out of fear that growing anti-Semitic feeling in American society would place all Jews — old and new — into one negative category. Soon, however, the established community developed organizations that helped the newcomers adjust to their surroundings. Additionally, they made strenuous efforts to settle the newcomers in widely dispersed farm communities, away from the congested urban centers.[53]

ANTI-SEMITISM

Anti-Jewish stereotyping spread in the arts and the media as it had for other immigrant groups, such as the Irish and Asians. On stage the Jew was sometimes depicted as either a scoundrel or a comic character. Newspapers and magazines at times ran cartoons and editorials that were clearly anti-Semitic in nature. One example was *Life* magazine, published in New York City, where the Jewish population rose from 4 percent in 1880 to 25 percent in 1910. The magazine called the city "Jew York" and attacked the ostensible Jewish clannishness, pushiness, and domination of the theater. In the early twentieth century about half of the actors, songwriters, publishers, and entrepreneurs in New York City were Jewish; this included those who worked in the flourishing Yiddish language theater serving the immigrant community. *Life*'s editors launched a ten-year attack on the "Jewish Theatrical Trust," accusing it of poisoning American values, of lowering the moral tone by

FIGURE 5.10

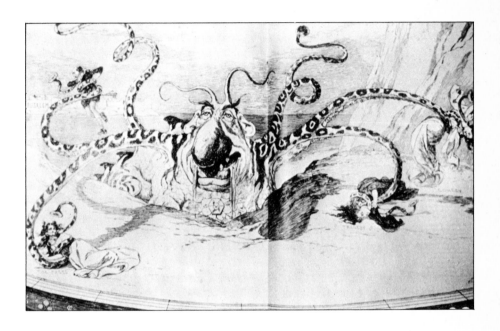

"OUR OLD FRIEND THE OCTOPUS IN HIS GREAT CHARACTER, THE
THEATRICAL TRUST"

The press, tragedy, and comedy are caught in the tentacles of the Trust Octopus. The alleged international Jewish conspiracy is symbolized by
Jerusalem, looming in the distance. Cartoon appeared in *Life*, December
9, 1897. (The Distorted Image, Anti-Defamation League. John and Selma
Appel Collection)

running lascivious plays for profit. The accusations were false or distorted. The Yiddish theater may have catered to a specific ethnic group and thus have been "different," but the plays were not lewd or lascivious.

Two notorious incidents emphasize the heights anti-Semitic feelings reached in the late nineteenth and early twentieth centuries. In the first instance, Joseph Seligman, an eminent banker and frequent guest of President Grant at the White House, was denied accommodations in 1877 at a fashionable resort hotel in Saratoga Springs, New York. Although he and his family had stayed there several times before, the hotel's new policy of "not accepting Israelites" made headlines across the country. This incident brought latent anti-Jewish attitudes into the open, and many other establishments quickly followed suit.

The second incident concerned Leo Frank, the manager of an Atlanta pencil factory, who was hastily convicted, on very flimsy evidence, of murdering a young factory girl. Many felt that he was convicted because he was a Jew. His case in 1913 led directly to the formation of the B'nai B'rith's Anti-Defamation League. With prominent Georgia newspapers and clergymen calling for a new trial and many Jews financing his appeal, anti-Semitic feelings intensified in the state. When the governor commuted Frank's execution to life imprisonment, an act praised by the Georgia press, some of the dead girl's friends and neighbors abducted Frank from the state prison, transported him 175 miles to the girl's home town, and lynched him.

It was more than a local episode. The nationwide press coverage of the incident included comments about racial nationalism and antagonism toward the "Parasite Race." Anti-Semitism of varying intensity has continued to the present day. It ebbed in the 1920s and flourished again during the Depression. The Silver Shirts, led by William Pelley, and the Christian Front, headed by Father Charles Coughlin, were two of the most active movements against the Jews in the late 1930s. Anti-Semitic behavior has declined since World War II, in part because of revulsion against Nazi genocide and in part because pluralism has become more generally accepted. Incidents still occur at rare intervals, mostly acts of vandalism or desecration. Some analysts suggest that the roots of anti-Semitism can be found in the teachings of Christianity (now renounced in the Catholic Church by Vatican II), which had blamed the Jews for the death of Christ.[54] Latent anti-Semitism may manifest itself for many reasons, such as status or economic rivalries.

UPWARD MOBILITY

Like other "new" immigrants, many of the East European Jews who came here were very poor. Most thus settled in great numbers in the

large cities that were ports of entry (Boston, New York, and Philadelphia). A great many went to work in the garment industry, while others
became street peddlers until they saved enough capital to open their
own stores. Since two-thirds of the Jewish male immigrants were skilled
workers, compared with an average of 20 percent of the males from
other immigrant groups, their absorption into the American economy

FIGURE 5.11

Boys from immigrant families attend class in New York's condemned Essex Market School in the early 1890s. (Photograph by Jacob A. Riis, Jacob A. Riis Collection, Museum of the City of New York)

was eased somewhat.[55] Many social scientists cite this immigrant group as one that climbed the socioeconomic ladder more quickly and more widely than most other groups,[56] although prejudices have limited their ascent to middle-management positions.

Several cultural factors have contributed to the success of some first- and many second-generation Jewish-Americans. First, because of discrimination in Europe, they had been relegated to such self-sustaining occupations as merchant, scholar, and self-employed artisan. Thus they brought with them skills and knowledge useful in an industrial society, together with values that encouraged deferred gratification, seriousness of purpose, patience, and perseverance — precisely those virtues stressed by the Protestant Ethic of middle-class America. Second, during the period of great immigration, 1880 to 1920, most Jews came here along with members of their families; in many other ethnic groups males usually came first and then either returned to the old country or else sent for their families.[57] Jews had traditionally placed a heavy emphasis on family responsibility, and having the entire family unit together from the outset gave them greater emotional stability and an advantage in cooperative efforts to start a new life. Sometimes the immigrant experience produced emotional and psychological strain within families, however. Third, and perhaps most important, was the Jewish people's traditional emphasis on learning — especially for boys. Even if the children were illiterate in the language of their country of origin, and this was less often true than with many other immigrant groups, they had learned Hebrew and, as a result, the discipline of study. By the time he was thirteen, a Jewish boy, if raised in a religious family, was prepared to read from the Torah for his bar mitzvah. Today, a large number of Jewish girls also participate in this ceremony (called bat mitzvah, for girls). Within the Jewish culture this positive orientation toward learning carried over to American public education and secular studies. While parents toiled in low-status factory jobs, they were encouraging their children to further their education and then enter the professions. The high percentage of Jewish youth attending public and private colleges in the first few decades of the twentieth century is all the more remarkable because of their limited residency in the United States and because most Americans placed less emphasis upon a college education in those times.[58]

Gordon reports that by the 1940s the occupational distribution of Jews was comparable to that of members of high-status Protestant denominations.[59] Yet Jews have been virtually unrepresented in some industries, such as steel, oil, banking, and insurance. Not all experienced upward mobility. Thousands of Jewish poor, especially the aged, exist on a level far from the stereotyped portrait of the successful Jews.

SOCIAL INTERACTION

Social ostracism often accompanied the economic successes of the Jewish people. Higher economic status did not necessarily mean a comparable increase in social prestige. Even when Jews gained positions with higher levels of income, they still found themselves excluded from social and recreational clubs and were forced to establish parallel social and recreational organizations for themselves. They also encountered restrictions in housing; admissions quotas for colleges, universities, and professional schools; and other obstacles designed to keep them at a social, economic, and educational distance from white Protestants.

Although many Jewish middle-class families moved to the suburbs after World War II, in keeping with a trend in the larger society, many social scientists reported continuing social segregation in the 1950s and 1960s. Social distance is sometimes measured by the degree of primary relationships between Jews and Gentiles. In his Detroit study, Gerhard Lenski found that the frequency of close associations between the two groups declined after adolescence, particularly at the time of choosing a mate.[60] In his study of Elmira, John P. Dean found that approximately 75 percent of his Jewish sample socialized occasionally with their closest non-Jewish friends, but few were regular participants in a mixed social clique.[61] Herbert J. Gans reported that the Jewish suburban housewives of Park Forest, outside of Chicago, participate in the daytime social activities of the entire neighborhood, but that in the evening and on weekends their social relationships are confined to other Jews.[62] Albert Gordon suggested that this pattern of relative isolation in suburban evening or weekend social gatherings is fairly common and not necessarily a voluntary choice.[63] Milton Gordon, echoing the concept of the triple melting pot,[64] suggested that Catholics, Protestants, and Jews each tend to interact in meaningful primary relationships with members of their own religio-ethnic group.[65]

The situation appears to be changing. Many social scientists believe that the degree of intermarriage is an excellent indicator of assimilation and primary group relationships, and some significant increases have occurred in this area. In 1974 the National Jewish Population Study reported a 500 percent increase in the Jewish intermarriage rate from the 1955–1960 period to the 1966–1972 interval. The actual increase in exogamy was from 5.9 percent to 31.7 percent.[66]

JEWISH IDENTITY

The synagogue, whether the congregation was Reform, Conservative, or Orthodox, played a significant role in the Jewish community struc-

BOX 5.5

*"People still believed the streets were paved with gold.
All what you needed was a shovel."*

"I heard a lot about the streets in America being paved with gold but I knew one thing, because I came in contact with GI's and I saw they came from different backgrounds in different parts of the country, and I knew one thing — that I was going to have to work in the United States. People didn't actually still say the streets were paved with gold, but this was still the belief in Europe because, you know, the dollar was the Almighty. In Europe you could buy five-six times with the dollar what you could buy in the United States. So this was why people still believed the streets were paved with gold. All what you needed was a shovel. But I knew. I was prepared. I never was disappointed in coming here to the United States.

"What is to me the American Dream? To some people maybe it's a bigger car or a bigger house. This is their dream. Take more vacations. Sure, we need vacations, but I think our way of life should be to practice just what we preach, just what we have in our Constitution. I mean, not to discriminate against people of all kinds, because this country — if it really is a melting pot — for this one reason, because it is so great this country, because from so many countries, the idea can be put together."

Polish Jewish immigrant who came to the United States in
1948 at age 35

ture. At the same time it had to compete with a variety of cultural, ideological, and self-help organizations that were supported by many Jews. Classes offered by organizations such as the Educational Alliance, on New York's Lower East Side, provided opportunities for Americanization. Together, the synagogues and organizations served as cohesive bonds and laid the foundation for community organization, social activities, and a feeling of belongingness.[67] More recently, the formation of the state of Israel and its continuing conflicts with its Arab neighbors have served as a focal point cementing Jewish identity among diverse Jewish Americans. Jews are by no means united on the Middle Eastern question, however. The American Council for Judaism, for example, is quite vociferous in its opposition to Zionism and the state of Israel. Another positive influence upon Jewish identity has been the ethnic renascence in America.[68]

THE ITALIANS

Though few in number, the first Italians to come to the New World were significant among the early explorers. Cristoforo Colombo (Columbus), Giovanni Cabotto (John Cabot), Amerigo Vespucci, and Giovanni da Verrazano all explored and charted the new land. Father Marcos da Nizza explored Arizona in 1539, and other Italians were among the settlers throughout the Colonies. Filippo Mazzei was an influence upon the writings and the farming of his neighbor Thomas Jefferson. Many Italians fought in the Revolution, the Civil War, and the other wars that followed. Antonio Meucci invented the first primitive version of the telephone 26 years before Alexander Graham Bell, and Constantino Brumidi painted the frescoes in the rotunda of the United States Capitol building.

Throughout the nineteenth century the parallels and relationship between Italians and blacks were somewhat unusual. In some pre–Civil War Southern localities futile efforts were made to replace black slaves with Italian workers. In other areas Southerners barred Italian children from the white schools because of their dark complexions. General Edward Ferraro commanded an all-black combat division during the Civil War. In 1899 five Sicilian storekeepers were hanged in Tallulah, Louisiana, for the unforgivable crime of treating black customers the same as whites.

THE GREAT MIGRATION

The major story of the Italian immigrants began after great numbers of them arrived between 1880 and 1920. Of the more than 5 million Italians who have come to the United States throughout its history, 80 percent came during this 40-year period. Many Italian males engaged in "shuttle migration," going back and forth between America and Italy. Fleeing abject poverty and economic disaster in the harsh "Mezzogiorno" east and south of Rome, they quickly became so visible to American society that they were subject to vicious anti-Italian bigotry.

The Italian immigrants were peasants from rural areas who were ill prepared for the occupations of an industrial nation. They therefore labored in low-status, low-paying manual jobs. They worked as railroad laborers, as miners, on the waterfront, and in construction. They dug ditches, laid sewer pipes, and built roads, subways, and other basic structures in urban areas.

SOCIETAL HOSTILITY

Strong negative attitudes against the Italians sometimes resulted in violence and even killings. Several Italians were lynched in West

FIGURE 5.12

Italian mother with her three children after arrival at Ellis Island. One of the greatest pictures taken by Lewis Hine. (The Bettmann Archive)

Virginia in 1891. In the same year, when 10 Sicilians were tried and acquitted of killing the New Orleans police chief, an angry mob that included many of the city's leading citizens stormed the prison and executed them, adding an eleventh victim who had been serving a minor sentence for a petty crime. Four years later coal miners and other residents of a southern Colorado town murdered six Italians. The following year three Italians were torn from a jail in Hahnsville, Louisiana, and hanged. After a street brawl in 1914, in a southern Illinois mining town, that left one Italian and two native-born Americans dead, a lynch mob hanged the only survivor, an Italian, with the apparent approval of the town's mayor. A few months later another Italian was lynched in a nearby town because he had been arrested on suspicion of conspiracy to murder a mining supervisor. Actually there was no evidence to substantiate the charge other than his nationality.

In Massachusetts, Nicola Sacco and Bartolomeo Vanzetti — an immigrant shoe factory worker and a poor fish peddler — were charged with and convicted of robbery and murder in 1920. The prosecutor insulted Italian defense witnesses and appealed to the prejudices of a bigoted judge and jury. Despite someone else's later confession and other potentially exonerating evidence, their seven-year appeals fight was futile, and they were executed in 1927. The point here is not their guilt or innocence, but that racism should never have figured in the case. At his sentencing in 1927, Vanzetti gave his famous address to presiding Judge Webster Thayer. At one point in his moving speech, he said:

> I would not wish to a dog or a snake, to the most low and misfortunate creature of the earth — I would not wish to any of them what I have had to suffer for the things that I am not guilty of. . . . I have suffered because I was an Italian, and indeed I am an Italian.[69]

These incidents are extreme examples of society's reaction to the Italian immigrants. Because they came in sizable numbers, the public became increasingly aware of their presence, and they quickly became the stereotype of all that was objectionable in the "swarm" of immigrants coming here. When an Italian got into trouble, newspaper headlines often magnified the event and stressed the offender's nationality.[70] Italians, like Jews, found certain occupations, fraternities, clubs, and organizations closed to them; and they were excluded from certain areas of the city and suburbs by restrictive covenants.

SOCIAL PATTERNS

The Italians mainly settled in the eastern cities in "Little Italies," the North End of Boston and Mulberry Street on the Lower East Side of New York City being two of the better known areas. In the west, San Francisco's North Beach area became and remains an Italian enclave. Often groups from the same village would live together in the same tenement. Earning poor wages because they were part of the unskilled labor force, they moved into rundown residential areas vacated by earlier immigrants whose children and grandchildren had moved up the social ladder and were out of the slum. Because of their numbers, they were able to create an Italian community replete with Italian stores, newspapers, theaters, social clubs, parishes, and schools. However, because of their village, family, and communal orientations, they failed to establish group-wide institutions.[71]

A variant of the extended-family system of southern Italian society was adapted to Italian life in America. Relatives were the principal focus of social life, and non-Italians were usually regarded as outsiders. True interethnic friendships rarely developed. Moreover, individual achievement (an American tradition) was not heavily encouraged. What mattered most were family honor, group stability, and social cohesion and cooperation. Each member of the family was expected to contribute to the economic well-being of the family unit.

In the old country, absentee landowners had usually exploited Italian tenant farmers, and priests and educators had silently supported this less than equitable system. Peasant children were rarely welcome in the schools. Landowner resistance to the political unification of Italy, which finally came about in 1870, further increased the hardships of tenant farmers and small landholders. Consequently, Italian immigrants generally distrusted priests and educated people.[72] In America, as in Italy, there was little involvement with the church, especially among males, and schooling was regarded as of only limited practical use. Children were permitted to attend school, for the most part, only as long as the law demanded; then they were sent to work to increase the family income. A few children were exceptions, but most second-generation Italian-Americans attending college did so in conflict with their families.

> The studies of the immigrant would suggest that the move to America resulted in little change in the pattern of adult life. The social structure which the immigrants brought with them from Italy served them in the new country as well. Those who moved to the cities, for example, settled in Italian neighborhoods, where relatives often lived side by side, and in the midst of people from the same Italian town. Under these conditions, the family circle was maintained much as it had existed in Southern Italy.
>
> The outside world continued to be a source of deprivation and exploitation. . . . Situated on the lowest rung of the occupational hierarchy, they were exploited by their employers and by the "padrone," the agent who acted as a middleman between the

immigrants and the labor market. Moreover, the churches in the immigrant neighborhoods were staffed largely by Irish priests, who practiced a strange and harsh form of Catholicism, and had little sympathy for the Madonna and the local saints that the Italians respected. The caretaking agencies and the political machines were run by Yankees and other ethnic groups. As a result of the surrounding strangeness, the immigrants tried to retain the self-sufficiency of the family circle as much as they could. They founded a number of community organizations that supported this circle, and kept away from the outside world whenever possible.[73]

MARGINALITY

First-generation Italian-Americans, reinforced by so many of their compatriots, retained much of their language and customs. The second generation became more Americanized, producing a strain between the two generations. Those Italians who did not settle or remain long in the "Little Italies" assimilated much more quickly. Some changed their names and religion to accelerate the process.

In his study *Street Corner Society*, William Foote Whyte commented upon the problems of marginality experienced by Italian-American boys:

Some ask, "Why can't those people stop being Italians and become Americans like the rest of us?" The answer is that they are blocked in two ways: by their own organized society and by the outside world. Cornerville people want to be good American citizens. I have never heard such moving expressions of love for this country as I have heard in Cornerville. Nevertheless, an organized way of life cannot be changed overnight. As the study of the corner gang shows, people became dependent upon certain routines of action. If they broke away abruptly from these routines, they would feel themselves disloyal and would be left helpless, without support. And, if a man wants to forget that he is an Italian, the society around him does not let him forget it. He is marked as an inferior person — like all other Italians. To bolster his own self-respect he must tell himself and tell others that the Italians are a great people, that their culture is second to none, and that their great men are unsurpassed.[74]

SOCIAL MOBILITY

Upward mobility occurred more slowly for the Italians than for other groups coming at about the same time, such as the Greeks, Armenians, and Jews. Many factors, already discussed, contributed to this situation — a retreatist life style, disregard for education, negative

"We heard a different language.... We didn't know what they were saying, maybe they were talking about us."

"We came here on a large ship in 1910. We had a rough time coming here with storms and all, and my big sister was deadly sick. She never lifted her head up from her berth. It was a very long trip, about thirteen days, and the waters were rough. And when we got to Ellis Island, we were so happy to get out of that ship.

"When we got there my daddy was waiting for us and we got some nice gifts from the attendants in Ellis Island. Who got a doll, who got a jumping jack. But the funniest part was when they were selling bananas in the room, and my brother thought they were peppers and he wanted a pepper and discovered they were bananas.

"When my father took us down to the street, we heard a different language. We looked at each other. We went to my mother. We didn't know what they were saying, maybe they were talking about us. My father said, 'Don't worry. That's the language they speak here and you'll learn it yourself very fast.'

"Then my dad took us on a train to Old Forge, Pennsylvania, where he had rented rooms for us and we lived there six months. They were mostly all Polish people and German, and my mother didn't feel at home with no Italians around. My mother wanted to move to Paterson, New Jersey, because there were more Italian people there, but here she didn't understand anybody. And that's what we did. There were all Italians on the street where we lived. My dad was a musician but the other Italian immigrants worked on the trolley tracks, digging trolley tracks or to make streets.

"I got in right away with all the kids. They were all very friendly with me. As soon as recess used to come, they used to be in a playground. They would all come around me and they would talk to me in English, which helped me pick it up right away."

Italian immigrant who came to the United States in 1910
at age 8

stereotyping, and overt hostility protracted by the continuing flow of new Italian immigrants. Sheltered within their ethnic communities in many large U.S. cities, the Italians adapted to an industrial society. They joined the working class and encouraged their children to do likewise as soon as they were able.

Second-generation adults, although drawn to *la via nuova* — the new way — through the schools, movies, and other cultural influences, still adhered to an extended-family-centered social structure. Most of them were employed in unskilled or semiskilled occupations. In 1976, Andrew Greeley reported that Italian Catholics ranked third behind Jews and Irish Catholics in terms of family income, but his data, as we shall discuss in Chapter 11, are somewhat misleading.[75]

Third-generation Italian-Americans are experiencing greater upward mobility than their parents or grandparents. They are going to college and entering the professions and white collar fields. However, even though married sons and daughters move to the suburbs, the close-knit family ties remain. Frequently, the move includes two generations, not just the young.[76]

Nathan Glazer and Daniel P. Moynihan suggest that suburban Catholicism is stronger than that of the old neighborhood because the separate ethnic identities are merged into a common identity, that of American Catholics. No longer is there as much Italian antagonism to an Irish-run church. Instead, the suburban Catholic church serves more as an expression of middle-class status and acceptability than as an expression of a particular ethnic identity.[77]

THE GREEKS

Most of the Greeks who came to this country in the early twentieth century did not expect to stay long. They came as sojourners, planning to make money and then return to Greece. For many, the dowry system was an important "push" factor. Fathers and brothers found they could earn more money in the United States than in their homeland, and so these Greek men journeyed here to earn the money to provide substantial dowries for the prospective brides in their families. The fact that 95 percent of all Greek immigrants were male encouraged them to return home to their women.

OCCUPATIONAL DISTRIBUTION

Many Greeks worked as laborers on railroad construction gangs or in factories. Those who did were often under the control of a padrone who, like the Italian *padroni*, acted as a labor agent and paternal figure. Abuses were common in such a system. Other Greek immigrants operated their own small businesses of many types, although Greeks came to be identified particularly with candy stores and restaurants.

The association of Greeks with candy and food was proverbial. Chicago became the center of their sweets trade, and in 1904 a

Greek newspaperman observed that "Practically every busy corner in Chicago is occupied by a Greek candy store." After World War II the Greeks still maintained 350 to 450 confectionary shops and eight to ten candy manufacturers in the Windy City. Most Americans still connect the Greeks with restaurants and for good reason. Almost every major American city boasts of its fine Greek eating establishments, a tradition that goes back more than half a century. After World War I, for example, estimates were that the Greeks owned 564 restaurants in San Francisco alone.[78]

For many Greeks the restaurant provided a more stable economic base and a higher social status. Restaurant owners enjoyed more esteem than peddlers or manual laborers. Because so many immigrants sought a career in the restaurant business (and still do), they were continuously interacting with the general public. A 1901 government survey showed Greeks faring better than Poles; at present, most Greeks, except for the newest arrivals, are economically secure, and many are in the upper middle class.[79]

SOCIAL PATTERNS

Although they came from a mostly agricultural country, the Greeks settled primarily in the cities. Like so many other ethnic groups, they resided in ethnic enclaves or "Greek colonies" within the major cities. A *kinotis*, or community council, served as the governing body; it was responsible for establishing and staffing schools and churches, and for the general welfare of the community. The *kaffeneion*, or coffeehouse, played a very important role, as Theodore Saloutos reports:

It was to the coffeehouse that the immigrant hurried after his arrival from Greece or from a neighboring community. It was in the coffeehouse that he sought out acquaintances, addresses, leads to jobs, and solace during the lonely hours. . . .

The coffeehouse was a community social center to which the men returned after working hours and on Saturdays and Sundays. Here they sipped cups of thick, black Turkish coffee, lazily drew on narghiles, played cards, or engaged in animated political discussion. Here congregated gesticulating Greeks of all kinds: railroad workers, factory hands, shopkeepers, professional men, the unemployed, labor agitators, amateur philosophers, community gossips, cardsharks, and amused spectators.[80]

Because of the favorable working conditions, many Greek males chose to remain in America. Since they preferred endogamous marriage, these men either returned home to marry a Greek woman or else sent money home to pay for the passage of a wife or wife-to-be. Like other immigrant peoples of this period, family ties among the Greeks in America

FIGURE 5.13

Greek coffeehouses were an important social gathering place for the male sojourners. The above scene is on Washington Street, New York, in 1919. (United Press International)

were very close. The father was the unchallenged head of the household. Children were raised to be strictly obedient and had specific
chores assigned to them. They studied Greek in addition to their regular
studies in American public schools, and were frequently admonished to
work hard and take advantage of the opportunities their parents had not
had. The Greeks placed a high value on education and encouraged their
children to enter the professions.

The Greek church — the Eastern Orthodox Church — and the Greek
press bolstered Greek-American solidarity. Additionally, many organizations encouraged cohesiveness. The most notable of these was the
American Hellenic Educational Progressive Association (AHEPA),
founded in 1922. Its purpose was both to preserve the Greek heritage
and to help the immigrant understand the American way of life.

Greek-Americans have blended certain aspects of pluralism (fierce
love of homeland, pride in their heritage, slowness to become citizens,
endogamy, institutional agencies) with some aspects of assimilation (geographic and occupational dispersion, low visibility, relatively high
socioeconomic status). Cultural pluralism has been an important element in their adaptation to American society.

SOCIETAL REACTION

Not all Greek immigrants adjusted to American society smoothly.
Many young males, away from family discipline and village controls,
got into trouble with the law. Sociologist Henry Pratt Fairchild held a
prejudiced and stereotyped view of the Greeks and other foreigners in
America. He was concerned about the large overrepresentation of Greek
immigrants among law violators and was pessimistic about the possibility of their assimilating or even being a benefit to American society. His
comments about the effects of concentration in Greek colonies contain
elements of the culture-of-poverty thesis developed in the 1960s with
respect to Puerto Ricans, Mexicans, and blacks. Fairchild states that the
negative values within the community are not likely to be overcome unless there is effective interaction with members of the better (that is,
middle) class. He also favored deconcentration and dispersal of Greeks.

> It seems likely that the presence of this race (Greeks) in the country
> will add to, rather than diminish, the growing indifference to law as
> such, which is one of the most threatening signs of the times. This
> lack of reverence for law, and every form of authority, seems to be
> characteristic of every race. But the Greeks appear to have it when
> they come. What the character of their children will be in this re-
> spect we can only conjecture. . . . It has been frequently remarked in
> the course of the preceding discussion, that the evil tendencies of
> Greek life in this country manifest themselves most fully when the

immigrants are collected into compact, isolated, distinctively Greek colonies, and that when the Greek is separated from the group and thrown into relations with Americans of the better class, he develops and displays many admirable qualities.[81]

Today few negative comments about Greek-Americans are heard. When Greeks are singled out as an ethnic group at all, the reference is usually positive or neutral. They often serve as a model of a nationality group that has been accepted, has achieved economic security, and has become Americanized, yet has also retained a strong pride in their ethnicity.

THE PORTUGUESE

Though it is a relatively small country, Portugal has provided the United States with immigrants of varying economic and cultural backgrounds. Whether their manner of adaptation was assimilationist or nonassimilationist has depended upon the part of the United States to which they migrated.

EARLY IMMIGRANTS

The fondness of many Portuguese for the sea was reflected in their early contributions to the United States. In the sixteenth century Portuguese mariners explored the California coast. In the eighteenth and nineteenth centuries, immigrants, primarily from the Azores Islands, settled in New England and became an important part of the fishing industry. Mostly of Flemish stock, these Portuguese had been whalers and fishermen for many generations. Recruited by business agents to bring their expertise to America, they came and settled in such coastal port cities as New Bedford and Newport. Though the Portuguese were predominantly Catholic, the Jews among them erected one of the first synagogues in the United States in Newport in 1763. Other Portuguese, some from the mainland and of Moorish lineage, worked on farms and in dairies. They started as farm laborers, then rented and eventually bought the old New England farms that became available. As the Portuguese continued to come and American industry grew, the newcomers turned to factory work; the majority of New England's Portuguese were working in factories shortly after the turn of the century.

A few Portuguese went to California, lured by the gold rush. Others followed in typical chain migration fashion. Thousands of other Portuguese went to the Hawaiian Islands in the late nineteenth century. By

1920 about 84,000 Portuguese lived in New England; the rest lived in California and Hawaii. Since transportation for laborers and their families was guaranteed and since they had labor contracts from the plantation owners, they were willing to make the long journey. Those in Hawaii assimilated, while those in California, encountering little conflict, retained their ethnic identity and sense of community to a much greater degree. The reason for this difference appears to be that the Portuguese quickly became a sizable working force on the pineapple and sugar plantations — about 12 percent of the population. The dominant group, from northern Europe, identified themselves separately through a special census classification and stereotyped the Portuguese as inferior. The Portuguese reacted by continuing to work hard, moving into crafts and skilled trades that paid better, and intermarrying and surrendering the usual accouterments of ethnic visibility — language, customs, residential clustering, and sometimes even their names — to achieve a respected status.

> There is a wide cultural differentiation between the Portuguese in the Island setting and those in California today. Four decades of separation have shown the influence that environment can have in remolding a people. Although there have been changes in the cultural patterns of the Portuguese in California, it is in Hawaii, where the Portuguese people have gone through the processes of competition, conflict, and accommodation, and assimilation and have broken down social distance, that the distinction from old-world family patterns [is most evident.][82]

As the experiences of other groups have already shown, the adaptation of strangers in a new land moves along a continuum that may or may not end in total assimilation. The Portuguese in Hawaii and California exemplify two successful patterns under differing structural conditions.

LATER IMMIGRANTS

As with other immigrant groups, the greatest number of Portuguese were encouraged to migrate here by the Industrial Revolution. Beginning in the late nineteenth century and peaking in 1921, after which immigration quotas restricted their numbers, 200,000 came, many to work in the mills of Massachusetts and Rhode Island. Their adaptation, as rural peasants in an urban setting, parallels that of other ethnic groups. They clung to the old ways and restricted their social relations to their own kind.

In an analysis of two Portuguese communities in New England in the late 1920s, Donald Taft noted a high infant mortality rate and low level of educational achievement. This lack of interest in education may have been due to their occupational preference for farming and fishing as well as to their high rate of illiteracy.[83] In the following passage note the ethnocentric outlook, patronizing tone, and stereotyping.

There seems no doubt that for the majority of Portuguese, immigration to New England has meant an improved status. Granting that they are poverty-stricken here, that they live far below our standards of comfort and decency, that women often work outside the home and that children leave school as soon as the law allows, that homes are unattractive and wages low; nevertheless their lot is far better than in the homeland, except perhaps in its picturesqueness. America gives the Portuguese a small wage but a higher one, a poor house but a better one, a meager sixth grade education but more than they know enough to want, and it is universal and compulsory.

... The presence of these people undoubtedly handicaps the public health organizations, increases the births where they should be fewest, and the death rates of all ages but especially of little children. It also makes possible economic and political exploitation whether by unscrupulous natives or by their own leaders. Indeed the presence of the Portuguese goes far to account for the poor record of our two communities [Fall River and Portsmouth] in official statistics and for the not altogether enviable reputation which they may have among sociologists.[85]

Though they are scattered throughout the nation, Portuguese-Americans are concentrated in Massachusetts, Rhode Island, California, Hawaii, and Newark, New Jersey, where *Luso-American*, the only Portuguese national weekly newspaper, is still published. A steady flow of new immigrants from Portugal has replenished the Portuguese communities. In the 1960s the numbers of arrivals increased sharply because of political unrest and worsening economic conditions in Portugal. As the situation there has become more stable in recent years, the numbers departing for America have declined.

THE ARMENIANS

Armenia, now absorbed within the Soviet Union, is a land with a long history. A mountainous region, situated by the Caspian, Black, and Mediterranean seas, Mount Ararat is famed as the resting place of Noah's Ark after the great deluge.

There is evidence that Armenian immigrants settled in Jamestown in 1619. In that year Armenian workers, together with some Germans and Poles, struck to secure the political rights being denied them as "inferiors." The Virginia House of Burgesses granted them their freedom in response to this early civil rights protest in America.[85]

CONFUSION OVER REFUGEE IDENTITY

A number of factors appear to have initiated Turkish persecution of the Armenians, who had come under the rule of the Ottoman Empire after 1375. As Christians in a Moslem country, the Armenians became a special target for the authoritarian, religiously intolerant rulers. Moreover, they were often better educated and more prosperous than the Turks, who therefore suspected them of wanting political power. Over the years Armenians migrated for religious, political, and economic reasons, but the Turkish government's genocidal campaign against them between 1894 and 1916 was the primary reason for their movement to America. In 1915–1916 alone, the Turks killed 1 million Armenians.[86]

Because they traveled with Turkish passports and the U.S. government identified immigrants by country of origin, Armenian and Syrian Christians were classified as Turks. It is therefore difficult to determine exactly how many Armenians came here in the late nineteenth century. However, government estimates placed the number of Armenian immigrants between 1895 and 1899 at 70,982. The Turkish government then cut off further emigration until 1915. Because of the war, only a few thousand came until the 1920s, when 26,000 Armenians arrived in America.[87] After that, although Armenians continued to emigrate, their actual numbers were further obscured because the U.S. government identified them by their points of departure: usually Egypt, France, Lebanon, Iraq, Iran, Turkey, or Syria. Despite their high degree of ethnic consciousness, church records, and special censuses, the number of Armenians remained only an estimate. That estimate presently ranges from 350,000 to 500,000 Armenian-Americans currently residing in the United States.

SOCIETAL REACTION

As indicated in the social distance scales of Emory Bogardus, American public opinion and stereotypes of the Turks were quite negative, partly as a result of the atrocities committed against the Armenians.[88] Still, when Armenians attempted to become United States citizens, the federal government tried to stop them. The issue was resolved in 1925 in the U.S. District Court with the case of Tatos O. Cartozian, an Armenian rug merchant in Portland, Oregon. The government argued that Armenians were of Asiatic descent and thus not eligible for citizenship under the 1790 Naturalization Act, which allowed only whites to become citizens. By this time Asians were the only group ineligible for citizenship; persons of African descent were given the right to citizenship by the Fourteenth Amendment and changes in the naturalization laws. After hearing expert testimony to the effect that they were Indo-European in language and origin, the court ruled in favor of the Armenians.

CULTURAL DIFFERENCES

Armenians have had a long, continuous history because of their resiliency in maintaining their cultural identity. Two contributing factors have been language and religion. Not only do Armenians have their own language, they also have their own alphabet, increasing ingroup solidarity. A second source of ethnic cohesion among the Armenian people, both in their homeland and in America, has been the Armenian Apostolic Church. As the first national Christian church in the world, dating from the third century, it never sought converts among other nationalities and functioned as much more than a religious institution. As Gary Kulhanjian reports:

> The Armenian Church was and still is a fortress for preserving the cultural identity of Armenians in the world. Religion, social organizations, ethnocentrism, family life, and endogamy had all been potent social forces by which Armenians or Americans of Armenian descent have been culturally identifiable.[89]

Armenian art, architecture, literature, philosophy, and music are heavily interwoven within the fabric of the Church.

Another important factor in Armenian cohesiveness has been family life. But, as Kulhanjian observes, the assimilation process appears to be weakening some traditional influences.

> The patriarchal family life of Armenians has played a major part in the cultural identification of these people throughout the world. Family life has traditionally advocated endogamy of the young generation. The young people have rebelled against many traditional ways of doing things, including endogamy. Americans of Armenian descent have drifted away from marrying within their minority, although some do; however, a great many still retain their subcultural identity with the Church, although they have married Americans from various backgrounds. This young group of second- and third-generation Armenian-Americans has not been as ethnocentrically

minded as their parents or grandparents, who are foreign-born Americans. Cultural differentiation has been predominant among the older foreign-born Armenian-Americans.[90]

ARMENIANS TODAY

The 1970 census identified 100,495 Armenians, as determined by nativity or parentage, living in the United States. However, the Armenians claim an ethnic community here and in Canada numbering between 350,000 and 500,000. They are scattered throughout the country, with larger concentrations in New England, New York, New Jersey, Michigan, and California. Whether they be Armenian celebrities such as writer William Saroyan; Ara Parsegian, former head coach at Notre Dame; Garo Yepremian of the Miami Dolphins; photographer Yousuf Karsh; TV stars Mike Connors (*Mannix*) and Arlene Francis; or the Armenian candy firm of Peter Paul (*Mounds, Almond Joy*); or the many rug merchants, factory hands, storeowners, and business people, the Armenians have become an integral part of the American scene while retaining their sense of ethnic identity.

RETROSPECT

Without question, the period from 1880 to 1920 was the greatest immigration epoch in American history, as 23 million persons left everything behind for the promise of "Golden America." Social and economic forces at work on both continents combined to encourage this mass migration. Europe's inability to offer a decent standard of living and America's need for great quantities of industrial labor were the major push-pull factors. Recruited or attracted to America because of its rapid industrialization, European immigrants fulfilled an important need in the growth and development of the United States.

Yet the "new" immigrants were hardly welcomed with open arms. Ethnocentric preconceptions of how an "American" should look and behave prejudiced large segments of the society against them. Their physical and cultural differences identified them as strangers and heightened nativist fears of an undesirable element populating America. By 1900 one-third of the total population were first- or second-generation Americans, a fact that spurred demands to close the "floodgates" to stem the "immigrant tide." Finally, in 1921 the first restrictive legislation against Europeans was enacted. Not until the late 1960s would the discriminatory quota system based on national origins be terminated entirely.

Many of the theoretical considerations in majority-minority relations apply to the European immigrants. Their cultural and structural differences set the stage for stereotyping, all three levels of prejudice, and discrimination. Progressive stages of culture shock, community organization, development of subcultural areas, and marginality were often the norm. Dominant patterns of nativism, antagonism, social and spatial segregation, and legislative controls were common, as were the minority responses of avoidance, deviance, defiance, and acceptance.

The immigrants settled in ethnic clusters and established their own institutions, and they generally followed the broad patterns of earlier groups of immigrants. The various new peoples differed from one another in language, customs, and value orientations, although Americans frequently found those who were not Italians or Jews indistinguishable, and lumped them all together. Not all of them wanted to stay, and not all of those who did stay assimilated. The immigrants in their ethnic clusters exhibited the same sort of cultural pluralism as, in more isolated settings, the "old" immigrants had shown. But the times were different. Urbanization had brought about a greater degree of functional interdependence, a reliance on one another for exchange of goods and services. Thus, the newcomers were not as isolated as the earlier immigrants had often been. Their numbers were great, and the dominant society wanted them to assimilate, although it also feared they could not do so.

For many, the transition from an agrarian to an industrial society was difficult. Those who had either come from an urban background or had to adapt to being a subordinate minority group in Europe, such as the Greeks, Jews, and Armenians, were able to adjust to city life more easily. They took advantage of educational opportunities, climbed the socioeconomic ladder when they or their children could, and adjusted to American society. Others, being mostly illiterate peasants, took longer to get established. Not all the immigrants became citizens, nor were they all successful. Some did not learn English. Today, the poorer areas of the cities, which originally housed newcomers, contain a number of poor and aged immigrants, for whom the American Dream, in economic terms at least, has proved elusive.[91]

American industry employed the immigrants because it needed them. The work was hard, the hours long, and the pay low, but most believed that the opportunities were better in America than in their homelands. Exploitation of workers led to labor unrest and the growth of the union movement. Some immigrants were attracted to radical movements, others returned home, but most toiled, indoors or outdoors, to succeed in their adopted land for themselves and their children.

QUESTIONS FOR DISCUSSION

1. How had structural conditions in America changed for the "new" immigrants?

2. What factors aroused dominant antagonism against the newcomers? In what ways was this hostility expressed?

3. Were there any similarities in the ways in which the various ethnic groups adapted to American society?

4. Apply the concepts of stereotyping and the vicious circle to the immigrant experience during this period.

5. How does the power differential relate to these immigrants' experiences and the labor union movement?

6. How and why were the Jewish and Italian experiences similar? dissimilar?

SUGGESTED READINGS

Barzini, Luigi. The Italians. Atheneum, New York, 1964.

Birmingham, Stephen. Our Crowd. Harper & Row, New York, 1968.

Davis, Jerome. The Russian Immigrant. Arno Press and The New York Times, New York, 1969.

———. The Russians and Ruthenians in America. Doran, New York, 1922.

Gambino, Richard. Blood of My Blood. Doubleday, New York, 1974.

Gans, Herbert. The Urban Villagers. Free Press, New York, 1962.

Glazer, Nathan, and Daniel P. Moynihan. Beyond the Melting Pot, 2nd ed. M.I.T. Press, Cambridge, Mass., 1970.

Goldstein, Sidney, and Calvin Goldscheider. Jewish Americans: Three Generations in a Jewish Community. Prentice-Hall, Englewood Cliffs, N.J., 1968.

Halich, Wasyl. Ukrainians in the United States. University of Chicago Press, Chicago, 1937.

Higham, John. Strangers in the Land. Atheneum, New York, 1973.

Howe, Irving. World of Our Fathers. Harcourt Brace Jovanovich, New York, 1976.

Iorizzo, Luciano J., and Salvatore Mondello. The Italian Americans. Twayne, New York, 1971.

Krug, Mark. The Melting of the Ethnics: Education of the Immigrants, 1880–1914. Phi Delta Kappa, Bloomington, Ind., 1976.

Kulhanjian, Gary A. The Historical and Sociological Aspects of Armenian Immigration to the United States, 1890 to 1930. R. and E. Research Associates, San Francisco, 1970.

La Gumina, Salvatore J. "Wop!" A Documentary History of Anti-Italian Discrimination in the United States. Straight Arrow Books, San Francisco, 1973.

Lengyel, Emil. Americans from Hungary. Lippincott, New York, 1948.

Levenson, Sam. Everything but Money. Simon and Schuster, New York, 1966.

Lopata, Helena Z. Polish Americans: Status Competition in an Ethnic Community. Prentice-Hall, Englewood Cliffs, N.J., 1976.

Maas, Peter. King of the Gypsies. Viking, New York, 1975.

Rolle, Andrew F. *The American Italians: Their History and Culture.* Wadsworth, Belmont, Calif., 1972.

Soloutos, Theodore. *The Greeks in the United States.* Harvard University Press, Cambridge, Mass., 1964.

Selzer, Michael (ed.). *"Kike!" — Anti-Semitism in America.* World Publishing, New York, 1972.

Sklare, Marshall. *The Jews: Social Patterns of an American Group,* Free Press, Glencoe, Ill., 1958.

Thomas, William I., and Florian Znaniecki. *The Polish Peasant in Europe and America,* 2nd ed. Dover, New York, 1958.

NOTES

1. "From Farm to Factory: Immigrant Adjustment to American Industry," *Spectrum,* 1 (May 1975), 1.
2. Milton M. Gordon, *Assimilation in American Life,* Oxford University Press, New York, 1964, p. 136.
3. Madison Grant, *The Passing of the Great Race,* 1916; reprint edition, Arno Press, Inc., New York, 1920, p. 91.
4. Gordon, *Assimilation in American Life,* p. 97.
5. Ronald M. Pavalko, "Racism and the New Immigration: Toward a Reinterpretation of the Experiences of White Ethnics in American Society," paper presented at the 72nd annual meeting of the American Sociological Association, 1977.
6. Isaac A. Hourwich, *Immigrants and Labor,* B. W. Huebach, Inc., New York, 1922; quoted in Pavalko, "Racism and the New Immigration," p. 8.
7. Pavalko, p. 2.
8. *Ibid.,* p. 24.
9. See the discussion on pp. 47–48; see also Gordon, *Assimilation in American Life,* pp. 137–138.
10. Ellwood P. Cubberly, *Changing Conceptions of Education,* Houghton Mifflin, Boston, 1909, pp. 15–16.
11. John Higham, *Strangers in the Land: Patterns of American Nativism, 1860–1925,* Rutgers University Press, New Brunswick, N.J., 1955, pp. 137–138.
12. *Public Opinion,* I (1886), 82–86.
13. *The Age of Steel,* quoted in *Public Opinion,* I (1886), 355.
14. Henry Pratt Fairchild, *The Melting Pot Mistake,* Little, Brown, Boston, 1926, quoted in *American Observer,* 50 (November 29, 1971), 5.
15. Victor R. Greene, *The Slavic Community on Strike,* University of Notre Dame Press, South Bend, Ind., 1968, pp. 40–41.
16. *Ibid.,* pp. 49–50.
17. See the discussion on pp. 427–428; see also Robert Coles, *Uprooted Children,* University of Pittsburgh Press, Pittsburgh, 1970; Robert Coles, *Migrants, Sharecroppers, Mountaineers,* Little, Brown, Boston, 1971.
18. See Charles B. Nam, "Nationality Groups and Social Stratification in America," *Social Forces,* 37 (1959), 328–333.
19. Henryk Sienkiewicz, *Portrait of America, Letters of Henryk Sienkiewicz,* ed. & trans. Charles Morley, Columbia University Press, New York, 1959, pp. 272–273.
20. *Ibid.,* p. 279.
21. William I. Thomas and Florian Znaniecki, *The Polish Peasant in Europe and America,* 5 vols., B. G. Badger, Boston, 1918–1920.
22. "Immigrants and Religion: The Persistence of Ethnic Diversity," *Spectrum* 1 (September 1975), 2.
23. Helena Znaniecki Lopata, *Polish Americans: Status Competition in an Ethnic Community,* Prentice-Hall, Englewood Cliffs, N.J., 1976, p. 92.
24. *Ibid.*
25. *Ibid.,* p. 145.
26. Beverly Duncan and Otis Dudley Duncan, "Minorities and the Process

of Stratification," *American Sociological Review*, 33 (June 1968), 356–364; Stanley Lieberson, *Ethnic Patterns in American Cities*, Free Press, New York, 1963, p. 189.

27. Lopata, *Polish Americans*, p. 95.

28. Neil C. Sandberg, *Ethnic Identity and Assimilation: The Polish-American Community*, Praeger, New York, 1974.

29. See the discussion on pp. 87–88.

30. Lopata, *Polish Americans*, p. 148.

31. Emil Lengyel, *Americans from Hungary*, Lippincott, New York, 1948, p. 128.

32. *New York Tribune*, September 11–12, 1897, pp. 1, 3.

33. See Peter I. Rose, *They and We*, 2nd ed., Random House, New York, 1974, p. 135.

34. Peter Maas, *King of the Gypsies*, Viking, New York, 1975, p. 29.

35. Werner Cohn, "Some Comparisons Between Gypsy (North American Rom) and American English Kinship Terms," *American Anthropologist*, 71 (June 1969), 477–478.

36. Glen W. Davidson, " 'Gypsies': People with a Hidden History," in *The Rediscovery of Ethnicity*, ed. Sallie TeSelle, Harper and Row, New York, 1973, p. 84.

37. Allan Pinkerton, *The Gypsies and the Detectives*, G. W. Carleton & Company, New York, 1879, pp. 68–69.

38. Gulbun Coker, "Romany Rye in Philadelphia: A Sequel," *Southwestern Journal of Anthropology*, 22 (Spring 1966), 90–92.

39. Maas, *King of the Gypsies*, pp. 29–31.

40. *Ibid.*, p. 35.

41. *Ibid.*, pp. 33–34.

42. *Ibid.*, p. 29.

43. Wasyl Halich, *Ukrainians in the United States*, University of Chicago Press, Chicago, 1937; reprint edition by Arno Press and *The New York Times*, 1970, pp. 28–29.

44. Jerome Davis, *The Russians and Ruthenians in America*, Doran, New York, 1922; reprint edition by Arno Press and *The New York Times*,

1970, p. 104.

45. Based on data from Mark Wischnitzer, *Visas to Freedom*, prepared by Hebrew Immigration Assistance Society, World Publishing Company, Cleveland, 1956; U.S. Immigration and Naturalization Service, *Annual Report: 1976*, Washington, D.C., Table 13, p. 63.

46. Jerome Davis, *The Russian Immigrant*, Macmillan, New York, 1922; reprint edition by Arno Press and *The New York Times*, 1970, p. 98.

47. Edward T. Devine, "Family and Social Work," in Jerome Davis, *The Russians and Ruthenians in America*, p. 32.

48. Davis, *The Russian Immigrant*, pp. 173–174.

49. See Milton L. Barron, "Ethnic Anomie," in *Minorities in a Changing World*, ed. Milton L. Barron, Knopf, New York, 1967.

50. Brewton Berry and Henry L. Tischler, *Race and Ethnic Relations*, 4th ed., Houghton Mifflin, Boston, 1978, p. 30.

51. Nathan Glazer, *American Judaism*, 2nd ed., University of Chicago Press, Chicago, 1972, p. 14.

52. Milton L. Barron, "The Incidence of Jewish Intermarriage in Europe and America," *American Sociological Review*, 1 (February 1946), 11.

53. See Joseph Brandes, *Immigrants to Freedom*, University of Pennsylvania Press, Philadelphia, 1971; Fred Rosenbaum, *Free to Choose: The Making of a Jewish Community in the American West*, Berkeley, The Judah L. Magnes Memorial Museum, 1976.

54. See Jules Isaac, *The Teaching of Contempt: Christian Roots of Anti-Semitism*, Harcourt, Brace & World, New York, 1964; Malcolm Hay, *Europe and the Jews*, Beacon Press, Boston, 1960.

55. Leonard Dinnerstein and David M. Reimers, *Ethnic Americans*, Harper & Row, New York, 1975, p. 44.

56. See Bernard C. Rosen, "Evaluation of Occupations: A Reflection of Jewish and Italian Mobility Differ-

ences," *American Sociological Review*, 22 (1957), 546–553; Herbert J. Gans, "American Jewry: Present and Future," *Commentary*, May–June 1956, pp. 422, 430, 555, 563.

57. "Distribution of Immigrants," *Senate Documents*, 20 (61st Congress, 3rd Session), 47 ff.

58. Dinnerstein and Reimers, *Ethnic Americans*, p. 53: "By 1915 Jews comprised 85 percent of the student body at New York's free but renowned City College, one-fifth of those attending New York University and one-sixth of the students at Columbia."

59. Gordon, *Assimilation in American Life*, p. 185.

60. Gerhard Lenski, *The Religious Factor*, Doubleday, New York, 1961, pp. 33–34.

61. John P. Dean, "Patterns of Socialization and Association Between Jews and Non-Jews," *Jewish Social Studies*, 17 (July 1955), 252–254.

62. Herbert J. Gans, "The Origin and Growth of a Jewish Community in the Suburbs: A Study of the Jews of Park Forest," in *The Jews: Social Patterns of an American Group*, ed. Marshall Sklare, Free Press, Glencoe, Ill., 1958, p. 227.

63. Albert I. Gordon, *Jews in Suburbia*, Beacon Press, Boston, 1956.

64. See the discussion on p. 99.

65. Milton M. Gordon, *Assimilation in American Life*, pp. 173–224.

66. Fred Massarik, "Intermarriage: Facts for Planning," *National Jewish Population Study*, Council of Jewish Federations and Welfare Funds, New York, 1974.

67. See Hutchins Hapgood, *The Spirit of the Ghetto*, The Belknap Press of Harvard University Press, Cambridge, Mass., 1967.

68. See Yisrael Ellman, "The Ethnic Awakening in the United States and Its Influence on Jews," *Ethnicity*, 4 (June 1977), 133–155.

69. *The Letters of Sacco and Vanzetti*, ed. Marion D. Frankfurter and Gardner Jackson, Viking, New York, 1928, p. 377.

70. Higham reports, for example, that under the heading "Italians" in the 1902 *New York Tribune Index*, 55 of the 74 entries were clear accounts of crime and violence (*Strangers in the Land*, p. 363).

71. For an excellent insight into the Italian community of Chicago's West Side, see Gerald D. Suttles, *The Social Order of the Slum*, University of Chicago Press, Chicago, 1968.

72. See Rudolph Vecoli, *The Peoples of New Jersey*, Van Nostrand, Princeton, N.J., 1965, pp. 221–236.

73. Herbert J. Gans, *The Urban Villagers*, Free Press, New York, 1962, pp. 204–205.

74. William Foote Whyte, *Street Corner Society*, University of Chicago Press, Chicago, 1943, p. 274.

75. Andrew M. Greeley, *Ethnicity, Denomination, and Inequality*, Sage Research Papers in the Social Sciences, Vol. 4, Series no. 90-029 (Studies in Religion and Ethnicity), Sage Publications, Beverly Hills, 1976.

76. Nathan Glazer and Daniel P. Moynihan, *Beyond the Melting Pot*, 2nd ed., M.I.T. Press, Cambridge, Mass., 1970, p. 187.

77. *Ibid.*, pp. 203–204.

78. Dinnerstein and Reimers, *Ethnic Americans*, p. 43.

79. In 1972 a Boston city survey, the Omnibus Survey, revealed that its sizable Greek immigrant population had a zero unemployment rate, no one on welfare, and a median income $4,000 above the Boston average.

80. Theodore Saloutos, *The Greeks in the United States*, Harvard University Press, Cambridge, Mass., 1964, pp. 78–79.

81. Henry Pratt Fairchild, *Greek Immigration*, Yale University Press, New Haven, Conn., 1911, pp. 239, 241–242.

82. Gerald A. Estep, "Portuguese Assimilation in Hawaii and California," *Sociology and Social Research*, 26

(September 1941), 64.

83. Donald R. Taft, *Two Portuguese Communities in New England*, reprint edition, Arno Press, New York, 1969, p. 79.

84. *Ibid.*, p. 348.

85. See Louis Adamic, *A Nation of Nations*, Harper, New York, 1945, pp. 287–288.

86. Marjorie Housepian, *The Unremembered Genocide*, "A Commentary Report," American Jewish Committee, New York, 1965, p. 31.

87. Frank A. Stone, *Armenian Studies for Secondary Students*, Parousia Press, Storrs, Conn., 1975, p. 8.

88. Emory S. Bogardus, "Comparing Racial Distance in Ethiopia, South Africa, and the United States," *Sociology and Social Research*, 52 (1968), 149–156.

89. Gary A. Kulhanjian, *The Historical and Sociological Aspects of Armenian Immigration to the United States, 1890 to 1930*, R. and E. Research Associates, San Francisco, 1975, p. 25.

90. *Ibid.*, p. 29.

91. See Table 11.3 on p. 459 for U.S. Census data on the foreign-born poor.

SIX

THE NATIVE AMERICANS

⚔ Different in race, material culture, beliefs, and behavior, the Europeans and the Indians at first were strangers to each other. The Europeans who first traded with and then conquered the natives showed little interest in or understanding of them. Brutalized and exploited, the American Indians experienced all the dominant group response patterns — legislative action, segregation, expulsion, xenophobia, and, for some tribes and groups, annihilation. In turn, they reacted with varying patterns of avoidance, defiance, and acceptance, steadfastly remaining a numerous and persistent subculture leading a marginal existence.

HISTORICAL AND SOCIOLOGICAL PERSPECTIVES

From the first European contact with the original population in the New World to the present day, the Native Americans have usually not been understood. Columbus called them Indians, since he thought he had reached the islands off the coast of Asia known as the Indies. Today some object to this word, preferring to use *Native American* or a tribal name such as Cherokee, Shoshone, or Blackfeet.

Early European explorers and settlers, reflecting ethnocentric views, condemned those aspects of Indian culture that they did not understand and related to other aspects only in terms of their own culture. Some considered the Indians to be savages, even though Indian societies had a high degree of social organization. Others idealized them as uncorrupted children of nature who spent most of their time engaging in pleasurable activities. In Europe, intellectual debate raged over how the presence of people so isolated from other human beings could be explained. Were they descended from the inhabitants of Atlantis, Carthage, ancient Greece, East Asia; were they the Lost Tribes of Israel?[1] Were they no better than beasts, or were they intelligent, capable beings?

In colonial and frontier America, the stereotype of the Indians was often negative, especially when they were an obstacle to those Europeans who wanted to use the Indians' land. As a result of *self-justification*, the denigration of others to justify maltreating them, some whites viewed Indians as cruel, treacherous, lying, dirty heathens. Although that very negative stereotype no longer prevails, even today Indians are portrayed in films, television, and comic strips as colorfully dressed but unemotional, humorless, and uncommunicative individuals. Supposedly, all they desired during the frontier period was scalps, firearms, and "firewater." Indians are often stereotyped as backward, lacking ambition, or continually drunk, or they are regarded as romantic anachronisms.

Some people overgeneralize about Indians, thinking of the many tribes as one people even though the various tribes have always been quite different from one another in language, social structure, values, and practices. Of the approximately three hundred different Indian languages spoken in 1492 in what is now the United States, only about fifty to a hundred still exist. At present there are 267 Indian reservations under federal jurisdiction, as well as scattered pieces of land at 38 other locations maintained in federal trusteeship for Indians, Aleuts, and Eskimos. The Bureau of Indian Affairs recognizes 493 different tribal entities in the United States.[2] Figure 6.1 shows the principal Indian tribes living in the United States today.

Native Americans share several distinguishing physical characteristics. Most Native Americans have thick, black, straight hair but very little facial or body hair. They tend to be dark-eyed with rather prominent cheekbones. Beyond these similarities they generally vary greatly in physical stature and features. The term *redskin* is not at all accurate; their skin coloring ranges from yellowish to coppery brown.

The Indians' experiences in the American Colonies were unique in one respect: the whites, not the Indians, were the newcomers, and the whites were the minority for many years. The relationship between Indians and whites was often characterized either by wariness and an uneasy truce or by violent hostilities. Even in colonial Massachusetts, where peaceful coexistence initially prevailed, the situation deteriorated.

As the two peoples interacted more fully, each group became more disenchanted with the other. The Indians could not understand the English settlers' use of beatings, hangings, and imprisonment as means of social control. The settlers could not understand the Indians' resistance to Christianity and to the whites' more "civilized" way of life. These were but peripheral considerations, however: the major issue was whose way of life would prevail and whether the land would be further developed or allowed to remain in its natural state, replete with fish and wildlife.

The disenchantment grew as the settlers encroached more and more upon Indian lands. Eventually, hostilities broke out. Large-scale fighting, resulting in many killings, broke out in Virginia in 1622 and in Connecticut in 1637. Metacom, the leader of the Wampanoag, who was known as King Philip, united the Nipmuc and Narraganset behind him in 1675 and attacked 52 of the 90 New England settlements, completely destroying 12 of them. The Colonies seemed in danger of total defeat, but in 1676, Philip was killed and the Indian bands were wiped out one by one. Fighting between Indians and whites continued sporadically and locally throughout the westward movement until the 1880s. Dominant-group attitudes toward the Indians, consisting of a mixture of racial and cultural prejudices, led to intergroup tensions and marked the beginning of a pattern that would be repeated with the blacks, Asians, and Hispanics, although each group's experiences were different.

FIGURE 6.1

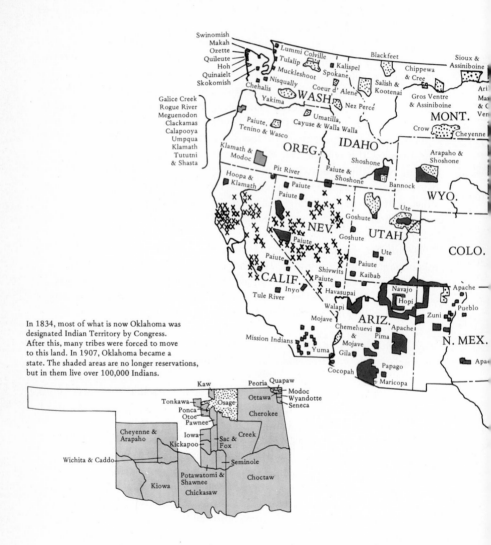

In 1834, most of what is now Oklahoma was designated Indian Territory by Congress. After this, many tribes were forced to move to this land. In 1907, Oklahoma became a state. The shaded areas are no longer reservations, but in them live over 100,000 Indians.

PRINCIPAL INDIAN TRIBES IN CONTINENTAL UNITED STATES, SHOWING WHERE THEY LIVE TODAY

Source: Based on data from "Indian Land Areas, General" (map), U.S. Department of the Interior, Bureau of Indian Affairs, U.S. Government Printing Office, 1971.

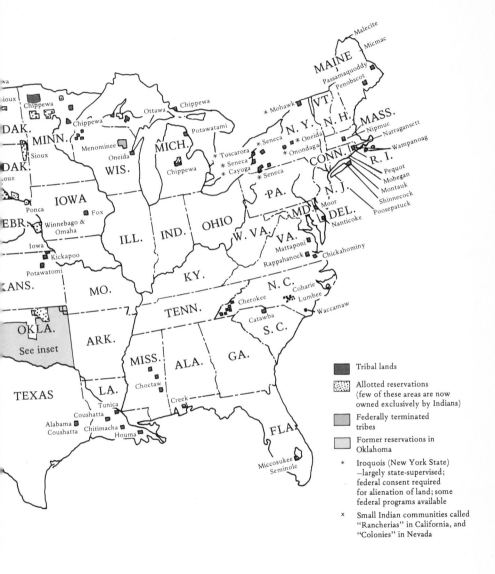

In the mid-nineteenth century, the government embarked upon a policy of containment as a means of controlling the Indians and encouraging westward expansion. The government used military force to displace the many tribes and resettle them on wasteland reservations, where they remained unless new settlement plans or the discovery of oil and valuable minerals resulted in further displacement. This program of forced segregation and dependency, compounded by attempts at forced "Americanization," reduced the Native Americans to the status of a subordinate colonized people — wards of the government — living at a subsistence level. Reflecting changing attitudes and interests in the late nineteenth and early twentieth centuries, Congress enacted various pieces of legislation ostensibly designed to help the Indians. These laws, to be discussed shortly, actually worked to the Indians' disadvantage and worsened their already low and dependent status.

Two short-lived Pan-Indian associations of the twentieth century, the Society of American Indians in the 1910–1920 decade and the National Congress of American Indians in the 1930s, failed to unify the tribes into an effective pressure group or to draw much outside support. New moves toward unity began in the 1960s, and new legislation and greater government sympathy helped the Indians' cause. The most significant factor in the Indians' new success, however, was the impact of the civil rights movement, for it created a greater social consciousness in the country and inspired the Indians to strive harder for self-determination. Though they had never been silent, they now became more vocal and organized, and they found non-Indians more receptive. They became more militant, as demonstrated by the occupation of Alcatraz Island in 1969, the takeover of the Bureau of Indian Affairs in Washington, D.C., in 1972, the long confrontation in 1973 at Wounded Knee, site of the 1890 massacre (discussed on p. 253), and the march on Washington in 1978. A new generation of Red Power advocates took up the fight for Indian rights. Some attempted to achieve their goals through a national or Pan-Indian movement, whereas others preferred an emphasis on individual tribal culture and practices.

Throughout the five-hundred-year history of Indian-white relations, the Indians have frustrated whites by their general refusal to believe that the whites' religions and life styles are better. To understand the nature of these relations between dominant and minority groups is to understand the important role of ethnocentrism, stereotyping, cultural differences, and power differentials in intergroup relations.

EARLY ENCOUNTERS

To appreciate the significance of the first encounters, it is important to note not only that two human races were seeing each other's physical distinctions for the first time, but also that the vast differences in culture, knowledge, and life style made each a source of wonder to the other. Columbus's first impressions of the Arawak Indians in the Caribbean reflected ethnocentrism:

> I knew they were a people who would better be freed and converted to our Holy Faith by love than by force . . . they are all generally of good height, of pleasing appearance and well built. . . . They must be good servants and intelligent, . . . and I believe that they would easily become Christians, as it appeared to me that they had no sect.[3]

Though he admired the Indians, Columbus essentially saw them as "creatures." He looked upon them as potential servants, and he assumed that they had no religious convictions because he found no trappings of religion or written codes such as he was accustomed to seeing in Europe.

As Europeans became more curious about Indians, an idealistic concept of the Indian as the Noble Savage took hold. Michel de Montaigne, a sixteenth-century French philosopher, after reading many travelers' journals and talking with explorers, wrote that the Indians were indeed Noble Savages, for they

> [have] no kind of traffic, no knowledge of letters, no intelligence of numbers, no name of magistrate, nor of politics, no use of service, or riches, or of poverty; no contracts, no successions, no partitions, no occupation but idle, no apparel but natural, no manuring of lands, no use of wine. The very words that impart a lie, falsehood, treason, covetousness, envy, detraction, were not heard among them.[4]

While some Europeans were romanticizing Indians and a positive mystique about the Indians swept Elizabethan England and other parts of Europe, others viewed the Indians as bloodthirsty barbarians and cruelly exploited them. The early phases of Spanish military activity, particularly in Mexico, Peru, and the American Southwest, included Indian enslavement, plunder, rape, and slaughter. The Spanish put the peaceful Arawak Indians of the Caribbean islands into forced labor, using them in land clearing, building, mining, and plantation work. Since they had no weapons comparable to those of their conquerors, the subjugated peoples often responded by committing mass suicide and mass infanticide. The Indian population began to decline rapidly as a result of disease, warfare, and self-destruction.

The dichotomy of views of the Indian either as a Noble Savage or as a bloodthirsty barbarian was epitomized in the great debate between Bartolome de las Casas, a bishop serving in the New World, and Juan Ginés de Sepúlveda, a Renaissance scholar. The latter considered the Indians no better than "beasts" who should be enslaved. Las Casas presented a picture of the Indians as innocent children, both artistically and mechanically inclined, with intellectual capabilities for learning and a willingness to coexist with the Spanish intruders.[5] In 1550, King Charles V appointed the Council of the Indies, a panel of distinguished theologians and counselors, which met at Valladolid. The Council heard the arguments of the two antagonists, agreed in large measure with Las Casas, and thereby redirected Spanish policy toward the Indians.

As part of his long struggle to protect the Indians, Las Casas had returned to Spain in 1517 to plead their case directly to the king. In doing so, he revealed the extent of their decimation: "At my first arrival in Hispaniola (1497), it contained a million inhabitants and now there remain scarce the hundredth part of them." He felt that the Indians could survive only if another labor force replaced them. By convincing the Spanish authorities that Africans were sturdier and better adapted to agricultural operations, he opened the doors for the subsequent massive slave trade of blacks to the Spanish possessions in the New World. It is cruelly ironic that the humane efforts of Las Casas on the Indians' behalf led to the brutalization and exploitation of black people and racial discrimination against them for over four hundred years.

The Indian populations in the United States and Latin America differ in their social, economic, and political status. Several factors, including habitability of terrain, migration patterns, degree of industrialization, and especially different attitudes in the various countries, have accounted for these differences. In the United States, the nineteenth-century policy of removal, containment, and Indian dependency upon the federal government prevented most tribes from becoming full participants in American society. In Latin America, however, Spain adopted a more benevolent policy toward the Indians in 1550, following the recommendations of the Council of the Indies, and greater interaction, intermarriage, absorption, and gradual acculturation occurred among the Indians and the Spanish. Except for those living in the central Andes and other remote areas, the Indians became fuller participants in their society than their counterparts in the United States, and lived in relative cultural and racial harmony with the white, black, *mulatto* (of mixed black and white ancestry), and *mestizo* (of mixed Indian and white ancestry) populations. Along with the other nonwhite groups, they were part of the large low-ranking social class, in sharp contrast to the small high-ranking class. Despite racial harmony, they have had very little opportunity for upward mobility, and most Latin-American nonwhites live in economic stagnation. In contrast, most North American Indians have experienced both economic stagnation *and* a lack of racial harmony.

Indian populations in Latin America and North America were decimated by various sicknesses that had resulted from earlier contact with white explorers or traders. When the early settlers in New England found deserted Indian villages, they rejoiced; they considered this to be mute testimony of the judgment of Divine Providence upon these "heathens" as well as upon their own undertaking. The Lord had smitten the pagan to make way for the righteous! This accidental annihilation had often resulted from a serious contagion such as smallpox, tuberculosis, or cholera. The Indians also were often fatally susceptible to such diseases as measles, mumps, and chicken pox because they had not developed immunities to these European illnesses.

CULTURAL STRAINS

When the white settlers were few in number and depended upon Indian assistance, the Indians were hospitable and the whites were receptive to them. The Indians along the Eastern Seaboard helped the colonists to get settled by teaching them what to plant and how to cultivate it as well as imparting to them the knowledge and skills they would need to survive in the wilderness. As the settlements became stabilized, the relations between the two races became more strained, as the following excerpt from Douglas Edward Leach's study of seventeenth-century New England reveals:

> Ever since the coming of the white men there had been economic intercourse between Indians and English traders. At first it had seemed that the flourishing trade in furs, tools, cloth, and foodstuffs was as beneficial to the Indians as to the colonists, but as time went on and the English extended their activities the Indians grew more and more dissatisfied with the situation. It became apparent that they were gradually sinking into a position of complete economic subservience. Indian villages which had once enjoyed almost total self-sufficiency were now increasingly dependent upon products of English manufacture. Individual Indians became enmeshed in debt, which degraded them still further in the eyes of the English. The wiser leaders among the Indians saw that if the trend were not reversed, the time would soon come when the natives of New England would be completely stripped of their independence.
>
> In the meantime, some of the Indians were exchanging their forest ways for the security and comfort of English habitations by engaging themselves as servants or laborers to the settlers, whose ambitious expansionism was fostering a continual shortage of labor. This meant that members of the two races were now being brought into frequent contact with each other on the streets of colonial villages, producing still more interracial friction. Furthermore, the migration of individual Indians to the English plantations was disturbing to

the other Indians who chose to cling to their old independence, and who saw with dismay the weakening of tribal and family bonds. . . .

At the same time, the English colonists were being hardened in the conviction that the Indians were a graceless and savage people, dirty and slothful in their personal habits, treacherous in their relations with the superior race. To put it bluntly, they were fit only to be pushed aside and subordinated, so that the land could be occupied and made productive by those for whom it had been destined by God. If the Indians could be made to fit into a humble niche in the edifice of colonial religion, economy, and government, very well, but if not, sooner or later they would have to be driven away or crushed.[6]

Throughout the westward movement, if contact led to cooperation between the two cultures, the resulting interaction and cultural diffusion usually worked to the disadvantage of the Indians. They lost their self-sufficiency and became economically dependent on whites. The whites in turn demanded full compliance as the price of continued peaceful relations. Even if the Indians complied with the whites' demands, however, many whites continued to regard Indians as inferior, destined for a subservient role in white society.

DIFFERING VALUES

Benjamin Franklin offered a classic example of different values in his account of a treaty signed between the whites and the Iroquois in 1744.

After the principal Business was settled, the Commissioners from Virginia acquainted the Indians by a Speech, that there was at Williamsburg a College, with a Fund for Educating Indian youth; and that, if the Six Nations would send down half a dozen of their young Lads to that College, the Government would take care that they should be well provided for, and instructed in all the Learning of the White People. . . . [The Indians'] Speaker began . . . "We are convinc'd . . . that you mean to do us Good by your Proposal; and we thank you heartily. But you, who are wise, must know that different Nations have different Conceptions of things; and you will therefore not take it amiss, if our Ideas of this kind of Education happen not to be the same with yours. We have had some Experience of it; Several of our young People were formerly brought up at the Colleges of the Northern Provinces; they were instructed in all your Sciences; but, when they came back to us, they were bad Runners, ignorant of every means of living in the Woods, unable to bear either Cold or Hunger, knew neither how to build a Cabin, take a Deer, or kill an Enemy, knew our Language imperfectly, were therefore neither fit for Hunters, Warriors, nor Counsellors; they were totally good for nothing. We are however not the less oblig'd by your kind Offer, tho' we decline accepting it; and, to show our grateful Sense of it, if the Gentlemen of Virginia will send us a Dozen of their Sons, we will take great Care of their Education, instruct them in all we know, and make *Men* of them."*

Almost one hundred years later, George Catlin offered insight into another manifestation of differing value orientations. Catlin, a nineteenth-century artist famous for his paintings of Indians and his sensitivity to their ways, observed in this passage how each of the two cultures viewed the other.

The civilized world look upon a group of Indians, in their classic dress, with their few and simple oddities, all of which have their moral or meaning, and laugh at them excessively, because they are not like ourselves — we ask, "why do the silly creatures wear such great bunches of quills on their heads? — Such loads and streaks of paint upon their bodies — and bear's grease? abominable!" and a thousand other equally silly questions, without ever stopping to think that Nature taught them to do so — and that they all have some definite importance or meaning which an Indian could explain to us at once, if he were asked and felt disposed to do so — that each quill in his head stood, in the eyes of his whole tribe, as the symbols of any enemy who had fallen by his hand — that every streak of red paint covered a wound which he had got in honourable combat — and that the bear's grease with which he carefully anoints his body every morning, from head to foot, cleanses and purifies the body, and protects his skin from the bite of mosquitoes, and at the same time preserves him from colds and coughs which are usually taken through the pores of the skin.

At the same time, an Indian looks at the civilized world, no doubt, with equal, if not much greater, astonishment, at our apparently, as well as really, ridiculous customs and fashions; but he laughs not, nor ridicules, nor questions, — for his natural good sense and good manners forbid him, — until he is reclining about the fireside of his wigwam companions, when he vents forth his just criticisms upon the learned world, who are a rich and just theme for Indian criticism and Indian gossip.

An Indian will not ask a white man the reason why he does not oil his skin with bear's grease, or why he does not paint his body — or why he wears a hat on his head, or why he has buttons on the back of his coat, where they can never be used — or why he wears whiskers, and a shirt collar up to his eyes — or why he sleeps with his head towards the fire instead of his feet — why he walks with his toes out instead of turning them in — or why it is that hundreds of white folks will flock and crowd round a table to see an Indian eat — but he will go home to his wigwam fireside, and "make the welkin ring" with jokes and fun upon the ignorance and folly of the knowing world.[7]

These two selections are excellent illustrations of how culture shapes an individual's view of reality. When people use their own group as a frame of reference in judging another group, the resulting ethnocentric judgments declare the outgroup to be strange and inferior.

WHITE AND INDIAN GOVERNMENTAL RELATIONS

In 1754 the English Parliament adopted a new policy of treating the Indian tribes as independent nations and denied the Colonies all jurisdiction over them. Thereafter, if the colonists wanted to obtain additional Indian land or negotiate any trade pacts, they had to do so through the English government and not directly. Historians cite enforcement of this policy as an indirect cause of the American Revolution. In addition to the delay in gaining approval caused by drawing up petitions, making ocean crossings, and waiting for bureaucratic processing, the colonists fumed over heathens being accorded higher official status than they, loyal British subjects. Yet when the Colonies declared their independence from England, they adopted the same policy in 1778, and the tribes had quasi-national status.

One Indian nation, the Iroquois, had a pronounced influence upon some of the provisions of the U.S. Constitution. Iroquois is a name given to five Indian tribes located in New York State and the Ohio River Valley — the Cayuga, Mohawk, Oneida, Onondaga, and Seneca — who united in a league in 1570. They added a sixth tribe — the Tuscarora — in 1722, and also took other groups, including the Delaware, under their protection.[8] The League had not yet reached its full extent when it was curtailed by the white settlers; by 1851 it had virtually disappeared.

In its time, the League's democratic processes were so effective that romanticists called the Iroquois the "Greeks in America," and many aspects of their system served as a model for the colonists. One example is the means by which a Senate-House conference committee works out the differences between bills passed in each house in order to enable a compromise bill to become law.

INDIAN VALUES AND SOCIAL STRUCTURE

Although there were, and still are, a great many tribes whose cultures differ from one another, some marked similarities have existed among them. For one thing, the Indians have lived in a close and intimate relationship with nature, respecting and not abusing the land. They maximize the use of any animal prey — using its skin for clothing and shelter, its bones for various tools and implements, its sinews for thread, its meat for food, its bladder for a container, and so on.

Indian attitudes toward possession of the land itself ranged from single to joint to tribal ownership, depending upon the tribe. More frequently, the land belonged to the tribe, and as tribal members individuals or families could live on and possibly farm certain portions. Land no longer cultivated by one Indian could be cultivated by another. However, the nominal owner could not dispose of the property without considering the land use rights of the current user. More emphasis was thus placed upon the rights of the user than upon the rights and power of the nominal owner.[9] This practice is somewhat comparable, at least in terms of shared access, to a law in present-day Sweden that roughly translates to "every man's right." In that country a landowner cannot deny others access to the land, since all are entitled to enjoy its beauty. Thus campers or hikers do not encounter no-trespassing signs; since all respect the land, littering and other forms of abuse are quite rare.

Concerning personal interaction, Indians established primary relationships either through a clan system (descent from a common ancestor) or through a friendship system, much like other tribal societies.

Kin relationships were the basic building blocks of Indian society. These blocks were formed into social and political structures ranging from nuclear families to vast empires. The Indians, in their initial attempts to establish a basis of cooperation with the immigrant whites, attempted to incorporate the newcomers into the familiar kinship system. When proffered marriage alliances were turned down by the whites, the Indians sought to establish relationships based on the reciprocal responsibilities of brother to brother, nephew to uncle, and, finally, children to father. The white man refused the proferred relationships, misinterpreted Indian speech as weakness, and increasingly imposed his will on the disheartened remnants of once proud Indian nations.[10]

Indian children grow up under the encouragement and discipline of the extended family, not just the nuclear family. A generalized love of all children in the tribe, rather than just their own progeny, has been common among the Indians.[11] This factor may help explain the permis-

BOX 6.1

"The greatest object of their lives seems to be to acquire possessions — to be rich. They desire to possess the whole world."

"I had heard marvelous things of this people. In some things we despised them; in others we regarded them as *wakan* (mysterious), a race whose power bordered upon the supernatural. I learned that they had made a 'fire-boat.' I could not understand how they could unite two elements which cannot exist together. I thought the water would put out the fire, and the fire would consume the boat if it had the shadow of a chance. This was to me a preposterous thing! But when I was told that the Big Knives had created a 'fire-boat-walks-on-mountains' [a locomotive] it was too much to believe.

"I had seen guns and various other things brought to us by the French Canadians, so that I had already some notion of the supernatural gifts of the white man; but I had never before heard such tales as I listened to that morning. It was said that they had bridged the Missouri and Mississippi rivers, and that they made immense houses of stone and brick, piled on top of one another until they were as high as high hills. My brain was puzzled with these things for many a day.

"Certainly they are a heartless nation. They have made some of their people servants — yes, slaves! We have never believed in keeping slaves, but it seems these *Washichu* [white men] do! It is our belief that they painted their servants black a long time ago, to tell them from the rest, and now the slaves have children born to them of the same color!

"The greatest object of their lives seems to be to acquire possessions — to be rich. They desire to possess the whole world. For thirty years they were trying to entice us to sell them our land. Finally the outbreak gave them all, and we had already spread over the whole country.

"They are a wonderful people. They have divided the day into hours, like the moons of the year. In fact, they measure everything. Not one of them would let so much as a turnip go from his field unless he received full value for it. I understand that their great men make a feast and invite many, but when the feast is over the guests are required to pay for what they have eaten before leaving the house [restaurant].

"I am also informed, . . . but this I hardly believe, that their Great Chief (President) compels every man to pay him for the land he lives upon and all his personal goods — even for his own existence — every year! I am sure we could not live under such a law."

Sioux youth during the 1870s

sive and indulgent child-rearing practices many Europeans reported.[12] Whether the Indian tribe was a hunting, a fishing, or a farming society, social scientists have found that the children were raised in a cooperative, noncompetitive, and affectionate atmosphere. Considered from the outset as an individual, the child developed a sense of responsibility and interdependency at an early age. Unrestrained displays of affection or temper and the use of corporal punishment have rarely been part of traditional Indian child care practices. Instead, the means of social control are shame and ridicule, and the Indian matures into an individual keenly aware of any form of conduct that would lead other members of the tribe to have such reactions. Sometimes the price of emphasizing these forms of social control is heavy, for a great deal of psychological harm can be caused by shame and ridicule.

Closely related to sensitivity to shame and ridicule is the Indian concept of personal honor, including the honor of one's word. Once pledged, whether to a white person or to another Indian, that word was never to be broken. Exceptions existed, for, Albert Britt reports, chiefs "lied only as a war measure, personal or tribal — later, in an attempt to please the white."[13] Some tribes had no word for *thief*, although an enemy's goods were always fair game. Sometimes, as among the Sioux, Crow, and Blackfeet, young men of one tribe would steal from another tribe as a form of sport or a joke, but normally they would not steal from one another.[14]

The Indian woman's role differed from the man's. Women's functions were to work and to raise children. However, the traditional view that women held a subservient position and labored long and hard while the men idled away their time is not completely accurate. Actually, there was a cooperative but not egalitarian arrangement between the sexes, with the men doing the heavy work and the women doing tasks that would not conflict with their child-rearing responsibilities. In hunting and fishing societies, the men would be away from the village for extended periods searching for food. In farming societies, the men cleared and cultivated the land, and the women tended the crops, collected edible foods, and gathered firewood as the men sought a fresh meat supply. Each member of the tribe, according to sexually defined roles, had responsibilities to fulfill for kin and tribe.

STEREOTYPING OF INDIANS

One popular misconception was that the Indian was a bloodthirsty savage. Some tribes, such as the Apache and Ute, were more warlike, but most sought to avoid conflict if they could. Rivalries did exist among various tribes, however, and the French, English, and Americans often exploited these rivalries for their own advantage. The Indians did believe strongly in retributive justice: a wrong had to be repaid, even if it took years, but not to a greater degree. Scalping, often depicted in films as a common Indian practice, in fact was not common. Even those tribes that did scalp frequently did so because of their belief in retributive justice. Some historians argue that the Indian first learned about scalping from white settlers.

> Whatever its exact origins, there is no doubt that scalp-taking quickly spread over all of North America, except in the Eskimo areas; nor is there any doubt that its spread was due to the barbarity of White men rather than to the barbarity of Red men. White settlers early offered to pay bounties on dead Indians, and scalps were actual proof of the deed. Governor Kieft of New Netherland is usually credited with originating the idea of paying for Indian scalps, as they were more convenient to handle than whole heads, and they offered the same proof that an Indian had been killed. By liberal payment for scalps, the Dutch virtually cleared southern New York and New Jersey of Indians before the English supplanted them. By 1703 the colony of Massachusetts was paying the equivalent of about $60 for every Indian scalp. In the mid-eighteenth century, Pennsylvania fixed the bounty for a male Indian scalp at $134; a female's was worth only $50. Some White entrepreneurs simply hatcheted any old Indians that still survived in their towns.*

Another side of the Indian stereotype is the portrayal of the Indian as silent or aloof. This image probably grew out of normal Indian behavior in ambiguous situations, such as those faced by Indians transported to Europe for exhibition, transported to Washington, D.C., for treaty negotiations, or interacting with strangers. Since they had developed from childhood a sensitivity to acting in any way that might bring about shame or ridicule, Indians often remained silent for fear of speaking or acting improperly. This practice is still common in courtship, in the greeting offered to children returning from boarding school, and in the face of harsh, angry words from a white. In each instance, the practice among most tribes is to allow some time, perhaps days or months, to elapse before the uncertainty is sufficiently reduced to permit conversation. Indian silence is a cautionary device to preserve respect and dignity on both sides.[15] The silence does not represent aloofness, and it is temporary, continuing only until the situation lends itself to speaking.

Hollywood has established the false Indian stereotype in the minds of many Americans. Ignoring their many ethnic identities, the movies have

*From *Man's Rise to Civilization as Shown by the Indians of North America from Primeval Times to the Coming of the Industrial State* by Peter Farb, p. 158. Copyright © 1968 by Peter Farb. Reprinted by permission of the publishers, E. P. Dutton.

created a single fictional identity, often called "Sioux" or "Apache," and portrayed "the Indian" as either a noble redskin or a vicious savage, either of whom denies the "white man his proper Christian right to this continent."[16] As Will Rogers once said, "The problem ain't ignorance, but everyone knowing something that ain't true."

THE CHEROKEE: A TRAGIC CASE STUDY

Of all the broken treaties, confiscation of Indian lands, and disregard for minority rights and property, perhaps none is as poignant or as indicative of racist antagonism toward all Indians as the tragic experience of the Cherokee nation. Here was an Indian tribe that had succeeded in adapting to the white people's ways, but was nonetheless brutally victimized by the whites.

When George Washington assumed the presidency in 1790, the federal government adopted the British policy of treating the Indian tribes as independent nations. This policy was continued until 1871, although if the Indians failed to accept the government's dictates, it frequently used military force against them. About 1790, the Cherokee, after some 14 years of warfare with the Americans, decided to adopt American customs and culture. In other words, they embarked upon an active program of assimilation in an effort to live harmoniously with a different civilization.

ACCOMPLISHMENTS

Over the next 40 years, their success in achieving this goal was remarkable. They converted their economy to one based on agriculture and commerce, strengthened their self-governing political system, and prospered. They cultivated farmlands in the fertile soil of the tri-state region of Georgia, Tennessee, and North Carolina, and reaped bountiful harvests. The Cherokee patterned themselves after the whites, setting up churches, schools, sawmills, grist mills, and blacksmith shops. They acquired spinning wheels, looms, plows, and all the other implements of white society.

Most extraordinary of all was the achievement of one Cherokee of part white ancestry named Sequoyah, after whom the redwoods and giant sequoia trees are named. In 1821, after a 12-year struggle, this crippled genius succeeded in inventing a phonetic syllabary notation system for the Cherokee language. This immense accomplishment was unprecedented in world history. An untrained man had been able to write a language by himself, and to do so in a way that could be easily learned.

What quickly followed is also remarkable. Within three years almost all the Cherokee could read and write their own language. By 1828, the tribe had its own newspaper and had adopted a written constitution and code of laws.

By American standards, the Cherokee were the most "civilized" tribe in the country. Driven by the desire for self-improvement, they had educated themselves, converted to Christianity, and learned the whites' ways of agriculture, business, and government. They had successfully acculturated. Just one problem remained: the whites wanted their rich land for cotton growing.

LEGAL MANEUVERS

After much debate in Congress, with many legislators from the North against it, the Indian Removal Bill passed in 1830 by a close vote. This act called for the expulsion of all Indians east of the Mississippi. Georgia removed the Creek nation, but the Cherokee and their supporters succeeded in having the matter considered by the United States Supreme Court. On February 28, 1832, Chief Justice John Marshall delivered the majority opinion in favor of the Cherokee on the basis of long-standing treaties. President Jackson's reported response was, "John Marshall has rendered his decision, now let him enforce it." Indeed, two of the three branches of government favored removal, and Jackson interpreted his overwhelming reelection in November as a mandate from the electorate.

With public opinion against the Cherokee, the voices of John Marshall, Daniel Webster, Henry Clay, Sam Houston, Davy Crockett, and others could not help the Cherokee cause. Georgia confiscated Cherokee land and redistributed it through land lotteries, with the state militia stationed in the region to preserve the peace should the Indians resist.

> The premeditated brutality of the militia's daily conducts suggested their commanders' hope of provoking a Cherokee reaction which might provide an excuse for their immediate physical expulsion. The carefully disciplined Cherokee instead patiently submitted even when the provocations extended to the burning of their homes, the confiscation of their property, the mistreatment of their women, the closing of their schools, and the sale of liquor in their churches.[17]

The Cherokee retreated into the forests and continued their desperate legal maneuvering to avoid removal. Although federal troops removed the Choctaw and Chickasaw in Mississippi and the Creek in Alabama, they did not move against the Cherokee, who had won worldwide sympathy and whose legal efforts to prevent removal were still successful. Instead, the federal government intensified its efforts to promote disunity among the Cherokee through bribery, jailings, persecution, and denial of the services and support guaranteed under treaties. Most of the Cherokee remained loyal to their president, John Ross, and rejected the proposed treaty of removal and its $5 million compensation payment.

Government officials finally succeeded in getting the treaty signed on December 29, 1835, by convening an ad hoc council of Ross's Cherokee opponents. Fewer than five hundred of the seventeen thousand Cherokee appeared, but they signed the treaty, and the Senate ratified it on May 18, 1836. Ross and the Cherokee people fought this pseudo-legitimate treaty, and in January of 1838 Ross presented the Senate with a petition signed by 15,665 Cherokee repudiating the treaty. The Senate rejected the petition by a 37–10 vote. A new wave of public protest in the North, including an impassioned open letter to President Van Buren from Ralph Waldo Emerson, had no result. On April 10, 1838, the president ordered General Winfield Scott to remove the Cherokee immediately, using whatever military force was necessary.

EXPULSION

What followed is one of the ugliest episodes in this country's history. The United States government, through its military forces, acted against an entire people who had willingly adapted to the changing world around them. Soldiers forced them at gunpoint from their homes, first to stockades and then westward, far from all that had been theirs.

Families at dinner were startled by the sudden gleam of bayonets in the doorway and rose up to be driven with blows and oaths along the weary miles to the stockade. Men were seized in their fields or going along the road, women were taken from their wheels and children from their play. In many cases, on turning for one last look as they crossed the ridge, they saw their homes in flames, fired by the lawless rabble that followed on the heels of the soldiers to loot and pillage. So keen were these outlaws on the scent that in some instances they were driving off the cattle and other stock of the Indians almost before the soldiers had fairly started their owners in the other direction. Systematic hunts were made by the same men for Indian graves, to rob them of the silver pendants and other valuables deposited with the dead. A Georgia volunteer, afterward a colonel in the Confederate service, said: "I fought through the Civil War and have seen men shot to pieces and slaughtered by thousands, but the Cherokee removal was the cruelest work I ever knew."[18]

The Cherokee suffered extensively during this mass expulsion. Beginning in October 1838, army troops marched the Cherokee westward, along what the Cherokee later called the Trail of Tears; ten to twenty Indians died each day from exposure and other miseries. By March 1839, less than nine thousand out of thirteen thousand survived to reach the Indian Territory, which is now Oklahoma. At the midpoint in this sad episode — December 3 1838 — President Van Buren's message to Congress announced:

> It affords me sincere pleasure to apprise the Congress of the entire removal of the Cherokee Nation of Indians to their new homes west of the Mississippi. The measures authorized by Congress at its last session have had the happiest effects. ... They have emigrated without any apparent reluctance.[19]

CHANGES IN GOVERNMENTAL POLICY

A shift in governmental policy in the mid-nineteenth century changed Indian life styles to such an extent that one can see its aftereffects today on any reservation. Instead of using annihilation and expulsion as means of dealing with the Indians, the government embarked on a policy of segregation and isolation. Between 1850 and 1880, it established most of the reservations, of which there are now almost three hundred.

In 1871 Congress tacked onto an appropriations bill a rider that ended federal recognition of the Indian tribes as independent, sovereign nations and made them wards of the government instead. Bureaucrats were now responsible for the welfare of the Indians, issued them food rations, and supervised every aspect of their lives. The results were devastating. Proud and independent people, who had been taught self-reliance at an early age, were now totally dependent on non-Indian government agents. Many of the tribes had been nomadic, and did not easily adjust to reservation life. Moreover, such problems as inadequate administration by the Indian agents and irregular delivery of food, supplies, and equipment only made matters worse.

The government was still not through restructuring the Indians' life styles, as leaders at the time believed that what they were doing was "for the best." Americanization became the goal. This meant destroying tribal organizations, suppressing "pagan" religions and ceremonies, allowing only the English language in the schools, requiring "white" hair and clothing styles, and teaching only American culture and history.

> Most of the attention of the Americanizers was concentrated on the Indian children, who were snatched from their families and shipped off to boarding schools far from their homes. The children usually were kept at boarding school for eight years, during which time they were not permitted to see their parents, relatives or friends.

Anything Indian — dress, language, religious practices, even out-look on life (and how that was defined was up to the judgment of each administrator of the government's directives) — was uncom-promisingly prohibited. Ostensibly educated, articulate in the Eng-lish language, wearing store-bought clothes, and with their hair short and their emotionalism toned down, the boarding-school graduates were sent out either to make their way in a white world that did not want them, or to return to a reservation to which they were now foreign. The Indians had simply failed to melt into the great American melting pot.*

One value that was promulgated was the rugged individualism of white society, rather than the cooperative, noncompetitive approach of the Indian. This was the purpose of the General Allotment Act of 1887. Its sponsor, Senator Dawes, genuinely believed that it would create in the Indian that spirit of self-interest that he considered the major force in white civilization.

What this legislation actually did was deprive the Indians of even more land. Its intent was to break the backbone of Indian culture by ending the communal ownership of reservation lands and giving each Indian a share. Many of the Indians had no technical knowledge of farming and neither the cash nor credit to obtain farm implements. Some Indian peoples believed it was sacrilegious to plow open the earth. Loopholes in the Dawes Act enabled unscrupulous whites to plunder the Indian land, either through low-cost long-term leases or by convincing the Indian owners to write wills leaving their property to white "friends." This practice was widespread, and a suspicious in-crease in the number of Indian deaths followed; some of these deaths were actually proven to have been murders.[20] By 1914 the 138 million acres of Indian land had been reduced to 56 million acres, all of it eroded and of poor quality.[21]

After 1933, the Roosevelt administration shifted from a policy of forced assimilation to one of pluralism. Secretary of the Interior Harold L. Ickes and Bureau of Indian Affairs Commissioner John Collier, in par-ticular, were deeply sympathetic to the Indian cause. One outcome was the Indian Reorganization Act of 1934, which ended the land allotment program, encouraged tribal self-government, extended financial credit to the tribes, gave preference in BIA (Bureau of Indian Affairs) employ-ment to Indians, and permitted consolidation of Indian lands split up through inheritance. Further, the Indians were encouraged to revive

*From *Man's Rise to Civilization as Shown by the Indians of North America from Primeval Times to the Coming of the Industrial State* by Peter Farb, p. 310. Copyright © 1968 by Peter Farb. Reprinted by permission of the publishers, E. P. Dutton.

their ancient arts and crafts, their languages, their religions and ceremonies, and their customs and traditions. In keeping with an administrative philosophy of treating the Indians with dignity, the act was
permissive, not mandatory; each tribe could vote to accept or reject the
new law. Most chose to accept it.

In the 1950s, new top administrative personnel in the Interior Department and the BIA who had a different philosophy caused a shift
back to attempts at assimilation. Some critics of the 1934 legislation had
thought it regressive. Now, these people, believing that the only way to
end the chronic poverty, disease, overpopulation, and hopelessness
among the Indians was to end the isolation of reservation life, tried
some new approaches.

RELOCATION

Beginning in 1952, the Bureau of Indian Affairs attempted to at least
partially resolve the problem of overpopulation on the reservations. The
BIA provided financial and other assistance to individuals or families
who wanted to secure jobs and living accommodations in urban areas.
For many Indians the word *relocation* had terrible connotations. That
was the euphemism that had been used for the prison camps in which
110,000 Japanese-Americans had been placed during World War II. Furthermore, Dillon S. Myer, the government administrator who had been
in charge of those camps, was now in charge of the Indian relocation
program.

Most of the Indians who utilized this program (about 40,000) went to
work in low-status unskilled or semiskilled jobs and to live in the
poorer sections of the cities. Some adjusted and became acculturated;
others felt uprooted and were driven to alcoholism. More than one-
fourth of the total number returned to the reservations. The program ta-
pered off after 1960, mostly because of other efforts to improve Indian
life.

TERMINATION

A series of bills passed in 1953–1954 sought to end federal responsibility for the Indians by ending all federal services and federal-liaison
tribal organizations, and dispensing assets among members of the tribe.
Two of the more prosperous tribes, the Klamath of southern Oregon and
the Menominee of Wisconsin, both of whom owned considerable tracts
of valuable timberland, some Paiute and Ute in Utah, and several other
tribes were the first to be affected by this legislation.

For the Klamath, a tribe of 668 families totaling some 2,000 individuals, termination even threatened to end their tribal identity. In the

spring of 1968, when 77 percent voted to withdraw from the tribe and receive a cash payment for their share of the land holdings, many government and business officials feared that liquidating tribal assets when the lumber market was already depressed would threaten the Pacific Northwest economy. Instead of selling the lumber, Congress voted to purchase the land, creating the Winema National Forest. A federal trusteeship for adults declared incompetent to handle their own affairs and for minors kept the government involved in 48.9 percent of the tribe members' affairs. With their tribal identity coming to an end, many Klamath are now professing interest in the Pan-Indian movement.[22]

In the case of the Menominee, the new policy brought economic disaster.

Almost overnight, many millions of dollars of tribal assets disappeared in the rush to transform the Menominee reservation into a self-supporting county. The need to finance the usual hospital, police, and other services of a county and pay taxes imperiled the tribe's sawmill and forest holdings, alienated tribal lands, threatened many Indians with the loss of their homes and life savings, and saddled Wisconsin with a huge welfare problem which it could not underwrite and which had to be met by desperate appeals for help from the same federal government that had thought it had washed its hands of the Menominees.[23]

Washington's hasty blunder cost the Menominee their hospital, their sawmill, and some of their best land, which they had to sell because they could not afford the taxes on it. President Nixon officially repudiated the termination policy in 1970 and Congress reversed the termination of all the tribes affected in December 1973, re-creating these reservations, but nobody gave the Menominee back their hospital or their sawmill. The following year the Menominee took over the abandoned 64-room Alexian Brothers monastery to serve as their hospital. It had been built on Menominee land at a time when any church group could take as much Indian reservation land as it needed to build religious structures. Local whites, who had bought tribal land cheaply when the tribe had to sell, objected, although the Alexian Brothers did not. When bloodshed seemed imminent, the governor of Wisconsin called out the National Guard to maintain order. Fortunately, a peaceful accommodation was reached, and the Menominee retained permanent possession of the building.

OTHER APPROACHES

In 1966 Lyndon Johnson appointed the first Native American — Robert L. Bennett, an Oneida from Wisconsin — to be Commissioner of

Indian Affairs. However, paternalistic federal bureaucrats continued to impose their will upon a still subjugated people, as President Richard Nixon indicated in his July 8, 1970, message to Congress repudiating termination.

The story of the Indian in America is something more than the record of the white man's frequent aggression, broken agreements, intermittent remorse and prolonged failure. It is a record also of endurance, of survival, of adaptation and creativity in the face of overwhelming obstacles. It is a record of enormous contributions to this country — to its art and culture, to its strength and spirit, to its sense of history and its sense of purpose.

It is long past time that the Indian policies of the Federal government began to recognize and build upon the capacities and insights of the Indian people. Both as a matter of justice and of enlightened social policy, we must begin to act on the basis of what the Indians themselves have long been telling us. The time has come to break decisively with the past and to create the conditions for a new era in which the Indian future is determined by Indian acts and Indian decisions.

. . . Of the Department of the Interior's programs directly serving Indians, for example, only 1.5 per cent are presently under Indian control. Only 2.4 per cent of HEW's Indian health programs are run by Indians. The result is a burgeoning Federal bureaucracy, programs which are far less effective than they ought to be, and an erosion of Indian initiative and morale.

. . . This, then, must be the goal of any new national policy toward the Indian people: to strengthen the Indian's sense of autonomy without threatening his sense of community. We must assure the Indian that he can assume control of his own life without being separated involuntarily from the tribal group. And we must make it clear that Indians can become independent of Federal control without being cut off from Federal concern and Federal support.

Some legislation beneficial to the Indians was enacted, notably the return of 48,000 acres to the Taos Pueblo Indians. However, there was no sweeping reform. The following sections will examine some of the changes as well as the problems that remain.

PRESENT-DAY NATIVE AMERICAN LIFE

Of all the minorities in America, according to HEW statistics on income, employment, and housing, the Native American is "the poorest of the poor." It is cruelly ironic that most of the Native Americans' problems are due not only to their subordinate position as a result of conquest, but also to their insistence on their right to be different, to continue living as Native Americans. In a society that has long demanded assimilation, this insistence has not been popular. Still, U.S. policy on assimilation has been vicissitudinary over the years.

POPULATION

The Native American population in the United States has grown significantly in the past few years. The number of Native Americans living on or near reservations in 1978, according to the Department of the Interior, was about 649,000. The 1970 census counted 340,000 urban Native Americans, so that the present number of people who identify themselves as Native Americans surpasses 1,000,000. Native American fertility rates were nearly double those for whites in 1970 and a third higher than those for other nonwhites. The Native American population is presently growing faster than any other subgroup, at 3 percent a year.[24] As population growth has been exceeding economic gains, most reservations are overcrowded and cannot offer adequate economic support to all their inhabitants.

EMPLOYMENT

The unemployment rate on reservations has been about 45 to 55 percent in recent years, sometimes reaching 80 percent in some places during certain seasons. This partially explains why the median Native American family income is about 40 percent of the national median.[25] In 1975, per capita income for Native Americans on reservations was only $1,573. Forty-six percent of all jobs on reservations are with various government agencies, more than three times the national average for government employment.[26] Government efforts to encourage industrial development on reservations have had only limited success. In addition, most new businesses are owned by outsiders and have a high attrition rate; the new industries prefer for the most part to hire women, thereby disrupting traditional family roles and injuring male pride.[27]

LIFE EXPECTANCY

The demographic statistics testify to the harshness and deprivation of reservation life, and the despair accompanying it.[28] The average life span of the Native American is about ten years less than the national average. The suicide rate among all Native Americans is twice the national average; that among young Native Americans, three times the national average; and that among boarding school students, five to seven times the national average. The infant mortality rate in 1970 was 30.9 per 1,000 live births for Indians, compared with 21.8 per 1,000 nationally.[29]

One explanation offered for the high suicide rate is the problems engendered by marginality.[30] Caught between two cultures, with assimilation unlikely and living as Native Americans difficult, the Native Americans are trapped in an unpleasant situation. According to Jack Bynum, inadequate acculturation and assimilation into the ways and society of whites has led to isolation, alienation, anomie, aggression, social disorganization of the minority subculture, and suicidal behavior.[31] Students at boarding schools are especially prone to suicide, as they experience extreme isolation and the denial of their culture and its values.

The most serious social problem among Native Americans on reservations, and a major factor in their high mortality rate, is alcohol consumption. Indians have a five times greater likelihood than the national average of dying of cirrhosis of the liver. The Indian Health Service reports that many accidents, suicides, and homicides are alcohol-related. Alcoholism is a major problem. The second greatest cause of death is accidents, usually by motor vehicle; this is three times the national average, and these deaths are also frequently alcohol-related.[32]

Excessive drinking among the Navaho, for example, is one of the tribe's greatest problems. Theodore D. Graves reported that their alcohol intake is almost seven times greater than that for Anglos and more than three times greater than that for persons of Spanish descent.[33] Frances N. Ferguson cited a distinguished Navaho medicine man who estimated that 30 percent of the Navaho population drink to excess.[34] Strong peer pressures — refusal to buy a drink is an affront subject to ridicule — and lack of strong sanctions in Navaho society — a reluctance to interfere in another's behavior — appear to be contributing factors.[35]

EDUCATION

From 50 to 60 percent of all Indian children drop out of school before completing the twelfth grade, compared with a national average of 23 percent. Reasons for this include an unresponsive educational system, a poor curriculum, and inadequately trained educational personnel, but some improvements are being made in these areas.[36] The major difficulties occur in BIA boarding schools, currently attended by over 30,000 Indian children. Still other students attend off-reservation public schools but are housed in BIA dormitories. Some children are sent several hundred miles from home (Alaskan Indian children thousands of miles) and are often kept away from their families for the entire school year. Many become runaways, suicides, or dropouts. Off-reservation schools appear to be a carryover from the past BIA practice of removing children from the main socializing agency — the family. Observers have reported seeing children rounded up at the beginning of the school year to be sent away. If they hide in the hills, BIA officials threaten to stop the parents' checks unless or until they produce their missing offspring for school.

In the fall of 1969, a Special Senate Subcommittee on Indian Education issued a scathing report on the BIA school system. This report, which was largely ignored, offered powerful arguments supporting Indian self-determination.

We are shocked at what we discovered. . . .

We have developed page after page of statistics. These cold figures mark a stain on our national conscience, a stain which has spread slowly for hundreds of years. They tell a story, to be sure. But they cannot tell the whole story. They cannot, for example, tell of the despair, the frustration, the hopelessness, the poignancy, of children who want to learn but are not taught; of adults who try to read but have no one to teach them; of families which want to stay together but are forced apart; or of 9-year-old children who want neighborhood schools but are sent thousands of miles away to remote and alien boarding schools.

We have seen what these conditions do to Indian children and Indian families. The sights are not pleasant.

We have concluded that our national policies for educating American Indians are a failure of major proportions. They have not offered Indian children — either in years past or today — an educational opportunity anywhere near equal to that offered the great bulk of American children. Past generations of lawmakers and administrators have failed the American Indian. Our own generation thus faces a challenge — we can continue the unacceptable policies and programs of the past or we can recognize our failures, renew our commitments, and reinvest our efforts with new energy.

. . . Creative, imaginative, and above all, relevant educational experiences can blot the stain on our national conscience. This is the challenge the subcommittee believes faces our own generation.[37]

In 1976 the American Indian Policy Review Commission issued a report on education criticizing the BIA for not acting to remedy any of the problems the subcommittee had pointed out.[38] Particularly singled out were the 19 boarding schools, which the Commission called "dumping grounds for students with serious social and emotional problems" that "do not rehabilitate" but "do more harm than good."[39]

The Commission reported that the official BIA policy of sending students to the school closest to home is in reality not practiced.[40] Alaskan Indian children have been sent to Fort Sill, Oklahoma. Others who are classified as "problems," such as the girl in Washington State who objected to a history test that called her ancestors "dirty savages," are also sent to distant boarding schools. In another report, the Commission also criticized the locations of the schools:

> The sites of these schools were determined not merely by financial considerations of the Government, but by the conscious intention of forcing a separation between Indian parents and children and between Indian children and the idea of the reservation.[41]

Others have frequently commented on the teaching of American culture and history in reservation schools and on insensitivity and nonreceptivity to Native American culture and history. One typical example is a composition given to Chippewa children at a reservation school in the Northwest: "Why we are all happy the Pilgrims landed."

HOUSING

One of the most visible signs of deprivation is reservation housing, which some have referred to as "open air slums." In 1967, 90 percent of Native American housing was unacceptable by any standard.[42] The 1970 census revealed that half the housing units had no bathrooms and a third lacked any interior water supply.[43] Most of those who obtain their water outside the house must haul it a mile or more.[44] Some small gains have been made since 1970, but the overall need for improvement is still significant.

RED POWER

As Alvin M. Josephy, Jr., a distinguished observer of Indian history and life, has noted, the Indians have never been silent about their needs and wishes.[45] Beginning with Seneca Chief Red Jacket's visit to Washington in 1792, Indians have repeatedly tried to tell the federal authorities what their people wanted and what was acceptable to them. Since they were seen as savages, the Indians found that government representatives usually ignored their views. When the forced removal programs and the bloodshed came to an end in the late nineteenth century, the government began trying to change the reservation Indians' way of life, to eliminate their poverty, and to encourage further integration. In the twentieth century, Indian militancy was quite rare until the

1960s. In the mid-1960s the Indians changed their approach, partly because the social climate was different. Many social forces were at work — the civil rights movement, the Vietnam protest, the idealism of the Great Society, and a growing social awareness in society itself. Perhaps taking their cue from other movements, a new generation of Native American leaders asserted themselves.

PAN-INDIANISM

This recent social movement, which attempts to establish an American Indian ethnic identity instead of just a tribal identity, has its roots in the past. The growing Iroquois Confederation of the seventeenth century, the mobility and social interaction among the Plains Indians in the nineteenth century, and the spread of the Ghost Dance religion were all early examples of Pan-Indianism. As Indian youths found comfort in one another's presence, first in boarding schools and later in urban areas, they found a commonality in their identity as Indians.

From this emerging group consciousness evolved several organizations dedicated to preserving Indian identity and gaining greater political clout. The Society of American Indians (SAI) and the National Congress of American Indians (NCAI) were the first twentieth-century attempts to organize. More recently, the National Indian Youth Council (NIYC) and the American Indian Movement (AIM) have attracted many young people who object to discrimination and white domination. The NIYC staged fish-ins to protest treaty violations of Indian rights in Washington State. In the ensuing legal battle, the Supreme Court ultimately ruled in favor of the Indians.

The Pan-Indian movement has not been completely accepted, however, even among young people. Many Native Americans are anxious to preserve their tribal identities and prefer to work for the cultural enrichment and social betterment of their own tribe rather than to engage in a national movement. As part of this tribal emphasis, these individuals also learn and teach their people silversmithing, pottery and blanket making, and other crafts that are part of their heritage. In an effort to increase tribal pride and economic welfare, they also establish cultural centers to exhibit and sell their artistic works and wares.

ALCATRAZ

On November 20, 1969, a group of 78 Indians under the name "Indians of all Tribes" occupied Alcatraz Island, a former federal prison. This move, the first militant Indian action in the twentieth century, was both symbolic and an effort to establish a cultural center. The sarcasm in this excerpt from their proclamation was meant to dramatize the plight of the American Indians and the forced assimilation they so deeply resented.

We will give to the inhabitants of this island a portion of that land for their own, to hold in perpetuity — for as long as the sun shall rise and the rivers go down to the sea. We will further guide the inhabitants in the proper way of living. We will offer them our religion, our education, our life-ways, in order to help them achieve our level of civilization and thus raise them and all their white brothers up from their savage and unhappy state. We offer this treaty in good faith and wish to be fair and honorable in our dealings with all white men.

We feel that this so-called Alcatraz Island is more than suitable for an Indian Reservation, as determined by the white man's own standards. By this we mean that this place resembles most Indian reservations in that:

1. It is isolated from modern facilities, and without adequate means of transportation.

2. It has no fresh running water.

3. It has inadequate sanitation facilities.

4. There are no oil or mineral rights.

5. There is no industry and so unemployment is very great.

6. There are no health care facilities.

7. The soil is rocky and nonproductive; and the land does not support game.

8. There are no education facilities.

9. The population has always exceeded the land base.

10. The population has always been held as prisoners and kept dependent upon others.

Further, it would be fitting and symbolic that ships from all over the world, entering the Golden Gate, would first see Indian land, and thus be reminded of the true history of this nation. This tiny island would be a symbol of the great lands once ruled by free and noble Indians.[46]

This militant action did not succeed. The group's cohesiveness collapsed when the 12-year-old daughter of its leader, Michael Oakes, a Mohawk, accidentally fell down an elevator shaft on the island and died. Oakes, the unifying and motivating force, left Alcatraz with his daughter's body. Federal authorities then stepped in and removed the Indians. Oakes himself was later shot to death in California, supposedly mistaken for a trespasser. Today Alcatraz Island is a tourist attraction as a former prison, and its conversion to a gambling casino has been discussed.

BLUE LAKE

The story of the sacred Indian lands at and near Blue Lake in New Mexico is noteworthy because it illustrates how Indian efforts within the system can occasionally be effective. In 1906 the federal government appropriated these lands, without compensation, to create a national forest. Since the fourteenth century the Taos tribe had regarded this land as a religious site. The Forest Service, which was managing the land, attempted to restrain Indian access and to encourage non-Indians to use the land. The Indian Claims Commission upheld the Taos claim to the area, but the Taos insisted upon getting their land back rather than accepting a money settlement. The Department of Agriculture strongly opposed this action as a dangerous precedent, although the Department of the Interior supported it. Finally, at President Nixon's urging, Congress enacted legislation in 1970 returning 48,000 acres to the Taos Pueblo Indians.

WOUNDED KNEE

On February 27, 1973, about two hundred members of the American Indian Movement seized control of the village of Wounded Knee, South Dakota, taking 11 hostages. The location was symbolic, since Wounded Knee had been the site of the last Indian resistance in 1890, when one hundred and fifty Sioux, including men, women, and children, were massacred by the U.S. Cavalry. Many were killed from behind, and the wounded were left to die in a blizzard the following night.[47]

A 71-day siege following the seizure was a staged media event aimed at directing national attention to the plight of the Native Americans. Some Native American leaders criticized the action as rash, but most Native Americans appeared to be in sympathy with it. The holdout ended May 8, 1973, with two Indians killed, injuries on both sides, including a U.S. marshal paralyzed, and $240,000 in damages to property.[48]

Several months later the leaders — Dennis Banks, a Chippewa, and Russell Means, a Sioux — were brought to trial on charges directly related to the siege at Wounded Knee. The presiding judge dismissed all charges, severely criticizing the FBI and the Justice Department for misconduct in withholding or doctoring documents, illegal wiretaps, and spending money on liquor and women for a Native American pro-government witness.

Among other things, the militants had demanded that the government deal with the Sioux on the basis of an 1868 treaty that guaranteed them dominion over the vast Northern Plains between the Missouri River and the Rocky Mountains, land which the U.S. government confiscated in

FIGURE 6.2

Top photo shows band of Indians led by Big Foot, assembled for a dance in August 1890. Nearly all were later killed at Wounded Knee. Bottom photo shows bodies on battleground at Wounded Knee following the massacre on December 29, 1890. (United Press International)

1876. That Indian land claim has been described by Sioux representatives as the "largest, most historically and socially significant and, in terms of time taken in the courts, the oldest Indian land claim on record." Although pending before various courts since 1920, it was not until July 1979 that the U.S. Court of Claims, in the largest court settlement ever awarded to Native Americans, awarded compensation payment of more than $100 million to 60,000 Sioux. However, many Sioux have demanded the return to them of the sacred Black Hills instead of a cash settlement.

THE COURTS

In recent years Native Americans have increasingly succeeded, from the Atlantic to the Pacific, when they have pressed their claims to land, water, and mineral rights based upon old laws and treaties. An early precedent occurred in July 1950, when the U.S. Court of Claims awarded $31,200,000 to the Colorado Ute for lands illegally taken from them. This amounted to about $10,000 for every man, woman, and child in the tribe.

In spring 1977 the Passamaquoddy and Penobscot laid claim to about 5 million acres, or nearly one-third of Maine. The Carter administration threw its support behind the Indians and in 1978 reached an out-of-court settlement: $25 million cash, $1.7 million a year for 15 years, and 300,000 acres at $5 an acre. The basis for these claims was that the Indian land had been bargained away in violation of the Nonintercourse Act of 1790, which reserved to Congress the power to negotiate with Indian tribes. Indians are pushing other claims throughout many other Eastern states and as far south as South Carolina. In the Pacific Northwest federal courts have been upholding Indian fishing rights to the steelhead and salmon, based upon treaties over one hundred years old.

BUREAU OF INDIAN AFFAIRS

The BIA, a government agency, can trace its origin to 1824. It has many critics, among Native Americans as well as among federal officials, sociologists, and anthropologists. Some view it as a bureaucracy staffed by some able, dedicated people who are restricted and frustrated by an inefficient organization and by self-serving, unsympathetic people who simply do not belong there.

There are undoubtedly weak, poor, and inefficient men within the Bureau. Some enter the system, especially at the area level, by patronage: some should never have been employed by the Bureau;

some are poor because of inadequate training and orientation after they were employed; and some were good originally but, after many frustrations and defeats, gave up.... One of the scores of "weaknesses," with which it appears unable to cope, is the continued presence within the Bureau of key personnel who long since should have been removed from it. ... Many members of Indian communities are driven to desperation, some even to suicide, as a result of ineptitude, indifference or lethargy on the part of a poor superintendent or area official. Yet the record of the 1960's contains documentation of Commissioner Nash turning down Indian appeals to relieve them of intolerable agency personnel by telling them he would not remove a man while he was under fire, and of Commissioner Bennett answering tribal complaints of frustration and negativism with the retort that he was not interested in discussing "criticism of the BIA."[49]

Native American hostility toward the BIA goes beyond complaints about unsympathetic, incompetent, or even patronizing personnel; it is directed against its very structure. Although different government agencies touch all Americans in some ways, few non-Indians realize how totally the BIA dominates Native Americans' lives, as President Nixon's address and the Senate Subcommittee Report indicated. Every tribal decision throughout the United States is subject to BIA veto. A BIA official's mere supposition that certain individuals cannot properly handle their money or their personal affairs is sufficient to require formal BIA approval of any transactions those persons make. The BIA makes all decisions about school locations, staffing, and student residence. Additionally, all other aspects of Native American life — such as housing and economic development — are also the domain of the BIA. Only by comprehending the total pervasiveness of this bureaucracy can one begin to fathom the dependence, despair, and frustration the system engenders.

The problems inherent in all bureaucracies exist in the Bureau of Indian Affairs as well, and therein lies the problem of a complex organization running people's lives. Robert K. Merton has pointed out that working in a bureaucracy has a tendency to affect one's personality.[50] The very structure of a formal organization, with its hierarchy of authority, limitations on individual responsibility, specified work procedures, and emphasis upon objective criteria, encourages conformity to ongoing practices. To ensure job security and the approval of superiors, employees tend to follow guidelines rigidly. The means of achieving goals, rather than the goals themselves, become the point of emphasis. When criticisms mount, organization members become defensive and engage in obfuscation to ward off the outside pressures.

FIGURE 6.3

About 500 occupied the Bureau of Indian Affairs building in Washington, D.C., in 1972 to protest broken treaties and other actions of the whites. (United Press International)

Yet Native Americans have mixed feelings about the BIA. They dislike many of its practices, but it is all they have, and so many oppose dismantling it. Vine Deloria, Jr., points out that dismantling the BIA would only lead to further deterioration of Native American conditions and loss of their remaining lands.[51] The disastrous termination policy showed what can happen when the government withdraws its support. Restoration of tribal sovereignty, or self-determination without termination as recommended by President Nixon, is the approach most favored today.

Still, little has changed since President Nixon's historic message to Congress in 1970, as Congress has failed to enact the necessary legislation. At that time there was a slight shakeup at the BIA, ostensibly to increase Indian self-determination. However, little really changed, as the American Indian Policy Review Commission, made up of 10 executives from private industry, indicated in its report to Congress in 1976. It concluded that every area of personnel management in the BIA was "inadequate" and recommended a massive restructuring to bring decision-making closer to the tribal level.[52]

URBAN NATIVE AMERICANS

Not all Indians live on reservations. Although it is difficult to locate and identify the Indians who live in the more urbanized regions of the West Coast and in the Eastern states and the Midwest, the government estimates that there may now be more than 400,000 of them. In New York City, a metropolis hardly considered to be Indian territory any longer, there are more than 10,000 Native Americans. Chicago, Cleveland, Denver, Detroit, St. Louis, Los Angeles, Minneapolis, Omaha, Phoenix, San Francisco, and Seattle all have large Native American populations also, many of them exceeding 10,000. Most live a non-Indian existence, with reservation life either a distant memory or known only through relatives' stories.

One interesting Eastern public image of the urban Native American is that of the Iroquois ironworkers, who regularly work high atop the structural steel frames of skyscrapers being built in the urban centers. While this group has a colorful image, most urban Native Americans are less visible to the non–Native American society. Consequently they have not received as much attention from sociologists as have those on reservations.[53] Urban living, however, helped to spawn the Pan-Indian movement. Contact with members of other tribes raised a group consciousness of being Indian, which led to an attempt to improve the lot of all by united action.

Though they are more widely scattered in residence than are the blacks or Chicanos, approximately three-fourths of the urban Native

Americans live in poverty in the poorer sections of the cities. Their migration to urban areas has intensified in the last 15 years; almost half of the nation's Native Americans, especially those from 20 to 40 years old, have left the overpopulated reservations to seek better economic opportunities.[54]

Although urban Native Americans are not gathered in ethnic enclaves, all their other behavior patterns are similar to those of European immigrants. Situated in a social arena where they are the minority, they experience the culture shock of urban living away from the solidarity of the tribe. This shock sometimes leads to personal disorientation, and they seldom get relief or assistance from the dominant society.

A recent incident in Los Angeles highlights the problem of adjustment. A newly-arrived Navaho, who spoke no English, became quite ill, and on the street approached a woman wearing a white uniform, in the belief that she was a nurse. The woman, a beautician, thought she was being attacked and had the Indian arrested. Unable to communicate with the man, the police placed him in a hospital where he was classified as an insane Mexican-American.[55]

The newcomers often seek out other Native Americans, usually of the same tribe, and frequent the same bars. Drunkenness is as serious a problem in the cities as on the reservations. The Native Americans suffer from lack of preparedness, disorientation, and lack of job skills, and as a result seek solace in drink from the harshness of the "cement prairies." In an in-depth study of Navaho migrants in Denver, Theodore D. Graves found drunkenness to be common as a result of structural and psychological variables. The Navaho had great difficulty adjusting to city life because their parents had not been role models for urban employment and because their cultural attitudes were dysfunctional for the work environment.[56] Custom and tradition, peer pressure, and drinking role models help to explain why they take out their frustration in drink.

Although urban Indians interact with whites, these relationships tend to be superficial and functional rather than intimate. Bruce A. Chadwick and Joseph H. Strauss, for example, found a fairly low level of assimilation among urban Indians in Seattle, especially in terms of political participation and conflict with the dominant power structure. They found no relation between length of time lived in the city and degree of structural assimilation. For almost all, assimilation was quite low.[57]

Indians who succeed in adapting to urban living, usually over a two- to three-year period, settle into semiskilled or skilled jobs. Once they have gained some economic security, they frequently move out of the city to racially mixed suburban areas. While this shows some degree of acculturation and convergent social adaptation, other evidence suggests this trend is a limited one. Many middle-class urban-adapted Indians form their own ethnic institutions, including churches, powwow clubs, social centers, and athletic leagues.[58]

From the Pueblo, the first penthouse dwellers in the United States, to the city-dwelling Native American of today, urban living does not appear to have encouraged more rapid movement into the mainstream of American society. Today's urban Native Americans are relatively invisible, but that does not necessarily mean they have assimilated. There may have been some degree of acculturation, but most urban Native Americans attempt to preserve their ethnic identity and do not interact socially with non–Native Americans to any noticeable degree.

ENERGY DEMANDS

Trappers, settlers, oil drillers, and large companies have continually encroached upon Indian territory to obtain natural resources or fertile land. The situation is no different today. The need for water and energy has led government and industry to look covetously at reservation land once considered worthless. In July 1978, two thousand Native Americans participated in a 2,700-mile march to Washington, D.C. There they demonstrated against several proposed bills that would have allowed strip mining and siphoning of ground water from tribal land, and increased state police jurisdiction over the reservations.

The 53 million acres held by 22 Western tribes contain much of the nation's richest reserves of natural gas, oil, coal, and uranium, worth billions of dollars. In fact, one-third of the nation's low-sulfur coal and almost all the known uranium deposits are on tribal land. For some tribes, such as the oil-rich Osage in Oklahoma, the benefits are real. Other impoverished tribes, such as the Navaho, are only now beginning to benefit, because for a long time the Indians did not gain much from their ownership. The government's own watchdog, the General Accounting Office, has criticized the Bureau of Indian Affairs for frequently failing to protect Native American interests when it encouraged and approved extraction of natural resources. The experiences of just two tribes, the Northern Cheyenne and the Navaho, illustrate present-day efforts to victimize the Native Americans for their land's riches.

NORTHERN CHEYENNE

Much of the 440,000-acre Cheyenne Reservation in Montana sits atop a 60-foot-deep deposit of high-quality coal. At BIA urging, the tribe approved a vaguely worded agreement that gave industry virtual carte blanche to use 243,808 acres — more than half the reservation. The company was free to strip mine and to build railroad lines, vast industrial complexes of power and conversion plants, and non-Indian towns for its workers. As the mammoth consequences became known to the Cheyenne and to environmentalists, organized, successful opposition arose to contain this development and protect the land.

NAVAHO

The Navaho were a small band when the Spaniards arrived, but today they number over 140,000. They live on 15 million acres of land, mostly barren and badly eroded, in Utah, Arizona, and New Mexico. Despite income from natural gas and uranium deposits, the Navaho are among the poorest Indians in the United States. Their family income is only about one-fourth that of the rest of the country. As late as 1970, only one home in three had electricity and only one in five had running water and indoor plumbing.

When the United States wanted large quantities of water from Navaho lands for the purpose of energy production, the Navaho suffered as a consequence. The Navaho, like the Pueblo and other Western tribes, have primarily an agricultural economy. The treaty of 1868 guaranteed them basic water rights, but costly dams and irrigation systems are necessary if their arid land is to be made more productive. Yet the U.S. Bureau of Reclamation and the Army Corps of Engineers, as they had done in other similar instances, built a dam upstream and diverted the water to non-Indian users. Not only was the economic growth of the underdeveloped Indian community thwarted, but the river water levels dropped and the fish were dying. Finally, in 1976, after completion of the first stage of a massive federal irrigation project, the Navaho began to get water to irrigate 110,630 arid acres of land in northwestern New Mexico.

CULTURAL IMPACT

Perhaps no other ethnic group has had as great an impact upon American culture as have the Native Americans, primarily because they were already here and the whites, who had to adapt to a new land, found it advantageous to learn from them. Cities, towns, counties, states, rivers, lakes, mountains, and other geographic entities by the thousands bear Indian names today. Over five hundred words in our language are Indian, including *wigwam, succotash, tobacco, papoose, chipmunk, squash, skunk, toboggan, oppossum, tomahawk, moose, mackinaw, hickory, pecan, raccoon, cougar, woodchuck,* and *hominy.*[59]

The Native Americans' knowledge of herbs and the more than eighty plants they domesticated brought whites a wide variety of new tastes. Native Americans introduced the Europeans to corn, white and sweet potatoes, kidney beans, tomatoes, peanuts, peppers, pumpkins, avocados, pineapples, maple sugar, chicle, and cacao, as well as tobacco and long-fiber cotton. The Native Americans' knowledge of medicinal plants is also part of their legacy.

At least fifty-nine drugs, including coca (for cocaine and no-vocaine), curare (a muscle relaxant), cinochona bark (the source of quinine), cascara sagrada (a laxative), datura (a pain-reliever), and ephedra (a nasal remedy), were bequeathed to modern medicine by the Indians.[60]

The Indians also made various other objects many Americans still use today. Some of these are canoes, kayaks, snowshoes, toboggans, moccasins, hammocks, pipes, parkas, ponchos, dog sleds, and rubber syringes. Indian influence upon jewelry, clothing, art, architecture, literature, and Scouting is substantial. "Iron Eyes" Cody, an Indian actor, appears in a television campaign against littering, and symbolizes the likeness between traditional Indian reverence for the land and the positions that conservationists support today. The Iroquois influence upon House-Senate conferences as detailed in the Constitution has already been mentioned. Additionally, a new appreciation and adaptation of Indian child-rearing practices, group-directed activities, cooperatives, and ministrations to a patient's mental state are occurring.[61]

RETROSPECT

The white strangers who came among the Indians eventually outnumbered them, overpowered them, and changed their way of life. Once a proud and independent people, they were reduced to a state of poverty, despair, and dependency. The land they had known so well and roamed so freely was no longer theirs. Forced to live within an alien society that dominated all aspects of their lives, the Indians became strangers in their native land. Misunderstood and categorized as savages, they observed the taken-for-granted world of the whites more keenly than most whites did theirs.

Physical and cultural differences quickly became the basis for out-group hostility as the groups competed for land and resources. Like other groups, the Indians faced the familiar patterns of stereotyping, prejudice, discrimination, and conflict because of their alleged inferiority and actual lack of power. Isolation on the reservations not only prevented the assimilation that most Indians did not desire anyway, but it also created for them a world of dependency and deprivation. Subsequent efforts at forced assimilation — boarding schools, relocation, termination — failed because of Indian resiliency and the BIA's lack of thoroughness in personal preparation, assistance, and follow-through.

The Native Americans are still misunderstood and exploited. One, two, or three hundred years ago, those who did not live near the Indians idealized them, and those who were closest often abused and humiliated them. It is no different today. Many people are oblivious to the Native Americans' problems and consider them quaint relics of the past, and others find them either undesirable or else in the way. Some still want their land and will use almost any means to secure it. Native Americans still encounter discrimination in stores, bars, and housing, particularly in cities and near the reservations. They are frequently beaten or killed, and their property rights are infringed upon.

In the 1970s, some Native Americans have become more aggressive. Many young, better-educated Indians are forgetting tribal differences and finding a common bond — Pan-Indianism — uniting in the struggle to protect what they have and to restore what they have lost. Others prefer a more individualistic approach within the tribe. Some gains have been made and more non–Native Americans are becoming aware of the facts, but at present the Native Americans are still one of the poorest American minorities.

QUESTIONS FOR DISCUSSION

1. Why do some social scientists call the Native Americans the first victims of racism? Is racism an integral part of their experiences? Why?

2. Cite examples of ethnocentrism and stereotyping regarding Native Americans.

3. Why is the power differential so crucial in understanding the Native Americans' past and present problems?

4. Why have most government efforts to "help" the Native Americans failed?

5. In what ways can it be said that little has changed in the exploitation of the Native Americans?

SUGGESTED READINGS

Bahr, Howard M., Bruce A. Chadwick, and Robert C. Day (eds.). *Native Americans Today: Sociological Per-* *spectives.* Harper & Row, New York, 1972.

Brown, Dee. *Bury My Heart at*

Wounded Knee. Holt, New York, 1970.

Deloria, Vine, Jr. *Custer Died for Your Sins.* Avon, New York, 1969.

————. *We Talk, You Listen: New Tribes, New Turf.* Macmillan, New York, 1970.

Embry, Carlos B. *America's Concentration Camps.* McKay, New York, 1956.

Farb, Peter. *Man's Rise to Civilization.* Dutton, New York, 1968.

Fritz, Henry E. *The Movement for Indian Assimilation, 1860–1890.* University of Pennsylvania Press, Philadelphia, 1963.

Hertzberg, Hazel W. *The Search for an American Indian Identity.* Syracuse University Press, Syracuse, 1971.

Jahoda, Gloria. *The Trail of Tears.* Holt, New York, 1975.

Josephy, Alvin M. *The Indian Heritage of America.* Knopf, New York, 1968.

La Farge, Oliver. *Laughing Boy.* Houghton Mifflin, Boston, 1929.

Levine, Stuart, and Nancy O. Lurie (eds.). *The American Indian Today.* Penguin, Baltimore, 1972.

Manypenny, George W. *Our Indian Wards.* 1880. Reprint edition, Da Capo Press, New York, 1972.

Momaday, N. Scott. *House Made of Dawn.* Harper & Row, New York, 1968.

Shorris, Earl. *The Death of the Great Spirit.* Simon and Schuster, New York, 1971.

Van Every, Dale. *Disinherited: The Lost Birthright of the American Indian.* Discus Avon Books, New York, 1966.

Washburn, Wilcomb E. *The Indian in America.* Harper & Row, New York, 1975.

Wax, Murray L. *Indian Americans: Unity and Diversity.* Prentice-Hall, Englewood Cliffs, N.J., 1971.

NOTES

1. See Lee E. Huddleston, *Origins of the American Indians: European Concepts, 1492–1729,* University of Texas Press, Austin, 1967.
2. Bureau of Indian Affairs, "You Asked About . . . Facts About American Indians and Alaskan Natives," Washington, D.C., 1976.
3. John Boyd Thacher (ed.), *Christopher Columbus,* Vol. 1, AMS Press, Inc., New York, 1967, I, 533.
4. Michel de Montaigne, "Of Cannibals," Book I, Ch. 31, in *The Complete Works of Montaigne,* translated by Donald M. Frame, Stanford University Press, Stanford, Calif., 1957, pp. 150–159.
5. See Lewis Hanke, *The First Social Experiments in America: A Study in the Development of Spanish Indian Policy in the Sixteenth Century,* Peter Smith, Gloucester, Mass., 1964.
6. Douglas Edward Leach, *Flintlock and Tomahawk, New England in King Philip's War,* Norton, New York, 1958, pp. 20–22.
7. George Catlin, *Letters and Notes of the Manners, Customs and Conditions of the North American Indians* (London, 1841), Dover, New York, 1973, I, 102–103.
8. Peter Farb, *Man's Rise to Civilization as Shown by the Indians of North America from Primeval Times to the Coming of the Industrial State,* E. P. Dutton, New York, 1968, p. 128.
9. Wilcomb E. Washburn, *The Indian in America,* Harper & Row, New York, 1975, p. 32.
10. *Ibid.,* pp. 39–40.
11. See D'Arcy McNickle, *They Came Here First: The Epic of the American Indian,* J. B. Lippincott, Philadelphia, 1949, p. 128.
12. Anthony F. C. Wallace, *The Death*

and Rebirth of the Seneca, Knopf, New York, 1970, p. 38; John Axtell, "The Scholastic Philosophy of the Wilderness," *William and Mary Quarterly,* 29 (1972), 359.

13. Albert Britt, *Indian Chiefs,* Books for Libraries Press, Freeport, N.Y., 1969, p. 8.

14. *Ibid.,* p. 26.

15. See Keith H. Basso, " 'To Give Up on Words': Silence in Western Apache Culture," *Southwestern Journal of Anthropology,* 26 (1970), 213–230.

16. Alice Marriott and Carol K. Rachlin, *American Epic: The Story of the American Indian,* Mentor, New York, 1969, p. 114.

17. Dale Van Every, *Disinherited: The Lost Birthright of the American Indian,* Discus Avon Books, New York, 1966, p. 163.

18. James Mooney, *Myths of the Cherokee,* 19th Annual Report, Bureau of American Ethnology, Washington, D.C., 1900, p. 130.

19. James D. Richardson, *Messages and Papers of the President,* Washington, D.C., 1897, III, 497.

20. Farb, *Man's Rise to Civilization,* p. 309.

21. *Ibid.*

22. See Theodore Stern, *The Klamath Tribe,* University of Washington Press, Seattle, 1966.

23. Alvin M. Josephy, Jr., *The Indian Heritage of America,* Knopf, New York, 1968, p. 354.

24. Sar A. Levitan, William B. Johnston, and Robert Taggart, *Minorities in the United States: Problems, Progress and Prospects,* Public Affairs Press, Washington, D.C., 1975, p. 86.

25. Richard J. Margolis, "A Long List of Grievances," *The New York Times,* Nov. 12, 1972; *The New York Times,* Feb. 19, 1967, p. 33; Josephy, *The Indian Heritage of America,* p. 359; Bureau of Indian Affairs, "You Asked About . . ."

26. Levitan, et al., *Minorities in the United States,* pp. 84–85.

27. *Ibid.,* p. 91.

28. For an excellent depiction of the harshness of reservation life, see Murray Wax, *Indian-Americans: Unity and Diversity,* Prentice-Hall, Englewood Cliffs, N.J., 1971, pp. 65–87.

29. *The New York Times,* Nov. 12, 1972.

30. See the discussion on pp. 49–51.

31. Jack Bynum, "Suicide and the American Indian: An Analysis of Recent Trends," in *Native Americans Today: Sociological Perspectives,* eds. Howard M. Bahr, Bruce A. Chadwick, and Robert C. Day, Harper & Row, New York, 1972, p. 375.

32. Levitan, et al., *Minorities in the United States,* p. 88.

33. Theodore D. Graves, "Acculturation, Access, and Alcohol in a Tri-Ethnic Community," *American Anthropologist,* 69 (April 1967), 306–321.

34. Frances Northend Ferguson, "Navaho Drinking: Some Tentative Hypotheses," *Human Organization,* 27 (Summer 1968), 159–167.

35. Graves, "Acculturation, Access, and Alcohol in a Tri-Ethnic Community."

36. See Alvin M. Josephy, Jr., *Red Power,* McGraw-Hill, New York, 1971, p. 3; *The Indian Heritage of America,* p. 359.

37. 1969 Report of U.S. Senate Committee on Labor and Public Welfare, Special Subcommittee on Indian Education, quoted in Josephy, *Red Power,* pp. 156–157.

38. American Indian Policy Review Commission, "Report on Indian Education," Washington, D.C., 1976, p. 253.

39. *Ibid.,* p. 245.

40. *Ibid.,* p. 123.

41. American Indian Policy Review Commission, "Report on Urban and Rural Non-Reservation Indians," Washington, D.C., 1976, p. 25.

42. Josephy, *The Indian Heritage of America,* p. 359.

43. Levitan, et al., *Minorities in the United States,* p. 84.

44. Josephy, *The Indian Heritage of America*, p. 359.
45. Josephy, *Red Power*, p. 4.
46. Quoted in Morris Freedman and Carolyn Banks (eds.), *American Mix*, Lippincott, Philadelphia, 1972, pp. 46–47.
47. See Dee Brown, *Bury My Heart at Wounded Knee*, Holt, New York, 1970.
48. "Wounded Knee: The Media Coup d'Etat," *Nation*, 216 (June 25, 1973), 807.
49. Alvin M. Josephy, Jr., "The American Indian and the Bureau of Indian Affairs," Special Report to the President, Feb. 11, 1969, Sec. V.
50. Robert K. Merton, *Social Theory and Social Structure*, Free Press, Glencoe, Ill., 1957, p. 197 ff.
51. Vine Deloria, Jr., *Custer Died for Your Sins*, Avon, New York, 1970, p. 145.
52. American Indian Policy Review Commission, "Report on Trust Responsibilities and Federal-Indian Relations, Including Treaty Review," Washington, D.C., 1976, pp. 3–6.
53. See Howard M. Bahr, "An End to Visibility," in *Native Americans Today*, pp. 404–407. One significant exception is Edmund Wilson, *Apologies to the Iroquois*, Farrar, Straus and Cudahy, New York, 1960. This book includes Joseph Mitchell's study, "The Mohawks in High Steel."
54. American Indian Policy Review Commission, "Report on Urban and Rural Non-Reservation Indians," p. 35.
55. John A. Price, "The Migration and Adaptation of American Indians to Los Angeles," *Human Organization*, 27 (Summer 1968), 168–175.
56. Theodore D. Graves, "The Personal Adjustment of Navaho Indian Migrants to Denver, Colorado," *American Anthropologist*, 72 (1970), 35–54.
57. Bruce A. Chadwick and Joseph H. Strauss, "The Assimilation of American Indians into Urban Society: The Seattle Case," *Human Organization*, 34 (Winter 1975), 359–369. See also Joan Ablon, "Relocated American Indians in the San Francisco Bay Area: Social Interaction and Indian Identity," *Human Organization*, 23 (Winter 1964), 296–304.
58. John A. Price, "North American Indian Families," in *Ethnic Families in America*, eds. Charles H. Mindel and Robert W. Haberstein, Elsevier, New York, 1976, p. 266.
59. Josephy, *The Indian Heritage of America*, p. 32.
60. *Ibid.*
61. *Ibid.*, p. 34.

SEVEN

THE ASIAN IMMIGRANTS

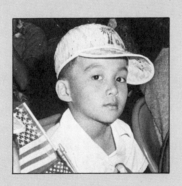

⨼ Asian immigrants experienced the same dominant-group reaction as many other immigrant groups. Readily perceived as strangers because of their physical and cultural differences, they were broadly categorized as a single entity — Orientals — despite their diversity of nationality, history, language, customs, religion, politics, personality, and subgroup variances. The Asian groups also differed in rural-urban spread, occupations, ghettoization, life styles, and experiences with prejudice. Because so many of them encountered racial discrimination and suffered from a generalized negative image, many Asian-Americans today object to the designation "Oriental," looking upon it as an ethnic slur.

HISTORICAL AND SOCIOLOGICAL PERSPECTIVES

Asians had some contact with the land and peoples of the Western Hemisphere before the beginning of recorded emigration in the mid-nineteenth century. Pottery and other archaeological finds suggest Japanese contact with Ecuador and Peru in 3000 B.C., and Chinese settlements in Mexico can be dated from the latter part of the Ming Dynasty (1368–1644). China played a role in early United States history, as New England merchants sought a monopoly on the lucrative China trade, an issue that became important in the struggle for American independence. Chinese sailors served on United States ships in the early 1800s, and a short-lived Chinese colony was established at Nootka Sound in 1792. The first United States Consul outside the Western Hemisphere was Samuel Shaw, assigned to Canton in 1794.

The Chinese first came to the United States during the gold rush (1849); Japanese, Koreans, and Pilipinos came to the West Coast at least a generation later to seek their fortune. Some came to stay, but many came as sojourners, intending to return home after a limited work engagement. This view of America as a temporary overseas job opportunity, together with the white racism they faced and, in the case of the Chinese, a tradition of separate associations wherever they went, led the early Asian immigrants to form subsocieties. Throughout the first third of the twentieth century, when many Asians sought permanent residence in the United States, structural discrimination sharply limited their work and life opportunities.

The several different peoples among the immigrants came from quite distinct cultural backgrounds and, depending upon when they migrated, encountered different socioeconomic situations in the United States. Three important considerations dominate their respective experiences as minority groups: structural conditions, economic competition, and racism.

STRUCTURAL CONDITIONS

The Chinese encountered racist hostility almost as soon as they arrived in California, despite the overwhelming need for manual labor in the mid-nineteenth century. They were often expelled from the mining camps, forbidden to enter schools, denied the right to testify in court, barred from obtaining citizenship, and even occasionally murdered. After the Civil War, anti-Chinese tensions increased, culminating in the Chinese Exclusion Act of 1882. The Japanese, Koreans, and Pilipinos who came to the West Coast later encountered racism and discrimination similar to that which the Chinese had faced. Many of them went to work as farm laborers in rural areas or as unskilled workers in urban areas.

A major social problem affecting most Asian immigrants through the 1940s was the shortage of women. Not only was this imbalance in the sex ratio significant in their personal, social, and community life; it also was the basis for racist complaints about prostitution or miscegenation. For the Chinese, the sojourner orientation, the custom that wives should remain in the household of the husband's parents, and subsequent immigration restrictions mostly account for this disproportionate sex ratio. By the turn of the century, the shortage of women had led to the rise of brothels in Chinatowns, and the Chinese were condemned for resorting to prostitutes. The Pilipinos were also mostly male and thus affected by the shortage of women. Whether the Asians patronized prostitutes or sought the company of white women, racists expressed moral indignation, and negative racial stereotypes resulted. Legislators in 14 states passed laws against miscegenation to keep Asians from marrying whites.

By 1920, the Japanese sex ratio was largely balanced. Following the Second World War, a greater number of females migrated to the United States, and the sex ratio for other Asian immigrant groups improved. Refugees and war brides from the Japanese, Korean, and Vietnamese wars account for part of the change, as do the brides of servicemen stationed overseas during the intervening years. The Immigration Act of 1965, in its relative-preference provisions, ensures both sexes equal opportunity to enter the United States.

After World War II, immigrants from these countries and from other parts of Southeast Asia were entering a much more industrialized American society. Many also came from lands that had been somewhat affected by Western influence. Some were political refugees, better educated and more skilled than earlier Asian immigrants. Many of these immigrants continued to prefer living in California, while others moved to the East Coast or elsewhere. Entering various occupations, these postwar immigrants were spared the violent hostility of previous times, although they still encountered resentment and discrimination.

ECONOMIC COMPETITION

Ethnic antagonism usually increases whenever the economy turns downward and jobs become scarce. Once the Chinese were accused of competing with whites, particularly in the post–Civil War period, vilification and hostility increased. Similarly, the experiences of the Japanese in the late nineteenth and early twentieth centuries resulted from labor antagonism as well as from fears of Japan's military power and industrial prowess. The negative comments of many Americans about permitting thousands of Vietnamese refugees to enter the United States were at least in part based upon fear of the effect their presence would have on an already depressed labor market. When there is economic competition among distinct racial or ethnic groups for a limited number of jobs, latent prejudices become overt, and discrimination often follows. Unless structural conditions can reduce or eliminate the source of the tensions (for example, if there is an economic upturn or government programs are started), open hostility, xenophobia, and violence may follow.

RACISM

Racism may be defined as linking the biological conditions of a human organism with its sociocultural capabilities and behavior. Race, in and of itself, becomes the basis for judgment, a simplistic "explanation" of a very complex situation. The chapters on the American Indians and the southern Europeans showed how much racism could affect relations between the minority group and the host society. The Asian experience in the United States is also a vivid example of how racism can be a key factor in influencing relations between groups that are physically different.

Many of the problems the Asian immigrants encountered, like the problems faced by blacks and American Indians, can, in large measure, be traced to the tendency to base attitudes on skin color. When accentuated by labor troubles, the racism becomes much more apparent in the dominant group's words and actions. If a racially distinct group is perceived as an economic threat, its members' distinguishing physical characteristics often become the basis for scapegoating as well as stereotyping.

THE CHINESE

Americans on both sides of the continent knew something about the Chinese long before they first came to the United States. The United

States had established trade relations with China as early as 1785, and a great many Protestant missionaries had been sent there after 1807. Newspaper reports and magazine articles, inspired by the Anglo-Chinese War (1839–1842) and subsequent rebellions and incidents, gave lurid descriptions of filth, disease, cruel tortures, and executions. The American people gradually developed an unfavorable image of the Chinese. In 1842, seven years before the gold rush, the *Encyclopedia Britannica* gave an unflattering portrait of the Chinese people:

> A Chinaman is cold, cunning and distrustful; always ready to take advantage of those he has to deal with; extremely covetous and deceitful; quarrelsome, vindictive, but timid and dastardly. A Chinaman in office is a strange compound of insolence and meanness. All ranks and conditions have a total disregard for truth.[2]

STRUCTURAL CONDITIONS

Most of the Chinese who came to the United States in the nineteenth century were farmers, artisans, craftsmen, political exiles, and refugees. The discovery of gold in California proved to be an opportunity not only for easterners and Europeans but also for the Chinese from Kwangtung, who could get out easily, and who sought to recoup their losses from flood, famine, and the Tai Ping Revolution (1850–1864). A combination of push-pull factors thus brought the Chinese to the United States. Chinese males set out alone, often leaving wives and children within the village and the kinship circle of the extended family. The first wave of migrants came as sojourners, intending to earn some money and then return home.

The Chinese were visible because of their race, and their appearance and behavior aroused both curiosity and suspicion. The sounds and characters of their language seemed most peculiar to the non-Chinese, as did their religions. Their "strange" clothes and hair worn in queues also seemed out of place in the crude pioneer surroundings. Since they had little or no command of English, kept mostly to themselves, and viewed California as a temporary workplace, the Chinese remained an enigma to most Americans.

When the Chinese began arriving in greater numbers in the late 1850s, the surface gold deposits were becoming exhausted. The white miners left these low-yield diggings to the Chinese, who in the 1860s moved on to become railroad construction workers, ranch hands, farm laborers, domestic servants, unskilled workers in the factories that had started to spring up, and anything else at which they could find work. Back in 1852, their industriousness had prompted Governor John MacDougall to praise them before the California legislature as the "most desirable of our adopted citizens" and to call for a land grant system to encourage more to come. However, the Chinese were not permitted to become U.S. citizens, and their reception in the years that followed could hardly be called a welcome.

By 1860, California's population had a large and varied ethnic segment. About 38 percent were foreign-born, and many others were Spanish-speaking natives or children of European immigrants.[3] The Chinese constituted about 9 percent of the state's population in 1860, but because they were mostly adult males, they represented close to 25 percent of the labor force at that time.[4] As the general population increased, the percentage of the total and working population that they represented decreased.

Hired as laborers who worked in gangs, the Chinese at this time helped to build the western portion of the transcontinental railroad for the Central Pacific. As many as nine thousand Chinese a year toiled through the High Sierra country, digging tunnels and laying tracks, and the task was completed sooner than expected. Leland Stanford, then president of the Central Pacific Railroad, described the Chinese as "quiet, peaceable, industrious, economical." While Chinese laborers received the same wages as non-Chinese, they fed and housed themselves, unlike the white workers, thereby costing the railroad company only two-thirds as much as whites.[5] The Chinese did not, however, pose an economic threat to the non-Chinese workers, who found their jobs upgraded.

> Hiring Chinese resulted not in displacement of non-Chinese but in their upgrading. To the unskilled white railroad laborer of 1865, the coming of the Chinese meant his own advancement into that elite one-fifth of the labor force composed of strawbosses, foremen, teamsters, skilled craftsmen. And one final reason was perhaps more cogent than all the others. No man with any choice would have chosen to be a common laborer on the Central Pacific during the crossing of the High Sierra.[6]

At the same time the railroad was being built, West Coast manufacturing was increasing. Wartime demands on Eastern industries and the high cost of transporting Eastern goods encouraged this growth.[7] A shortage of available women and children prompted the textile industry to hire many Chinese.[8] The end of the Civil War brought veterans seeking jobs and Eastern manufacturing concerns seeking West Coast markets, helped by efficient, low-cost shipment of goods over the transcontinental railroad. Fired when their work was completed, Chinese railroad laborers sought other jobs, but the economic conditions worsened, culminating in the Panic of 1873. Labor supply exceeded demand, and racist arguments of laborers, union organizers, and demagogues mounted against Chinese "competition."

Some of the ethnophaulisms directed against the Chinese during this period of labor agitation dealt with their being "dirty" and "disease-ridden." These epithets had originated decades earlier. In the 1840s Americans first became aware of the relationship between germs and dirt and disease. Negative stereotypes about the supposed Chinese preference for eating vermin, and crowded, unsanitary Chinatowns caused the Chinese to be associated with leprosy, cholera, and bubonic plague. By the 1870s the labor issue had become predominant, but as the labor unions joined together against the Chinese, they labeled them a menace to both the economy and the health of the society. The *real* issue by 1877 was race, disguised as labor conflict.

SOCIETAL REACTIONS

Racist attacks against the Chinese continued throughout the second half of the nineteenth century. Some compared their "racial inferiority" with that of the blacks, and others attacked the "vices" of the Oriental race. In the 1850s one anti-slavery Southerner had attempted to draw parallels among several groups that were supposedly inferior:

No inferior race of men can exist in these United States without becoming subordinate to the will of the Anglo-Americans. . . . It is so with the Negroes in the South; it is so with the Irish in the North; it is so with the Indians in New England; and it will be so with the Chinese in California. . . . I should not wonder, at all, if the copper of the Pacific yet becomes as great a subject of discord and dissension as the ebony of the Atlantic.[9]

Cries for restrictions on Chinese immigration increased as racial antagonism rather than economic competition became the issue. In 1865, *The New York Times* viewed with alarm the effect of the increase in Asian immigration on American civilization, religion, morals, and political institutions:

Now we are utterly opposed to the permission of any extensive emigration of Chinamen or other Asiatics to any part of the United States. There are other points of national well-being to be considered beside the sudden development of material wealth. The security of its free institutions is more important than the enlargement of its population. The maintenance of an elevated national character is of higher value than mere growth in physical power.

FIGURE 7.1

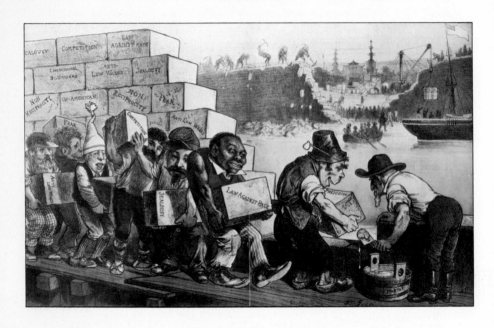

"THE ANTI-CHINESE WALL"

"The American wall goes up as the Chinese original goes down." Cartoon by
F. Gratz, *Puck*, March 29, 1882. (The Bettmann Archive)

... We have four millions of degraded negroes in the South ...
and if there were to be a flood-tide of Chinese population — a population befouled with all the social vices, with no knowledge or
appreciation of free institutions or constitutional liberty, with
heathenish souls and heathenish propensities, whose character, and
habits, and modes of thought are firmly fixed by the consolidating
influence of ages upon ages — we should be prepared to bid
farewell to republicanism and democracy.[10]

In 1867 California Democrats used an anti-Chinese platform to such
advantage that they swept the state elections, including the gubernato-
rial chair. Democrats elsewhere saw a bonanza in this subject, since
many Republicans were identified with the railroads and with companies that recruited and employed the Chinese, and because the
Democrats — identified with the defeated Confederacy and slavocracy
— could not use Negro-baiting effectively after 1865. Republicans secured the Burlingame Treaty of 1868 between China and the United
States, providing for free immigration and emigration to both countries
"for the purpose of curiosity, or trade, or as permanent residents." Still,
public hostility against the Chinese continued.

To some, the Chinese also posed the first real immigrant threat to the
idealized concept of the melting pot. Individuals who held this belief
argued that German and Irish Catholics at least were physically similar
to the Protestant northern and western Europeans. *The New York Times*
spoke of the undesirability of the Chinese:

Although they are patient and reliable laborers, they have characteristics deeply imbedded which make them undesirable as part of
our permanent population. Their religion is wholly unlike ours, and
they poison and stab. The circumstance would need be very favorable which would allow of their introduction into our families as
servants, and as to mixing with them on terms of equality, that
would be out of the question. No improvement of race could possibly result from such a mixture.[11]

As the prejudices of the 1850s developed into the sinophobia of the
1870s and 1880s, the negative stereotype of the "yellow menace"
broadened. Senator James G. Blaine of Maine, a party leader and presidential hopeful, attacked even the Chinese family structure, since the
Chinese, as sojourners, had temporarily left their families in China.

The Asiatic cannot go on with our population and make a
homogeneous element. This idea ... comparing European immigration with an immigration that had no regard to family, that does not
recognize the relation of husband and wife, that does not observe
the tie of parent and child, that does not have in the slightest

degree the enabling and civilizing influences of the hearthstone and the fireside.[12]

LEGISLATIVE ACTION

Several hundred thousand Chinese came to the United States between 1820 and 1882. As Chinese sojourners both came to America and returned to China in steady numbers, steamship companies found passenger trips a very profitable operation and so encouraged Chinese immigration. In 1881, 11,890 Chinese disembarked, and in 1882 the number jumped to 39,579.[13] Economic woes and labor agitation against the Chinese led to increasing pressures for restrictions. President Arthur vetoed the first restriction bill, which would have barred all Chinese immigration for 20 years. A few months later he signed a revised bill, barring Chinese laborers for a 10-year period, but permitting Chinese businessmen, clergy, students, and travelers to enter. The Chinese Exclusion Act of 1882 marked a significant change in national policy toward immigrants. For the first time the federal government had enacted a human embargo on a particular race of laborers. There were still sufficient exceptions to allow 8,031 legal Chinese immigrants in 1883, but legislative action in 1884 tightened the restrictions further, and the number of immigrants in 1885 dropped to 22.[14]

The exclusion law had a pronounced effect upon public opinion. Now that a ban on immigration of Chinese laborers was official policy, people's negative attitudes toward the Chinese became more and more evident in the media and in people's actions. Violence and killings, which had occurred prior to the legislation, continued. In 1871, 21 Chinese had been massacred in Los Angeles, and there had been anti-Chinese riots in Denver in 1880. Hostile actions became much more widespread after 1882. For example, at Rock Springs, Wyoming, in September 1885, a mob attacked and murdered 28 Chinese, wounded many others, and drove hundreds from their homes. What appeared to be a carefully organized plan against the Chinese was put into effect by labor unions and politicians in the western United States. In Tacoma, Seattle, Oregon City, and many smaller towns, angry mobs expelled hundreds of Chinese residents, with considerable loss and destruction of property.

Congress renewed the exclusion act for another 10 years in 1892, and extended it indefinitely in 1902. Other Anglo-Saxon countries on the Pacific rim also restricted Chinese immigration. Australia passed legislation in 1901, but Canada did not take such action until 1923. Americans frequently criticized Canada, especially British Columbia, because Chinese entered the United States from that province. The reverse migration also occurred after 1858, when the United States served as a point of entry into Canada for many Chinese.

FIGURE 7.2

THE ANTI-CHINESE RIOT IN DENVER, OCTOBER 31, 1880
Engraving by N. B. Wilkins. (The Bettmann Archive)

Organized labor's creation and instigation of the anti-Chinese issue is illustrated in an 1893 AFL (American Federation of Labor) convention resolution, which held that the Chinese brought to America "nothing but filth, vice, and disease." It also maintained they had corrupted "a part of our people on the Pacific Coast to such a degree that could it be published in detail the American people would in their just and righteous anger sweep them from the face of the earth."[15]

SEGREGATION

How did the Chinese react to all this abuse, vilification, and discriminatory legislation? Some reluctantly returned to China. Some sought redress in the courts, winning all cases involving state immigration restrictions but few involving assault or property damage complaints, as from 1854 to 1870, California courts did not allow Chinese to testify against whites. Expelled from various trades and occupations, as well as from many residential areas, the Chinese had little choice but to congregate in Chinatowns and rely on the benevolent and protective associations for assistance. A large number congregated in San Francisco, but others moved to the larger Eastern and Midwestern cities, forming ethnic enclaves there. These Chinatowns were in low-rent ghetto areas, usually situated near major means of transportation, which at least allowed the Chinese to be readily accessible to friends and relatives. For example, in New York City and San Francisco they are in close proximity to the docks, while in Boston, Pittsburgh, and St. Louis they are near the railroad station.

The Chinese sought redress of grievances through the courts, petitioning for equal rights. They won for their children the right to attend public schools; then they fought to desegregate the schools. Housing codes kept them in the ghetto, and they found themselves segregated both socially and spatially. Securing jobs through the associations or from Chinese merchants, most entered occupations either not in competition with whites (such as art and curio shops or Chinese restaurants) or serving only their own people. They settled disputes among themselves, partly because this was their custom and partly because they distrusted the white people's court. The traditional associations and the family clan offered them the familiarity and protection they needed. Chinese temples, newspapers, schools, and Old World festivals all were efforts to preserve their cultural and traditional practices.

Examining the early growth of the Chinatowns, and analyzing the present status of New York's Chinatown, D. Y. Yuan suggested that there was a four-stage process of development.[16] The first stage was marked by involuntary choice in response to societal prejudice and discrimination. Defensive insulation came next, as a mutual protection against racial hostility. As a group consciousness emerged, voluntary segregation became the third stage, sharing culture and problems of adjustment. The final stage is gradual assimilation, a process markedly slowed down by voluntary segregation and social isolation.

Albert Palmer drew from first-hand experience as a white boy growing up near San Francisco's Chinatown in the late nineteenth century in his social analysis of the stereotyped dominant view of these "foreign settlements":

> Those who know only the picturesque Chinatown of today can hardly realize what the Chinatown of the eighties and nineties was like. It was dirty, overcrowded, rat-infested, and often diseased. It was poorly built with narrow alleys and underground cellars and secret passages, more like a warren of burrowing animals than a human city. It seemed uncanny because inhabited by a strange yellow race who wore "pigtails," talked an outlandish lingo in high falsetto voices, were reputed to eat sharks' fins and even rats, and to make medicine out of toads and spiders, and who sprinkled garments for ironing by sucking their mouths full of water and then squirting it out over the clothes. And Chinatown was accounted vicious because it was the haunt of gambling, opium smoking, lotteries, tong wars and prostitution, where helpless little slave-girls were bought and sold. . . .
>
> Now, fear is a great disturber, and it largely created the old Chinatown. It did this partly, in fact, by herding Chinese into narrow, squalid quarters and surrounding them by hatred and suspicion; and partly in imagination, by creating the weird and distorted picture of their outlandish character. . . . Chinatown was never quite so bad as the prejudice and fear imagined it![17]

In an analysis of organizational life within San Francisco's Chinatown between 1850 and 1910, Stanford M. Lyman found that the traditional associations quickly came in conflict with one another.[18] As the clans (lineage bond), hui kuan (ethnic or regional bond), and secret societies (outlaw or protest bond) fought to secure the allegiance of immigrants and to dominate the community, the Chinese faced strife from both inside and outside their community.

> The organizational developments and internecine fights that took place in Chinatown from 1850 to 1910 indicate that forming an overseas Chinese community was not an easy task. Principles of clan solidarity, barriers of language and dialect, allegiance to rebellious secret societies, and their own competitive interest in making enough money to permit retirement in China divided the loyalties of the Chinese immigrants. Yet during the same period the depredations of anti-Chinese mobs, the difficulties and indignities imposed

by restrictive immigration legislation, the occupational discrimination created by state and local laws prohibiting or limiting the employment of Chinese, and the active opposition of the American labor movement to the Chinese workingman all seemed to call for a community united in the face of its enemies. What emerged out of this condition of pressures from without the ghetto and divisions within was a pattern alternating between order and violence. By 1910 this pattern had assumed a complex but recognizable sociological form: that of the community whose members are bound to one another not only because of external hostility but also because of deadly internal factionalism.*

The Chinese continued to encounter discrimination and hostility in the Caucasian world:

During most of this period, the lives of average Chinese in the United States were difficult and irregular. No matter how well educated they were, in their living quarters they were confined to a crowded Chinatown.... College training in engineering or other technical subjects did not guarantee decent positions to Chinese. If one should go out, dressed casually for a walk, or go to a club, or even to a church, he was liable to be picked up by the immigration officers on suspicion of illegal residence. For many years officials made a practice of picking up persons in the street or in public places on the suspicion that they were aliens illegally in this country. Such arrests were reported to be very common, especially in the late 1920's.... It was up to the Chinese to prove he was not an illegal alien or even an illegal citizen. But proof is sometimes difficult and takes time. Eventually he would solve his difficulty, but only after suffering much trouble and anxiety.[19]

Not all Chinese migrated to the crowded Chinatowns of the cities. A few hundred, many of whom became merchants, settled in the Mississippi Delta. Chinese grocers sold mostly to blacks, extending them credit and providing other essential services (such as assisting illiterate rural blacks with government forms and making telephone calls). Some Chinese married black women; others brought their families over from China. In this transition from sojourner to immigrant, the Chinese men with families tried to evade their "black" status and avoid discrimination against their children, who were attending white public schools. In the 1920s, however, as a result of segregationist actions, Chinese children were expelled from the white schools, and the action was upheld by the courts "to preserve the purity and integrity of the

*Stanford M. Lyman, "Conflict and the Web of Group Affiliation in San Francisco's Chinatown, 1850–1910," Pacific Historical Review, 43 (November 1974), 494–495.

white race, and prevent amalgamation." Separate schools for Chinese
were established, as the Mississippi Chinese developed parallel institutions when they were excluded from the white prototypes. By 1950,
however, their status had improved, and white churches and schools
were opened to them. In the 1970s the second-generation Mississippi
Chinese have been migrating to other parts of the United States.

SOCIAL FACTORS

Perhaps the most tragic element in Chinese life in the United States
was the scarcity of Chinese women. In the nineteenth century, single
Chinese women did not usually venture forth alone seeking economic
opportunity, and Chinese tradition demanded that the wife remain with
her husband's parents, even if he worked far from home. About half the
Chinese sojourners were married.[21] The imbalance in the male-female
ratio was very significant: 1,858:1 in 1860; 1,284:1 in 1870; 2,106:1 in
1880; 2,678:1 in 1890; and 1,887:1 in 1900. The 1890 ratio converts to
102,620 Chinese males and 3,868 females. By 1920 the sex ratio, while
still very much out of balance, had lessened to 695:1. By 1960 the disparity was still high but going down, with a total of 100,654 females
and 135,430 males.[21] This overabundance of Chinese males and scarcity
of Chinese females led to organized prostitution in Chinatowns. Numerous brothels dotted the Chinatowns, some of them run or protected by
the secret societies and staffed with girls kidnapped from their villages,
sold by impoverished parents, or lured abroad by the deceit of a proxy
marriage.[22]

> With the vast Pacific Ocean separating him from domestic joys and
> companionship, the Chinese sojourner relied on the tong-controlled
> brothels for sex, attending the gambling and opium dens for recrea-
> tion and respite from the day's toil, and paid homage and allegiance
> to his clansmen, Landsmänner, and fraternal brothers to secure
> mutual aid, protection, and a job.[23]

Intermarriage was also generally impossible for the Chinese, since 14
states had passed laws forbidding miscegenation. Furthermore, in 1884,
a federal court ruled that only wives of those males exempt from the
Chinese Exclusion Act of 1882, namely merchants and businessmen,
could emigrate to the United States. For nearly all the Chinese laborers
in America, establishing a family was impossible. By 1890, forty years
after the Chinese had first arrived, only 2.7 percent of the total Chinese
population was American-born. The figure climbed to 30 percent by
1920. Legislation in 1943 allowed Chinese women to enter the country,
enabling the American-born Chinese population to pass the halfway

point in 1950. By 1960, the American-born Chinese were approximately two-thirds of the total.[24]

Congress ended the ban on immigration from China in 1943, and began a quota system. But first there was a dispute that reflected the lingering anti-Chinese feeling in America. Speaking against repeal, Congressman White of Idaho condemned the Chinese as a race unable to accept American standards:

> The Chinese are inveterate opium-smokers most of the day. They brought that hideous opium habit to this country.... There is no melting pot in America that can change their habits or change their mentality.... If there are any people who have refused to accept our standard and our education, it is the Chinese.[25]

Actually, the 1943 legislation only permitted 105 Chinese to enter per year, and that quota included anyone in the world of Chinese descent, not just those from China. Special and separate legislative acts covering refugees, displaced persons, and brides allowed more Chinese to enter. However, not until the Immigration Act of 1965 would the Chinese be able to enter under regular immigration regulations.

The Chinatowns today are far from disappearing. The number of Chinese immigrants admitted has increased steadily since 1968, with 12,513 admitted in 1977.[26] San Francisco's Chinese population grew from 30,000 in 1953 to 65,000 in 1973.[27] New York's Chinatown now numbers approximately 50,000 people, at a conservative estimate.[28] A 1976 Census Bureau report said that about 300,000 people speak Chinese in this country, placing it behind Spanish and Italian as the fourth most common language spoken in the United States.

The San Francisco and New York Chinatowns, paradoxically, are both tourist attractions and slum communities. They are filled with over-crowded, dilapidated buildings, and troubled by the problems of youth gangs and high tuberculosis rates, but they retain historical, pictur-esque, and communal importance. Land values have skyrocketed, and during the business day a bustling community is evident. The New York City Planning Commission reported in 1976 that 10,000 people pass the corner of Mott and Bayard Streets in Chinatown every business hour.[29] All around that area are hundreds of restaurants, garment factories, and import-export houses. Not quite as apparent are the exploited labor, crime, and disease.

The Chinese are presently a sizable minority — about half a million of them currently reside in the United States. The large number of new ar-rivals each year since the immigration laws were liberalized in 1965 continue to experience problems of adjustment and poor living standards in the Chinatowns. Although hostilities and overt discrimination against the Chinese have lessened, to believe that prejudice and discrimination against the Chinese have completely disappeared would be a serious mistake. There is substantial evidence to demonstrate that more subtle, sophisticated forms of discrimination exist in employment opportunities, education, and city services.[30] For example, the Chinese are still highly underrepresented in executive, managerial, academic, sales, and personnel positions, and in such highly paid craft positions as ironworkers, operating engineers, plumbers, and electricians.[31]

A Chinatown concern in recent years has been the increasing rebelliousness, criminality, and radicalism of many Chinese youth. The formation of delinquent gangs, particularly in New York and San Francisco, has resulted in a growing number of gang wars and killings. The growing problem of youthful militancy and delinquency appears to reflect the marginal status of those in the younger generation, who experience frustration and adjustment problems in America. Recent arrivals from Hong Kong are unfamiliar with the language and culture, they are either unemployed or in the lowliest of jobs, and they live in overcrowded, slumlike quarters with no recreational facilities. Gang behavior serves as an alternative and a means of filling status and identity needs.[32]

THE JAPANESE

When Commodore Perry sailed into Tokyo Bay in 1853, his arrival marked the beginning of a new era for Japan. For more than two hundred years the Japanese had lived in government-enforced isolation. The emperors had prohibited travel and foreign visitors, though castaways were treated hospitably and allowed to leave. No one was permitted to build large boats, and any Japanese attempt to emigrate was punishable by death.

The situation began to change in 1860, when the Japanese government sent its first official emissaries to Washington.

With their first major debarkation in the New World, the Japanese appeared to Americans to lack emotional expression. [A San Francisco reporter observed:] "This stoicism, however, is a distinguishing feature with the Japanese. It is part of their creed never to appear astonished at anything, and it must be a rare sight indeed which betrays in them any expression of wonder."

In the 85 years which passed between the arrival of Japan's first embassy and the end of World War II, this "distinguishing feature" of the Japanese became the cardinal element of the anti-Japanese stereotype. Characterized by journalists, politicians, novelists, and film-makers as a dangerous enemy, the Japanese were also pictured as mysterious and inscrutable.[33]

Beginning in 1868, the Japanese began emigrating, first as laborers and eventually as permanent settlers. Their numbers on the U.S. mainland were small at first. United States Census records show only 55 in this country in 1870, and 2,039 in 1890. After that they came in much greater numbers, reaching 24,326 in 1900, 72,157 in 1910, and 111,010 in 1920.

STRUCTURAL CONDITIONS

Because many families in Japan still followed the practice of primogeniture (the eldest son inheriting the entire estate), many second and third sons came to the United States to seek their fortunes. They settled in the Western states, where anti-Chinese sentiment was still strong, most of them becoming farmers or farm laborers. Their growing numbers, their concentration in small areas, and their racial visibility in a racist region led to conflict with organized labor, vegetable growers, and shippers in California.

ECONOMIC COMPETITION

Early Japanese immigrants entered various manufacturing and service occupations. Hostility from union members, who resented Asians' willingness to work for lower wages and under poor conditions, produced the inevitable clashes. Members of the shoemaker's union attacked Japanese cobblers in 1890, and members of the union for cooks and waiters attacked Japanese restaurateurs in 1892. Finding work difficult to get, most Japanese gravitated to the outlying areas and entered agricultural work, first as laborers and eventually as tenant farmers or small landholders; some Japanese became contract gardeners on the estates of Caucasians.

The Japanese, whose industriousness and knowledge of cultivation placed them in serious competition with the native farmers, encountered further discriminatory actions. In 1913 the California legislature passed the first alien land-holding law, prohibiting any person ineligible for citizenship from owning land and permitting such persons to lease land for only three years. Under the United States Naturalization Act of 1790, then still in effect, citizenship was available to "any alien, being a free *white* person [italics mine]." In 1868, the government modified this law to extend citizenship to persons of African descent (the recently freed slaves), but the Japanese were still excluded. In a remarkable and unsuccessful case (*Ozawa* v. *U.S.*, 1921) the Japanese claimed to be Caucasoid.

Since their children, having been born in this country, were automatically United States citizens, the Japanese held land in their children's names, either directly or through land-holding companies in which they collectively owned the stock. After World War I, new agitation arose against the Japanese. In 1920, the California legislature passed a law prohibiting aliens from being guardians of a minor's property or from leasing any land at all. The United States Supreme Court upheld this law in 1923, and New Mexico, Arizona, Louisiana, Montana, Idaho, and Oregon passed similar laws. Because their opportunities were still best in agriculture, many Japanese continued in tenant or truck farming. Morton Grodzins suggests that their immense success (they raised 42 percent of California's truck crops by 1941) helps to explain why Caucasian vegetable growers and shippers pressed for their evacuation during the war.[34]

NATIONAL POLICY

Most non-Californians had no strong feelings about Japanese immigrants, but they were quite aware of Japan's growing military power after the Japanese defeated Russia in 1905. The catalyst that finally triggered a change in national policy toward the Japanese was a local incident. In 1906 the San Francisco Board of Education passed a resolution transferring 93 Japanese children, who were scattered throughout the city's 23 schools, into a segregated Oriental school in Chinatown. This action made national headlines and had international ramifications. Under pressure from the Japanese government, President Theodore Roosevelt instructed the attorney general to initiate lawsuits challenging the constitutionality of this action.

As a compromise, the school board rescinded its resolution, the government dropped its legal action, and Roosevelt issued an executive order, which remained in effect until 1948, barring the entry of Japanese from a bordering country or U.S. territory. Thus, Japanese who stayed even briefly in Hawaii, Canada, or Mexico could no longer enter the mainland United States. In addition, President Roosevelt secured the so-called Gentlemen's Agreement of 1908, whereby Japan agreed to restrict, but not eliminate altogether, the issuance of passports.

The big loophole in the Gentlemen's Agreement was permission for wives to enter. Many Japanese married by proxy and then sent for their "picture brides." Several thousand Japanese a year came until World War I, and almost six thousand a year after the war. As men brought their wives here and children were born, the Japanese birth rate became exaggerated. Questions about Japanese immigration began to shift from their economic competition to their "assimilability" because of their race, life style, and alleged birth rate. The anti-Japanese stereotype, long a part of dominant-group attitudes, played a key role.

The anti-Japanese stereotype was so widespread that it affected the judgements of sociologists about the possibilities of Japanese assimilation. Thus, in 1913 Robert E. Park was sufficiently depressed by anti-Japanese legislation and popular prejudice to predict: "The Japanese . . . is condemned to remain among us an abstraction, a symbol, and a symbol not merely of his own race, but of the Orient and of that vague, ill-defined menace we sometimes refer to as the 'yellow peril.'" Although Park later reversed his doleful prediction, his observations on Japanese emphasized their uncommunicative features, stolid faces, and apparently blank character.[35]

The Immigration Law of 1924, which severely restricted the number of southern, central, and eastern Europeans who could enter, specifically barred the Japanese, since it denied entry to all aliens ineligible for citizenship. The bill passed by large majorities (323 to 71 in the House and 62 to 6 in the Senate), indicating widespread support for limiting immigration to the supposedly "assimilable" peoples. The Japanese government vehemently denounced this legislation, taking it as a personal affront, a violation of the terms of the Gentlemen's Agreement, and an insult to a nation only recently courted by the United States. Nevertheless, the legislation remained in effect until 1952.

EXPULSION AND IMPRISONMENT

By 1940 there were about 127,000 Japanese in America, 94,000 of them in California. About 63 percent were American-born, and only 15 percent were of voting age. Japan's attack on Pearl Harbor in 1941 and the subsequent war led to what is now referred to as "our worst wartime mistake."[36] Approximately 110,000 Japanese, many of them second- and third-generation Americans, were removed from their homes and placed in what were euphemistically called relocation centers in Arkansas, Arizona, California, Colorado, Idaho, Utah, and Wyoming.[37]

The evacuees loaded their possessions onto trucks. . . . Neighbors and teachers were on hand to see their friends off. Members of other minority groups wept. One old Mexican woman wept, saying, "Me next. Me next."

. . . People were starting off to 7 o'clock jobs, watering their gardens, sweeping their pavements. Passersby invariably stopped to stare in amazement, perhaps in horror, that this could happen in the

FIGURE 7.3

Part of the 1942 mass evacuation, these Japanese-Americans are boarding a special train in Seattle under Army guard. Their destination is a "relocation center" in California. (United Press International)

United States. People soon became accustomed to the idea, however, and many profited from the evacuation. Japanese mortgages were foreclosed and their properties attached. They were forced to sell property such as cars and refrigerators at bargain prices.[38]

This mass expulsion of the Japanese from the West Coast was unnecessary for national security, although that was given as the primary justification. The traditional anti-Asian sentiment on the West Coast, fear of the "perfidious" character of the Japanese, and opposition to Japanese producing a sizable share of the area's agricultural products may all have been factors. There was no mass evacuation of the 150,000 Japanese in Hawaii, which was much more strategic and vulnerable to attack because of its location. The differences in the Japanese experience in Hawaii and on the mainland can perhaps best be understood by looking at the differences in structural discrimination. In Hawaii the Japanese were more fully involved in economic and political endeavors, partly because they lived in an environment of greater racial harmony. On the West Coast, the Japanese were more isolated from most of American society, and certain labor and agricultural groups saw them as an economic threat. Also, anti-Oriental attitudes and actions had prevailed in that area for almost a hundred years.

Besides the trauma that resulted from being uprooted and incarcerated, the Japanese had to make many cultural adjustments to their new surroundings. Instead of their preferred deep hot baths, they had only showers and common washrooms. Central dining halls prevented families from eating together intimately as a family unit. Outside and sometimes distant toilet facilities, not partitioned in the early months, were a hardship for the old and for the parents of small children. Almost six thousand babies were born while these centers were in existence, and proper hospital facilities were not always available. There were only partial partitions between rooms occupied by different families in the same barracks, and this did not allow for very much privacy. Ted Nakashima, a second-generation Japanese-American, offered a frightening portrait of what the early months of life in the Tule Lake camp were like:

> The resettlement center is actually a penitentiary — armed guards in towers with spotlights and deadly tommy guns, fifteen feet of barbed wire fences, everyone confined to quarters at nine, lights out at ten o'clock. The guards are ordered to shoot anyone who approaches within twenty feet of the fences. No one is allowed to take the two-block-long hike to the latrines after nine, under any circumstances.
>
> The apartments, as the army calls them, are two-block-long stables, with windows on one side. Floors are ... two-by-fours laid directly on the mud, which is everywhere. The stalls are about eight-

een by twenty-one feet; some contain families of six or seven persons. Partitions are seven feet high, leaving a four-foot opening above. . . .

The food and sanitation problems are the worst. We have had absolutely no fresh meat, vegetables or butter since we came here. Mealtime queues extend for blocks; standing in a rainswept line, feet in the mud, waiting for the scant portions of canned wieners and boiled potatoes, hash for breakfast or canned wieners and beans for dinner. Coffee or tea dosed with saltpeter and stale bread are the adults' staples. Dirty, unwiped dishes, greasy silver, a starchy diet, no butter, no milk, bawling kids, mud, wet mud that stinks when it dries, no vegetables — a sad thing for the people who raised them in such abundance. . . .

Today one of the surface sewage-disposal pipes broke and the sewage flowed down the streets. Kids play in the water. Shower baths without hot water. Stinking mud and slops everywhere.

Can this be the same America we left a few weeks ago? . . . What really hurts most is the constant reference to us evacuees as "Japs." "Japs" are the guys we are fighting. We're on this side and we want to help.

Why won't America let us?[39]

Although the harsh physical conditions and sanitation problems were improved somewhat, the Japanese-Americans remained prisoners because of their background. They tried to make life inside the barbed wire fences a little brighter by fixing up their quarters and planting small gardens. However, these "residents" of the "relocation centers" still lived, for the most part, in concentration camps. About 35,000 young Japanese-Americans had left these centers by the end of 1943, going voluntarily to the East and Midwest for further schooling or a job. For those obliged to remain in the camps, life was monotonous and unproductive. The evacuation brought financial ruin to many Japanese families; they lost property, savings, income, and jobs for which they were never adequately compensated.

By weakening Japanese subcommunities and institutions, the evacuation program encouraged acculturation. The traditional authority of the first-generation Japanese-Americans (Issei) lessened, family structure and husband-wife roles underwent changes and became more equal because of camp life, and those second-generation Japanese (Nisei) who resettled found new opportunities. The Japanese relocated in Chicago, New Jersey, and a few other places, but later many families returned to the West. Many became more a part of American society in the postwar period because they had been forced to do so.

Finally, in 1976, President Ford signed an executive order officially closing the camps, but such mass evacuations could conceivably recur,

FIGURE 7.4

This scene is of Fort Meade, Maryland, where several hundred German, Italian, and Japanese nationals were interned. The barbed wire and guard tower were at the perimeter of relocation centers. (United Press International)

because of the judicial precedent set by the United States Supreme Court in upholding the action. When the Supreme Court in 1944 upheld the Japanese evacuation by a 6–3 vote, the dissenting justices gave sharp minority opinions. Justice Francis Murphy called approving the evacuation "the legalization of racism." Justice Robert H. Jackson, who would later prosecute the Nazi war criminals at Nuremberg, wrote:

> Once a judicial opinion rationalizes such an order to show it conforms to the Constitution, or rather rationalizes the Constitution to show that the Constitution sanctions such an order, the Court for all time has validated the principle of racial discrimination in criminal procedure, and of transplanting American citizens. The principle then lies about like a loaded weapon ready for the hand of any authority that can bring forward a plausible claim of an urgent need. Every repetition imbeds that principle more deeply in our law and thinking and expands it to new purposes.[40]

RECENT PATTERNS

As internees and during the years following this mass incarceration, Japanese-Americans sought vindication and a redress of grievances. They have fought to obtain frozen bank deposits, receive compensation for land, and restore lost retirement benefits to Civil Service workers. A long campaign to clear Mrs. D'Aquino, the Japanese-American woman accused of being "Tokyo Rose," who broadcast propaganda messages to Allied troops during World War II, was finally successful in 1976.

Because homeland influences are important in understanding immigrant orientations, changes in Japan since World War II are worth mentioning. American occupation of the country and foreign aid led to significant and rapid social change in Japan. The westernization and industrialization affected Japanese values and life styles; it also altered American attitudes toward and relations with that country. The 25,000 war brides who accompanied returning GIs encountered suspicion and hostility, but such attitudes can no longer be so clearly seen. Some may not be accepted by the Japanese-American ethnic community, but Japanese wives of Caucasians are usually looked upon as exotic.[41]

Traditionally, Japanese parents have encouraged their children to get an education, and since 1940 the Japanese have had more schooling than any other group in the United States, including whites.[42] Japanese emphasis upon conformity, aspiration, competitiveness, discipline, and self-control help to explain the high Japanese educational attainment.[43] Encouraged by their parents, the upwardly mobile second- (Nisei) and third-generation (Sansei) Japanese-Americans entered the professional fields, especially engineering, pharmacy, and other technical fields.

They have, in fact, higher incomes than any other nonwhite group and are comparable to whites in occupational distribution and income.[44]

As another indication of structural assimilation, recent statistics show that about 50 percent of both males and females engage in outgroup dating and marriage.[45]

Another unusual dimension to the Japanese experience has been their very low rates of juvenile delinquency and mental illness. The Japanese adult and juvenile crime rate has been decidedly lower than that of any other group. Those youths who engage in delinquent behavior are usually in a marginal situation, not identifying with the major institutions of Japanese culture and not as effectively under their social control.[46] In 1969 Harry H. L. Kitano suggested that the social organization and social controls within Japanese culture were strong enough to overcome any problems of marginality, as evidenced by the low rates of crime, delinquency, mental illness, and suicide.

> The ability of the Japanese family and community to provide ample growth opportunities, to present legitimate alternatives, to provide conditions of relative tolerance and treatments, to provide effective socialization and control, as well as the relative congruence between Japanese culture and middle-class American culture, has aided the group in adapting to acculturative changes with a minimum marginal population. Relatively few Japanese seek social friendships in the social cliques and organizations outside their own ethnic group. And those who do seek outside contacts appear to have many of the necessary requisites for such activity — high education, good training, and adequate income.[47]

In the 1970s the rates of delinquency, mental illness, and suicide have increased somewhat. Among the reasons given for this increase are urbanization and less effective social control over the third (Sansei) generation, which feels more alienated from both white America and their parents' version of Japanese America.

One special group of Japanese in the United States is known as the Kai-sha — business people and employees of large corporations on two- or three-year assignments with their company's United States branch office. Their presence is more noticeable in the New York metropolitan region than ever before. Many suburban towns near New York City, particularly those across the Hudson River in Bergen County, New Jersey, have experienced a large influx of Japanese Kai-sha and their families. Long-time white residents, unaccustomed to Asian neighbors, have seen their neighborhoods racially integrated by a group they had not expected.[48]

Recent Japanese immigrants, of whom there have been more than 4,000 a year during the 1970s, are very different from their predecessors before World War II. Coming from an industrialized, urbanized nation, and most of them skilled and professional workers according to current immigration guidelines, they find many similarities between American society and their own. Many are Buddhists, and their religion, because of Japanese and other Asian immigration, is growing in the United States. The Japanese in the United States today enjoy a much more favorable image, but they are still a visible minority who remain stereotyped as an ethnic group.

THE PILIPINOS

Americans have traditionally called this ethnic group Filipinos. However, since there is no "F" sound in Tagalog, the second most widely spoken language in the Philippines, the shift to *Pilipino* is part of a very recent symbolic assertion of ethnic consciousness.[49] When racial or ethnic groups enter a stage of emerging self-consciousness and militancy, they often seek to transform their name to one representing greater racial or ethnic pride. Other examples are *Oriental* to *Asian*, *Negro* to *black*, *Mexican* to *Chicano*, and *Indian* to *Native American*.

EARLY IMMIGRANTS

After the Gentlemen's Agreement of 1908 curtailed Japanese emigration, the Hawaiian Sugar Planters' Association recruited laborers from the Philippines to work the plantations. The modest number of Pilipinos in the continental United States (there were only 5,603 here in 1920, according to census records) began to increase in 1923. Why? California growers, faced with the loss of Mexican labor because of quota restrictions in the pending Immigration Act of 1924, turned to the Pilipinos as an alternative labor source. By 1930 their numbers had increased to over 45,000, with more than two-thirds of them living in California.

The Pilipinos came to this country with a unique status. After 1898 the Philippines had become an American possession and the inhabitants were considered nationals, although not United States citizens. Consequently, they were not designated as aliens and there was no quota restriction on their entry until 1935. Their Spanish heritage confused their status, however, since the federal government held that they were not Caucasians. The United States Supreme Court upheld this official position in a 1934 ruling on a case challenging the 1790 naturalization law limiting citizenship to foreign-born whites.

"White persons" within the meaning of the statute are members of the Caucasian race, as Caucasian is defined in the understanding of the mass of men. The term excludes the Chinese, the Japanese, the Hindus, the American Indians and the Filipinos.[50]

OCCUPATIONAL DISTRIBUTION

Many Pilipinos worked in agriculture at first, particularly in California and Washington. However, the promise of educational opportunities and the lure of the big city attracted many young Pilipino males to urban areas, where they sought jobs. Discrimination and their lack of education and job skills resulted in their getting only low-paying domestic and personal service work in hotels, restaurants, businesses, and residences. They were employed as bellboys, waiters, cooks, bus boys, janitors, drivers, house boys, elevator operators, and hospital attendants. By 1940 their employment in these areas peaked, with nine out of ten Pilipinos so employed.[51] Feeling that they were being exploited by their employers, they often joined unions, or formed their own unions when denied membership in existing unions, and went on strike, which only intensified management resentment. Ironically, the union hierarchy also disliked them and later joined in efforts to bar them from the United States.

As the Depression of the 1930s worsened and jobs became scarcer, increased objections were made to the presence of the Pilipinos. Race riots erupted in Exeter, California, on October 24, 1929, and in Watsonville, California, on January 19, 1930, when one Pilipino was killed. In both instances several hundred white men beat Pilipinos, shattered windows in cars and buildings, and wrecked property. Other clashes occurred in San Jose and San Francisco. Then on January 28, 1930, someone bombed the Filipino Federation of America Center in Stockton — called "the Manila of California" because of its large Pilipino population.

THE SCARCITY OF PILIPINO WOMEN

Of every 100 Pilipinos coming to California between 1920 and 1929, 93 were male; almost 80 percent were single and between 16 and 30 years of age. Since there were few Pilipino women available, these males sought the company of women of other races. This situation enraged many Caucasian men, as the following racist statement illustrates.

The Filipinos have ... demanded the right to run dance halls under the alias of clubs, with white girls as entertainers. And the excuse they have openly and brazenly given for their demand is that the Filipinos "prefer" white women to those of their own race and that besides there are not enough Filipino women in the country to satisfy their lust. . . . If that statement is not enough to make the blood of any white man, or any other decent man boil, then there is no such thing as justified indignation at any advocacy of immorality.[52]

This prejudicial, demagogic statement reflects the sort of sexually oriented charges often directed against racial groups. Association with Caucasian women through intermarriage, dance halls, and affairs led to increased tensions in Pilipino-Caucasian relations. The Pilipinos' reputation as great lovers emerged as a stereotype, causing a San Francisco judge to comment:

Some of these boys, with perfect candor, have told me bluntly and boastfully that they practice the art of love with more perfection than white boys, and occasionally one of the girls has supplied me with information to the same effect. In fact, some of the disclosures in this regard are perfectly startling in nature.[53]

Pilipino responses were quick to follow. Sylvester Saturday, editor of the Filipino Poets League in Washington, D.C., stated:

We Filipinos are tickled at being called "great lovers." Surely, we are proud of this heritage. We love our women so much that we work ourselves to death to gain and keep their affections.[54]

Another Pilipino from Chicago chided:

And as for the Filipinos being "great lovers," there is nothing surprising about that. We Filipinos, however poor, are taught from the cradle up to respect and love our women. That's why our divorce rate is nil compared with the state of which Judge Lazarus is a proud son. If to love and respect our womenfolks [sic] is savagery, then make the most of it, Judge. We plead guilty.[55]

White America was not amused. Several Western states passed laws prohibiting marriages between Pilipinos and Caucasians. The Tyding-McDuffie Act in 1935 granted deferred independence to the Philippines and imposed an immediate rigid quota of 50 immigrants a year. Repatriation efforts in 1935–1937 succeeded in returning only 2,190 to the Philippines.[56]

Because of the lack of Pilipino women and legal restrictions on intermarriage, many Pilipino males remained single. These early immigrants are now lonely old men with no family ties, living in poverty after years of hard work, although a small number did intermarry among Mexicans, Indians, mulattos, Asians, and Caucasians.[57]

Unlike the Chinese, who had a tradition of being sojourners and who formed benevolent and protective associations, the Pilipinos did not establish the institutions usually found in immigrant communities. Their lack of families and the seasonal, transitory nature of their employment were primary reasons for this. As a result of housing discrimination, they lived in hotels and rooming houses in less desirable sections of town. The pool hall and taxi-dance hall became their recreational outlets.[58]

POSTWAR IMMIGRANTS

Many Pilipinos circumvented the immigration quota by enlisting in the U.S. Armed Forces, particularly the navy and army, as completion of active military service entitles an alien to become a U.S. citizen. These Pilipino males emigrated with their families. It is mostly the children of these immigrants who lead the movement for increased Pilipino ethnic pride and identity.[59]

With the Philippines an ally during World War II, the social climate on the mainland became more liberal for Pilipinos. In January 1942, legislation was passed enabling Pilipino residents to become naturalized American citizens. They could buy land in California, and many did, often from Japanese-Americans who were being removed from such areas as Los Angeles. Many Pilipinos bought farms in the San Fernando Valley and the San Joaquin Valley as well as in the Torrance-Gardena area.[60]

Since the Immigration Act of 1965, Pilipino immigration has been quite high. Hawaii now has the largest concentration of Pilipinos living outside the Philippine Islands. In 1976 a total of 20,895 came to the United States, including Hawaii. For several years preceding 1976 the number had been only slightly lower (19,238 in 1974, 18,938 in 1975). Many of those who come to the mainland are professional people, particularly doctors and nurses, and they often go to the East Coast to live and work. Many are underemployed because they have difficulty securing jobs comparable to their education, skills, and experience.

CURRENT STATUS

Pilipinos rank below all other Asian-American groups in median family income and educational level.[61] The 1970 Census identified 343,000 Pilipinos in the United States. Allowing for over 100,000 immigrants since then, the Pilipino community has increased in size by one-third in 10 years. As a major port of entry, San Francisco has received a great many of the new arrivals, particularly in its South of Market area.

THE KOREANS

Korea, because of its strategic location, has been a pawn in the expansionist efforts of several nations. Voyagers visited Korea frequently from the late seventeenth century onward. By the middle of the nineteenth century, English, French, and Russian whaling ships sailed Korean waters, and many Catholic missionaries had come to Korea. The United States, however, became the first Western nation to sign a treaty with Korea in 1882, when it formalized a relationship of friendship and trade. Other nations quickly followed suit, and all attempted to remove the Chinese influence from Korea. In 1910 Japan gained control of Korea as a result of a conflict with China.

Although various treaties and declarations by the different nations guaranteed Korea's independence, Japanese encroachment, both political and economic, continued. Japan's victory over Russia in 1905 solidified Japanese domination of Korea, and Japan retained colonial control until the end of World War II. Korea still did not gain national independence, however, for the Allied military strategy in 1945 was that Soviet troops would accept the Japanese surrender north of the thirty-eighth parallel and United States troops would do the same south of it. This temporary line, created out of military expediency, became a permanent delineation that still exists.

EARLY IMMIGRANTS

The Hawaii Sugar Planters' Association, needing laborers to replace the Chinese excluded by the 1882 legislation, recruited 7,226 Koreans, 637 of them women, between 1903 and 1905.[62] This was the first large group of Koreans to migrate to the United States. The Koreans, mostly peasants, sought economic relief from the famines plaguing their country at the turn of the century. In Hawaii they worked long hours for meager wages under harsh conditions.[63] Of this original group, about 1,000 returned to Korea, 2,000 males and 12 women went on to the mainland United States, and the rest remained in Hawaii.[64] The males were almost all between the ages of 20 and 40.[65]

Between 1907 and 1924 several thousand more Korean immigrants, mostly "picture brides," political activists fighting Japanese oppression, and students, migrated to the United States. As a result of the age disparity between the picture brides and the older males, many second-generation Korean-Americans spent a good portion of their formative years with non-English-speaking, widowed mothers who had had limited formal schooling.[66]

BOX 7.1

"My mother and sister-in-law . . . scrubbed, ironed, and mended shirts for a nickel apiece. . . . Their knuckles became . . . raw from using the harsh yellow . . . soap."

[The following comments, through the courtesy of Harold and Sonia Sunoo, are a composite of interviews with three Korean women who were among the first 12 women to come to the mainland.]

"We left Korea because we were too poor. We had nothing to eat. . . . There was absolutely no way we could survive.

"At first we were unaware that we had been 'sold' as laborers. . . . We thought Hawaii was America in those days. . . . We cut sugar canes, the thing you put in coffee. . . .

"I'll never forget the foreman. No, he wasn't Korean — he was French. The reason I'll never forget him is that he was the most ignorant of all ignoramuses, but he knew all the cuss words in the world. . . . [I] could tell by the sound of his words. He said we worked like 'lazy.' He wanted us to work faster. . . . He would gallop around on horseback and crack and snap his whip. . . . He was so mean and so ignorant!

". . . If all of us worked hard and pooled together our total earnings, it came to about fifty dollars a month, barely enough to feed and clothe the five of us. We cooked on the porch, using coal oil and when we cooked in the fields, I gathered the wood. We had to carry water in vessels from water faucets scattered here and there in the camp area. . . .

"My mother and sister-in-law took in laundry. They scrubbed, ironed, and mended shirts for a nickel apiece. It was pitiful! Their knuckles became swollen and raw from using the harsh yellow laundry soap . . . but it was still better than in Korea. There was no way to earn money there."

[On the mainland the Koreans encountered even worse problems than in Hawaii because of the more highly charged racial tension and the severe weather conditions, as the following account indicates.]

"We had five children at that time — our youngest was three and a half. I was paid fifteen cents an hour for weeding. Our baby was too young to go to school, so I had to take him along with me to the fields — it was so early when we started that he'd be fast asleep when we left so I couldn't feed him breakfast. Returning home, he'd be asleep again because he was so tired. Poor child, he was practically starved. He too suffered so much. . . . [In February] the ground . . . was frozen crisp and it was so cold that the baby's tender ears got frozen and blood oozed from him. . . . For all this suffering, I was paid fifteen cents an hour. . . ."

Three Korean immigrants, ranging in age from 19 to 25, who came to Hawaii between 1903 and 1905

RECENT IMMIGRANTS

Not until the Korean War and passage of the Refugee Relief Act in 1953 did Koreans migrate in substantial numbers. As refugees or as war brides, Koreans came to the United States in growing numbers beginning in 1958. The continued presence of U.S. troops in South Korea, and the cultural influence that resulted, was a constant inducement to the Koreans to intermarry or think about living in America. Also, the liberalized immigration law of 1965 opened the doors to Asian immigrants and allowed relatives to join family members already in the United States. In 1976, for example, there were 19,852 new arrivals, 15,359 of whom had relatives in this country. In 1970 the Bureau of the Census reported the Korean population in the United States to be about 70,000. With Korean-Americans now numbering over 200,000, their population has tripled since that time.[67]

One researcher, Hyung-Chan Kim, has determined several general trends regarding Korean immigrants to the United States during the 1959–1971 period. The immigrants were overwhelmingly female, most of them wives and children of U.S. servicemen. They settled more in the highly urbanized and industrialized states.[68] U.S. government figures for 1976 show Koreans settling in California, New York, Maryland, and Illinois, in that order.[69] The proportion obtaining U.S. citizenship is higher than that of immigrants from Japan, China, India, and Mexico.

SOCIAL MOBILITY

The majority of adult Korean immigrants since 1968, excluding housewives, held professional, technical, or managerial jobs in their home country. It appears that many who do not enter these fields in the United States start small businesses. On Olympic Boulevard in Los Angeles, on Clark Street in Chicago, and in lower Manhattan, these small Korean businesses are especially conspicuous.[70] In the Los Angeles area, which has the largest Korean-American population (about 80,000) perhaps one-fourth of the Korean families operate their own businesses.[71] Many other Koreans are employees of these firms, which penetrate the black and Hispanic markets.[72] Because the Koreans, themselves a minority group, occupy an intermediate position in trade and commerce between producer and consumer, elite and masses, the role they play is that of a *middleman minority*.[73]

Overall, Koreans are more highly educated than most other nonwhite groups. Their income, in proportion to their number of college graduates, lags behind that of native-born Americans, although their earnings are similar to those of other Asian-American groups.[74] Koreans have not fared so well in social as in economic status, if recent studies are any indication. Korean-Americans have never scored high in any measures of social distance, an important indicator of structural assimilation. In studies conducted in 1956 and 1966, Emory S. Bogardus found Koreans at or near the bottom in preference ranking, below other Asian peoples.[75] In a small replication study at Western Illinois University in 1976, Won Moo Hurh also found a near-bottom social distance ranking for Koreans.[76] Bad publicity over the "Koreagate" scandal in Washington and the controversial preacher Moon Sun Myung has not helped. Many Korean-Americans report that in social and business interactions they are considered — sometimes in jest, sometimes in earnest — guilty by association.[77]

THE VIETNAMESE

When the Vietnam war ended with the rapid fall of the capital, Saigon, in the spring of 1975, the United States evacuated nearly 140,000 refugees who feared for their safety. In late April 1975, U.S. military forces were airlifting more than 5,000 each day from Saigon to Guam and other interim locations.

Like the Cuban exiles, many of the Vietnamese refugees were members of the middle class who were migrating for political rather than economic reasons. Some were doctors, lawyers, storeowners, and professional people; however, the majority were nonworking women and children. In fact, only 35,000 of the total were heads of households.[78] Many were well educated, with marketable skills, and nearly half spoke English.[79] They were a cosmopolitan people, most from the Saigon region, and many had previously lived elsewhere, especially in North Vietnam.

Eventually, the refugees came to seven relocation centers in the United States. Approximately 6,600 went to France or Canada to live, and 1,546 decided to return to Vietnam. About 127,000 Vietnamese and 4,000 Cambodians waited in the centers for an American sponsor in order to be resettled somewhere in the United States.[80] Between April 1975 and July 1979, 220,000 Indochinese refugees were granted permanent residence in the United States.[81] In July 1979, President Carter, responding to the growing flood of Vietnamese "boat people" seeking refuge, doubled the U.S. quota to 14,000 refugees a month. These new immigrants will increase the Vietnamese-American population by nearly 200,000 by the end of 1980.

SOCIETAL RESPONSE

At first American public opinion appeared to oppose the federal government's decision to admit the Vietnamese refugees. The arrival of such a large number all at once at a time when the national economy was depressed caused some people to react negatively to what they saw as an economic threat. Government officials concluded that some of this reaction was also due to the traditional racial opposition to Asian immigrants and to the fierce antipathy to the war itself.

The initial public response was hostile. In early May 1975, the telephone calls, letters, and telegrams to the White House ran 2 to 1 against admitting the Vietnamese. Public opinion polls showed that the majority of Americans, especially the working class, were convinced that the refugees would take jobs away from Americans. Labor and state officials raised serious objections to "flooding" the labor market and welfare rolls with so many aliens at a time when the economy was depressed. Whether a dramatic shift in public attitude then occurred or whether other Americans came to be heard from is uncertain. Offers of help, particularly from church groups, poured in from all over the country. On December 20, 1975, just seven months after the relocation centers had opened, the last one — Fort Chafee, Arkansas — closed. Not only had all the refugees been placed, but there were more potential sponsors than there were refugees. Some sponsors exploited the refugees but, fortunately, this was not a widespread practice, according to government observers.

RESETTLEMENT

The federal government scattered the Vietnamese throughout every state, even placing 81 refugees in Alaska. The largest concentration was in California (27,300), followed by Texas (9,300), Pennsylvania (7,400), Florida (5,300), and Washington State (4,200).[82] Over 2,000 settled in New Orleans, whose semitropical climate and French traditions may have reminded them of their homeland. Other large concentrations located in the Arlington, Virginia–Washington, D.C. area and in Los Angeles. Because they were scattered, the refugees, unlike other immigrant groups, were usually unable to establish ethnic communities to ease their adjustment in America.

One observer who was deeply involved in the resettlement program contrasted it with the experience of other immigrants and refugees:

The first stage of resettlement is over. "My own dad," exclaimed John McCarthy [executive director of Migration and Refugees Services], "was a refugee. Can we do less for these people than someone did for our forefathers?" He was too generous; no such agency was around to do for our Irish, Italian, German, Polish or other American ancestors. I recall my own Acadian forebears, brutally exiled from Nova Scotia, with no help from anyone, requiring

FIGURE 7.5

Vietnamese refugees await final processing before being flown to the United States mainland from Guam. (United Press International)

some 10 years of wandering before they found a haven in the bayous of Louisiana. Thanks to [computer records of relocation settling], no Vietnamese Evangeline would be forever lost to her Gabriel.[83]

It is remarkable that the first group of Vietnamese refugees was so rapidly resettled. The Cuban migration may have been larger, but resettling them took many years, whereas resettling the Vietnamese took only seven months. Government officials had benefited from their experience with the Cuban refugees, and were better prepared to handle large numbers of people effectively without causing major problems to any one area. This pattern appears to be continuing with the recent arrival of the boat people. Like many strangers in a new country, the Vietnamese have sometimes encountered difficulty, resistance, suspicion, and discrimination in adjusting to their situation.

CULTURAL DIFFERENTIATION

Unlike Americans, who commonly believe in one's ability to establish one's own destiny, many Vietnamese believe life is essentially predetermined, with individual control over what occurs partial at best.[84] Two of the more important aspects of existence that the Vietnamese believe determine one's destiny are *phuc duc* and astrology. These are core elements within the family infrastructure of filial piety and ancestor worship, and they provide important insights into the Vietnamese ability to adapt to a new society with a minimal amount of emotional anxiety.

The concept of *phuc duc* refers to the amount of good fortune that comes from meritorious or self-sacrificing actions. This accumulation of rewards, primarily secured by the women for their family, also affects the lives of succeeding generations into the fifth generation. *Phuc duc* is quantifiable in that improper conduct diminishes the amount one has, while the nature of one's actions and one's degree of personal sacrifice determines the amount of *phuc duc* one acquires.

To a great extent *phuc duc* acts as the social conscience of the nation, a collective superego. The children are conscientiously instructed in the ways of living that result in *phuc duc*. It is, in great part, related to the Confucian concept of *Li*, although it is actually Buddhist-Confucian in origin and unique to Vietnam. It has its place in future reincarnations but primarily it relates to the family and to future generations of the family. Thus the responsibility that it represents is impressively exacting: the future destiny of one's loved ones and of those yet unborn depends upon one's conduct.[85]

So strong is the Vietnamese belief in horoscopes that parents accept no responsibility for a child's personality, believing that the configuration of the celestial bodies at the moment of conception has fixed the character of that individual. At the time of birth a Vietnamese astrologer specifically predicts the personality and events to come for the newborn infant. This often becomes a self-fulfilling prophecy, as the predictions influence actual behavior (parental child-rearing practices as well as the child's own actions, including mate selection as an adult). Thus the prophecy is confirmed by its result.

The important thing here is that the Vietnamese way of life includes belief in a deterministic life force over which one has minimal control. This concept has greatly influenced the accommodation of the Vietnamese to the United States.

> For many this is the second or third time that they have been refugees. It is not something that one ever gets used to, but there is a philosophic acceptance of fate. And this the Vietnamese can accept. It is assigned to bad *phuc duc*, to the heavens, to the land on which one's ancestors are buried, or whatever. The cause, however, is externalized and inasmuch as this is universally concurred in by one's peers, these adverse events are integrated into one's psychic apparatus with a minimum of emotional dislocation.[86]

In one of the first sociological studies of "Vietnamericans," Han T. Doan identified six areas of differentiation: attitudes toward human nature, humanity and nature, time, space, activity, and human interrelations.[87] Rather than perceiving human nature as basically evil but perfectible, Vietnamese believe it is basically good but corruptible. Diligence is thus necessary in all activity: one must exercise caution, self-control, meditation, honor, modesty, and moderation. Vietnamese are strongly tradition-bound, revering their ancestors, homeland, and family traditions. They tend to live in harmony with nature rather than to dominate it. Instead of favoring individualism, Vietnamese culture is oriented toward group goal achievement, primarily within the extended family.

> The doctrine of the "Golden Mean" of Confucius and that of the "Middle Path" of Buddha have been ingrained in the Vietnamese thinking and have dominated Vietnamese thoughts. These doctrines account for the harmony maintained in social relationships among Vietnamese and between Vietnamese and other peoples. In their relations with others, Vietnamese, in order to maintain the "just middle," try to avoid injuring others and hurting their susceptibility; they compromise. They are also delicate and tactful, gentle, polite, and flexible: what belongs to others is pretty and what belongs to them is ugly. Also, it is desirable for Vietnamese to show respect to

BOX 7.2

"I had the feeling I would never come back here. . . . I felt that I was losing the things that I really love. . . . It's a very lonely and scary feeling."

"I came to the U.S. for the adventure. I had heard much about this country and seen many American films. My parents are Chinese and migrated to Thailand about twenty years before I was born. My father is a very successful businessman, having his own lumber business and a few hotels. So I really came here only to satisfy my own curiosity, but I stayed here for my undergraduate and graduate course work and I haven't returned yet.

"It's almost as if I sensed this before I left. I was going to America because I wanted to see that country, but before my parents took me to the airport, I cried. At the airport a lot of people came to say farewell to me and I just waved to them. I had the feeling I would never come back here. Especially when I got into the airplane, I felt that I was losing the things that I really love, and I wanted to get off. It's a very lonely and scary feeling. . . .

"Things seemed strange to me at first. Oriental people all have dark hair. Here I saw many people with different features, with blond hair, brown hair, and so on. At that time they looked funny to me. I had seen some American soldiers in Thailand, but they were a small minority. Now everyone around me was so very different. Another thing was being driven [so fast] on the highways. . . . We have few good highways in Thailand and this was a new experience.

"I can't describe to you how lonely and depressed I was in this country. I at first wished I had never come. The family I stayed with in New Hampshire was friendly and tried to teach me about America, but the language and cultural barriers were overwhelming in those first six or eight months. I was withdrawn because I was afraid of the people and didn't know how to do. Most people were impatient with me and so avoided me. I was sad and didn't like this country, but I felt obliged to my parents to stay for the year even though I was very homesick.

"At the end of the school year I went back home. I discovered I had changed. I was more independent and stubborn, and I enjoyed doing some things that Thai people thought were silly, like getting a suntan. Also, I really wanted to be somebody and make my parents proud, and I thought the best way was to get an education in the U.S. So I came back here and earned my bachelor's degree. This summer I'll finish my master's degree and then I'll go back home to my parents and give them my diplomas. They really belong to my parents because they gave me material and emotional support. I'll come back here . . . and maybe someday be a college professor."

Thai immigrant who came to the United States in 1971 at age 19

their superiors and kindness to their inferiors. The desire to please others can be found in old folk sayings that "since one does not have to buy nice words, one should choose those pleasant to others' ears." To make others happy, one sometimes has to bend low and to live up to their expectation.[88]

According to Confucian thinking, a hierarchical system is the natural order of things. It is necessary, therefore, that individuals know their position in the system, and behave as befits that position.[89]

ACCULTURATION

Once resettled, the Vietnamericans often formed their own self-help organizations to help those who could not communicate well in English learn to do so. Some of the refugees had a fairly good command of English because they had had contact with United States military or civilian personnel stationed in Vietnam. However, about half, usually relatives of former United States employees, had great difficulty with the language.

Some Vietnamese initially lived in the homes of their sponsors and later found their own lodgings. Others obtained separate lodging at the outset, with assistance from their sponsors. Although few, if any, entire families succeeded in leaving Vietnam, many of the Vietnamese came to the United States with enough members of their extended family to continue the traditional family structures. However, early studies show that the change in structural conditions has resulted in tension between the vivid and persistent extended family image and emotional reality.[90] In American society, many Vietnamericans establish separate households, often at a considerable distance from other relatives, although they continue to have occasional contacts and visits and to assist in time of need in a modified extended family arrangement.

In an effort to gain some insight into the degree of acculturation in the first two years, Han T. Doan obtained, from a systematic random sample of 245 respondents now living in eight eastern or western states, information about their changing cultural patterns and language improvement. In a factor analysis of such acculturation outcomes as increased cultural pursuits, leisure activities, and social contacts, feeling at home, language improvement, higher standard of living, more varied diet, proximity to non-Vietnamese, and general acceptance, Doan found that a higher level of education, prior travel abroad, and a greater degree of Americanization prior to emigration were the major factors influencing ease in the acculturation process.[91]

Certainly the composition of the Vietnamerican population suggests that they would have an easy adjustment to American society. About one-fourth of them had been employed in professional, technical, and managerial occupations.[92] Over three-fourths of the adults were high school graduates, and one-fourth had at least one college degree.[93] Only a few years have passed since the first Vietnamese refugees arrived. In areas where they have concentrated, some signs of an ethnic community (organizations, stores, restaurants) have appeared. It remains to be seen whether this ethnic group will become a more cohesive and organized community, or whether their adaptation will follow a different pattern.

OTHER ASIAN-AMERICANS AND PACIFIC ISLANDERS

Other Asian immigrants have come to the United States from Bangladesh, Burma, Cambodia, Indonesia, Laos, Malaysia, Pakistan, and Thailand. There are also Pacific Islanders from Guam, Samoa, Fiji, Tonga, and other parts of Micronesia. Each of these peoples has immigrant populations in the United States ranging in size from a few thousand to tens of thousands. Enumerated information about them is scanty, as little empirical data from either government or other sources exists.

RETROSPECT

As a result of a combination of racial and non-Western cultural differences, a great many Asian immigrants from 1850 to 1940 remained outside the American mainstream all their lives. Lack of acceptance and social interaction in the dominant society, and frequent hostile actions directed against them, made the Asians acutely aware of the differences in the people and culture around them. Each succeeding wave of Asian immigrants, from whatever country, encountered some degree of hostility because of racial and cultural visibility. To some Americans, the Asians posed a serious challenge to the cherished notion of a melting pot because of their race, their non-Christian faith (though some were Christians), their language and alphabet, and their customs and practices. That many chose to settle on the West Coast near their port of entry, much as European immigrants had in the East, only accentuated their presence and led whites to overemphasize their actual numbers. Many also believed that these immigrants posed an economic threat to American workers, and this further encouraged racist reactions.

Many white Americans came to accept negative stereotypes, first about the Chinese and later about the Japanese and Pilipinos. Normal ethnocentric judgments about a culturally distinct people, coupled with racial visibility that served as a distinct link to the stereotype, caused a generalized societal antagonism toward the Asians. The vast differences in culture and physical appearance, augmented by imagined racist fears of threats to economic security or to white womanhood from "lascivious Orientals," led to frequent hostility.

The Japanese were mostly concentrated in rural areas on the West Coast until 1940. On the mainland, racist antagonisms and fears culminated in 1942 with the removal of Japanese-Americans from their homes and jobs. Although a few Japanese-Americans were rounded up in Hawaii, there was no mass evacuation, because the Japanese lived in a less racist environment, with fuller political and economic participation. Pilipinos also encountered overt racial discrimination prior to 1940. Since the changes in the immigration law in 1965, over 250,000 Pilipinos have migrated to the United States. Although many are underemployed, they and the Chinese and Japanese encounter less hostility today than did their predecessors.

Koreans, Vietnamese, Cambodians, and Thais are among the more recent Asian immigrants. Some are war refugees, but all are from non-Western cultures and are racially distinct from white and black Americans. They enter an America far less racially hostile toward Asians than it was in the past. Many are either dependents of U.S. servicemen or individuals with marketable job skills. Most come from a region of the world where patience, stoicism, quiet industriousness, and the cohesiveness of the extended family are long-standing traditions. These traditional values aid the newcomers' transition to a new life.

Asia is presently the major supplier outside this hemisphere of immigrants to the United States. While the figure includes others besides Asians, it is still rather significant that approximately one out of every three immigrants in 1977 came from Asia. Obviously, that part of the world is having a profound effect upon the composition of our population. In the years ahead America will become even more a land of racial and cultural diversity.

QUESTIONS FOR DISCUSSION

1. Discuss the interrelationship between labor conflict and racism with regard to the Chinese, Japanese, and Pilipinos.

2. How did the Chinese of the late nineteenth century respond to hostility and discrimination?

3. How can we explain the different treatment of Japanese-Americans in Hawaii and those on the mainland during World War II?

4. Discuss the legislation and court rulings that were directed against Asian-Americans.

5. How do today's Asian immigrants differ from their predecessors? How and why does society respond to them differently?

SUGGESTED READINGS

Barth, Gunther. *Bitter Strength.* Harvard, Cambridge, Mass., 1964.

Conroy, Hilary, and T. Scott Miyakawa (eds.). *East Across the Pacific.* Clio Press, Santa Barbara, Calif., 1972.

Coolidge, Mary R. *Chinese Immigration.* Henry Holt and Company, New York, 1909.

Cressey, Paul G. *The Taxi-Dance Hall.* University of Chicago Press, Chicago, 1932.

Daniels, Roger. *Concentration Camps U.S.A.: Japanese Americans and World War II.* Holt, New York, 1971.

———. *The Politics of Prejudice.* Atheneum, New York, 1972.

———, and Harry H. L. Kitano. *American Racism: Exploration of the Nature of Prejudice.* Prentice-Hall, Englewood Cliffs, N.J., 1970.

Hsu, Francis L. K. *The Challenge of the American Dream: The Chinese in the United States,* Wadsworth, Belmont, Calif., 1971.

Hundley, Norris Jr. *The Asian American.* American Bibliographic Center — Clio Press, Santa Barbara, Calif., 1976.

Ignacio, Lemuel F. *Asian Americans and Pacific Islanders.* Pilipino Development Associates, San Jose, Calif., 1976.

Kashima, Tetsuden. *Buddhism in America.* Greenwood Press, Westport, Conn., 1977.

Kim, Hyung-Chan. *The Korean Diaspora.* Clio Press, Santa Barbara, Calif., 1977.

Kitano, Harry H. L. *Japanese Americans: The Evolution of a Subculture.* Prentice-Hall, Englewood Cliffs, N.J., 1969.

Loewen, James W. *The Mississippi Chinese.* Harvard, Cambridge, Mass., 1971.

Light, Ivan. *Ethnic Enterprise.* University of California Press, Berkeley, 1972.

Lyman, Stanford M. *The Asian in the West.* Desert Research Institute, Reno, Nev., 1970.

———. *Chinese Americans.* Random House, New York, 1974.

———, *The Asian in North America.* Clio Press, Santa Barbara, Calif., 1977.

McWilliams, Carey. *Brothers Under the Skin.* Little, Brown, Boston, 1951.

Myer, Dillon S. *Uprooted Americans.* University of Arizona Press, Tucson, 1971.

Petersen, William. *Japanese Americans.* Random House, New York, 1971.

Saxton, Alexander. *The Indispensable Enemy: Labor and the Anti-Chinese Movement in California.* University of California Press, Berkeley, 1971.

Sung, Betty Lee. *Mountain of Gold.* Macmillan, New York, 1967.

Weglyn, Michi. *Years of Infamy: The Untold Story of America's Concentration Camps.* Morrow, New York, 1976.

Wu, Cheng-Tsu (ed.). *"Chink!"* — *Anti-Chinese Prejudice in America.* World Publishing, New York, 1972.

NOTES

1. Edwin P. Hoyt, *Asians in the West,* Nelson, New York, 1974, p. 123.

2. "China," *Encyclopedia Britannica,* 7th ed., 1842, Vol. 6.

3. Otis Gibson, *The Chinese in America*, Hitchcock and Walden, Cincinnati, 1877, pp. 51–52.
4. *Ibid.*
5. Alexander Saxton, *The Indispensable Enemy: Labor and the Anti-Chinese Movement in California*, University of California Press, Berkeley, 1971, p. 63.
6. *Ibid.*
7. Mike Hilton, "The Split Labor Market and Chinese Immigration, 1848–1882," presented to the 72nd annual meeting of the American Sociological Association, 1977, p. 7.
8. *Ibid.*, p. 5.
9. Hinton Helper, *The Land of Gold: Reality Versus Fiction*, Baltimore, 1855, pp. 94–96, quoted in Saxton, *The Indispensable Enemy*, p. 19.
10. "The Growth of the U.S. Through Emigration — The Chinese," *The New York Times*, Sept. 3, 1865.
11. *The New York Times*, June 7, 1868.
12. Senator James G. Blaine, *Congressional Record* (Feb. 14, 1879), p. 1301.
13. U.S. Immigration and Naturalization Service, *Annual Report*, U.S. Government Printing Office, Washington, D.C.; 1926, pp. 170–181.
14. *Ibid.*
15. American Federation of Labor, Proceedings, 1893, p. 73.
16. D. Y. Yuan, "New York Chinatown," in *Minority Problems*, eds. Arnold M. Rose and Caroline B. Rose, Harper & Row, New York, 1965, pp. 277–284.
17. Albert W. Palmer, *Orientals in American Life*, Friendship Press, New York, 1934, pp. 1–2, 7.
18. Stanford M. Lyman, "Conflict and the Web of Group Affiliation in San Francisco's Chinatown, 1850–1910," *Pacific Historical Review*, 43 (November 1974), 473–499. This work is based upon Georg Simmel's two theoretical essays, "Conflict" and "The Web of Group Affiliation."
19. S. W. Kung, *Chinese in American Life*, University of Washington Press, Seattle, 1962, p. 89.
20. Stanford M. Lyman, "Marriage and the Family Among Chinese Immigrants to America," *Phylon*, 29 (Winter 1968), 324.
21. *Ibid.*, pp. 322–323.
22. *Ibid.*, p. 327.
23. *Ibid.*, p. 330.
24. *Ibid.*, p. 328.
25. *Congressional Record*, Oct. 21, 1943, p. 8626.
26. U.S. Immigration and Naturalization Service, *Annual Report*, 1977, U.S. Government Printing Office, Washington, D.C., 1977, p. 42.
27. *The New York Times*, June 17, 1973, p. 49.
28. *The New York Times*, July 18, 1976, Sec. 8, p. 1.
29. *Ibid.*, pp. 1, 6.
30. See Cheng-Tsu Wu (ed.), *"Chink!" —Anti-Chinese Prejudice in America*, World Publishing, New York, 1972, pp. 213–269.
31. *Ibid.*, p. 225.
32. Lucy Jen Huang, "The Chinese American Family," in *Ethnic Families in America*, eds. Charles H. Mindel and Robert W. Habenstein, Elsevier, New York, 1976, p. 144.
33. Stanford M. Lyman, "Generation & Character: The Case of the Japanese-Americans," in *East Across the Pacific: Historical and Sociological Studies of Japanese Immigration and Assimilation*, eds. Hilary Conroy and T. Scott Miyakawa. Reprinted by permission of American Bibliographical Center — Clio Press, Inc., Santa Barbara, Calif., © 1972, p. 279. Also in Lyman, S., *The Asian in North America*, Clio Press, Santa Barbara, Calif., 1977, pp. 151–176.
34. Morton Grodzins, *Americans Betrayed*, University of Chicago Press, Chicago, 1949.
35. Lyman, "Generation & Character: The Case of the Japanese-Americans," pp. 279–280. Reprinted by permission of ABC-Clio, Inc., Santa Barbara, California, © 1972.
36. Eugene V. Rostow, "Our Worst Wartime Mistake," *Harper's Magazine*, 191 (September 1945), 193–201.

37. See Michi Weglyn, *Years of Infamy: The Untold Story of America's Concentration Camps*, Morrow, New York, 1976.

38. Esther B. Rhoads, "My Experience with the Wartime Relocation of Japanese," in *East Across the Pacific: Historical and Sociological Studies of Japanese Immigration and Assimilation*, eds. Hilary Conroy and T. Scott Miyakawa, pp. 131–132. Reprinted by permission of ABC-Clio, Inc., Santa Barbara, Calif., © 1972.

39. Ted Nakashima, "Concentration Camp, U.S. Style," *The New Republic*, June 15, 1942, 822–823.

40. Justice Robert H. Jackson, dissenting opinion, *Korematsu v. United States of America*, Vol. 65, Supreme Court Reporter, 1944, pp. 206–208.

41. Harry H. L. Kitano, *Japanese Americans: The Evolution of a Subculture*, Prentice-Hall, Englewood Cliffs, N.J., 1969, p. 132.

42. William Petersen, *Japanese Americans*, Random House, New York, 1971, p. 113.

43. Kitano, *Japanese Americans*, pp. 23–24, 107–108.

44. *Ibid.*, pp. 1–2, 47–48.

45. Akemi Kikumura and Harry H. L. Kitano, "Interracial Marriage: A Picture of the Japanese Americans," *Journal of Social Issues*, 29 (1973), 1–9.

46. Harry H. L. Kitano, "Japanese-American Crime and Delinquency," *Journal of Social Psychology*, 66 (1967), 253–263.

47. Kitano, *Japanese Americans*, p. 127.

48. Vincent N. Parrillo, private interviews with community residents, 1976.

49. Lemuel F. Ignacio, *Asian Americans and Pacific Islanders*, Pilipino Development Associates, San Jose, Calif., 1976, pp. 3–4.

50. *Morrison et al. v. California* (1934), No. 487, Vol. 291, United States Supreme Court Reports, U.S. Government Printing Office, Washington, D.C., 1934, pp. 85–86.

51. Davis McEntire, *The Labor Force in California: A Study of Characteristics and Trends in Labor Force, Employment and Occupations in California, 1900–1950*, University of California Press, Berkeley, 1952, p. 62.

52. Carey McWilliams, *Brothers Under the Skin*, Little, Brown, Boston, 1951, p. 239.

53. Sylvain Lazarus, San Francisco Municipal Court, January 1936, quoted in Manuel Braken, *I Have Lived with the American People*, Caxton, Caldwell, Calif., 1948, pp. 136–138.

54. Letter from Sylvester Saturday, in *Time*, 27 (May 11, 1936), 4.

55. Letter from Ernest D. Ilustre, in *Time*, 27 (April 27, 1936), 3.

56. McWilliams, *Brothers Under the Skin*, p. 244.

57. Bernicio T. Catapusan, "Filipino Intermarriage Problems in the United States," *Sociology and Social Research*, 22 (1938), 265–272.

58. For an excellent sociological study of Pilipinos in dance halls, see Paul G. Cressey, *The Taxi-Dance Hall*, University of Chicago Press, Chicago, 1932, pp. 145–176.

59. Ignacio, *Asian Americans and Pacific Islanders*, p. 7.

60. R. T. Feria, "War and the Status of the Filipino Immigrants," *Sociology and Social Research*, 31 (1946), 50.

61. Department of Health, Education, and Welfare, *A Study of Selected Socioeconomic Characteristics of Ethnic Minorities Based on the 1970 Census. Volume II: Asian Americans*, Washington, D.C., 1974, pp. 105, 134, 145.

62. Harold H. Sunoo and Sonia S. Sunoo, "The Heritage of the First Korean Women Immigrants in the United States: 1903–1924." *Korean Christian Journal*, 2 (Spring 1977), 144.

63. *Ibid.*, p. 146.

64. *Ibid.*, pp. 144, 165.

65. Bernice H. Kim, "The Koreans in Hawaii," *Social Science*, 9 (1934), 409.

66. Lee Houchins and Chang-su Houchins, "The Korean Experience in America, 1903–1924," *Pacific Historical Review*, 43 (November

1974), 560.

67. Won Moo Hurh, "Comparative Study of Korean Immigrants in the United States: A Typology," *Korean Christian Journal*, 2 (Spring 1977), 75.

68. Hyung-Chan Kim, "Some Aspects of Social Demography of Korean Americans," *International Migration Review*, 8 (Spring 1974), 23–42.

69. U.S. Immigration and Naturalization Service, *Annual Report*, U.S. Government Printing Office, Washington, D.C., 1976, pp. 57–61, 123–127.

70. Kwang C. Kim, "Intra- and Inter-Ethnic Group Conflicts: The Case of Korean Small Business in the United States," presented to the 11th annual meeting of the Korean Christian Scholars, 1977, p. 3.

71. Edna Bonacich, Ivan Light, and Charles Choy Wong, "Small Business Among Koreans in Los Angeles," presented to the 71st annual meeting of the American Sociological Association, 1976, p. 10.

72. Kim, "Intra- and Inter-Ethnic Group Conflicts: The Case of Korean Small Business in the United States," p. 23.

73. See Edna Bonacich, "A Theory of Middleman Minorities," *American Sociological Review*, 38 (1973), 583–594.

74. Department of Health, Education, and Welfare, *A Study of Selected Socioeconomic Characteristics of Ethnic Minorities Based on the 1970 Census. Volume II: Asian Americans*, pp. 105, 134, 142.

75. Emory S. Bogardus, "Comparing Racial Distance in Ethiopia, South Africa, and the United States," *Sociology and Social Research* 52 (1968), 149–156.

76. Won Moo Hurh, "Comparative Study of Korean Immigrants in the United States: A Typology," p. 68.

77. Richard Halloran, "Koreans in the U.S. Suffer Effects of Bribe Affair," *The New York Times*, April 12,

1977, p. 16; see John Lofland, *The Doomsday Cult: A Study of Conversion, Proselytization, and Maintenance of Faith*, rev. ed., Prentice-Hall, Englewood Cliffs, N.J., 1975, for a discussion of the "Moonies."

78. "Future of Refugees: The Furor and the Facts," *U.S. News and World Report*, May 19, 1975, 16.

79. *Ibid.*, pp. 16–17.

80. "Christmas Brings Happy Ending for Vietnamese Refugees," *U.S. News and World Report*, Dec. 29, 1975, 14–15.

81. UN High Commissioner on Refugees, reported in *Newsweek*, July 2, 1979, 48.

82. *Ibid.*

83. C. J. McNaspy, "The New Faces at Fort Chafee," *America*, 134, No. 5 (1976), 99.

84. The author acknowledges a substantial debt and gratitude to Walter H. Slote, Ph.D.; and Stephen Young, J. D., for sharing their expertise about the Vietnamese and Vietnamericans.

85. Walter H. Slote, "Adaption of Recent Vietnamese Immigres to the American Experience: A Psycho-Cultural Approach," paper presented at the 29th annual meeting of the Association for Asian Studies, March 1977, p. 9.

86. *Ibid.*, p. 11.

87. Han T. Doan, "Vietnamericans: Bending Low or Breaking in the Acculturation Process?" presented to the 72nd annual meeting of the American Sociological Association, 1977, pp. 14–15.

88. *Ibid.*, p. 12.

89. *Ibid.*

90. See Walter H. Slote, "Psychodynamic Structures in Vietnamese Personality," *Transcultural Research in Mental Health*, 2 (1972).

91. Doan, "Vietnamericans: Bending Low or Breaking in the Acculturation Process?", pp. 9–11, 15.

92. Department of Health, Education,

and Welfare, Refugee Task Force, *Report to the Congress*, March 15, 1976.

93. Department of Health, Education, and Welfare, Refugee Task Force, *Report to the Congress*, March 21, 1977.

EIGHT

OTHER NON-WESTERN IMMIGRANTS

◢ Other peoples from the non-Western world have come to the United States as permanent immigrants, students, or sojourners. They come from that part of the world situated between the area of Western thought and history on the one side, and the area of Eastern thought and the history of the Orient on the other. In other words, these are the peoples from Africa, the Middle East, and other Asian countries, such as India and Turkey.

Although some of these peoples migrated before 1965 and had encounters similar to those of other racial and ethnic groups of earlier times, most have come in the past fifteen years. Their acceptance as strangers and their adjustment to American life has differed from those of pre-1920 immigrants because structural conditions in both the sending and host countries have changed. Because of the occupational preference ranking of the 1965 legislation, many of those who have come were professional, managerial, or technical workers. Some are underemployed, but others are accepted in their occupational roles. Either way, most are generally isolated from informal social contact with others outside their nationality group. Thus the theoretical framework used in examining the experiences of past immigrant groups is not completely applicable to this group of immigrants, as we shall see.

HISTORICAL AND SOCIOLOGICAL PERSPECTIVES

Aside from special legislation allowing political or war refugees to enter, the immigration regulations prior to 1965 effectively limited the number of immigrants from the non-Western world. Eliminating the restrictive national origins quota system opened the door to America to many different peoples who had previously been denied entry. Since few had migrated to the United States prior to 1890, the year upon which the 1924 immigration legislation based its quotas, very few non-Western immigrants had been able to gain approval to migrate to the United States.

After the immigration laws were changed in 1965, there was a perceptible change in the types of newcomers arriving. For instance, European migration decreased by 34.7 percent, from 113,424 in 1965 to 74,048 in 1977, while Asian immigration increased by 629.3 percent, from 20,683 in 1965 to 150,842 in 1977, and African immigration rose 184.4 percent, from 3,383 in 1965 to 9,612 in 1977.[1]

THE PUSH-PULL FACTORS

For many non-Western immigrants, overpopulation and poverty have so seriously affected the quality of life in their homelands that they have sought a better life elsewhere. Sometimes restrictive governmental actions or limited socioeconomic opportunities have pushed the people to look elsewhere. America, with its cultural diversity, economic opportunities, and higher living standards, makes its influence felt throughout the world and is a powerful lure to those who are dissatisfied with their situation. For others, the United States offers educational or professional or career opportunities. Rapid air travel, which reduces the psychological distance from one's native country, has been a further inducement.

STRUCTURAL CONDITIONS

The non-Western immigrants discussed in this chapter have followed the same patterns as other ethnic groups who have emigrated to the United States. They usually settle in urban areas in close proximity to their compatriots, with whom they develop close, primary social contacts. Because many are trained professionals or skilled technicians, however, their job situation is quite different from that of the unskilled poor, who made up the majority of the 1880–1920 immigrant groups. Nor do they usually settle in decaying sections of cities, since with their income they can find better places to live. Wherever they congregate to live and work, one can find the various support facilities: churches or temples, food stores and restaurants specializing in their native victuals, social clubs or organizations, and perhaps their own schools and newspapers. They soon send for other members of their family or write home telling of their good fortune, and this stimulates others to come to the United States. The chain migration pattern of earlier immigrants is once again in evidence.

A great many of the new immigrants do not fit the acculturation patterns that worked so well for other immigrant groups. For instance, Middle Eastern prosperity and the new international image of the Arabs have not only strengthened that group's ethnic solidarity in the United States, but have also encouraged some to plan to return to their native country eventually. A Saudi Arabian, for example, might return from the United States after acquiring an advanced education or experience that would be preparation for a better life back home. Saudi Arabia collects no taxes whatsoever and offers free education and medical care, and its standard of living is improving rapidly. Arab recruitment of those with American know-how and an Arab background might even generate a "reverse brain drain."[2] Still, although immigration from Saudi Arabia may be extremely low, a greater number of newcomers from other Arab countries are seeking permanent residence here, as indicated in Table 8.1.

Because of new circumstances and conditions in the United States and because of the special character of this immigration, the theoretical

TABLE 8.1

ARAB IMMIGRANTS ADMITTED TO THE UNITED STATES

COUNTRY	1973	1974	1975	1976
Egypt	2,016	1,642	1,513	1,560
Iran	2,013	1,576	1,514	1,814
Iraq	892	2,059	2,603	3,276
Jordan	1,957	2,306	2,120	2,118
Lebanon	1,503	1,857	1,737	2,397
Morocco	244	261	235	195
Saudi Arabia	a	a	a	246
Syria	941	897	1,074	1,108
Yemen	1,002	477	185	451

[a]Figures not available.

SOURCE: U.S. Immigration and Naturalization Service, *Annual Report*, U.S. Government Printing Office, Washington, D.C., 1976, Table 7, p. 53; *Annual Report*, 1977, p. 1B.

framework for dealing with this new breed of immigrants needs revision. The emphasis is still upon structural conditions and the differentials of power, culture, and class, but the model is different.

Since many of this group of non-Western immigrants have marketable skills, they can get professional and salaried jobs without first having to play a subservient role in the economy. They need not yield to pressures to conform to the American way of life in order to gain middle-class respectability. Their income is high enough to enable them to enjoy the life style they want, and they are thus free to continue their own cultural behavior patterns. Some Americanization will undoubtedly occur, but these immigrants do not have to make substantial adaptations in order to "make it" in American society.

Another sizable segment of non-Westerners in the United States is the nonimmigrant students, workers, and business people. Although they usually remain for only two to five years, their growing numbers make their presence of significant concern in the field of race and ethnic relations. In 1976, for example, 47,878 Asian and 9,368 African students arrived in the United States to study, and 16,004 Africans and 148,295 Asians came to this country for business purposes.[3]

In many respects, these temporary visitors, although visible to others in work, residential, shopping, and entertainment settings, are similar to Americans who work for a multinational corporation overseas. Even if assigned to another country for a considerable number of years, they seldom lose their sense of ethnic identity. They live within the culture and enjoy the available opportunities without any thought of abandoning their own cultural ties and becoming assimilated in the country in which they work. Many aliens working here have the same orientation, whether they work for one of their own country's multinational corporations or for some American employer. U.S. citizenship and assimilation are not part of their plans. Many of today's sojourners may be more sophisticated than their predecessors, but their resistance to assimilation is just as strong.

SOCIETAL REACTION

Some, although very few, non-Western immigrants from Africa, the Middle East, Turkey, and India did come to the United States in the late nineteenth and early twentieth centuries. They encountered far more prejudice and discrimination than their compatriots experience in America today. Americans are now more tolerant of what may seem to them to be the strange appearance and customs of the non-Western immigrants. Tolerance, though, is not the same thing as acceptance. People do categorize others and make judgments based on visible impressions, which often lead to stereotyping. Racial distinguishing features and distinctive apparel, such as a dashiki, turban, or sari, set these newcomers apart. Although there is no more overt discrimination than that along racial lines or among racial purists, other visible differences offer additional grounds for preferential treatment and limited social interaction.

In recent surveys of social distance among various minority groups,[4] the racially distinct non-Western immigrants have all scored at the bottom. Many newcomers find themselves accepted in their professional, managerial, and technical occupational roles by members of the dominant society, but usually not included in personal social activities.

THE SYRIAN-LEBANESE

A number of factors have contributed to a confusion of ethnic identities and a lack of accurate official statistics covering the immigrants from this part of the world. In the late nineteenth and early twentieth centuries, the Arabian peninsula was part of the Ottoman Empire; its inhabitants were Turkish citizens until the end of World War I. Although there was a great deal of cultural diversity in this single geographic region, all the inhabitants spoke Arabic and, except the Egyptians, used the term *Syrian* to identify themselves. Still, the immigrants had Turkish passports, and so United States officials identified them as Turkish until 1899, when a separate category for Syrians was begun. While approximately 85 percent of the immigrants came from the area known as Lebanon, only in the 1930s did the term *Lebanese* gain acceptance. Some Lebanese resisted, preferring to continue calling themselves Syrians, while some authentic Syrians began calling themselves Lebanese.

ETHNIC IDENTITY

Neither political authority nor specific regional residence determined group affinity; rather, religion defined the goals and boundaries of the "Syrian" community, as here indicated:

> Theological differences of Jews, Christians and Moslems have become translated into social and structural realities with each community becoming socially separate from the others. What the people believe is not so important as the fact that people who believe similarly are considered to belong to some social order qualitatively different from that of the rest. Since religion deals with things of primary importance, a different religious persuasion turns others into members of a somewhat distinct society or "nation."
> ... Since the religions of the Middle East were all structurally and socially separate from one another, the Jewish community and the immigrant Moslem and Christian community continued this pattern of separation in the United States.[5]

MIGRATION AND SETTLEMENT

Although religious differences kept the three groups separate, the push-pull factors that led them to emigrate to the United States affected them similarly. In the main a combination of harsh living conditions — hunger, poverty, disease — and Turkish oppression — particularly against the Christians — led many Syrians to leave. The pull of the United States was the result of reports by missionaries and steamship agents of economic opportunities and religious and political freedom. Emigration to the United States began in the 1870s, reaching substantial proportions between 1890 and 1914 as Turkish oppression increased. The peak years were 1913 and 1914, when over 9,000 migrated to avoid conscription into the Turkish army, then being prepared for combat in the First World War.

A seven-block area on Washington and Rector Streets in lower Manhattan became a thriving Syrian community in the late nineteenth century. Other Syrians settled in downtown Brooklyn and elsewhere throughout the entire country. Most Syrian immigrants came either from cities or from densely populated villages; they usually located in American cities of 100,000 or more, and had little difficulty adjusting to urban life.

CULTURE CONFLICTS

Syrians often replaced the Irish in old city neighborhoods. This is an example of the sociological concept of *invasion-succession*, in which one group experiencing vertical mobility gradually moves out of its old residences. It is then replaced by another group at the previous residents' original socioeconomic level. Sometimes there may be hostility between the old and new groups. In the case of the Syrians, religious tension resulted in a clash with the Irish, as this 1920 account about the Dublin District of Paterson, New Jersey, reveals:

> When the Syrians came to live there, the rentals became higher. This caused hard feelings between the Irish and the Syrians, which developed into a feud between the two nationalities. The fight started in the saloon on Grand and Mill Streets, first with bitter arguments and harsh words, and then threatening fist fights. From the saloon, the fight came out to the streets. It was like two armies in opposition facing each other. . . . The police force was called in to put an end to this fight. All they could do was to throw water on them to disperse them. These fights continued for three days in the evening. Finally, a committee of Syrians went to talk to Dean McNulty of St. John's, explaining to him that they were Christians coming from the Holy Land, not Mohammedans or Turks, as the Irish used to call them. They were good Catholics and they wanted to live in peace with everybody. Then the good Dean, at Sunday masses, urged the Irish to stop fighting with the Syrians, who were like them, Catholics. He succeeded in stopping this fighting better than the police.[6]

To be called a Turk was a bitter insult to the Syrian Christians, who had suffered religious persecution by the Moslem Turks. Americans frequently thought the Syrians were Turks, but they also frequently used the word in a derogatory sense, as an ethnophaulism much like "Jap," "kike," or "wop." Although these enthnophaulisms are still in evidence to a lesser degree today, Syrians no longer encounter this form of prejudice.

Another problem the Syrian immigrants encountered before World War I was racial classification. In 1909 the U.S. District Court in St. Louis ruled them ineligible for naturalization on the basis of the 1790 legislation, declaring them to be nonwhite. Many Syrian Christians

FIGURE 8.1

The Syrian Colony, Washington Street, New York. Drawing by W. Bengough.
(Museum of the City of New York)

were blond and blue-eyed, but the racial barrier was determined by country of origin. The Circuit Court of Appeals reversed this decision. Shortly thereafter the matter was again raised, this time in the United States District Court in New York, which ruled that they could be naturalized.

EARLY PATTERNS

Syrian males usually came alone and then sent for their wives and children. Though poor, they were mostly literate and insisted that their children complete primary school. The wife was more emancipated and less dependent on her husband than her counterparts in other ethnic groups at that time. She and the children, after they completed grade school, all worked together for the family's economic welfare. The family structure proved to be an important factor in the Syrians' economic success.

Generally, Syrians preferred to work at trade and shopkeeping, as trading was a time-honored occupation in their native land. Many Syrians became peddlers and traveled throughout the country, bringing both essential and exotic goods to many Americans. In the late nineteenth and early twentieth centuries, the peddler filled an economic need and was a welcome visitor to the home and community. About one out of three Syrian men became peddlers; others tried various ventures in commerce, started restaurants, or, in a few cases, worked in factories.

UPWARD MOBILITY

The Syrians achieved economic security quickly, often in the first generation. This is especially significant since less than one-fourth of those who came were professional or skilled workers. What aided them in their adjustment, acceptance, and upward mobility was (1) wide dispersal, negating any significant opposition to their presence; (2) business expertise and selection of self-employment, which allowed them greater rewards; and (3) cultural values of thrift, industriousness, and investment that were comparable to the middle-class values of the host society.

Even while they were still in the lower income brackets and in working class occupations, the "Syrians" displayed the social characteristics of the middle classes in American urban centers. Studies of these Arab immigrants in Chicago, Pittsburg and the South reveal a common pattern: low crime rates, better than average health, higher I.Q.'s, and more regular school attendance among the children, few intermarriages and divorces.[7]

Coming from a country in which nearly every man owned the house he lived in, determined to be independent, and highly motivated to suc- ceed, the Syrians accumulated money rapidly and invested it either in property or in business ventures. By 1911 there were Syrians in almost every branch of commerce, including banking and import-export houses, and the government reported that their median income was only slightly lower than the $665 annual income of the adult native-born male.

Unlike other immigrant groups who had to wait two or three gener- ations to exert their independence from ghetto life and to satisfy their desire for mobility, it was the Syrian immigrants (first genera- tion) who amassed the wealth that their sons used as a lever for bringing themselves into wider contacts with society.[8]

The story of Michael A. Shadid, an 1890 immigrant, typifies not only first-generation upward mobility, but also early efforts to help others on the part of the ethnic elite.[9] Beginning as a door-to-door jewelry peddler in the Southwest, Shadid saved $5,000 to pay for his medical education. After he became a successful doctor, he wanted to repay his debt to his adopted country by helping others. With the enthusiastic cooperation of other Arab immigrants in western Oklahoma, he founded the first cooperative hospital in the United States, providing inexpensive medi- cal care. A modern parallel is entertainer Danny Thomas, a second- generation Lebanese-American, who founded St. Jude Children's Research Hospital in Memphis, Tennessee, which has become the greatest single rallying point for the Arab-American community for fund-raising and a source of ethnic pride.[10]

Rapid economic success and the lack of either unfavorable stereotypes or discrimination barriers once they were known as Syrians, not Turks, allowed the Syrian-Lebanese to assimilate into American society quite easily, so that they did not need to duplicate the host society's institu- tions. True, they had social organizations and their own newspapers, but their mobility, wide dispersal, differing religions, and emphasis on the extended family rather than on ethnic organizations resulted in their being assimilated rather easily.

By the mid-1950s the Syrian-Americans had completely abandoned their "nomadic" occupations. They had entered the mainstream of American economic and social life and were represented in virtually every industry and profession.[11] Because they were prosperous, their children were able to enter the sciences, the professions, politics, and the arts, and many have distinguished themselves in each of these fields.

Ethnicity among the Syrian-Lebanese is not very viable, except perhaps among the most recent arrivals. Large-scale intermarriage has

BOX 8.1

"Sometimes in class I might say something with a super-heavy accent, and perhaps even say it completely wrong, and they would laugh at me."

"I am of Circassian origin, having been born in Syria. My father worked in government with the interior ministry. When the government changed from a moderate socialist to a radical socialist government following the Arab-Israeli War in 1968, my father was arrested as a pro-western sympathizer. He escaped from jail, and we all fled to Jordan, where we received asylum. We migrated to West Germany, but very few Circassians live there, and so we came to the U.S. where other Circassians who had fled from Russia now lived.

"Before we came here, the idea I had about America was that the people were the same, that everybody was an American except the blacks because they were different in color. I thought everybody would be an American, but when we came here — especially as soon as I went to high school — I found everyone identified with their parents' origin. In other words, they would call themselves Italian-American, Dutch-American, and so on. It was a little confusing to me because I expected them to say they were Americans. Instead they said their nationality first and then said American.

"Most Circassians live in northern New Jersey or in California, and so we settled in New Jersey where my father already knew some people. I did have a lot of trouble with the language here. I spoke two languages — Circassian and Arabic — but starting as a sophomore in high school I had trouble relating to the people. You know how high school kids are. They're immature. Sometimes in class I might say something with a super-heavy accent, and perhaps even say it completely wrong, and they would laugh at me. I didn't have many friends in high school because I worked after school, and besides, we didn't interact very much with the Americans because the Circassian community had its own activities and clubs. Our language and culture were different and the Americans weren't so friendly. Besides, once you know you have an accent, that does stop you from even trying to make friends. It's a barrier. You're still trying to learn a language and it's hard. With my brothers I spoke Arabic, with my parents who were so nationalistic we had to speak Circassian, and in school I had to learn English, and it was all very confusing."

Syrian immigrant who came to the United States in 1968
at age 15

been occurring in recent years despite en masse family moves, vacations, and social activities, and this, Milton Gordon maintains, is usually the last stage of the assimilation process.[12] Less than two thousand new Lebanese immigrants have been coming to the United States in recent years, except in 1976 when many people fled the raging civil war in that country.

Although exact figures are hard to establish because of past use of Turkish passports, researchers suggest that the current Syrian-Lebanese population in the United States is about 200,000. In 1976 there were 1,108 Syrian, 2,118 Jordanian, and 2,397 Lebanese immigrants admitted.[13] Under current immigration laws, most of these were relatives — wives, children, brothers, and sisters — of people already here.

THE IRANIANS

Immigrants from Iran, or Persia, as many preferred to call their homeland during the reign of Shah Mohammed Reza Pahlevi, are in some ways similar to other recent ethnic groups. They are mostly of the middle class, coming here as either students or skilled professionals. They dislike the political climate or the standard of living in their own country and are seeking a better quality of life somewhere else. Coming from a highly Westernized country, they are generally familiar with the English language and American values, having learned them in school and through contact with American business people.

LACK OF COMMUNITY

Many European, Asian, and Western Hemisphere immigrants who have come to the United States have not planned to remain here permanently. Indeed, tens of thousands have returned to their native land over the years. Many of the Iranians currently residing here are sojourners, and this appears to contribute to a lack of community among them. In a study of Iranian professional, middle-class immigrants living and working in the New York metropolitan region, Abdoulmaboud Ansari found that most do not intend to remain in the United States.[14] They do not form a territorially compact community, nor do they develop close personal ties with their compatriots other than their families. Most Iranian immigrants are physically and socially distant from other Iranians in this country and do not come together except at Now-Rooz, the Persian New Year, celebrated on the first day of spring.

The Now-Rooz party (which takes place in many major American cities) is the only major national event for Iranians in America. As the only publicly visible ceremony, it creates an atmosphere of national identity and a sense of belonging. However, it seems that somehow the ceremony has lost the meaning originally attached to it. For example, one of the most important aspects of Now-Rooz is to review or to extend friendships. The Iranians who attend the festivities in America are apt to come together as strangers and leave without exchanging any addresses or gaining any new friendships. Most of the festivities are characterized by a lack of intimacy and excessive self-consciousness in maintaining of social distance.[15]

Among Iranian students in the United States, of whom there were about 50,000 in the 1975–1976 academic year, there is likely to be more personal interaction, formation of associations, such as the political organization Iran House, or a sense of community. The minority emigrants from Iran — the Armenians, Bahais, and Jews — show greater group cohesiveness and intend to become U.S. citizens, but these are less than a tenth of the immigrants from Iran. For students, political difficulties at home, causing fear of returning, have been important factors in both their cohesiveness and their desire to stay here. Shortly before and after the fall of the Shah of Iran, hundreds of Iranian students did return home.

MARGINALITY

Many of Ansari's respondents described themselves as *Belataklif*[s], or ambivalent persons. Unable to choose between the two countries, they have become alienated in both. In Iran, their social prestige is much higher, but they have become Americanized enough to feel like foreigners in their own land. In America they are emotional aliens.

Here in America, not only is his social recognition limited to areas such as hospitals and universities, but as an alien he is subject to a discriminatory treatment because of his particular identity; he is an alien professional. It is as a result of such lowering of status that this type of immigrant finds his professional success has not completely satisfied his social needs.

A large proportion of the members of this group seem to be considering the idea of leaving this country. Such tendency to re-emigration is one of the main characteristics of this type of immigrant. While some of the advantages of the present environment may exert pressure upon him to remain in America, personal ties, status aspirations, and cultural attachment constantly evoke the hope of returning home. The image of home, of course, is an over idealized image. From a distance of time and space, life at home is romanticized, thus intensifying the tendency to re-emigration. At the same time, the idea of returning gives the immigrant a convenient self-assurance against the creeping thought of his abandonment of home. But since his state of mind is one of skepticism and uncertainty, accompanied by an earlier alienation from home, many are likely to remain, up to a certain point, an undecided immigrant. The more he remains as an undecided immigrant, the less likely will he be to return, because as time passes, he becomes more convinced that he cannot afford another readjustment.[16]

Oppression at home and opportunity abroad are common push-pull factors, and so some members of other nationalities are what Ansari terms "dually marginal men" — those who find themselves on the periphery of both their native and host societies. This point became quite evident when, after American hostages were taken at the U.S. Embassy in Iran in November 1979, Iranian-Americans and visiting students became victims of verbal abuse, boycotts, arson, and physical attack because of their nationality. In a manner painfully reminiscent of the experiences of Japanese-Americans in the 1940s, Iranians in the United States became scapegoats, suffering indignities and discrimination.

THE IRAQIS

It is necessary to distinguish between the immigrants from Iraq who came here before and after the Second World War because the political, social, and economic changes in the Middle East made these groups of immigrants very different. Studying one Iraqi subcultural group of Chaldeans living in the Detroit metropolitan area, Mary Sengstock observed its pre- and postwar changes due to the evolution of Iraq into a modern nation-state and the heightened Arab consciousness caused by Arab-Israeli tensions.[17]

The early immigrants had formed a community of village-oriented entrepreneurs with their religious traditions as their primary identification. They maintained a *gemeinschaft* subsociety within American society. Family orientations were strong, and a great many Iraqis were self-employed, operating grocery stores and other small businesses. They were, for the most part, a self-enclosed ethnic community.

Not only have recent Iraqi immigrants to Detroit had different value orientations than their predecessors, reflecting their increased education and their more urbanized backgrounds; they have also affected the self-perceptions and behavior of the earlier immigrants. Although the Chaldeans are Christian, they feel the pull of Arab nationalist loyalties,[18] and this national consciousness is infectious. Most now think of themselves as Arabs or Iraqis, not as Chaldeans or Telkeffes, another Iraqi subcultural group. Recent immigrants are less likely to be self-employed and more likely to be involved in bureaucratic endeavors that bring them into contact with many persons of different backgrounds.

In short, recent Iraqi immigrants rely more on formal organizations and interact more with outsiders. They are likely to join non-Chaldean organizations and to develop social relationships, including close friendship ties and marriage, with people from other backgrounds. With new immigrants arriving all the time (this particular community exceeds 6,000), these patterns may well continue and be the norm.

THE SAUDI ARABIANS

In recent years the close, friendly political and business relations between Saudi Arabia and the United States have encouraged a very small but steady stream of Saudi Arabians to come to the United States. Economic conditions are so favorable at home, though, that very few of those who emigrate seek permanent residence; however, many temporary visitors (students, business people, travelers) come. In 1976, for example, there were 246 immigrants from Saudi Arabia. Yet the number of Saudi Arabians here is much higher; the Saudi Arabian embassy estimates that about 7,500 Saudi citizens are in the United States.[19]

Most of those who come to the United States seek higher education or professional training, and most of the Saudi Arabian students attend colleges in Arizona, California, and Colorado. Generally they cluster together and share many things in common. One might easily walk down a street near the University of Denver and smell *Kabsa,* a popular Saudi dish of lamb stew with rice and tomatoes. When their training or education ends, almost all return to Saudi Arabia. A small fraction remain, usually because they have taken an American spouse.

Saudi Arabia has few permanent emigrants. Urbanization is proceeding smoothly in this tribal society and is generating many opportunities for its citizens, particularly the college-educated. In this oil-rich economy, there is no need for an income tax; education and medical services are free to all citizens. There is freedom of speech, and anyone may offer suggestions or air grievances through personal appointments with government leaders, by letter, or in the press. Because economic opportunities are excellent, the standard of living rapidly improving, and the Moslem religion a strong unifying force in their society, few Saudis seek permanent residence elsewhere.

OTHER ARAB IMMIGRANTS

The number of Arab immigrants other than the Syrian-Lebanese who came to the United States prior to 1965 was extremely small. Some early immigrants became peddlers, like the Persian peddler immortalized in the musical *Oklahoma!* Even before World War I, these immigrants were usually well-educated in medicine, engineering, and commerce. There are relatively few of these immigrants, as Table 8.1 indicates, but because many enter American society at a higher social level, they are making substantial contributions in sophisticated fields of work.

Tens of thousands of Arab students come to study in the United States, often with generous allowances from their families, and seem to adjust well to their new environment. Interviews and economic trends suggest that an increasing percentage of the newcomers will choose to return to the Middle East after they have completed their education here, or even after they have made a niche for themselves in one of the professions.[20]

THE RAMALLAH FEDERATION

One example of an ethnic organization that exists to help those of its people who lack the financial wherewithal and expertise to adjust to and establish themselves in the United States is the Ramallah Federation. Named after a town of 25,000 inhabitants just north of Jerusalem, it is made up of local and regional social clubs in all major cities in the United States. This is not a Pan-Arab organization, but one oriented to people tracing their heritage back to Ramallah.

In addition to providing scholarships and supporting schools, a library, a hospital, and Boy Scout troops in Ramallah, the organization also assists people from Ramallah who come to the United States, of whom there are now ten thousand scattered throughout the country.[21] Realistically reasoning that newcomers are not ready for sophisticated business ventures, the clubs guarantee them bank loans and provide seed money for mom-and-pop-type grocery, liquor, and variety stores. The newcomer repays the loan with proceeds from the business, then adds a small percentage so that the club may help Ramallahans yet to come. It is estimated that Ramallahans now own a quarter — perhaps more — of San Francisco's small convenience stores. With them they are preparing their children for more sophisticated businesses, building their future with help from the past.[22]

CULTURAL DIFFERENTIATION

Edward Hall identified differences in the value orientations of most Arabs and Americans. Although the Arab nation-states are changing and other variables (such as specific nationality, socioeconomic status, or residence) may also shape Arabs' values, knowledge of these traditional values may help in understanding the perspective of some first-generation Arab-Americans. Hall indicates four principal areas of difference: rights to body space; privacy; facing; and olfaction.[23] To the Arab, all individuals have rights in their moving about, no one more than another. For example, pushing and shoving in public places is not considered rude or intrusive. What the Arab does consider rude or aggressive is an American's cavalier regard for moving space, such as some drivers' callousness toward pedestrians. All have rights in their movement. Physical privacy is rare in the Arab world; there is no Arabic word for the concept. Arabs enjoy lots of space within their homes, avoiding partitions so as not to be alone. Personal privacy is being alone with one's thoughts, not talking to others. Using the "silent treatment" on an Arab to show anger will not work, for the Arab will simply feel that the silent party wants to be in thought and not in conversation. Arabs consider it impolite to converse in one's peripheral view. Thus, speaking while walking side by side is not acceptable; the Arab will probably edge ahead, turn, and stop to see and to be involved in face-to-face contact. Perhaps most intriguing to Westerners is the prominent place of olfaction in traditional Arab life.

> Not only is it one of the distance-setting mechanisms, but it is a vital part of a complex system of behavior. Arabs consistently breathe on people when they talk. However, this habit is more than a matter of different manners. To the Arab good smells are pleasing and a way of being involved with each other. To smell one's friend is not only nice but desirable, for to deny him your breath is to act ashamed. Americans, on the other hand, trained as they are not to breathe in people's faces, automatically communicate shame in trying to be polite. . . . Smell is even considered in the choice of a mate. When couples are being matched for marriage, the man's go-between will sometimes ask to smell the girl, who may be turned down if she doesn't "smell nice." Arabs recognize that smell and disposition may be linked.

> In a word, the olfactory boundary performs two roles in Arab life. It enfolds those who want to relate and separates those who don't. The Arab finds it essential to stay inside the olfactory zone as a means of keeping tab on changes in emotion. What is more, he may feel crowded as soon as he smells something unpleasant.[24]

PRESENT TRENDS

Although a few thousand new Arab immigrants arrive each year, it does not seem likely that their numbers will increase significantly in the foreseeable future. Some Arab countries, such as Egypt, do have serious economic problems, and others, like Iran and Lebanon, have political problems, but the oil-producing countries have been using their revenues to upgrade living standards. As a result, there would seem to be no compelling reason for any change in current migration patterns.

THE TURKS

According to immigration figures, a total of 384,271 Turkish immigrants came to the United States between 1820 and 1977. That number would normally place Turkey among the top twenty countries from which immigrants came to this country. However, as indicated in the section on the Syrian-Lebanese, subjugated peoples of the Ottoman Empire with different languages and cultures used Turkish passports, and so immigration officials identified them as Turkish. In reality, only a few thousand Turks actually migrated here before World War II, and only about 23,000 have come since that time.

FACTORS AGAINST IMMIGRATION

Several factors explain this low level of emigration in comparison with other poor, undeveloped nations during the great migration period. Perhaps foremost, Moslem Turks had waged a relentless campaign against the Christians within their empire and would hardly be favorably inclined toward settling in an almost exclusively Christian country. Second, the Turks had traditionally always migrated in large groups. Consequently, there was little outside the country to attract families or individuals. In 1923 Turkey barred any emigrant from ever returning, even as a visitor. This law remained in force until 1950. With laws against emigration, few Turks decided to seek a better life elsewhere. Since 1965, however, a small but steady trickle of Turkish immigrants have migrated to the United States.

SOCIETAL ATTITUDES

Although relatively few Turks emigrated to the United States, feelings toward the Turks in this country were mostly negative, primarily because of the Ottoman Empire's political and religious repression.

Such sentiment towards Turkey as existed in America was largely anti-Turkish. We had of course inherited the ordinary western

European prejudice against the Turks as champions of Islam. In addition, many groups in America had espoused the cause of one or another of those Ottoman subject peoples who in the nineteenth century were fighting to gain their independence from the Empire. Immigrants from that Empire had helped foster pro-Greek or pro-Macedonian or pro-Bulgarian sentiments in this country. What had principally aroused American interest in Turkey, however, and what had especially directed that interest towards the non-Turks were certainly the long-standing presence and activities of American missionaries in the Ottoman world. It was chiefly the Armenians' aspirations and woes to which those missionaries gave currency.[25]

The Ottoman Empire was often brutal in its attempts to suppress the Armenian and Syrian-Lebanese Christians. Annihilation of enemies was frequent, and Turkish massacres of thousands of Armenians in the 1890s and again in 1915 stirred the wrath of many Americans. To this day many Americans of Armenian descent mark the anniversary of these Turkish pogroms. American hostility toward the Turks was common during those times, and this helps explain further the initial hostility the Syrian-Lebanese encountered in this country when they were confused with Turks. In his survey of social distance in 1926, Emory S. Bogardus found that Turks ranked twenty-seventh out of thirty, above only Chinese, Koreans, and Indians from India. In 1946, 1956, and 1966, Turks shifted a position or two, finishing twenty-sixth in 1966, above Koreans, Mexicans, blacks, and East Indians.[26] In the same surveys Armenians ranked from five to eleven positions higher than Turks.

IMMIGRANT PATTERNS

When the Balkan War of 1912 began, many young unmarried males came to the United States to avoid military service. When war-ravaged Europe was at peace again in 1918, over 30,000 of them returned to Turkey. The few thousand who remained settled primarily in New York, Massachusetts, Michigan, Illinois, and Indiana.

Most of the Turkish immigrants who came before World War II were illiterate and secured jobs as unskilled laborers. They settled mostly in New York City and Detroit, and they kept to themselves. Some gradually became acculturated, while others remained socially segregated within American society.

The more recent Turkish immigrants have been much better educated than their predecessors. They are often professionals or experienced business people, and they usually adjust fairly easily. The poor tend to migrate to places like West Germany where they can find work as laborers. There are still relatively few Turkish immigrants to the United States; the 1975 total of 1,071 was in fact a 25 percent decline from the 1973 and 1974 totals of 1,447 and 1,433, respectively. In 1976 the figure declined by another one-third to 956, increasing to 991 in 1977.

THE EAST INDIANS

Emigration from India to the United States took place in two distinct phases. In the early twentieth century several thousand poorly educated Indian agricultural laborers migrated to the West Coast and settled in rural regions in Washington and California. They experienced much discrimination because of the then prevailing anti-Asian attitudes. Since 1965, a second group of immigrants — better educated, more urbanized and affluent — has come to the United States.

EARLY IMMIGRANTS

Between 1820 and 1900, fewer than eight hundred immigrants came to the United States from India. In the next two decades a small wave of almost seven thousand agricultural laborers from northern India journeyed to the West Coast of the United States, and still others chose Canada. Almost entirely male, this group — like so many other immigrant groups — intended to accumulate some savings and then return home. Between 1908 and 1920, a total of 1,656 did leave, and another 249 were deported as "undesirable" aliens.[27]

SOCIETAL REACTION

Even though the Japanese, Chinese, and Pilipinos far outnumbered the East Indians, the latter group also experienced discrimination and aggression because of their visibility and identification as Asians. Near a lumber camp in Bellingham, Washington, several hundred whites raided the living quarters of Hindu workers on September 5, 1907, forcing about seven hundred of them to flee across the Canadian border. Two months later, in Everett, Washington, several hundred whites drove the Hindu workers out of town. Racial prejudice manifested itself in Port Angeles, where real estate brokers published in the local newspaper the terms of their covenant not to sell to "Hindoos or Negroes." They justified their action on the grounds that wherever these groups settle, they "have depreciated [the] value of adjacent property and injured the reputation of the neighborhood, and are generally considered as undesirable."[28]

The San Francisco–based Asiatic Exclusion League quickly included the East Indians among their targets and warned the public that they were a "menace." League officials declared that the East Indians were untrustworthy, immodest, unsanitary, insolent, and lustful.[29] These pressures against the East Indians were effective from 1908 to 1910, when immigration officials rejected 1,130 immigrants at their ports of entry. Pressure from the Western Pacific Railroad in 1910 enabled 1,462 to enter between 1911 and 1920, but another 1,762 were denied entry, mostly on the grounds that they would become public charges.[30] The popular magazine *Collier's*, influenced by the Asiatic Exclusion League's exaggerated claim that there were 10,000 East Indians living in California, printed an article warning its readers about the "Hindu invasion."[31]

In this atmosphere of marked hostility toward Asians, the few thousand East Indians gradually established themselves primarily in California and relied chiefly on agriculture as a means of livelihood. Typically the Indians sought work in groups with a leader serving as their agent in negotiating with employers. Owing in part to the desire of many farmers to break the Japanese monopoly on the labor supply in those areas, they had little difficulty finding employment in the Sacramento and San Joaquin valleys. Also, Indians moved into the Imperial Valley, another rapidly growing agricultural area.[32]

In 1923 the U.S. Supreme Court reversed previous lower court decisions and ruled that East Indians were nonwhites and thus ineligible for citizenship under the terms of the 1790 naturalization act. The government then canceled the naturalization certificates that had previously been granted to sixty or seventy East Indians. This decision also prevented the East Indians from owning or leasing land in their own names because of state legislation against alien land-holding. The East Indians thus became itinerant farm laborers. Few of them had any family life because of the itinerant nature of their work and the lack of women they could marry.

MINORITY RESPONSE

About 3,000 East Indians returned home between 1920 and 1940. A few hundred more were deported. The population dwindled from 5,441 in 1920 to 3,138 in 1930 and to 2,405 in 1940.[33] A few of those who remained married Mexican women. Most, however, lived in communal groups apart from the rest of society. Some congregated in Stockton, California — site of a large Pilipino community — and built a temple there for worship.

Physical appearance was an important factor setting these immigrants apart. In the early twentieth century, the long hair and full beards prescribed by the Sikh religion were not fashionable. Moreover, all the men wore turbans and were sometimes castigated as "ragheads." Those Indian women who had come before the Depression, as well as those who have come since the more liberal Immigration Act of 1965, were quite distinct in their wearing of the *sari*, a lightweight outer garment with one end wrapped about the waist and the other draped over the shoulder or covering the head. Most of the cultural differences — appearance, food taboos, social interaction — were an integral part of either the caste system or the religions of India. Therefore, the East Indians not only seemed strange to the Americans, but also had difficulty assimilating because they were reluctant to abandon their customs and practices.

Gary R. Hess reports that by the mid-1950s the East Indian community in Sutter County in north central California numbered about 900, and had grown stronger and more unified.[34] This had come about because the men preferred to marry East Indian women and because the caste system in India had a negligible influence in the United States, except perhaps in terms of status. Because of the small amount of intermarriage and the retention of important aspects of their culture, the rural East Indians, Hess concludes, remain only slightly acculturated even though they have adopted certain material comforts, dress, and other features of American life.

RECENT IMMIGRANTS

The dramatic change in the number of immigrants from India can be seen in the following statistics: from 1901 to 1965 there were 15,513 immigrants, from 1966 to 1970 the total was 24,587, and from 1971 to 1975 the total was 66,650.[35] In 1976, the peak year thus far, there were 17,487 immigrants, but in 1977 the total dropped to 16,849.

Since 1965, the immigration laws have allowed in an increased number of Asian immigrants, but this alone does not explain the increase in migration. Conditions in India are an important factor. India is the world's second most populous country after mainland China, with 15 percent of the world's population on 2.5 percent of the world's land mass. This means that the population density is seven times greater than that of the United States.

FIGURE 8.2

At the Gurdwara Temple in Queens, New York, worshipping Sikhs receive the distribution of "parshad" after the service. (Katrina Thomas, Photo Researchers)

The problem of overpopulation is quite serious. India's population has grown from 439 million in 1960 to 550 million in 1971 to 610 million in 1976.[36] The rapid growth is not due to any spurt in the birth rate (about 22 million babies a year), but rather to a decline in the mortality rate. The population is increasing by about 1.2 million people each month.

With over two-thirds of the population engaged in agriculture, a literacy rate of only 30 percent, and problems of severe poverty, hunger, and inadequate resources, India does not have very much to offer in terms of economic security. However, many of the recent immigrants have been professional workers — 1,500 physicians, surgeons, and dentists have come to the United States in each of the past several years — with the result that America is getting the very people India needs most to retain if the quality of life there is to improve.

Many East Indian immigrants have settled in the northeastern United States. In addition to medicine, they are also in other professions, such as teaching, in white collar business positions, and in various skilled trades. Some agricultural workers still come, of course, but relatively few; they are more likely to settle in the southwestern United States.

A total of about 250,000 East Indians now live in the United States. With their education and occupational skills, they can achieve economic security, but there are cultural strains. For example, they are uneasy with America's sexual mores. Parents have considerable difficulty convincing their children that the Indian custom of not dating before marriage has merit. As a result of societal pressures, many either wear American clothes or rarely venture out alone. Immigrants may also be lonely at holiday times and may feel guilty when their compatriots in India accuse them of having sold their skills to an already rich country.[37]

THE AFRICANS

Although many white Americans simply use Negroid racial features as the basis of group classification, there is much cultural diversity among blacks in America. Generalizing about them is just as inaccurate as generalizing about whites. Regional and social class differences create distinctions among American blacks, and cultural differences make West Indian black immigrants unlike native-born blacks. Black immigrants from Africa are culturally distinct not only from the two former groups but also from one another when they have different countries of origin. Also, although many native-born American blacks call themselves Afro-Americans, in reality a wide cultural gulf separates them from the African immigrants.[38] This fact is often demonstrated at the student level when two separate groups form on college campuses.

It has not been uncommon to see, for example, both a black student union and an African students' association at the same college.

VALUE ORIENTATIONS

Professor Muruku Waiguchu, himself an immigrant from Kenya, has contrasted some of the value orientations of black American and African college students in the United States.[39] He has found that African students tend to show some degree of contempt for and arrogance toward black students, commonly using such terms as "Negro" or "nigger" to refer to them. Africans are frequently more achievement-oriented, competitive, and opportunistic than black American students, partly because they have help from white supporters and no "history of denials and exclusion" from white America. The African student is also less racially conscious in the American sense and therefore is more likely to participate in interracial primary relationships (parties, dating, marriage) than black American college students. Waiguchu argues that the two black groups do not share a greater trust and understanding because both have been victimized by white social conditioning:

Unlike any other people, much of our history, and therefore our cultural continuity, has been written by our detractors and oppressors. The inevitable consequence has been that we look at one another through the eyes given and provided to us through the education process and other forms of communication owned and operated by white people.... We do not articulate our interests collectively because we oftentimes do not understand one another and waste valuable time labelling one another with the stereotypes we have collected from the white man.[40]

Whether whites are the ultimate cause of black American–African misunderstanding is disputable. It is true, though, that differing cultural orientations and ethnocentrism play important roles. Just as dominant and minority white groups have often mistrusted each other, so might different black groups display an outgroup negativism despite racial similarity.

As Tables 8.2 and 8.3 indicate, African immigration has been increasing. When one looks at the breakdown by countries, however, the totals are relatively small. Africa has only recently emerged from generations of colonial rule, and the now independent developing countries are attempting to change from tribal societies into modern nations. For this reason, most Africans in America are foreign students, not immigrants.

ADJUSTMENT TO AMERICAN LIFE

Black African immigrants frequently face a double handicap in adjusting to American society. First, they encounter racial prejudice and discrimination in various social settings and on the job. Second, because of their own cultural distinctions, they do not identify with American blacks. Successful American blacks who are interested in helping the less fortunate usually concentrate on the American black poor, not on newcomers from Africa. African immigrants seek one another for mutual comfort and security.

TABLE 8.2

AFRICAN IMMIGRATION TO THE UNITED STATES
BY COUNTRY OF ORIGIN, 1973–1976

COUNTRY	1973	1974	1975	1976
Ghana	145	135	148	157
Ethiopia	a	a	a	205
Kenya	253	322	390	371
Liberia	a	a	a	282
Nigeria	497	372	424	439
Republic of South Africa	316[b]	343[b]	437[b]	588[b]
Tanzania	238	207	275	269
Uganda	308	283	828	332
Zambia	a	a	a	217
Other Africa, excluding Egypt and Morocco	508	481	541	633
Total	2,265	2,143	3,043	3,493

[a]Figures not available.
[b]Most of these immigrants were white.
SOURCE: U.S. Immigration and Naturalization Service, *Annual Report*, U.S. Government Printing Office, Washington, D.C., 1976, Table 7, p. 53.

Since many African states have only recently been freed from colonial rule, their political boundaries are not as significant as tribal allegiances. Thus, when Biafra attempted to gain independence from Nigeria, each side found that whether their cause was supported by Nigerians in this country or not depended on where those Nigerian immigrants had formerly lived. The starvation and slaughter that ensued in Biafra, when it was brought to public attention, only hardened people's earlier stances. Similarly, other boundary disputes, invasions, or surreptitious aid to rebels, such as Angola's invasion of Katanga Province in Zaire, or Kenya's logistical assistance to the Israeli commando unit rescuing hijacked Jewish passengers from Entebbe Airport in Uganda, all have consequences for the attitudes of Africans in the United States toward one another. Grouping these immigrants into one category is as much a mistake as generalizing about the eastern and central Europeans. As a result of the preference classifications in current immigration law, a great many of the immigrants from Africa are educated, with occupational skills that place them at a middle-class socioeconomic level. Many also come to attend institutions of higher learning, planning to return to Africa. Some do return, but a substantial number remain.

TABLE 8.3

AFRICAN IMMIGRATION TO THE UNITED STATES[a]

1901–1910	7,368
1911–1920	8,443
1921–1930	6,286
1931–1940	1,750
1941–1950	7,367
1951–1960	14,092
1961–1970	28,954
1971–1977	43,283

[a]Includes Egypt, Libya, and Morocco.
SOURCE: U.S. Immigration and Naturalization Service, *Annual Report*, U.S. Government Printing Office, Washington, D.C., 1977, pp. 86–88.

RETROSPECT

Relatively few members of the racial and ethnic groups mentioned in this chapter came to the United States before 1940. The experiences of those who did were generally similar to those of other non-Western peoples here, and depended on the then prevailing American policies and regional attitudes.

For the most part, the immigrant experience of people from this part of the world is current. Although they are still identifiable because of physical and cultural differences, they usually have little difficulty with

Americans because of their occupational status, their urban locale, and the relaxation of American norms about newcomers. Nevertheless, as strangers they are keenly aware of the society in which they find themselves, and Americans generally tend to avoid interacting with them in meaningful primary relationships. The non-Westerners are somewhat unusual in that many are able to secure a respectable social status in terms of education, occupation, income, and residence, but because of their cultural differences and their resistence to assimilation, they have little social participation with native-born Americans. This is often a two-way arrangement.

As larger numbers of immigrants from the non-Western world come to the United States, they are making their presence felt more and more. One aspect of this impact is in religion. Waves of immigrant peoples have changed the United States from an almost exclusively Protestant country to one of three major faiths. Now this Judeo-Christian population composition, if present trends continue, may be modified further as the numbers of Moslems, Hindus, Buddhists, and adherents of other Eastern religions swell.

As the United States becomes culturally diverse in the areas of religion, physical appearance, and value orientations, more Americans are becoming conscious of the differences in the people around them. Some argue that Americans today are more tolerant because of a resurgence of ethnicity and a more liberal government attitude toward cultural pluralism. Others contend that the past nativistic reaction to Asians in the West and to southern and eastern Europeans in the East is being replicated today against the non-Western immigrants. There may not be riots and violent confrontations, but there are more subtle and sophisticated acts of discrimination, in keeping with the changing times.

How accurate this analysis is has not yet been determined. What is known is that recent non-Western immigrants are better educated and better trained; they often speak English before they arrive; and thus they enter American society at a higher socioeconomic level than earlier immigrants did. They follow the usual pattern of residential clustering, organizational life, and ingroup socializing common to all new ethnic groups, but they seem to adjust fairly easily to living in America. Perhaps we are still a generation away from being able to measure the full impact of their role within American society.

QUESTIONS FOR DISCUSSION

1. Explain why the differences in economic power between non-Western immigrants and earlier immigrants make assimilation less necessary now than before.

2. How have structural conditions at home reshaped ethnic identity and attitudes among Arab immigrants to the United States?

3. What parallels are there between the East Indian and Asian immigrant experiences, both past and present?

4. How are the cultural orientations of African immigrants dissimiliar to those of black Americans?

SUGGESTED READINGS

Elkholy, Abdo A. *The Arab Moslems in the United States: Religion and Assimilation.* College and University Press, New Haven, Conn., 1966.

Kayal, Philip M., and Joseph M. Kayal. *The Syrian-Lebanese in America.* Twayne, New York, 1925.

Neidle, Cecyle S. *The New Americans.* Twayne, New York, 1967.

Thomas, Lewis V., and Richard N. Krye. *The United States and Turkey and Iran.* Harvard, Cambridge, Mass., 1952.

NOTES

1. U.S. Immigration and Naturalization Service, *Annual Report*, 1977, U.S. Government Printing Office, Washington, D.C., p. 10.

2. Abdo A. Elkholy, "The Arab American Family," in *Ethnic Families in America*, eds. Charles H. Mindel and Robert W. Habenstein, Elsevier, New York, 1976, pp. 166–167.

3. U.S. Immigration and Naturalization Service, *Annual Report*, 1976, U.S. Government Printing Office, Washington, D.C., p. 92.

4. Emory S. Bogardus, "Comparing Racial Distance in Ethiopia, South Africa, and the United States," *Sociology and Social Research*, 52 (1968), 149–156; Won Moo Hurh, "Comparative Study of Korean Immigrants in the United States," *Korean Christian Journal*, No. 2 (Spring 1977), 60–99.

5. Philip M. Kayal and Joseph M. Kayal, *The Syrian-Lebanese in America*, Twayne, New York, 1925, pp. 50, 61.

6. Rev. Cyril Anid, *I Grew with Them*, Paulist Press, Jounieh, Lebanon, 1967, p. 18.

7. Morris Berger, "America's Syrian Community," *Commentary*, 25, No. 4 (1958), 316.

8. *Ibid.*, p. 111.

9. Cecyle S. Neidle, *The New Americans*, Twayne, New York, 1967, pp. 248–253.

10. Philip Harsham, "Arabs in America: A Special Contribution," *Aramco World Magazine*, 26, No. 2, (1975), 35.

11. Kayal and Kayal, *The Syrian-Lebanese in America*, p. 108.

12. *Ibid.*, pp. 197–200.

13. U.S. Immigration and Naturalization Service, *Annual Report*, 1976, p. 53.

14. Abdoulmaboud Ansari, "A Community in Process: The First Generation of the Iranian Professional Middle Class Immigrants in the United States," *International Review of Modern Sociology*, 7 (Spring 1977), 96.

15. *Ibid.*, p. 99.

16. Abdoulmaboud Ansari, "The Dually Marginal Man: The Iranian Immigrant in the United States," unpublished doctoral dissertation, New School for Social Research, 1974, pp. 12–13.

17. Mary C. Sengstock, "Social Change in the Country of Origin as a Factor in Immigrant Conceptions of Nationality," *Ethnicity*, 4 (March 1977), 54–69.

18. *Ibid.*, p. 61.

19. Vincent N. Parrillo, personal interview with Ali M. Baluchi, Saudi Arabian businessman, July 1977.

20. Philip Harsham, "Arabs in America: The Transplanted Ones," *Aramco World Magazine*, 26, No. 2 (1975), 11.

21. *Ibid.*, p. 6.

22. *Ibid.*

23. Edward T. Hall, *The Hidden Dimension*, Doubleday, Garden City, N.Y., 1966, pp. 144–153.

24. *Ibid.*, p. 149.

25. Lewis V. Thomas and Richard N. Krye, *The United States and Turkey and Iran*, Harvard, Cambridge, Mass., 1952, pp. 139–140.

26. Bogardus, "Comparing Racial Distance in Ethiopia, South Africa, and the United States," p. 152.

27. Gurdial Singh, "East Indians in the United States," *Sociology and Social Research*, 30 (1946), 210–211.

28. Joan M. Jensen, "Apartheid: Pacific Coast Style," *Pacific Historical Review*, 38 (1969), 335–340.

29. Gary R. Hess, "The Forgotten Asian Americans: The East Indian Community in the United States," *Pacific Historical Review*, 43 (1974), 580.

30. Singh, "East Indians in the United States," pp. 210–211.

31. "Hindu Invasion," *Collier's*, 45 (March 26, 1910), 15.

32. Hess, "The Forgotten Asian Americans: The East Indian Community in the United States," pp. 583–584.

33. *Ibid.*, p. 590.

34. *Ibid.*, pp. 593–594.

35. U.S. Immigration and Naturalization Service, *Annual Report*, U.S. Government Printing Office, Washington, D.C., 1977, Table 13, pp. 62–64.

36. "India," *Deadline Data on World Affairs*, DMS Inc., Greenwich, Conn., June 30, 1977.

37. George Becker, "Asian Spice in the Melting Pot," *New York Sunday News Magazine*, Nov. 28, 1976, pp. 7–21.

38. For a comparative analysis of native-born and foreign-born blacks, see Ira De Augustine Reid, *The Negro Immigrant*, 1939, reprint ed., Arno Press and *The New York Times*, New York, 1969.

39. Muruku Waiguchu, "Relations Between African and Afro-American Students in the United States," paper presented at the 7th annual meeting of the African Heritage Studies Association.

40. *Ibid.*, pp. 5, 16.

NINE

BLACKS IN AMERICA

◄ Most Africans who arrived in America from 1619 until the end of the slave trade in 1808 were unwilling immigrants, but twentieth-century black voluntary emigration to the United States has been substantial. Between 1899 and 1922, 115,000 African blacks and over 25,000 West Indian blacks were admitted. The restrictive immigration law of 1924 reduced the number of new immigrants from these groups; Africans, for example, were limited to only 122 annually.[1] In recent years black Africa has been averaging over 3,000 immigrants a year, while over 60,000 West Indians have been emigrating to the United States each year.

Differences in culture have prevented any unifying racial bond from forming between black immigrants and native-born blacks. The newcomers are strangers in a new land, the native-born blacks — like the Indians — are strangers in their own land, and both groups are strangers to each other. The new arrivals have come from an area where their race was the majority, or where a tripartite color system prevailed, or where color was not a primary factor in group life, into a society where color is an important determinant. They find that white Americans identify Africans with a partially assimilated and socially restricted native black population that itself does not accept or relate well to them.

The role of blacks in American society, together with the recurring racial problems of prejudice and discrimination, has often been discussed, particularly in the past two decades. This chapter attempts to place black-white relations in perspective by showing the similarities in and differences from the patterns of dominant-minority interaction of other racial and ethnic groups. Other major themes are the long-lasting impact of cultural conditioning and the changes wrought by the civil rights movement.

THE BLACK EXPERIENCE

During the age of exploration, black crew members served under Columbus and sixteenth-century Spanish explorers such as Balboa, Cortez, Pizzarro, and de Soto. The first known group of African immigrants were 20 voluntary immigrants who landed in Jamestown in August 1619, a year before the Pilgrims landed at Plymouth Rock. They came as indentured servants, as did many whites, worked off their debt, and became masters of their own destiny. They were the fortunate few, for the labor demands of the Southern colonies soon resulted in the enslavement of millions of other Africans and their forced migration to the United States. Slavery replaced indentured servitude in the South. Blacks were forcibly taken from their African homelands and sold into a lifetime of slavery in a land they did not choose and in which they had no opportunity to advance themselves because they were not free.

THE YEARS OF SLAVERY

To ease the transition, other ethnic groups re-created in miniature the society they left behind, but the Africans were not allowed to do so. Other groups could use education to give themselves and their children a better future, but Southern state laws made the education of black slaves a criminal offense. Other groups may have encountered various degrees of hostility and discrimination, but through hard work and perseverance many were able to overcome nativist fears and prejudices. For the blacks, however, two hundred years of master-slave relations did much more than just prevent their assimilation; they shaped values and attitudes about the two races that are still visible today.

As the industrial North and the slave-holding, agrarian South evolved into different societies, they developed different norms. Since norms are shared expectations of what does and does not constitute proper behavior, intergroup relations in these two regions might be expected to vary greatly. They did, but not in the way many Americans assume. To be sure, the institution of slavery created an inferior status for blacks and led to much prejudice and discrimination. Yet there were free blacks in the South too (nearly half a million by 1860) — those who had been set free by their owners, those who had purchased their freedom, or those who were descendants of free mothers. They lived in such urban areas as New Orleans, Mobile, and Charleston; in the tidewater regions of Virginia and Maryland; or in the Piedmont mountains of North Carolina and Virginia. Those who lived in the Southern cities worked in a wide variety of skilled and unskilled occupations; some were architects, teachers, store and hotel managers, clerks, and milliners. In the North, although there was some variance, the blacks faced considerable discrimination in education, housing, employment, and voting rights. Since in the North no operative caste system delineated norms and interaction patterns, many whites reacted more strongly to blacks in their midst. As a result, Northern blacks had considerable difficulty achieving economic security.

RACISM AND ITS LEGACY

Although ancient civilizations considered themselves superior to others, they did so on the basis of culture, not race. Most historians agree that racism did not emerge until the sixteenth and seventeenth centuries.² This was the period of European exploration and imperialism, during which Europeans were brought into contact with many physically different, less technologically advanced peoples. Their physical characteristics, values, and ways of life were different, and so the Europeans naively concluded that there must be some relationship between how the people looked and how they behaved. This was another instance in which prejudices and stereotyping resulted from ethnocentric rationalization. W.E.B. DuBois interpreted this rise of racism as follows:

> Labor was degraded, humanity was despised, the theory of "race" arose. There came a new doctrine of universal labor: mankind were of two sorts — the superior and the inferior; the inferior toiled for the superior; and the superior were the real men, the inferior half men or less. . . . Luxury and plenty for the few and poverty for the many was looked upon as inevitable in the course of nature. In addition to this, it went without saying that the white people of Europe had a right to live upon the labor and property of the colored peoples of the world.
>
> In order to establish the righteousness of this point of view, science and religion, government and industry, were wheeling into line. The word "Negro" was used for the first time in the world's history to tie color to race and blackness to slavery and degradation. The white race was pictured as "pure" and superior: the black race as dirty, stupid, and inevitably inferior; the yellow race as sharing, in deception and cowardice, much of this color inferiority; while mixture of the races was considered the prime cause of degradation and failure in civilization. Everything great, everything fine, everything really successful in human culture, was white.
>
> In order to prove this, even black people in India and Africa were labeled as "white" if they showed any trace of progress; and, on the other hand, any progress by colored people was attributed to some intermixture, ancient or modern, of white blood or some influence of white civilization.³

Racism may be defined as establishing a link between the biological conditions of a human organism and its sociocultural capabilities and behavior. Previous chapters on the American Indians and the Asians showed how important this concept was in their relations with the dominant society.

Myths about black racial inferiority emerged as a rationalization of slavery. Although slavery had existed under earlier systems, the ancient civilizations did not link skin color and social status. Statues and paintings from ancient Egypt, for example, depict slaves and rulers alike as both white and black.⁴ Speculation about the causes of the rise of racism includes the rise of seagoing power among European nations and increased contact with red, brown, black, and yellow peoples; the influence of Christianity, linking slavery and skin color with the Curse of Ham; and European technological and military superiority over native peoples throughout the world. In the nineteenth century, evolutionary theory was also used to support racist thinking, as some argued that the white race was more highly evolved than the others.

Although an extremely small percentage of white Southerners actually owned slaves, they were the most influential, and other Southern whites were strong supporters of the system. The total separation of American slaves from the rest of society, unlike the partial separation of slaves in Latin American countries (where they had greater family stability and gradated freedom conditions), had important social consequences. As the dominant element of the Southern economy, plantation slavery affected the cultural life style and the shape of societal institutions. Illiteracy, nonexistent social and economic organizations, itinerant preachers, only local white law enforcement and protection, lack of medical and learning facilities, isolation, and dependency were the lot of the blacks.

As a result of the racial ideology, stereotyping, and social isolation that survived the end of slavery, blacks in the United States — despite their adaptability, willingness, and competence — were more excluded from participation in the free community than were the ex-slaves of Latin America. Once established, the impact of a master-slave social system and the concomitant theory of racial inferiority conditioned values, attitudes, and development of capacities that were to last well beyond the Civil War. Treated as if they were biologically inferior, the blacks became socially inferior, first as a result of slavery and then as a result of discrimination in jobs, housing, and education.

Overcoming two hundred years of social conditioning is not easy. A generation after the close of the Civil War, many blacks were making economic progress in the South, but the whites still held deep-seated beliefs of racial superiority. Previous discussions of the vicious circle and the long-lasting effects of stereotypes help explain the continuance of institutionalized racism long after the end of slavery.[5]

In 1876, when Reconstruction ended and the status of blacks became a Southern question rather than a national matter, blacks were given a formalized inferior status. Segregation, disfranchisement, "black codes," job discrimination, and occupational eviction took place. Not until the 1960s did many deliberate segregationist practices end in the South.

Although there are now many laws to protect people against discrimination, racist beliefs continue to exist; they can be seen in the reasons people give for moving out of racially changing neighborhoods or for their attitudes toward cities, crime, and welfare. While fear of crime, violence, and other evils of the inner city is justified, some individuals attribute such problems to race. Deviance, it must be remembered, occurs among all groups who are poor, powerless, and victims of discrimination.[6]

The problem with racism is twofold: its legacy and its subtlety. *Legacy* here refers not only to its institutionalization within society, but also to its transmission from one generation to the next. Slavery may end, segregation may end, but some people still believe blacks are inferior. This is part of the subtlety of racism, because people usually draw such conclusions from their observable world. They are not aware that this "objective" reality has been socially constructed over generations. The alleged inferiority is a myth, except as a social product. One sees primarily the effects of prolonged racist attitudes and actions. Even one's own attitudes, actions, and reactions may unwittingly contribute to the existence of racism.[7]

THE QUESTION OF RACIAL SUPERIORITY

Belief in white supremacy has existed for a long time in the United States. There have been, and still are, people who believe that blacks are biologically inferior to whites. This was the justification for segregation and for the Jim Crow laws, and this is the reason for many of the social problems of today. It is not only uneducated people who feel this way; some scientists and scholars also believe there are innate differences among the races. For example, in 1928 the noted American sociologist Pitirim Sorokin observed:

> That there are mental differences among races seems to be definitely established. . . . No partisan of a belief in the uniformity of all races can disregard the differences in the historical role and in the cultural achievements of the different races. . . . The difference in the cultural contributions and in the historical roles played by different races is excellently corroborated by, and is in perfect agreement with, the experimental studies of race mentality and psychology. . . . So far as I know, all studies of the comparative intelligence of the contemporary Negro and white races . . . have unanimously shown that the I.Q. of the blacks, or even the Indians, is lower than that of the white or yellow. . . .
>
> The only conclusion which it seems possible to make from the above and similar studies is that the mentality of various races . . . is different.[8]

Scientific attempts to prove racial superiority and inferiority have traditionally followed three primary approaches: anatomical, historical (or comparative achievement), and psychological.[9]

FIGURE 9.1

PHRENOLOGICAL SIGNS OF CHARACTER. 41

The ORANG-OUTANG has more forehead than any other animal, both perceptive and reflective, with some moral sentiments, and accordingly is called the "half-reasoning man," its Phrenology corresponding perfectly with its character.

PERCEPTIVES LARGER THAN REFLECTIVES.

THE VARIOUS RACES also accord with phrenological science. Thus, Africans generally have full perceptives, and large Tune and Language, but retiring Causality, and accordingly are deficient in reasoning capacity, yet have excellent memories and lingual and musical powers.

Fowler's *Phrenological Signs of Character* was based on the popular notion that one's character could be read from the "bumps" on one's head. This illustration from the 1857 edition shows how this notion could support the prejudicial belief in the biological inferiority of blacks. (The Distorted Image, Anti-Defamation League. John and Selma Appel Collection)

THE ANATOMICAL APPROACH

It has been mentioned elsewhere in this text that in many parts of the world, the group lowest on the socioeconomic ladder is often viewed as lowest on the evolutionary ladder as well. Some scientists have tried to use physical characteristics to show that whites are further evolved than blacks. The blacks, they argue, most resemble the ape; they have a receding forehead, prognathous jaw, and broad, flat nose. What these proponents conveniently ignore is that the hair texture, body hair, and lip form of whites are closer to apes than are those of blacks. Also, underneath their fur most simians have white skin. Using physical characteristics to rank the races in any evolutionary order is simply impossible, because no race is consistently more simian than another.

Whites generally have larger brains than blacks, and some have contended that this proves they have superior intellectual capabilities.[10] However, physical size or cranial capacity is not in itself an indicator of mental capacity. Not only is there a wide range of size among all groups, but some peoples not particularly noted for their intellectual achievements (preliterate Eskimos and Neanderthals) have possessed larger-sized brains. Physical characterizations of skin pigmentation, hair texture, and brain size do not correlate with a comparative evolution of the human races.

THE COMPARATIVE ACHIEVEMENT APPROACH

In other attempts to prove racial superiority, the achievements of different races have been compared. Some argue that since not all races have made "important" contributions to the world's culture and produced gifted artists, inventors, philosophers, geniuses, explorers, and conquerors, or built great civilizations and vast empires, they are not all equal. After all, they argue, a race that has produced all the engineering feats of today in architecture, computers, electronics, medicine, and space-age technology surely surpasses a primitive, illiterate, underdeveloped race of people, such as the Australian aborigines or Amazon jungle natives or African villagers.

Stanford M. Lyman attacks any attempt to measure the "contributions" of any ethnic group, since this involves a retrospective analysis of what has and has not been widely adopted or popularly acclaimed.

The uselessness of contributions as a sociological concept is clear because its designative capacity is always post hoc. It forces a bifurcation of a natural class — the activities of a minority group — at an unnatural joint: those that are contributions and those that are not. When a minority is evaluated according to its contributions, its activities are classified in accordance with a concept that cannot be derived from their actual context. A people's activities should be regarded as contributions only when it can be shown that they were intended as such. Sociology should be faithful to the actual nature of its subject matter — people in active and creative existence.[11]

Another problem with this line of reasoning is that one should not confuse performance with potential. To do so is to misunderstand the dynamics of civilization as well as to lack perspective and to be ignorant of the history of culture. How, for example, do we measure achievement? Most of us would measure it by our standards, that is, using an ethnocentric approach. We may boast of our scientific knowledge and accomplishments, failing to realize that other people may not admire these things or consider them criteria for excellence. As Berry and Tischler point out:

> We would not come out so well in proving our superiority if our opponents insisted on using as criteria, not science and machines, but ability at sand painting, physical endurance, complexity of grammar, multiplicity of taboos, respect for the aged, ability in hunting, closeness to nature, fear of the deity, reverence for the soil, freedom from authority, disregard for material goods, the absence of neuroses, or peace of mind. The fact is that no racial or ethnic group excels in all things, but each has its own interests and values, goals toward which it strives, and channels into which its efforts are directed.[12]

Even if someone were to argue that some peoples are superior because of the flowering of their civilization, time would show that attainment also to be relative. Some civilizations have exceeded others, only to be surpassed in later years by those very ones thought to be inferior. The history of some world civilizations — those of the Sumerians, Egyptians, Greeks, Romans, and English — is testimony to this fact. From the ninth century, when marauding tribes were still roving through parts of Europe, through the fifteenth century, various African kingdoms were building such sophisticated and affluent cities as Timbuktu, the intellectual capital of Western Sudan, with its stone palaces, many-windowed homes, city university, and busy marketplace; or Benin, Nigeria, with wide streets and civic splendor and a huge, magnificent palace; or the numerous tall stone towns on the East African coast. Early explorers noted some of these achievements, but ethnocentric misconceptions and the debilitating effects of enslavement distorted, dulled, and destroyed this knowledge of the Africans and their varied social systems. In the following passage, Basil Davidson presents an undistorted picture of African civilizations:

> Some of these systems produced societies whose standard of living — in terms of food, personal safety and freedom — equaled

that of contemporary societies in Europe. In some instances they were even more advanced: African societies practiced a simple but effective social welfare in their concern for widows and orphaned children.

This is the Africa . . . that Europeans began to see for themselves in the latter half of the fifteenth century. Instead of a primeval wilderness, these visitors found prosperous, self-contained cities linked to each other by a busy, carefully ordered trade. Their inhabitants — merchants, artisans, laborers, clerks — lived comfortable lives. . . .

Though far behind Europe in their technical knowledge, Africans developed tropical farming techniques that have scarcely been bettered to this day. They were good miners and metalworkers. . . . They were astute businessmen. . . . They operated political systems of considerable flexibility and sophistication. They were superb sculptors. . . .

But the record of achievement is not confined to big political systems alone. In the shadow of their pomp and glory rests the modest but impressive achievement of village-level Africa. In community attitudes that join man to man in a brotherhood of equals, in moral rules that guided social behavior, in beliefs that exalted the spiritual aspects of life above the material, the African village achieved a kind of social harmony that often functioned without any need for centralized authority. This, in fact, was where Africa best displayed its real genius — in its capacity for social organization.[13]

In the United States and Africa, the subjugation of the African people and the creation of a social structure in which they were assigned a dependent, inferior status effectively hindered their further achievements. Civilizations flourish and wane for a variety of social, economic, political, and military reasons, not because of the superiority of a race or ethnic group.

Like all civilizations, the African civilizations ebbed, partly as a result of imperialism, colonialism, and slavery. The subjugation of blacks in the United States, first through slavery and then through continued discrimination and denial, effectively limited their advancement and thereby kept them from having as substantial an impact upon American society as they might have had until the mid-1950s. Individual black poets, authors, inventors, craftspeople, engineers, actors, and others flourished under slavery and in the following period, but black people as a whole had little or no education, poor-paying jobs and poor housing, and little upward mobility. Life for them was survival; there was not much opportunity for anything else.

Another counterargument to this historical approach to racial superiority is cultural diffusion. Each civilization is the beneficiary of the inventions and discoveries of others, and white civilizations are no exception; they have evolved further from the contributions of nonwhite civilizations. Whatever the United States has accomplished in world leadership and in achievement as a nation, it owes much to various other peoples for many of the elements within its culture.[14]

THE PSYCHOLOGICAL APPROACH

The intelligence test, first developed by Alfred Binet in 1905, became a popular means of comparing the intelligence of different racial and ethnic groups, although that was not Binet's intention. Supposedly, this objective, scientific instrument would measure innate intelligence and not be influenced by any beneficial or detrimental effects of environment. Any question or claim of one group's intellectual superiority could now be determined. Early studies showed that northern and western Europeans, and often the Chinese and Japanese, scored consistently and decidedly higher than southern and eastern Europeans, blacks, Mexicans, and American Indians.[15] Conveniently ignoring the results for Asians, nativists and segregationists seized upon these studies as arguments for immigration restrictions against "inferiors," for the Americanization of Indians, and to justify Jim Crow laws in the South.

Gradually, as nativist antipathy against the "new" immigrants abated, the argument shifted primarily to intelligence differences between blacks and whites. The disparity in the test results, actually reflecting a cultural bias within the tests, now became a basis for claiming white intellectual superiority.

In 1958 Audrey Shuey's book *The Testing of Negro Intelligence* appeared and caused a furor. Shuey surveyed some 240 studies of 60 different intelligence tests that had been given over a 44-year span to hundreds of thousands of servicemen from World Wars I and II and thousands of schoolchildren of all ages through college, from all regions of the country. She concluded:

> The remarkable consistency in test results, whether they pertain to school or preschool children, to high school or college students, drafts of World War I or World War II, to the gifted or mentally deficient, to the delinquent or criminal; the fact that the colored-white differences are present not only in the rural South and urban South, but in the border and northern areas; the fact that relatively small average differences are found between the I.Q.'s of northern-born and southern-born Negro children in northern cities; the evidence that the tested differences appear to be greater for abstract than for practical or concrete problems; the evidence that the differences obtained are not due primarily to a lack of language skills, the colored

averaging no better on non-verbal tests than on verbal tests; the fact that differences are reported in all studies in which the cultural environment of the whites appeared to be no more complex, rich, or stimulating than the environment of the Negroes; the fact that in many comparisons (including those in which the colored appeared to best advantage) the Negro subjects have been either more representative of their racial group or more highly selected than are the comparable white subjects; all point to the presence of some native differences between Negroes and whites as determined by intelligence tests.[16]

For any scientist, interpretation of findings is as critical as the findings themselves and the methods employed to obtain them. Shuey was accurate in observing the consistent lower scoring of blacks on intelligence tests. However, many disagreed with her conclusion that this was due to intellectual inferiority of the race. This conclusion of innate or generic differences was a quantum leap from her findings, which did not prove any such thing.

More recently, the IQ controversy has centered around two California professors: Arthur R. Jensen, an educational psychologist at the University of California (Berkeley), and William B. Shockley, a Nobel Prize–winning physicist at Stanford University. Jensen argued that the 10- to 20-point IQ differential between blacks and whites involves only certain mental functions. He pointed out that blacks and whites test equally well in such brain functions as rote learning and memory, but that blacks test poorer in problem-solving, in seeing relationships, and in abstract reasoning. Since this material does not depend on specific cultural information, he maintained, the only conclusion is that the blacks' lower scores are due to their genetic heritage.[17] Shockley also declared in the mid-1960s that the conceptual intelligence of blacks, as measured by many different IQ tests, is significantly lower than that of whites, and that some of this variance is genetically caused and therefore cannot be corrected.

In a recent article, Thomas Sowell effectively summarized the arguments against the Shockley-Jensen school of thought.[18] White ethnic groups, such as the Poles, Jews, and Italians, scored in the 80s during the tests of the 1920s, but gained 20 to 25 points by the 1970s after experiencing upward mobility. Those groups of European ancestry who have not experienced upward mobility, as well as the Mexican-Americans and the Puerto Ricans, continue to score in the 80s on IQ tests. Most significantly, at various times and places other low-IQ groups have also done poorly on the abstract portions of mental tests. Studies of immigrant groups in 1917, of white children in isolated mountain communities, of working-class children in England, and of early Chinese immigrants all show marked deficiencies on the abstract sections. Concerning the Chinese-Americans, recent studies show them to be strongest on the abstract portions of the mental tests, suggesting that upward mobility helps to improve powers of abstract reasoning. Other patterns — children's IQ scores declining as they become adults, and females consistently scoring higher than males — are also common among low-IQ groups, not just blacks. Again, these results change once the group achieves a higher socioeconomic status.

In the late 1960s a number of tests were developed that were deliberately culturally biased in favor of blacks, to protest culture-loaded tests and demonstrate how they can produce invalid scores. Among these were the BITCH test ("Black Intelligence Test to Counter Honkeyism") and the "Dove Counterbalance Intelligence Test," which became a part of the Air Force's race relations course for its personnel. It is important to note that some blacks scored low on even these tests because their socioeconomic status, age, or residence made the questions unfamiliar to them.

Another problem with IQ tests is that they measure only some forms of intelligence — analytical, conceptual, and verbal. Very recently, neurobiologists have suggested that this type of intelligence appears to reside in the left hemisphere of the brain, and intuitive, artistic intelligence in the right hemisphere. Just as we have a tendency to be right-handed or left-handed, so too we may have a tendency to be right-brained or left-brained, although the average person uses either or both brain hemispheres depending upon the situation.[19] If a child can be trained to use one hand instead of the other (and many parents suppress their child's use of the left hand), might it not be possible for an individual's life experience to influence development of one brain hemisphere over the other? That is, if an individual matures in an environment that is not conducive to learning the skills IQ tests measure, might not that individual become "life-smart," relying on intuitive powers, on the right brain hemisphere? Recent neurobiological research has suggested that outside experiences of the human organism may influence how ribonucleic acid (RNA) acts upon the molecular structure of the brain.[20]

We are only beginning to understand how and why the brain functions as it does. Until we know more, any assumption of intellectual superiority or inferiority based on IQ scores is conjecture. Moreover, the only proven value IQ scores have is in predicting how well students will do in a traditional school setting. They do not predict performance in nontraditional approaches to education or in any job situation. Does a professor with a 135 IQ teach better than one with 120? Not necessarily, and that is another reason why IQ scores should not be a factor in questions of social interaction.

LANGUAGE AS PREJUDICE

Words are symbols connoting meanings to the world about us. That the very words used to describe the two races — white and black — usually convey positive and negative meanings, respectively, is unfortunate. For example, *white* often symbolizes cleanliness, purity, or heroes (clothes, armor, hats, horses), and *black* often stands for dirty, evil, or villains. A snow-covered landscape is beautiful, but a sky laden with black smoke is not. Black clouds are seen as threatening, but white clouds are not.

The power of words is such that the pervasiveness of such meanings for these two words can easily influence minds and attitudes. Ossie Davis had such concerns in mind when he said:

A superficial examination of Roget's *Thesaurus of the English Language* reveals the following facts: the word "whiteness" has 134 synonyms, 44 of which are favorable and pleasing to contemplate. For example: "purity," "cleanness," "immaculateness," "bright," "shiny," "ivory," "fair," "blonde," "stainless," "clean," "clear," "chaste," "unblemished," "unsullied," "innocent," "honorable," "upright," "just," "straightforward," "genuine," "trustworthy," and only 10 synonyms of which I feel to have been negative and then only in the mildest sense, such as "gloss-over," "whitewash," "gray," "wan," "pale," "ashen," etc.

The word "blackness" has 120 synonyms, 60 of which are distinctly unfavorable, and none of them even mildly positive. Among the offending 60 were such words as "blot," "blotch," "smut," "smudge," "sullied," "begrime," "soot," "becloud," "obscure," "dingy," "murky," "low-toned," "threatening," "frowning," "foreboding," "forbidding," "deadly," "unclean," "dirty," "unwashed," "foul," etc. In addition, and this is what really hurts, 20 of these words — and I exclude the villainous 60 above — are related directly to race, such as "Negro," "Negress," "nigger," "darkey," "blackamoor," etc.

If you consider the fact that thinking itself is subvocal speech (in other words, one must use words in order to think at all), you will appreciate the enormous trap of racial prejudgment that works on any child who is born into the English language.[21]

When *black* has so many negative connotations — blackening the reputation, being black-hearted, blacklisting or blackballing someone, being a blackguard, using black magic, running a black market, and so on — it is easy to see how language by itself can precondition a white person's mind against black people and can lead a black person's mind into possible self-hatred.

INSTITUTIONALIZED RACISM

During the Reconstruction period and almost to the end of the nineteenth century, Southern blacks generally had greater access to stores, restaurants, public transportation, bars, and theaters than in the first half of the twentieth century. A typical pattern was for whites to live on one street in large homes, while next to them on the parallel street were the lesser dwellings of blacks, many of whom worked as domestics. Although there was a clear status distinction, in most places, no severe social distance occurred between the two races. Blacks lived in close proximity to whites, and frequently interacted with them in secondary relationships through their occupational roles as domestic or service workers. In education, marriage, political participation, and major economic enterprises, however, blacks did not share a commonality with whites.

IMMIGRATION AND JIM CROW

The change in black-white relations in the late nineteenth and early twentieth centuries is an example of *cultural drift,* a gradual and pervasive change in a people's values. Economic problems, scandals, and frustrations on the part of Southern whites appear to be some of the factors that reshaped Southern attitudes. In a region in which they had long been considered inferior, many blacks were achieving socioeconomic respectability and becoming economic competitors. Resentment of black upward mobility, flowing from the historical undercurrent of racist attitudes, was increased by economic troubles (declining cotton prices and unemployment). Since they were racially distinct, the blacks were a convenient scapegoat for the frustrations and hostility of Southern whites.

Less liberal attitudes in the North were also a factor increasing the number of racist acts of discrimination in housing, labor, associations, unions, schools, and churches in both North and South.[22] What caused this change in the North? It is not just coincidence that this change in racial attitudes occurred just when great numbers of southern and eastern European immigrants were settling in Northern urban areas. The arrival of so many dark-eyed, dark-haired, dark-complexioned newcomers set in motion a nativist reaction culminating with restrictive immigration laws. Northerners became more sensitive to the influx of foreigners and "anarchists" as well as to Southern blacks coming to the North to seek work. There were racial overtones to the North's ethnocentric reaction to the "new" immigrants, and the South's reaction to the blacks received greater sympathy from Northern nativists. The North ceased to

BOX 9.1

*"In the South we had whites live here, colored live
there and everybody would speak to you whether they
knowed you or not. . . . People are not as friendly
up here."*

"I had heard so much talk about New York. People would say
things were so good in New York until I felt that if I would get to
New York, I would find money on the streets and wouldn't have no
more worries. All my problems would be solved. When I got to New
York, things were much different than that. Jobs were very hard to
find, and the people were very different than in West Virginia.

"Finally I did get a job through the State Employment Office,
working as a cook in the Brooklyn Navy Yard in a private canteen. I
stayed there a year and then the war closed up — was over. Then I
got another job in a seafood house on 34th Street and 3rd Avenue
and I stayed there a year. Then a friend of mine and I went into our
own business selling raw fish. Opened a store in Brooklyn selling
raw fish. And, of course, it didn't pan out that way. The problem
with that business was that we didn't have enough capital to carry
us over the rough spots. And then my wife started having babies
and so I had to give up that job and seek another, which I did, and
finally I got a job right away at another seafood house.

"In the South we had whites live here, colored live there and
everybody would speak to you whether they knowed you or not.
But when I got to the North, I'd be out on the street, maybe walking
around, before I got the jobs, looking around, trying to find my way
around, and I would be saying, 'Good morning,' and 'Good evening,' whichever way the situation was, and people would look at
me as if I was some dope or something. People would say, 'What's
wrong with him?' People are not as friendly up here.

"And I also found out when we bought a house here, that the
whites started right away moving out. They started selling their
houses, putting up signs for sale. That didn't bother me any. Only
thing was that I was just saying to myself that I thought New York
was so great. Why should this be happening? And in the South,
where I was living, it didn't happen that way. Blacks and whites
lived side-by-side there, and we didn't have no problems with that.
That kind of upset me that in New York, after hearing so much
about it, this did go on."

Black migrant from West Virginia who came North in 1944
at age 26

pressure the South regarding blacks, and allowed the Jim Crow laws to emerge without a challenge.

In the 1870s and 1880s, the Californians succeeded in making the Chinese question a national issue, and cleverly related it to that of the blacks whenever necessary. Political deals were made, and later, Southern representatives voted overwhelmingly in favor of the Chinese Exclusion Act of 1882 and the 1921 immigration bill restricting southern and eastern Europeans, most of whom were settling in the North.

In 1896 the Supreme Court ruling on *Plessy* v. *Ferguson* upheld the principle of "separate but equal" railroad accommodations and education for blacks and whites. Only a few Southern states had had mandatory segregation laws covering train passengers before the turn of the century. Between 1901 and 1910 most Southern states passed many different Jim Crow laws. What followed was the "snowball effect" of such legislation. Segregation became the norm in all areas of life — bars, barber shops, drinking fountains, toilet facilities, ticket windows, waiting rooms, hotels, restaurants, parks, playgrounds, theaters, and auditoriums. Through literacy tests, poll taxes, and other measures, the Southern states also succeeded in disfranchising black voters.

EFFECTS OF JIM CROW

The segregation laws, mostly of twentieth-century vintage, reflected racist attitudes that were still current throughout the South decades after slavery had ended. When the 1954 Supreme Court ruling overturned school segregation laws, 17 states had mandatory segregation: Alabama, Arkansas, Delaware, Florida, Georgia, Kentucky, Louisiana, Maryland, Mississippi, Missouri, North Carolina, Oklahoma, South Carolina, Tennessee, Texas, Virginia, and West Virginia. Four other states — Arizona, Kansas, New Mexico, and Wyoming — permitted segregation as a local option.

THE SOUTH It is impossible to exaggerate the impact upon a society of legalizing such discriminatory norms. These laws existed for two generations. During that time both white and black children grew up in a society in which the two races were distinguished from one another and treated differently simply because of that racial difference. Since the white world of reality was one in which differential treatment was the norm, the inferior status of blacks was taken for granted. For most whites growing up in such an environment and in turn transmitting values and attitudes to their children, this was objective reality.

Structural discrimination in the South was pervasive. Despite challenges by the NAACP and by other groups and individuals, most blacks and whites appeared to accept the situation. To whites, the inferior

FIGURE 9.2

An Appalachian father and son sit on the porch steps of their home. (Milton Rogovin, Photo Researchers)

status of blacks in Southern society appeared to justify continued differential treatment. It was, as Gunnar Myrdal concludes in his study of American race relations, a perfect example of the vicious circle in which "discrimination breeds discrimination."[23] As blacks' education and job opportunities were restricted, the end result of that action was to reinforce the attitude supporting the action. Thus, suffering the consequences of deprivation and limited opportunity only aggravated the blacks' situation. They were an easily recognizable group that did not hold better-paying jobs or become educated; they lived in squalor amidst poverty, disease, crime, and violence; they were not "good enough" to use the same facilities as whites. This gave whites more reason for their aversion to blacks and increased their prejudicial attitudes and discriminatory actions. Myrdal calls this intensification a *cumulative causation*, in which there is an almost perpetual sequence of reciprocal stimuli and responses.[24]

THE NORTH But what about the North, where few segregationist laws existed? Although there had been some migration to the North earlier, prior to 1914 almost all blacks resided in the South; but then large numbers of blacks began to migrate to the Northern urban areas. Clearly, the Jim Crow laws and poor economic conditions were the major "push" factors for moving north, while better wages, education, and political freedom were the primary "pull" factors.

By 1915, the North needed labor. The war was under way in Europe and Northern industry was reaping the benefits from it. The large supply of foreign immigrant labor was rapidly dwindling. In the fourteen years after 1900, over twelve million immigrants found their way to the United States. More than one million immigrants reached the United States in 1914 alone. The next year this figure was cut to about one third, in 1916 to about one fourth, and, by 1918, only 110,618 new arrivals landed on the shores of the United States, while 94,585 left. Other sources of labor were needed and Southern Negroes appeared as an available and willing substitute. . . .

The larger pay and increased economic opportunities in the North were heady inducements to migrants. But it was not only for economic reasons that the desire to come North existed in so many. . . . The desire of adults to see their children able to obtain an education caused many to move North. . . . According to a *New York Times* editorial (January 21, 1918), higher wages:

would have been far less attractive if the colored man had not felt, and felt for a long time and bitterly, that in the North and West he would not, as in his southern home, be reminded of his black skin every time he met a policeman, entered a street car, railway station or train, and in a hundred other less conspicuous ways in the course of a day.[25]

So the existence of Jim Crow in the South was an important cause of the migration to the North. By 1925 there were over 1½ million blacks living in the North, three-fourths of them concentrated in the following metropolitan regions:[26]

New York	251,300
Philadelphia	248,300
Chicago	131,600
St. Louis	102,600
Columbus–Cincinnati	89,600
Pittsburgh	88,300
Kansas City	65,400
Cleveland–Youngstown	58,800
Detroit–Toledo	55,900
Indianapolis	47,500

As their counterparts on the West Coast had done in response to Asian immigrants, the labor unions in the North organized against the blacks. Seeing them either as an undesirable element or as economic competition, many workers quickly became antagonistic toward them. It was one more instance of people being liberals from a distance but reactionaries at close range. Although there was greater freedom in the North, the animosity led to majority patterns of avoidance and discrimination.

Race riots, basically an urban phenomenon reflecting the growing animosity in the North, swept through a number of cities during World War I. In 1917 in East St. Louis, Illinois, thirty-nine blacks and eight whites were killed, and hundreds seriously injured, in one of the worst riots. In 1919 the situation became even worse, with returning war veterans seeking jobs and more blacks moving north.

That year there were race riots large and small in twenty-six American cities including thirty-eight killed in a Chicago riot of August; from twenty-five to fifty killed in Phillips County, Arkansas; and six killed in Washington. For a day, the city of Washington, in July, 1919, was actually in the hands of a black mob fighting against the aggression of the whites with hand grenades.[27]

The riots intensified the hostile racial feelings even more. The South had de jure segregation, but Jim Crow — as a cause of black migration and a model for Northern attitudes and actions — played an important role in the development of de facto segregation in the North. With race the determinant for various life opportunities in both the North and the

South, succeeding generations of blacks encountered the same obstacles to upward mobility. So the effects of Jim Crow upon black assimilation into the mainstream of American society went beyond the South and lasted longer than just the first half of the twentieth century.

THE KU KLUX KLAN

Once an organization primarily designed to intimidate blacks, the Ku Klux Klan reorganized in the twentieth century with a broader range of target groups. As a social organization, the Klan has experienced several phases of popularity and decline, and several different sets of goals and objectives. Ex-Confederates had organized the original Klan during the Reconstruction period to frighten and discourage blacks and carpetbaggers. In 1915 William J. Simmons resurrected the movement, formalized its rituals and organization, and dedicated it to white supremacy, Protestant Christianity, and Americanism.

Protest or reactionary groups generally do not become popular unless there is a shared awareness of the problems or concerns to which the group addresses itself within a segment of the society. The Klan was no exception, both in the 1870s and again in the 1920s, when a combination of factors — the agricultural depression, Prohibition, immigration, and isolationism — brought it to a period of rapid expansion. By 1923 the Klan claimed 3 million enrolled members and operated in virtually every state in the union, with public ceremonies and parades.

At first the Klan concentrated on maintaining white supremacy by intimidating white employers as well as black workers and potential voters. While this remained an important theme, as the Klan spread northward, its racist orientation broadened into a more general nationalism and nativism. Fears and condemnation of Jews and foreigners, especially Catholics, led the Klan into a campaign of promoting an Anglo-Saxon version of Americanism with evangelical zeal. In almost puritanical fashion the hooded Klansmen used mass raids, tarring and featherings, floggings, and other strong-arm tactics aimed at either moral regulation or a stabilization of the old order. In reality they accomplished neither, since their actions only fomented additional strife and cruelty.

After a series of internal struggles, exposés of corruption, and mounting anti-Klan opposition, the Klan empire came apart. Although it retained some influence in rural regions of New York, Pennsylvania, Indiana, Texas, and North and South Carolina, its heyday ended in the mid-1920s. It is still very active, however, particularly during times of racial troubles. Ironically, in the 1970s the Klan sought to recruit Catholics — one of its major targets in the past — from the South Boston area who were against school busing.

In the early 1920s, the Ku Klux Klan attracted a large following, partly in reaction to the recent influx of immigrants. Pictured above is a 1924 demonstration in Binghamton, New York. (United Press International)

The Ku Klux Klan, then, evolved into a multi-xenophobic organization in which southern and eastern European Catholics and Jews, as well as blacks, were seen as a threat to the American character. The Klan's enormous popularity in the early 1920s is a reflection of the times, since these minority peoples were felt to present an economic threat. As prosperity increased and immigration decreased, thereby reducing the tensions, support for the Klan also ebbed. Its success, like the success of the Native American Party and the Know-Nothing Party of the nineteenth century, indicates that many people were receptive to its philosophy and goals.

THE WINDS OF CHANGE

After World War II, several events accelerated the pace of change in the status of blacks in American society. Blacks organized, there was a massive civil rights movement, the Jim Crow laws were struck down by the courts, and civil rights legislation improved life opportunities.

Blacks had been migrating to the North since 1914, and, although they encountered discrimination there as well, they did have greater opportunities in jobs and in education. As their health, longevity, literacy, and occupational status improved, blacks in both the North and the South began to realize that things could be different and better for them.

DESEGREGATION: THE FIRST PHASE

In the past, blacks had made many concerted efforts to improve their lot. The Colored National Farmers' Alliance claimed 1,250,000 members in 1891, but had faded from the scene by 1910. In the twentieth century several black leaders arose to rally their people: Booker T. Washington, W. E. B. DuBois, Marcus Garvey, and A. Philip Randolph. In the 1920s, 1930s, and 1940s, the NAACP and other groups filed court cases that had limited success but laid the basis for the 1954 desegregation ruling. None of these attempts, however, resulted in as massive a restructuring of black-white relations as the events of the mid-twentieth century.

Having experienced life outside their cultural milieu, many blacks who fought in World War II returned home with new perspectives and aspirations. The GI Bill of Rights, Veterans Authority, and Federal Housing Authority offered increased opportunity for education, jobs, and housing. Expectations increased, and the growing popularity of television sets brought into more and more homes insights into life styles that previously could only be vaguely imagined.

Several court cases challenging the school segregation laws in Delaware, Kansas, South Carolina, and Virginia reached the U.S. Supreme Court in 1954. Consolidating the several suits, the Justices ruled unanimously on May 17, 1954, that the "separate but equal" doctrine was unconstitutional. Social science data, through amicus curiae briefs, played an important role in the decision.[28] The following year the Court established means of implementing its decree by giving the federal district courts jurisdiction over any problems relating to enforcement of the ruling. The Court insisted that the states move toward compliance with "all deliberate speed," but this guideline was vague enough to allow them to circumvent the ruling at first.

Although the National Association for the Advancement of Colored People (NAACP) quickly began a multipronged challenge to school districts in the 17 states in which school segregation existed, their efforts met with mixed success. Many whites, seeing their values, beliefs, and practices threatened by outsiders, resisted desegregation. State legislatures passed bills to stave off integration, whites used economic and social pressures to intimidate any blacks who attempted to integrate local schools, and the school districts themselves procrastinated in dealing with the problem. For three years the battle of wills resulted in continuation of the status quo despite the Supreme Court ruling.

On another front, an event occurred in Montgomery, Alabama, in 1955 that foreshadowed other minority actions in the 1960s. Mrs. Rosa Parks, a tired black seamstress on her way home from work, refused to give up her bus seat in the section reserved for whites and was arrested. Through the organizing efforts of Martin Luther King, Jr., in the black community, a successful bus boycott occurred. Four months later the NAACP argued the case in the Federal District Court, which ruled against segregated seating on municipal buses. The U.S. Supreme Court upheld the decision.

The confrontation in the fall of 1957 at Little Rock Central High School in Arkansas was a watershed in desegregation. Here the state's defiance of the Supreme Court could not be ignored, since the governor called out the National Guard to forcibly block a concerted effort to integrate the high school. President Eisenhower, who had personally been against the 1954 ruling, acted decisively by federalizing the National Guard and sending regular army troops to assure compliance.

With all legal avenues of appeal exhausted and the federal government insisting that all citizens, including black children, be accorded equal rights, Southern resistance ebbed. Desegregation in the public schools, though sometimes merely tokenism, became the norm throughout the Southern states. That is not to say that everything was harmonious. Some whites established private academies to avoid sending their children to integrated schools, and some Southern leaders publicly committed themselves to upholding Southern tradition at all costs. Still,

FIGURE 9.4

In 1957, paratroopers of the 101st Airborne Division enforced the integration of Little Rock High School in Arkansas. Many analysts consider this event a watershed in the school desegregation movement. (United Press International)

Jim Crow had been dealt a severe blow, and opponents readied themselves for the next assault.

DESEGREGATION: THE SECOND PHASE

In the 1960s the civil rights movement gained momentum, attracted many more followers, and moved against all other Jim Crow legislation. Sit-in demonstrations began in Greensboro, North Carolina, on February 1, 1960, when four freshmen from the all-black Agricultural and Technical College sat at the all-white lunch counter at the local Woolworth's store and refused to leave. During the spring of 1960, there were sit-ins throughout the South. From the sit-ins evolved a fourth social organization — the Student Nonviolent Coordinating Committee (SNCC, pronounced *snick*) — to compete with the NAACP, the Congress on Racial Equality (CORE), and the Southern Christian Leadership Conference (SCLC), which Dr. King had formed after the bus boycott.

The success of the sit-ins convinced many people that direct action was a quicker and more effective means of achieving total desegregation. James Farmer of CORE organized Freedom Rides from Washington, D.C., to selected Southern locations in 1961 to challenge the segregated facilities in bus terminals. These were followed by freedom marches, voter registration drives, and continued attacks upon Jim Crow legislation.

All the movements were symptomatic of the times. Kennedy's election as President in 1960 and his speaking of "a new generation of leadership" had inaugurated a period of high hopes and ideals. It was a time of commitment and change, of Vista and the Peace Corps, of promise and reachable goals. As the civil rights movement grew, "We Shall Overcome" became the rallying theme song, and Bob Dylan's "Blowin' in the Wind" captured the spirit of the times.

Civil rights activity met with fierce resistance. Dr. King urged nonviolence, but younger black activists grew impatient with such an approach.

Nonviolence was for him [King] a philosophical issue rather than the tactical or strategic question it posed for many younger activists in SNCC and CORE. The aim was "to awaken a sense of moral shame in the opponent." Such a philosophy presumed that the opponent had moral shame to awaken, and that moral shame, if awakened, would suffice. During the 1960's many civil rights activists came to doubt the first and deny the second. The reasons for this did not lie primarily in white Southern terrorism as manifested in the killing of NAACP leader Medgar Evers, of three civil rights workers in Neshoba, Mississippi, of four little girls in a dynamited church in Birmingham, and many others. To a large extent, white Southern violence was anticipated and expected. What was not expected was the absence of strong protective action by the federal government.

Activists in SNCC and CORE met with greater and more violent Southern resistance as direct action continued during the sixties. Freedom Riders were beaten by mobs in Montgomery; demonstrators were hosed, clubbed, and cattle-prodded in Birmingham and Selma. Throughout the South, civil rights workers, black and white, were victimized by local officials as well as by night-riders and angry crowds. It was not surprising, then, that student activists in the South became increasingly disillusioned with nonviolent tactics of resistance.[29]

Two events in 1963 — the March on Washington and the integration of the University of Alabama — gave two civil rights activists — King and Kennedy — the opportunity to express the mood of the times. On August 28, 1963, tens of thousands of marchers of all races from all over the country and many walks of life gathered before the Lincoln Memorial. King addressed them (in part) as follows:

There are those who are asking the devotees of civil rights, "When will you be satisfied?" We can never be satisfied as long as the Negro is the victim of the unspeakable horrors of police brutality. We can never be satisfied as long as our bodies, heavy with the fatigue of travel, cannot gain lodging in the motels of the highways and the hotels of the cities. We cannot be satisfied as long as the Negro's basic mobility is from a smaller ghetto to a larger one. We can never be satisfied as long as a Negro in Mississippi cannot vote and a Negro in New York believes he has nothing for which to vote. No, no, we are not satisfied, and we will not be satisfied until justice rolls down like waters and righteousness like a mighty stream. . . .

I say to you today, my friends, that in spite of the difficulties and frustrations of the moment I still have a dream. It is a dream deeply rooted in the American dream.

I have a dream that one day this nation will rise up and live out the true meaning of its creed: "We hold these truths to be self-evident; that all men are created equal." . . . I have a dream that my four little children will one day live in a nation where they will not be judged by the color of their skin but by the content of their character.

On April 4, 1968, an assassin's bullet prevented Martin Luther King from seeing his dream move closer to reality. President Kennedy died on November 22, 1963, before the passage of the civil rights legislation

FIGURE 9.5

Tens of thousands from the 1963 March on Washington jammed the area in front of the Lincoln Memorial and on either side of the Reflecting Pool to hear Dr. Martin Luther King, Jr. (United Press International)

he proposed after he sent troops to enforce the integration of the University of Alabama in that same year. In explaining his actions, Kennedy had told the American public in a television address:

> This nation was founded by men of many nations and backgrounds. It was founded on the principle that all men are created equal, and that the rights of every man are diminished when the rights of one man are threatened. . . .
>
> It ought to be possible, therefore, for American students of any color to attend any public institution they select without having to be backed up by troops. It ought to be possible for American consumers of any color to receive equal service in places of public accommodation, such as hotels and restaurants, and theaters and retail stores without being forced to resort to demonstrations in the street.
>
> And it ought to be possible for American citizens of any color to register and to vote in a free election without interference or fear of reprisal.
>
> It ought to be possible, in short, for every American to enjoy the privileges of being American without regard to his race or his color.
>
> In short, every American ought to have the right to be treated as he would wish to be treated, as one would wish his children to be treated. But this is not the case. . . .
>
> One hundred years of delay have passed since President Lincoln freed the slaves, yet their heirs, their grandsons, are not fully free. They are not yet freed from the bonds of injustice; they are not yet freed from social and economic oppression.
>
> And this nation, for all its hopes and all its boasts, will not be fully free until all its citizens are free.

The Civil Rights Act of 1964 was the most far-reaching legislation against racial discrimination ever passed. It provided for equal standards for all voters in federal elections. It prohibited racial discrimination and refusal of service on racial grounds in all places of public accommodation, including eating and lodging establishments and places of entertainment, recreation, or service. It gave the attorney general broader powers to intervene in private suits regarding violation of civil rights. It banned racial discrimination by employers or unions or by any recipient of federal funds, and it directed federal agencies to monitor this and to withhold funds from any recalcitrant state or local agency. Unfortunately, black workers still meet resistance from many unions when they apply for membership.

Congress passed additional legislation in 1965 to simplify judicial enforcement of the voting laws and to extend them to state and local elections. In 1968 further civil rights legislation barred discrimination in housing and gave the American Indians greater rights in their dealings with courts and government agencies at all levels. Congress also set stiff federal penalties for those convicted of intimidating or injuring anyone who was exercising any of the civil rights provided by congressional action.

The effect of the legislation upon attitudes is difficult to measure, but it did give blacks equal life opportunities. By the end of the 1960s, the number of black registered voters in the South had increased dramatically. Through political activity blacks came to hold many local and regional elective offices and thus gained influence in the decision-making process. Interaction in public places further increased their participation in society, thereby providing long-term opportunities for the social conditioning of people's attitudes toward racial harmony.[30]

URBAN UNREST

As the civil rights movement gained momentum, it spread northward as well. Protests against discrimination in employment and housing and against de facto segregation in the schools began in the early 1960s in New York and Philadelphia and quickly spread.

None of the problems of the blacks in the North — slum schools, unemployment or residential segregation — were new, but an intensified awareness of them had grown. Part of this new awareness reflected the economic cramp that developed during the latter part of the fifties, particularly in the burgeoning ghettoes of northern and western cities. Ideological cramp was being felt outside the South, too. The promise of a new equality for all blacks, the struggle of southern blacks to realize this promise, and the complacency of white America as the white South turned the new equality into token equality spread disillusionment into black neighborhoods all over the nation. Ironically, the plaintive and oft-repeated plea of white southerners that the problem of race relations was not just a Southern problem finally began to be heard — but only because it was now sounded by black voices.[31]

In the North, ideological support for the black cause waned as the distance from the conflict diminished with increasing percentages of blacks in Northern cities (Table 9.1). Changes were demanded nearer home, in particular open housing and busing. By 1964 Charles Silberman observed:

And so the North is finally beginning to face the reality of race. In the process, it is discovering animosities and prejudices that had been hidden in the recesses of the soul. For a brief period following the demonstrations in Birmingham in the spring of 1963 — a very brief period — it appeared that the American conscience had been

TABLE 9.1

PERCENTAGE OF BLACKS IN CENTRAL CITIES
OF TWELVE LARGEST SMSAS *, 1950–1970

CITY	1950	1960	1970
New York	10	14	21
Los Angeles	9	14	18
Chicago	14	23	33
Philadelphia	18	26	34
Detroit	16	29	44
San Francisco	6	10	13
Washington, D.C.	35	54	71
Boston	5	9	13
Pittsburgh	12	17	20
St. Louis	18	29	41
Baltimore	24	35	38
Cleveland	16	29	46

SOURCE: U.S. Bureau of the Census, Census of Population: 1960 and 1970, General Population Characteristics, Washington, D.C.
*Standard Metropolitan Statistical Area: a city of at least 50,000 inhabitants and its surrounding region.

touched; a wave of sympathy for the Negro and of revulsion over white brutality seemed to course through the nation. But then the counteraction set in, revealing a degree of anti-Negro prejudice and hatred that surprised even the most sophisticated observers.[32]

As blacks experienced some gains and some frustrations, a pattern of increased alienation, cynicism, hostility, and eventual violence ensued. When a social movement achieves some goals, its expectations are increased and so are its frustrations, leading to greater militancy.[33] Militant leaders like Malcolm X, Eldridge Cleaver, Huey Newton, and Bobby Seale emerged to speak of the grievances of Northern blacks. New organizations such as the Black Panthers and older ones such as the Black Muslims attracted many followers as they set out to meet the needs of Northern blacks in the ghettoes.

In the summer of 1964, blacks rioted in the tenement sections of Harlem, Philadelphia, and Rochester, attacking both police and property. The following summer, the violence and destruction were more massive; outbursts occurred first in the Watts section of Los Angeles and then in Chicago, Springfield, Massachusetts, and Philadelphia. Ghetto violence continued; in the summer of 1966 there were 18 different riots, and in the summer of 1967, 31 cities experienced riots, of which those in Newark (26 killed) and Detroit (42 killed) were the worst.

The increase in the number and intensity of riots in 1967 prompted an in-depth study of 75 of the disorders, including those in Newark and Detroit, by the National Advisory Commission on Civil Disorders. It found that, although specific grievances varied somewhat from city to city, there were consistent patterns in who the rioters were, how the riots originated, and what the rioters wanted. The most intense causal factors were police practices, unemployment and underemployment, and inadequate housing.

> Disorder did not erupt as a result of a single "triggering" or "precipitation" incident. Instead, it was generated out of an increasingly disturbed social atmosphere, in which typically a series of tension-heightening incidents over a period of weeks or months became linked in the minds of many in the Negro community with a reservoir of underlying grievances. At some point in the mounting tension, a further incident — in itself often routine or trivial — became the breaking point and the tension spilled over into violence. . . .
>
> The typical rioter was a teenager or young adult, a lifelong resident of the city in which he rioted, a high school dropout; he was nevertheless, somewhat better educated than his nonrioting Negro neighbor, and was usually underemployed or employed in a menial job. He was proud of his race, extremely hostile to both whites and middle-class Negroes and, although informed about politics, highly distrustful of the political system. . . .
>
> What the rioters appeared to be seeking was fuller participation in the social order and the material benefits enjoyed by the majority of American citizens. Rather than rejecting the American system, they were anxious to obtain for themselves a place in it.[34]

The deaths, injuries, burnings, and extensive property damage in all the cities — Watts, Newark, and Detroit being the worst hit — produced government action at municipal, state, and federal levels to correct the conditions that encouraged violence. But the riots also caused a white backlash. The exodus of the white middle class from the cities, which had begun in the 1950s, now had added impetus. The migration increased, with some stores and businesses also moving to the suburbs. There are a number of complex reasons for the urban-suburban migration, but in the late 1960s urban violence was clearly a major factor for many people.

In 1966 Stokely Carmichael, the head of SNCC, advanced the slogan "Black Power," which became subject to many interpretations since it was never clearly defined. For many, it was not a wild cry of radicals, but rather a declaration that civil rights goals could be achieved only through concerted black efforts. It symbolized the attainment of what Kurt Lewin called a "sense of peoplehood" and Franklin Giddings identified as a "consciousness of kind." The word "black" rather than "Negro" quickly became the accepted way of referring to this racial group.

Two factors contributed to the cooling of black urban violence. First, a new social movement protesting the war in Vietnam, to which many black youths were being sent, became a focus for public concern. Second, many black leaders were either assassinated (King, Medgar Evers, Malcolm X) or imprisoned (Carmichael, Newton, Seale), or went into exile (Cleaver). Many blacks redirected their energies toward community self-help programs, as other leaders were co-opted in leadership roles within the system and many blacks began to strive for the Black Power goal Carmichael had enunciated.

SOCIAL INDICATORS OF BLACK PROGRESS

Sociologists frequently use three variables — level of education, amount of income, and type of occupation — to measure a group's achievement and mobility in the stratification system of society. Since blacks in the United States had an inferior status in the past, the degree to which the gap between the two races has been narrowed is an indication of how far blacks have advanced.

EDUCATION

Without question blacks have made considerable gains in level of education attained. Even though the national average for years of completed schooling has been rising, the percent change for blacks from 1950 to 1975 has been far more dramatic than that for whites. The percentage figures in Table 9.2 reflect the increase in black educational levels. Since the percentage figures represent numerical comparisons, they are affected by population growth, greater emphasis on education, and increased educational opportunities. The first column indicates that fewer whites lacked a high school diploma in 1975 than in 1950, but that there was a slight increase in the number of black males and females who did not complete high school. Population growth may explain part of this increase, but the fact that there continues to be a large number of blacks who do not complete high school is significant.

Fewer blacks than whites attained the other levels of education in 1950. The 1975 percentage changes are much more dramatic for blacks because they show the beneficial effects of action to improve their edu-

TABLE 9.2

YEARS OF SCHOOLING COMPLETED IN 1975
AS COMPARED TO 1950

BY PERCENT

	LESS THAN FOUR YEARS OF HIGH SCHOOL	FOUR YEARS OF HIGH SCHOOL	ONE TO THREE YEARS OF COLLEGE	FOUR YEARS OF COLLEGE
BLACK MALES	9.0	390.1	387.8	379.7
WHITE MALES	−30.0	125.4	140.4	209.6
BLACK FEMALES	2.9	415.5	333.1	315.2
WHITE FEMALES	−20.0	131.0	104.5	177.0

Source: U.S. Department of Commerce, Bureau of the Census, "Educational Attainment in the United States: March 1975," *Current Population Reports*, Series P20, No. 295, June 1976.

cational opportunities. In Table 9.3, which shows the median years of schooling, this closing of the gap between the races becomes more apparent. In 1950 there was a spread of 2.9 years between black and white males, which had gradually lessened to 1.8 years by 1975. For females the gap of 2.9 years in 1950 had narrowed to 1.2 years by 1975.

While median scores help to establish one basis of comparison, a more detailed breakdown of years of schooling reveals the differences in educational attainment that remain. Table 9.4 shows that the percentage of whites completing higher levels of education is still greater than that of blacks. Approximately 75 percent of all whites, compared with slightly more than 50 percent of all blacks, have completed at least eight years of schooling. Despite recent gains, blacks as a group are not yet equal to whites in educational level.

TABLE 9.3

MEDIAN YEARS OF SCHOOLING COMPLETED
SELECTED YEARS, 1950–1975

	1950	1960	1970	1975
BLACK MALES	6.4	7.9	9.6	10.7
WHITE MALES	9.3	10.7	12.2	12.5
BLACK FEMALES	7.1	8.5	10.2	11.1
WHITE FEMALES	10.0	12.1	12.2	12.3

Source: U.S. Department of Commerce, Bureau of the Census, "Educational Attainment in the United States: March 1975," *Current Population Reports*, Series P20, No. 295, June 1976.

TABLE 9.4

YEARS OF SCHOOLING COMPLETED IN 1975
FOR AGES TWENTY-FIVE AND OLDER
BY PERCENT

	EIGHT YEARS ELEMENTARY	FOUR YEARS HIGH SCHOOL	ONE TO THREE YEARS COLLEGE	FOUR YEARS COLLEGE	FIVE OR MORE YEARS COLLEGE	TOTAL % EIGHT OR MORE YEARS
BLACK MALES	7.4	25.6	10.2	6.0	4.7	53.9
WHITE MALES	10.5	33.1	13.6	9.8	8.6	75.6
BLACK FEMALES	8.6	29.3	9.0	5.4	2.5	54.8
WHITE FEMALES	10.6	41.1	12.1	7.3	3.6	74.7

SOURCE: U.S. Department of Commerce, Bureau of the Census, "Educational Attainment in the United States: March 1975," *Current Population Reports,* Series P20, No. 295, June 1976.

INCOME

Historically, black family income has been less than that of white families, although differences between the two have narrowed slightly over the past ten to fifteen years. There has been virtually no gain in median real income, however, since increases have been offset by the higher cost of living. More black families have a female head (35.3 percent in 1975, compared with 10.5 percent for whites), and both they and many semiskilled black male workers are affected more by cyclical slowdowns in the economy. This greater sensitivity to economic conditions has on occasion, as in 1969–1970 and in 1973–1975, widened the income gap between whites and nonwhites. Table 9.5 shows how the gap has widened in terms of real income, although it has narrowed in percentage terms.

TABLE 9.5

MEDIAN INCOME OF FAMILIES BY RACE OF HEAD

YEAR	WHITE	BLACK	BLACK INCOME AS A PERCENT OF WHITE INCOME	ACTUAL INCOME GAP
1964	$ 6,858	$3,724	54.3	$3,134
1974	$13,356	$8,265	61.9	$5,091

SOURCE: National Commission for Manpower Policy.

Median family income statistics, while helpful, do not give a very accurate picture of general financial conditions among all black families.
The distribution of income, sources of income, and poverty rates of
blacks and whites are not the same, and these differences (shown in Tables 9.6, 9.7, and 9.8) illustrate some of the problems that still remain.

If the population, either as a whole or by race, is divided into fifths
(Table 9.6), we can see that the top two quintiles receive about two-
thirds of the total income in the United States. The top two quintiles of
blacks receive a larger proportion of the total black income than the top

TABLE 9.6

PERCENTAGE SHARE OF AGGREGATE INCOME BEFORE TAXES
RECEIVED BY EACH FIFTH AND TOP FIVE PERCENT OF FAMILIES
BY RACE OF HEAD

SELECTED YEARS, 1947–1974

INCOME RANK	1947	1960	1974
ALL RACES			
Lowest quintile	5.1	4.8	5.4
Second quintile	11.8	12.2	12.0
Middle quintile	16.7	17.8	17.6
Fourth quintile	23.2	24.0	24.1
Highest quintile	43.3	41.3	41.0
Top 5 percent	17.5	15.9	15.3
Total percent	100.0	100.0	100.0
WHITE			
Lowest quintile	5.5	5.2	5.8
Second quintile	12.2	12.7	12.3
Middle quintile	16.9	17.8	17.6
Fourth quintile	22.8	23.7	23.8
Highest quintile	42.6	40.7	40.5
Top 5 percent	17.4	15.7	15.1
Total percent	100.0	100.0	100.0
BLACK			
Lowest quintile	4.8	3.7	4.6
Second quintile	10.2	9.7	10.0
Middle quintile	15.7	16.5	16.2
Fourth quintile	23.6	25.2	25.0
Highest quintile	45.8	44.9	44.2
Top 5 percent	17.0	16.2	15.9
Total percent	100.0	100.0	100.0

SOURCE: U.S. Department of Commerce, Bureau of the Census, "Money Income in 1974 of
Families and Persons in the United States," *Current Population Reports*, Series P60, No.
101, January 1976, Table 22, p. 37.

TABLE 9.7

SOURCES OF INCOME IN 1974

BY PERCENT

SOURCE	BLACKS	WHITES
Earnings from work	82.9	84.0
Social security	6.3	5.6
Dividends, interest, trusts, etc.	0.7	4.9
Public assistance and welfare	5.9	0.8
Unemployment, workers' compensation, and public pensions	2.8	2.8
Private pensions, annuities, and alimony	1.4	1.9
Total percent	100.0	100.0

SOURCE: U.S. Department of Commerce, Bureau of the Census, "Population Profile of the United States: 1975," *Current Population Reports*, Series P20, No. 292, March 1976.

two quintiles of whites do of white income. This means that not only do blacks earn less money than whites, but blacks at the lower socioeconomic levels have an even smaller share of the income within their race than do whites at these levels.

Except for a slight decrease in the share of income earned by the highest quintile, there has been no significant change in the distribution

TABLE 9.8

POVERTY RATE IN SELECTED YEARS, 1959–1975

BY PERCENT

	1959	1969	1975
Black — all	55.1	32.2	31.3
White — all	18.1	9.5	9.7
Total U.S.	14.1	12.1	12.3
Black — age 65 and older	62.5	50.2	36.3
White — age 65 and older	33.1	23.3	13.4
Total U.S. — age 65 and older	35.2	25.3	15.3

SOURCE: U.S. Department of Commerce, Bureau of the Census, "Population Profile of the United States: 1975," *Population Characteristics, Current Population Reports*, Series P20, No. 292, March 1976, p. 35.

over the 27 years. True, the fourth quintile of the black population has gained somewhat, but this only further emphasizes the disparity. In other words, in terms of income, the black poor have not benefited as much from civil rights actions as have the black middle class.

The percentage of blacks whose work provides their income is comparable to that of whites: approximately 83 percent of all black income, in comparison with 84 percent of all white income, derives from labor. However, as Table 9.7 shows, there are significant differences in other sources of income as a result of the variance in economic security between the two races. More whites than blacks are in a position to make money on their money through savings and investments. Also, more blacks are at the lower socioeconomic level.

Changes in family composition are an important consideration in understanding income trends, since an increasing proportion of women are heads of families. Families with only one parent often have a lower median family income than families with two parents present. Females aged 25 to 44 constituted 5 percent of white family heads and 15 percent of nonwhite in 1960. By 1975 these proportions had grown to 9 percent white and 32 percent nonwhite.[35] Nonwhite women have experienced greater upward mobility than nonwhite men, to the extent that their incomes are now comparable to those of similarly qualified white women. Overall, however, there is still a very large gap between whites and nonwhites in occupational distribution.[36]

Another critical factor is the vitality of the labor market. In the 1970s the unemployment rate peaked in 1975 with 7 percent of the white and 13 percent of the nonwhite males 16 and over out of work.[37] In the major cities, with their heavy concentrations of nonwhite poor, this often meant an unemployment rate as high as 40 percent among nonwhites.[38] The very high unemployment rate among young black males suggests that many of them have great difficulty in beginning a self-sufficient working career.

These frustrations in securing the minimum essentials of life make blacks impatient. In the summer of 1977, Vernon Jordan of the National Urban League criticized the Carter administration for its slowness in dealing with the problem of black unemployment. Clayton Riley pointed out the gap between the promise and the reality:

> We are increasing our manufacture of luxury automobiles while failing to provide substance to the dreams we have told everyone to believe, the dreams of nothing more than shelter, clothes, food, and some occasional fun.
>
> This has been promised by Presidents and other politicians, by planners and thinkers and visionaries. But inside the cities, the systems don't work.

. . . We are living in a country without a national personality,
without a real sense of what the term "American" is supposed to
mean, or whom.[39]

The inability of the labor market to absorb a greater proportion of the
nonwhite population clearly impedes upward mobility. However, black

family income has risen slightly more rapidly than white family income since World War II.[40] Also, the number of blacks living in poverty has dropped substantially, although blacks are still disproportionately represented among the poor. Table 9.8 shows the gains achieved in recent years. Most of the nonwhite poor are concentrated in urban areas and thus are highly visible. In contrast, the white poor are more widely dispersed, residing in less densely populated areas, of which Appalachia is most commonly cited. Others live in New England, the Great Lakes region, and throughout the South.

OCCUPATION

For many Americans occupation is a primary measure of status. Accordingly, measurements of changes in occupational classification are a good indication of the progress or lack of progress, in terms of social mobility, that a group is making. Table 9.9 lists the major occupational groupings for nonwhites and whites in 1967, shortly after the civil rights legislation barring job discrimination, and in 1975. In many instances one can see a greater net gain for nonwhites than for whites. Again, remember that these statistics represent catch-up activity, since the numbers of nonwhites were much smaller at the outset.

Some of the occupational shifts represent advances in technology and societal trends, such as the decline in the number of farm workers, operatives, and private household workers. In professional and white collar positions, as identified in the first three categories in Table 9.9, the increase among nonwhites has been proportionally greater than that among whites. Among nonwhite females, the most dramatic change is the decrease in the percentage employed as private household workers and the increase in the percentage of sales and clerical personnel, clearly a sign of upward mobility. For nonwhite males the most significant shifts are the reduction of farm workers and of nonfarm laborers (fewer operatives being a nationwide trend). While the distribution of white males remained relatively stable among craft and kindred workers, nonwhite male representation in this area increased by 2.2 percent. This category includes trade union workers in construction, mechanics, and metals.[41]

OVERVIEW

From the three social indicators, education, income, and occupation, it would appear that blacks are making progress toward achieving a more equitable position in American society. The gap has been narrowed in many areas, and the educational pattern bodes well for continued progress in the future. Still, a substantial number of blacks have not made much improvement, as the median income disparities and dispropor-tionate poverty rates indicate. While many blacks have benefited from wider opportunities, a great many others — locked into a poverty cycle and trapped in the ghettoes — have yet to realize the American Dream.[42]

Achieving middle-class status does not necessarily mean, however, that the life situation of blacks is comparable to that of middle-class whites. Brigitte Erbe found quite different patterns when she examined segregation by socioeconomic status among whites and blacks in the Chicago SMSA in 1970.[43] Because of residential patterns, the black middle class were more likely to live in the same neighborhoods as lower-class laborers than were the white middle class. This situation carried over into education, where the black middle-class student was at a disadvantage because more lower-class students, who had lower motivation, a lower achievement rate, and a higher dropout rate, were in the school. The assumption here is that despite their middle-class in-comes, many blacks still do not enjoy the same environmental stimuli as their white counterparts.

Achieving political power is an important means by which a minority group strengthens its position in society. Since the mid-1960s, voter reg-istration drives and collective efforts have paid off, and the numbers of elected black legislators and public officials at all levels of government have increased substantially. The trend in the 1970s appears to be less toward black separatist or radical movements and more toward eventual integration, although there are divergent opinions about how rapidly this should be attained.[44]

RETROSPECT

Through two hundred years of slavery and one hundred additional years of another form of subjugation, blacks have found society unre-sponsive to their needs and wants. Negatively categorized by skin color, they have seen clearly that there are two worlds in this country: the white and the nonwhite. Many blacks remain trapped in poverty and isolated in urban ghettoes; others, who have achieved upward mobility, often find, at least in meaningful primary relationships, that they are still not accepted in white society.

There are many similarities between the black experience in the United States and the experiences of other minority peoples. Like the Asians and Indians, blacks have frequently been judged on the basis of their skin color, not their individual capabilities. They have experi-enced, as have many immigrant groups, countless instances of stereotyping, scapegoating, prejudice, discrimination, social and spatial segregation, deprivation, and violence. When they have become too vis-ible in a given area or have moved into economic competition with

TABLE 9.9

OCCUPATIONAL DISTRIBUTION OF U.S. LABOR FORCE,
1967 AND 1975

BY PERCENT FOR RACE

Classification	1967		1975		CHANGE	
	Nonwhite	White	Nonwhite	White	Nonwhite	White
MALES						
Professional, technical workers	6.2	13.8	9.9	15.1	+3.7	+1.3
Managers, administrators	3.4	14.4	5.9	14.8	+2.5	+0.4
Sales and clerical workers	8.8	13.2	10.3	12.9	+1.5	−0.3
Craft and kindred workers	12.8	20.9	15.0	21.0	+2.2	+0.1
Operatives	28.1	19.4	23.8	9.8	−4.3	−9.6
Nonfarm laborers	18.8	5.9	14.9	6.6	−3.9	+0.7
Private household workers	0.2	0.1	0.1	a	−0.1	−0.1
Service workers	14.7	6.1	16.2	7.7	+1.5	+1.6
Farmers, including managers, supervisors, and laborers	11.8	8.1	6.6	6.7	−5.2	−1.4

Classification	1967 Nonwhite	White	1975 Nonwhite	White	CHANGE Nonwhite	White
FEMALES						
Professional, technical workers	9.1	14.4	13.3	16.0	+4.2	+1.6
Managers, administrators	1.5	4.8	2.6	5.5	+1.1	+0.7
Sales and clerical workers	18.6	43.4	28.1	44.0	+9.5	+0.6
Craft and kindred workers	0.6	1.1	1.3	1.5	+0.7	+0.2
Operatives	17.1	15.3	15.4	11.1	-1.7	-4.2
Nonfarm laborers	0.8	0.4	1.7	1.1	+0.9	-0.7
Private household workers	24.5	3.9	10.6	2.4	-13.9	-1.5
Service workers	24.8	14.5	26.6	17.1	+1.8	+2.6
Farmers, including managers, supervisors, and laborers	5.8	4.0	2.0	2.5	-3.8	-1.5

aLess than 0.05 percent.
SOURCE: U.S. Department of Labor, *Annual Report*, U.S. Government Printing Office, Washington, D.C., 1976.

whites, the dominant group has seen them as a threat and reacted accordingly. All of this is a familiar pattern in dominant-minority relations.

More than two hundred years of slavery exacted a heavy toll upon the black people of America, and exploitation and discrimination did not end with the abolition of slavery. As a result of generations of social conditioning, many whites continued to have a master-slave mentality long after the Civil War. Two generations later, when blacks had made some progress, the Jim Crow laws eliminated those gains and reestablished unequal treatment and life opportunities, thereby increasing prejudice.

A change in values and attitudes became evident with the historic Supreme Court decision of 1954. Although school integration was slow, it did come about, and both blacks and whites were encouraged to seek even more changes. The growth of the civil rights movement — an idea whose time had come at last — peaked in the mid-1960s, when a broad range of laws were passed to offer black people a more equitable life experience.

A quarter of a century has elapsed since the 1954 decision. A great number of changes have taken place in the land, and there have been observable improvements in all aspects of life for many blacks. Still, many problems remain. A disproportionate number of nonwhite poor continue to be concentrated in the cities, frequently trapped in a cycle of perpetual poverty. Despite all the legislation and court decisions, most blacks still engage in primary relationships only with other blacks. Social distance between blacks and whites in informal and private gatherings is still great. De facto segregation is still a problem, with the majority of whites living in suburbs and the majority of blacks living in urban areas.

Greater interaction occurs between the two races in places of public accommodation, and this may eventually reshape white attitudes. That, together with improved educational opportunities, may lead to greater structural assimilation for blacks. One element crucial to black progress is the condition of the economy. Its ability to absorb blacks into those positions in the labor force that permit upward socioeconomic mobility will, in large measure, determine the future status of blacks in American society.

QUESTIONS FOR DISCUSSION

1. In what ways is the black experience in the United States unique?
2. What similarities exist among the experiences of the blacks, Amer-

ican Indians, and Asians in the United States?

3. What similarities are there between the responses of blacks and of European immigrants to prejudice and discrimination?

4. What factors have delayed blacks in gaining economic and political power as European and Asian immigrant groups did?

5. How justified is the individual who says that blacks are now, through affirmative action and other policies, obtaining too much at the expense of whites?

SUGGESTED READINGS

Billingsley, Andrew. *Black Families in White America*. Prentice-Hall, Englewood Cliffs, N.J., 1968.

Clark, Kenneth B. *Dark Ghetto*. Harper & Row, New York, 1965.

Frazier, E. Franklin. *Black Bourgeoisie*. Free Press, Glencoe, Ill., 1957.

————. *The Negro Family in the United States*. University of Chicago Press, Chicago, 1939.

————. *The Negro in the United States*. Macmillan, New York, 1949.

Glazer, Nathan, and Daniel P. Moynihan. *Beyond the Melting Pot*, 2nd ed. M.I.T., Cambridge, Mass., 1970.

Gutman, Herbert. *The Black Family in Slavery and Freedom, 1750–1925*. Pantheon, New York, 1976.

Hill, Herbert. *Black Labor and the American Labor System, Vol. I: Race, Work, and the Law*. Bureau of National Affairs, Washington, D.C., 1977.

Killian, Lewis M. *The Impossible Revolution, Phase II*. Random House, New York, 1975.

Kronus, Sidney J. *The Black Middle Class*. Merrill, Columbus, Ohio, 1971.

Lyman, Stanford M. *The Black American in Sociological Thought: A Failure of Perspective*. Putnam, New York, 1972.

Myrdal, Gunnar. *An American Dilemma*. McGraw-Hill, New York, 1964.

Pinkney, Alphonso. *Black Americans*. Prentice-Hall, Englewood Cliffs, N.J., 1969.

Scanzoni, John. *The Black Family in Modern Society*. Allyn and Bacon, Boston, 1971.

Silberman, Charles. *Crisis in Black and White*. Random House, New York, 1964.

Sowell, Thomas. *Race and Economics*. McKay, New York, 1975.

Staples, Robert. *The Black Woman in America*. Nelson-Hall, Chicago, 1973.

Willie, Charles V. *A New Look at Black Families*. General Hall, New York, 1976.

NOTES

1. Ira De Augustine Reid, *The Negro Immigrant*, 1939, reprint ed., Arno Press and *The New York Times*, New York, 1969, p. 32.

2. See James O. Buswell, III, *Slavery, Segregation and Scripture*, Eerdmans, Grand Rapids, Mich., 1964; George D. Kelsey, *Racism and the Christian Understanding of Man*, Scribner's, New York, 1965; W. E. B. DuBois, *The World and Africa*, International Publishers, New York, 1965; Keith Irvine,

The Rise of the Colored Races, Norton, New York, 1970.

3. DuBois, *The World and Africa,* pp. 19–20.

4. Irvine, *The Rise of the Colored Races,* p. 13.

5. See the discussion on pp. 48–49, 20–25.

6. See the discussion on pp. 42–44.

7. See the discussion on pp. 70–75.

8. Pitirim A. Sorokin, *Contemporary Sociological Theories,* Harper, New York, 1928, pp. 291–301.

9. The following three sections are partly drawn from Brewton Berry and Henry L. Tischler, *Race and Ethnic Relations,* 4th ed., Houghton Mifflin, Boston, 1978, pp. 48–52.

10. See Kenneth Pearson, "On Our Present Knowledge of the Relationship of Mind and Body," *Annuals of Eugenics,* 1 (1925–1926), 382–406; Otto Klineberg, *Race Differences,* Harper & Row, New York, 1935, pp. 84, 86.

11. Stanford M. Lyman, *Chinese Americans,* Prentice-Hall, Englewood Cliffs, N.J., 1974.

12. Berry and Tischler, *Race and Ethnic Relations,* p. 51.

13. Basil Davidson, *African Kingdoms,* Time-Life, New York, 1966, pp. 21–22.

14. See the discussion on pp. 75–77.

15. See Thomas Sowell, "New Light on Black I.Q.," *The New York Times Magazine,* March 27, 1977, p. 57.

16. Audrey Shuey, *The Testing of Negro Intelligence,* J. P. Bell, Lynchburg, Va., 1958, p. 318.

17. Arthur R. Jensen, "How Much Can We Boost I.Q. and Scholastic Achievement?" *Harvard Educational Review,* 39 (1969), 1–123. In December 1979, Jensen re-examined this issue, claiming that assumptions about biased tests are inaccurate, since mean differences remain despite attempts to raise black test scores; see Arthur R. Jensen, *Bias in Mental Testing,* Free Press, New York, 1980.

18. Sowell, "New Light on Black I.Q.," p. 57 ff.

19. See Robert E. Ornstein, *The Psychology of Consciousness,* 2nd ed., Harcourt Brace Jovanovich, New York, 1977, pp. 16–39.

20. See J. W. Zemp, J. E. Wilson, and E. Glassman, "Brain Function and Macromolecules: Site of Increased Labeling of RNA in Brains of Mice during a Short-Term Training Experiment," *Proceedings of National Academy of Science: United States,* 58 (1967), 1120–1125; also, H. Hyden and E. Egyhazi, "Nuclear RNA Changes of Nerve Cells During a Learning Experiment in Rats," *Proceedings of National Academy of Science: United States,* 48 (1962), 1366–1373.

21. Ossie Davis, "The English Language Is My Enemy," *IRCD Bulletin,* 5 (Summer 1969), 13.

22. See C. Vann Woodward, *The Strange Career of Jim Crow,* 2nd ed., Oxford University Press, New York, 1966.

23. Gunnar Myrdal, *An American Dilemma,* McGraw-Hill, New York, 1964.

24. *Ibid.,* pp. 25–38.

25. Dewey H. Palmer, "Moving North: Migration of Negroes During World War I," *Phylon,* 27 (Spring 1967), 52–62.

26. *The New York Times,* March 9, 1925, p. 16.

27. W. E. B. DuBois, *Dusk of Dawn,* Harcourt, Brace, New York, 1940, p. 264.

28. The Supreme Court specifically cited Kenneth B. Clark's study on negative self-image among black school children. For detailed information on the social scientists' role in the decision, see Kenneth B. Clark, *Prejudice and Your Child,* 2nd ed., Beacon Press, Boston, 1963.

29. Jerome H. Skolnick, *The Politics of Protest: Violent Aspects of Protest and Confrontation,* National Commission on the Causes and Prevention of Violence, Washington, D.C., 1969, pp. 101–102.

30. See Alphonso Pinkney, *Black Americans,* Prentice-Hall, Englewood

Cliffs, N.J., 1969.

31. Lewis M. Killian, *The Impossible Revolution, Phase II*, Random House, New York, 1975, p. 70.

32. Charles Silberman, *Crises in Black and White*, Random House, New York, 1964, p. 8.

33. See Robin M. Williams, Jr., "Social Change and Social Conflict: Race Relations in the United States, 1944–1964," *Sociological Inquiry*, 35 (Winter 1965), 20–24. Also, Stanley Lieberson and Arnold R. Silverman, "The Precipitants and Underlying Conditions of Race Riots," *American Sociological Review*, 30 (1965), 887–898.

34. From the Report of the National Advisory Commission on Civil Disorders, U.S. Government Printing Office, Washington, D.C., 1968.

35. U.S. Bureau of the Census, *Census of Population: 1960*, PC(2)-4B, 1964, Table 2; *Current Population Reports*, Series P20, No. 287, 1975, Table 2.

36. Reynolds Farley, "Trends in Racial Inequalities: Have the Gains of the 1960s Disappeared in the 1970s?" *American Sociological Review*, 42 (April 1977), 196–198.

37. U.S. Bureau of Labor Statistics, *Employment and Earnings*, Vol. 22, No. 7, 1976, Table 1.

38. See Tom Wicker, "A Prophecy Fulfilled," *The New York Times*, July 17, 1977, p. E21.

39. Clayton Riley, "Time Is No Longer Running Out; It's Gone," *The New York Times*, July 17, 1977, p. E21. Copyright © 1977 by The New York Times Company. Reprinted by permission.

40. Sar A. Levithan, W. Johnston, and R. Taggart, *Still a Dream: The Changing Status of Blacks Since 1960*, Harvard University Press, Cambridge, Mass., 1975.

41. See Arthur M. Ross and Herbert Hill (eds.), *Employment, Race and Poverty*, Harcourt, Brace & World, New York, 1967, for a discussion of occupational discrimination.

42. For a more complete analysis of black status improvements, see Farley, "Trends in Racial Inequalities: Have the Gains of the 1960s Disappeared in the 1970s?"

43. Brigitte Mach Erbe, "Race and Socioeconomic Segregation," *American Sociological Review*, 40 (December 1975), 801–812.

44. See Luther P. Gerlach and Virginia H. Hine, "The Social Organization of a Movement of Revolutionary Change: Case Study, Black Power," in *Afro-American Anthropology*, eds. Norman E. Whitten, Jr., and John F. Szwed, Free Press, New York, 1970.

TEN

THE HISPANIC IMMIGRANTS

⊀ Perhaps no group attracts more public attention these days than do the Hispanic people. Their large numbers, their residential clustering, the bilingual programs and signs provided for them, and their poverty and its concurrent social problems make them a recognizable ethnic group. Although there are many differences in their cultural background, social-class status, and length of residence in the United States, they have one thing in common: the Spanish language. Because of this one factor, non-Hispanic-Americans often lump them all together despite the many differences among them.

HISTORICAL AND SOCIOLOGICAL PERSPECTIVES

Spanish influence has long been felt in the United States. Long before the English settled in their colonies in the New World, Spanish explorers, missionaries, and adventurers roamed through much of the Western Hemisphere, including Florida and the southwestern United States. In the same year (1609) as the first permanent English settlement (Jamestown) was established, the Spanish founded Santa Fe, in what is now New Mexico. Spanish cultural influence was extensive throughout the New World in the areas of language, religion, customs, values, and town planning (for example, locating church and institutional buildings next to a central plaza).

STRUCTURAL CONDITIONS

The Hispanic-American experience varies greatly, depending upon the particular ethnic group, area of the country, and time period. In the American Southwest, agricultural needs and the presence of Mexican-Americans are crucial factors in dominant-minority relations. In the East, industrial employment, urban problems, and the presence of Cubans or Puerto Ricans provide the focal points of attitudes and actions. Figure 10.1 shows the percentage of Hispanics living in the 48 states in 1970.

Most low-skilled immigrant groups, including such Hispanic peoples as the Puerto Ricans and Mexicans, have at first obtained jobs that have low status, low pay, and little mobility. Unlike past groups, however, recent Hispanic immigrants have entered an industrial society in which the economy is no longer growing rapidly. Many Hispanic immigrants come from less industrialized nations and have few of the skills they would need in order to adjust easily to working in America. Technological progress has eliminated many of the jobs earlier immigrants could obtain to achieve some degree of economic security (such as unskilled

FIGURE 10.1

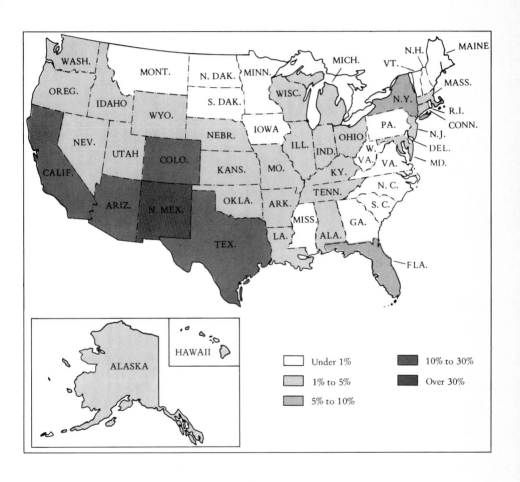

PERCENTAGE OF HISPANICS IN THE UNITED STATES, 1970

factory work). The suburbanization of industry has meant that in older cities, where poor immigrants have traditionally lived and worked out of economic necessity, there are no longer enough manufacturing jobs for the newcomers. Unions once helped European immigrants to obtain job security, better wages, and improved working conditions, but to-day's unions often exclude or restrict the "new" minorities.

Like all low-skilled workers, the Hispanic labor force is highly suscep-tible to a downturn in the economy. For example, from 1973 to 1975, as the recession intensified, the Hispanic unemployment rate went from 7.5 percent to 12.2 percent. This latter figure was higher than the rate for whites, 7.8 percent in 1975, but below the rate for blacks, 14.7 per-cent. Like the blacks, the Hispanics were overrepresented among the unemployed. While they were only 4.4 percent of the total labor force (4.1 million), they constituted 6.3 percent of the total number of unem-ployed (500,000) in 1975.[1]

Overpopulation throughout Latin America is a highly significant fac-tor in the continued migration of large numbers of Hispanics to the United States (Table 10.1). High birth rates, improved sanitation, the re-duction of child mortality, and negative attitudes toward birth control have led to population booms in countries whose resources and habita-ble land cannot support this many people. The Economic Commission for Latin America reports that the total population of Latin America grew from over 129 million in 1940 to over 284 million by 1970. Cur-rent projections are that the population will reach about 500 million by 1990 and be over 650 million by the year 2000.[2] Suffering from poor liv-ing conditions, inadequate schools, limited job opportunities, and other aspects of poverty, many Latinos journey to the United States, legally or illegally, for a better life.[3] The United States has a 2,000-mile border with Mexico and open migration for Puerto Ricans, and many other Hispanic nationalities use these routes to enter illegally. The U.S. gov-ernment estimated that there were 6 to 8 million illegal aliens in the United States in 1977, almost all of them Hispanics. This large number of illegal aliens has an adverse effect upon the labor market, living con-ditions for poor people, and social service costs.

CULTURAL DIFFERENTIATION

The cultures of the peoples from the various Caribbean and Central and South American countries differ. Value orientations within a par-ticular country also vary, depending on such factors as degree of urbanization, amount of outside contact, and social class. With these qualifications in mind, we shall examine some general cultural tra-ditions, shared to a greater or lesser degree by most Hispanics, that dif-fer from traditional American values. Before we do so, we should also

TABLE 10.1

IMMIGRANTS ADMITTED TO THE UNITED STATES
FROM WESTERN HEMISPHERE, FISCAL YEAR 1976

Mexico	58,354
West Indies	65,734
Cuba	28,433
Dominican Republic	12,473
Jamaica	8,743
Haiti	5,266
Trinidad & Tobago	4,922
Barbados	1,701
Other West Indies	4,196
Central America	10,097
El Salvador	2,405
Guatemala	1,964
Panama	1,794
Honduras	1,296
Costa Rica	1,199
Other Central America	1,439
South America	23,565
Colombia	5,701
Ecuador	4,404
Guyana	3,217
Argentina	2,650
Peru	2,433
Brazil	1,362
Chile	1,194
Other South America	2,604

SOURCE: U.S. Immigration and Naturalization Service, Annual Report,
U.S. Government Printing Office, Washington, D.C., 1976, p. 46.

note that in areas of considerable acculturation, such as New Mexico, some of these cultural traits are muted, and Hispanics have adopted many Anglo (the Hispanics' term for American) behavior patterns.

THE COSMIC RACE   One cultural concept that is associated with Hispanics — especially Mexicans — is that of *La Raza Cosmica*, the cosmic race. The Mexican intellectual José Vasconcelos coined the term to refer to the amalgamation of the white, black, and Indian races, which he believed was occurring in Latin America.[4] Though in his old age he dismissed the idea as a juvenile fantasy, the concept evolved into a group categorization similar to what Kurt Lewin calls a recognition of an "interdependence of fate." In essence, *La Raza Cosmica* suggests that all the Spanish-speaking peoples in the Western Hemisphere share a cultural bond and that God has planned for them a great destiny that has yet to be realized. Recent studies of Mexican-Americans have found that this cultural belief is still significant, either directly or in terms of the behavioral values associated with it.[5] Reflecting centuries of European dominance, the concept is also one of fatalism; it implies that one should submit to the things of the present and not plan for the future. Younger Hispanics appear to subscribe less to such fatalism than do their elders.

MACHISMO Overstated in the Anglo stereotype, *machismo* is a basic value covering various qualities of masculinity. To Hispanic males, such attributes as inner strength in the face of adversity, personal daring, bravado, leadership, and sexual prowess are all measures of one's manhood.[6] The role of the man is to be a good provider for his family, to protect its honor at all times, and to be strong, reliable, and independent. He should avoid indebtedness or charity and any kind of relationship, formal or informal, that would weaken his autonomy. The culture and family system are male-dominated. The woman's role is within the family, and she is to be guarded against any onslaught upon her honor.

The result of these values can be not only a double standard of sexual morality but also difficulty adjusting to American culture. Women have more independence in the United States than in most Hispanic countries. Instead of males being the sole providers, females can also find employment here, sometimes earning more money than the men of the family. The labor-force participation of Spanish women appears to be related to educational level. The U.S. government has reported that the more highly educated Cuban and Central and South American women have labor-force participation rates similar to those of all white women in the United States, whereas Mexican and Puerto Rican women have especially low rates.[7]

DIGNIDAD This cultural value is the basis of social interaction; it assumes that the dignity of all humans entitles them to a measure of respect. It is primarily "a quality attributed to all, regardless of status, race, color or creed."[8] Regardless of status, each person acknowledges others' *dignidad* in a taken-for-granted reciprocal behavior pattern. Therefore, Hispanics — particularly Puerto Ricans — expect to be treated in terms of *dignidad*. Because it is an implicit measure of respect, one cannot demand it from others. Instead, one concludes that others are rude and cold if they do not acknowledge one's *dignidad*. More broadly, the concept includes a strong positive self-image.

RACIAL ATTITUDES

In most Latin American countries skin color is less important as an indicator of social status than is social class. There seems to be a correlation between darker skin color and low social standing, but the sharp racial line between whites and blacks found in the United States is deemphasized in Latin America. A great deal of color integration takes place in social interaction, intermarriage, and shared cultural value orientations. There is also a much wider range of color gradations, which helps to blunt any color prejudice. Still, in some places, such as Puerto Rico, color prejudice has increased, perhaps as a result of social and economic changes from industrialization.[9]

Color is often an unexpected basis of discrimination for Latinos coming to the United States. Being stereotyped, judged, and treated on the basis of one's skin color is essentially unknown to these brown-skinned peoples. Therefore, encountering prejudice and discrimination based on their skin color is a traumatic experience for them. Before long they realize the extent of this regrettable aspect of American society. Some adapt to it, others forsake it and return home, but practically all resent it.

OTHER CULTURAL ATTRIBUTES

Latinos generally have a more casual attitude toward time, and a negative attitude toward hurrying about. Another cultural difference that could easily lead to misunderstanding is their attitude about making eye contact with others. To them, not looking directly into the eyes of an authority figure such as a teacher or police officer is an act of respect, but Americans may interpret it as shyness, avoidance, or guilt. Like some Europeans, they regard physical proximity in conversation as a sign of friendliness, but Anglos are accustomed to a greater distance between conversationalists. One can envision an Anglo made uncomfortable by the "unusual" nearness of an Hispanic person and backing away, the latter re-establishing the physical closeness, the Anglo again backing away, and the Hispanic concluding that the Anglo is a cold or aloof individual. Each has viewed the situation from a different cultural perspective and thus interpreted the incident quite differently.[10]

CURRENT PATTERNS

Hispanic-Americans are a very sizable minority, totaling 11,202,000 in 1975, according to Census Bureau estimates. Although that is only slightly more than 5 percent of the total population, some experts predict that within a decade the Hispanics will outnumber blacks and will be the largest minority group in the United States.[11] This projection is based upon their high birth rate (almost twice that of other Americans), their low average age (half are under 21), and the fact that one-third of all legal immigrants come from Spanish-speaking lands. Finally, there is the problem of the illegal immigrants. The U.S. Immigration and Naturalization Service estimates that at any one time there are probably 8 million or more illegal immigrants in this country, about 60 percent of them from Mexico and the others from other Latin American and Caribbean countries.

Of the 8 million Americans older than four who speak a language other than English, about 4 million speak Spanish, making it the second most common language in this country, according to 1976 Census Bureau statistics. Geographically, there are many Hispanic-Americans outside the large concentrations in California, Florida, and New York City. The Census Bureau reports that more Hispanics live in Illinois than in New Mexico and more live in New Jersey than in Arizona.[12] A large Mexican-American population in Chicago gives that city over 250,000 Latinos. Detroit has a mixture of almost 20 Spanish-speaking nationalities.

The degree of harmony in dominant-minority relations and of Hispanic assimilation varies by region and with the people and their culture. One pattern is relatively consistent, however, and that is the strong cultural vitality of various Hispanic-American groups. Mexican-Americans, for example, have long insisted on retaining their ethnic identity. Their large numbers in this country, their proximity to Mexico, and the fact that their predecessors in the Southwest were living in lands that had long been Spanish-controlled are undoubtedly all factors that reinforce cultural pluralism. Similarly, several influences encourage other Hispanic groups to retain their cultural identities. Primary among these are current migration patterns of newcomers from Spanish-speaking countries, psychological ties to the homeland because of rapid transportation and communications, actual proximity, endogamy, and high birth rates. Since there is less societal pressure for assimilation than there once was, and since Americans are more receptive to ethnicity, the Hispanics may become the first major immigrant group to be a lasting exception to the melting pot.[13]

THE MEXICAN-AMERICANS

About 80 percent of the 6.7 million Mexican-Americans in the United States live in the Southwest. Los Angeles, whose very name indicates its Spanish origin, has more than a million Mexican-American residents, making it second only to Mexico City in Mexican population. A great deal of diversity exists among this ethnic group in terms of degree of assimilation and socioeconomic status. For example, there is a very small group of old-family Spanish-Americans in northern New Mexico and southern Colorado who follow the old traditions and speak very little English.

Throughout New Mexico, which, unlike Texas and California, has not had constant contact with Mexico through border crossings, the employment pattern is brighter. In fact, Hispanic-Americans there are heavily represented in civil service occupations at the local, state, and federal levels. In a sense, they are like many recent non-Western immigrants in that they retain a cultural heritage (such as their diet, child-rearing philosophy, stress on the family, and extended family contacts), but hold economically secure occupational positions.

Second-generation Mexican-Americans living in Los Angeles are far more likely to be assimilated than their counterparts in Corpus Christi.[14] However, most present-day Mexican-Americans, whether they live in an urban or a rural area, are extremely poor, struggling to survive from day to day in a land that does not always look kindly upon them.

When the United States secured the southwestern region after the Mexican-American War of 1846–1848 and then added a small boundary section through the Gadsden Purchase of 1853, there were a relatively small number of Mexicans living in these areas. Most of these, quickly outnumbered by Anglos, lost their lands through legal maneuvering and became a subordinated population.

RECRUITING MEXICANS

In the second half of the nineteenth century a great need for agricultural labor developed and Mexicans from south of the border helped to fill it. Railroad lines were being built; cotton, fruit, and vegetable farms were expanding. The Chinese Exclusion Act of 1882 curtailed one source of laborers, and later the Immigration Acts of 1921 and 1924 curtailed another. But the demand for labor, especially for agricultural workers, increased, and the Mexicans left their poverty-stricken country for the economic opportunities available here.

It is important to understand the cultural milieu in their native land in order to understand the Mexicans' situation in the United States for over a hundred years. Most Mexicans were poor, illiterate peasants, virtually serfs, who eked out an existence laboring for the *hacendados*, the large landholding aristocracy of Mexico. Exploited by the hacienda owners and the Mexican government for years, and ignorant of the language and laws of this country, the Mexicans worked in the United States under servile conditions for meager wages. The degree of poverty in their native country is reflected in the fact that even though they worked for very low wages, they were still earning a great deal more than they could at home.

Although there were restrictions on immigration, it was easy for Mexicans to cross the largely unpatrolled border and enter the country illegally, and many did so. They were known as "wetbacks" because they had waded or swum across the Rio Grande. Some Mexican aliens also entered the United States legally as contract laborers. Under the *bracero* program, Mexican aliens were temporarily brought into the United States, then returned to Mexico after the harvest. This system provided the needed workers without the accompanying expenses of educating their children, giving them welfare during nonworking periods, and providing other social services. The program lasted from 1942 until 1964, when farm mechanization, labor shortages in Mexico, and the protests of native Hispanics in the United States ended it.

EXPULSION

Although Mexican labor was a boon to the Southwestern economy, during a downturn in the national economy Mexicans usually were not welcome. One such time was the 1930s, when a great many Americans were jobless. Some Mexicans returned home voluntarily; others were pressured to do so by local residents. A great many more were rounded up and deported.

During the depression the U.S. Government and public agencies, in what was called a "repatriation program," deported literally hundreds of thousands of Mexicans and Mexican Americans to cut down on welfare costs. Roundups extended through southern California, to most cities of the Southwest, and as far north as Chicago and Detroit.

In Los Angeles, official trucks would grind into the barrios — the Mexican American neighborhoods — and the occupants would be herded into them. There was little or no determination of national origin. Citizenship or noncitizenship was not considered. Families were divided; the bringing of possessions was not permitted. . . .

"They pushed most of my family into one van," one of the victims, Jorge Acevedo, remembers bitterly. "We drove all day. The driver wouldn't stop for bathroom nor food nor water. Everyone knew by now we had been deported. Nobody knew why, but there was a lot of hatred and anger. . . . We had always known that we were hated. Now we had proof."[15]

During the recession of the mid-1950s, the U.S. Immigration and Naturalization Service launched "Operation Wetback" to find and return all

FIGURE 10.2

This Mexican man was caught as he tried to cross the border illegally under the hood of an automobile; he was later returned to Mexico. (United Press International)

illegal Mexican aliens. Concentrating on California and Texas, but ranging as far as Spokane, Chicago, Kansas City, and St. Louis, between
1954 and 1959 government officials found and expelled 3.8 million
Mexicans, only 63,515 of whom had a formal hearing.[16] Not all were illegal aliens. Many American citizens, if they "looked Mexican," were
stopped and questioned. If they could not immediately prove their legal
status, they were often arrested and "sent home" without anyone even
checking into their status.[17]

VIOLENCE

One infamous incident in which prejudices against the Mexicans erupted
into violence is the Zoot Suit Riot of 1943. It was named thus because many
Mexican-American youths at that time followed the then current fad of
wearing long, loose-fitting jackets with wide shoulders; high-waisted,
baggy trousers with tight cuffs; and flat-topped hats with broad brims. The
gamblers in the original show and the film version of *Guys and Dolls*
dressed in this fashion.

On June 3, 1943, two events occurred that triggered the riot. Some Mexican boys, returning from a police-sponsored club meeting, were assaulted
by a group of non-Mexican hoodlums from the neighborhood in Los
Angeles. That same evening, 11 sailors on leave were attacked, and one
sailor was badly hurt. The sailors said that their assailants were Mexican
youths who outnumbered them 3 to 1. When the police, responding late,
found no one to arrest in the area, about 200 sailors decided to settle the matter themselves the following evening. Cruising through the Mexican section in a caravan of 20 taxicabs, they savagely beat every Mexican they
found. The police did nothing to stop this, and the press gave these events
wide publicity.

The stage was now set for the really serious rioting of June seventh and
eighth. Having featured the preliminary rioting as an offensive
launched by sailors, soldiers, and marines, the press now whipped public opinion into a frenzy by dire warnings that Mexican zoot-suiters
planned a mass retaliation. To insure a riot, the precise street corners
were marked at which retaliatory action was expected and the time of
the anticipated action was carefully specified. In effect these stories
announced a riot and invited public participation. . . .

On Monday evening, June seventh, thousands of *Angelenos,* in response to twelve hours' advance notice in the press, turned out for a
mass lynching. Marching through the streets of downtown Los
Angeles, a mob of several thousand soldiers, sailors, and civilians, pro-
ceeded to beat up every zoot-suiter they could find. Pushing its way
into the important motion picture theaters, the mob ordered the man-

FIGURE 10.3

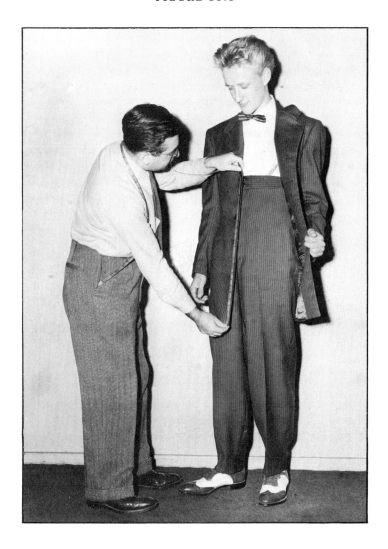

In the early 1940s, zoot suits were a very popular fashion, especially among Mexican-American youth. Because this style consumed too much wool, the war shortages ended its production. (United Press International).

agement to turn on the house lights and then ranged up and down the aisles dragging Mexicans out of their seats. Street cars were halted while Mexicans, and some Filipinos and Negroes, were jerked out of their seats, pushed into the streets, and beaten with sadistic frenzy. . . .

Here is one of the numerous eyewitness accounts written by Al Waxman, editor of *The Eastside Journal:*

> Four boys came out of a pool hall. They were wearing the zoot-suits that have become the symbols of a fighting flag. Police ordered them into arrest cars. One refused. He asked: "Why am I being arrested?" The police officer answered with three swift blows of the night-stick across the boy's head and he went down. As he sprawled, he was kicked in the face. Police had difficulty loading his body into the vehicle because he was one-legged and wore a wooden limb. . . .
>
> At the next corner a Mexican mother cried out, "Don't take my boy, he did nothing. He's only fifteen years old. Don't take him." She was struck across the jaw with a night-stick and almost dropped the two and a half year old baby that was clinging in her arms. . . .

A Negro defense worker, wearing a defense-plant identification badge on his work clothes, was taken from a street car and one of his eyes was gouged out with a knife. Huge half-page photographs, showing Mexican boys, stripped of their clothes, cowering on the pavements, often bleeding profusely, surrounded by jeering mobs of men and women, appeared in all of the Los Angeles newspapers. . . .

When it finally stopped, the Eagle Rock *Advertiser* mournfully editorialized: "It is too bad the servicemen were called off before they were able to complete the job. . . . Most of the citizens of the city have been delighted with what has been going on."[18]

This bloody incident, like the Know-Nothing riots, the anti-Chinese race riots, lynchings, and other past acts of violence, was the result of increasing societal tensions and prejudices against a minority, which erupted into aggression far in excess of the triggering incident. Whatever Mexicans thought about Anglo society before this wartime incident, they would long remember this race riot waged against them with official sanction from the police, the newspapers, and city hall.

URBAN LIFE

For the past thirty years or so, most Mexican-Americans have lived in cities. In some places, like Los Angeles and New Mexico, they are better integrated into the mainstream of society. There they have higher inter-marriage rates, nuclear instead of extended family residence patterns, and less patriarchal male roles. They are entering more diverse occupations, and many are attaining middle-class status and moving from the barrio to the suburbs and outskirts of the city. In other areas of the Southwest, particularly in smaller cities and towns, Mexican-Americans reside in large ethnic enclaves, virtually isolated from participation in Anglo society. Even those middle-class individuals whose families have resided in this country for generations choose to live among their own people and interact only with them.

Many Mexican-Americans live in substandard housing under crowded conditions. In the five Southwestern states their housing is more crowded than that of nonwhites — in Texas, twice as many Mexicans as blacks live in overcrowded housing. Segregated in the less desirable sections of town, with their children attending schools that warrant the same criticisms as inner-city schools in the major cities, they experience many forms of discrimination.

In general, the sudden disappearance of ordinary urban facilities when a visitor enters exclusively Mexican poverty areas is striking. Streets are unpaved; there are no curbs and sidewalks or street lights; traffic hazards go unremedied, and the general air of decay and neglect is unmistakable. (In many cities in the Southwest, "improvements" considered normal and essential in other neighborhoods are financed by per capita assessments of local property owners. These special assessments are often impossible to obtain in poor neighborhoods.) Abandoned automobiles, uncollected refuse, hulks of burned out buildings and the famous cactus fences symbolize the civic status of these neighborhoods. In addition, it is typical of Mexican-American neighborhoods in the Southwest that they are carelessly zoned. Thus cheap shops, small factories, small tumble-down houses and even tiny urban farms sprawl together in unregulated confusion.[19]

Recent challenges to overt forms of discrimination have succeeded, but covert methods still persist. One landmark case protecting the civil liberties of Mexican-Americans was the 1953 U.S. Supreme Court decision concerning Peter Hernandez. This decision, which preceded the better-known *Brown* v. *Board of Education* segregation case, held that a community's laws cannot be written or applied against a particular class of people if this results in their being treated differently. The ruling, which had a far-reaching impact on discriminatory actions by public officials, was based on a case in which a nonrepresentative jury (Mexican-Americans never served on juries in that region) convicted a Mexican-American.

FIGURE 10.4

With air and light streaming into her house, this Mexican-American woman
stands on a floor of wooden planks covering the ground. Many rural poor live
here in Texas and throughout the Southwest. (Don Getsug, Photo Researchers)

STEREOTYPING

Negative stereotypes of Mexican-Americans persist in American society. Such categorizations as their being lazy, unclean, treacherous, sneaks, or thieves frequently appear in the mass media. Even advertisements had used these derogatory stereotypes until adverse reaction forced advertisers to discontinue this practice. Consider from recent years the "Frito-Bandito" of potato chip fame; a Camel cigarette ad showing a sleepy Mexican village; an Arrid commercial showing a Mexican spraying his underarm while a voice says, "If it works for him, it will work for you"; a Liggett & Myers ad saying "Paco" never "feenishes" anything, not even a revolution.[20]

Sometimes scholarly works inadvertently contribute to the stereotype. Some people used Florence Kluckhohn's study of a remote village in New Mexico as the basis for generalizations about the values of all Mexicans.[21] Thus such cultural attributes as present-time orientation, emphasis on intangible gratification rather than material rewards, and emphasis on enjoyment rather than working hard became synonymous with being Mexican.[22] In reality, the values of most urban Mexican-Americans are quite similar to those of other Americans: they want upward mobility, a better life for their children, and community interaction.[23]

Like blacks and Puerto Ricans, the Mexican-Americans also suffer from the culture-of-poverty beliefs of the dominant society.[24] All too often they are blamed for their low socioeconomic standing because of their supposed cultural values. However, it is much more likely that dominant-minority interactions, rather than the minority's cultural variations, cause a minority group's problems in achieving economic security.

CHICANO POWER

The term *Chicano* was originally a derogatory name applied to the "lower" class Mexican-Indian people, rather than to the Mexican-Spanish. Most Mexican-American youths and some older people have now adopted the term as a symbol of pride and peoplehood. Chicanos look to the past to reaffirm their ethnic identity, but they also look to the future, aiming at becoming more organized, collectively independent within the system, and stronger in socioeconomic status.

Leaders have emerged — Cesar Chavez and his United Farm Workers Union, Rodolfo Gonzales and his La Raza Unida movement, Reies Lopes Tijerina and his Alianza group seeking to recover land lost or stolen over the years, David Sanchez and his Brown Berets. The awakening Chicanos are making their presence known in a society that has previously either exploited or ignored them. Today they are seeking to restore their people's pride and dignity, but they have had only limited success. The very diversity of the Mexican-American population makes it difficult to develop a unified, cohesive social or political action program that will appeal to the various classes within the community and to the diverse regional groupings within the nation, particularly in the Southwest.

CURRENT PATTERNS

Today's Mexican newcomers are mostly males from central Mexico; they are younger and less skilled and educated than other immigrants.[25] The median age of all Mexican-Americans residing in the United States is 19.6 years. Families tend to be large, reflecting the high fertility rate, and there are also high rates of separation without divorce.[26] Mexicans are disproportionately represented among those arrested and convicted, particularly in youth crimes. In large urban areas, vicious gangs frequently get into trouble because of narcotics offenses and other actions.[27]

In the predominantly Protestant Southwest, Mexicans' identification with Catholicism has further increased their social isolation. Since there were too few priests and since too few Mexicans became priests, in the past the church was not very effective in protecting or helping the Mexicans, or in providing leadership on social issues that affected their well-being.[28] This situation has changed in recent years as social-action-oriented clergy groups, such as the PADRES, based in San Antonio, have emerged.

Perhaps the most significant factor contributing to many of the socioeconomic problems of the Mexican-Americans, and one of long duration, is the number of illegal aliens in the country. Mexico has about 63 million people and one of the world's highest birth rates. More than half of its labor force is unemployed or underemployed. Getting across the lightly patrolled border is easy; only one illegal entrant in five gets caught, and those who are returned to Mexico try again, often on the same day. The number of illegal aliens, of whom about 80 percent are Mexican, is now estimated to exceed 8 million. As a result, the U.S. government has increased its efforts to find and deport illegal aliens. In 1966 the Immigration and Naturalization Service expelled 133,000; in 1976 the number expelled reached 793,000.[29] Some employers encourage illegal aliens to come because these aliens will accept lower wages, and it is not illegal to employ them. The actual impact of illegal aliens on job displacement and the economy is a matter of debate, but many people cite them as the cause of crime, welfare, and economic troubles.[30]

In April 1977 Leonel J. Castillo became the first Mexican-American Commissioner of the Immigration and Naturalization Service. Through him the Carter Administration hoped to find ways to resolve the problem of illegal aliens and to curtail the abuse of illegal alien workers. There are no easy solutions to this highly sensitive social and economic issue.

THE PUERTO RICANS

Puerto Ricans frequently refer to their island as the "true melting pot," unlike the mainland, which has only claimed to be so. Originally inhabited by the Arawak and Caribe Indian tribes, Puerto Rico came under Spanish domination in 1493 and remained so for 400 years. When the Indian population was decimated, black slaves were imported. Miscegenation was quite common, resulting in a society that de-emphasized race. Today Puerto Rico is not only a relatively harmonious multiracial society, but it also has a high degree of structural assimilation. Clara Rodriguez points out that in terms of housing, institutional treatment, government policy, and cultural identification, there is no difference between differently colored Puerto Ricans.[31] Because of the high degree of intermarriage, for example, those who can be classified as white, black, or tan are often found to have close sibling and kin relationships with other races, either by blood line or by adoption.

> The racial scene in Puerto Rico has also been characterized by what I would call a high degree of two-way integration, while in the U.S. one-way integration has been and is the norm. That is, Blacks are usually sent to White schools, not vice-versa. Blacks integrate into White America, not Whites into Black America. . . . In this country it rarely happens that a Black couple adopts a White child. The number of White babies available for adoption and the limited income of many Blacks tend to discourage this action. In most agencies the action is not permitted and the reverse is encouraged. In Puerto Rico, it is a fairly common occurrence to rear other people's children as one's own. These "hijos de crianza" come in all colors. Thus, a "White" couple may rear the darker, orphaned children of a neighbor and vice-versa.[32]

EARLY RELATIONS

In 1898, when the United States first annexed Puerto Rico after the Spanish-American War, there was an attempt at forced Americanization. The United States discouraged anything associated with the Spanish tradition and imposed the use of the English language. Presidents appointed governors, usually from the mainland, to rule the territory. The inhabitants were granted U.S. citizenship in 1917, but otherwise the island was virtually ignored and remained an undeveloped land with many poor people. Citizenship brought open migration because it eliminated passports, visas, and quotas, but it did not give the people the right to vote for President or to have a voting representative in Congress. By 1930 approximately 53,000 Puerto Ricans were living on the mainland. During the Depression and the war years, immigration virtually halted until the mass migration of the post–World War II era.

In the 1940s several improvements occurred. Luis Muñoz Marin's Popular Democratic Party (*Partido Popular Democratico*) emerged as a powerful force. President Franklin Roosevelt, as part of his Good Neighbor Policy, set about finding a new status for the island. Puerto Rico became a commonwealth, with the people writing their own constitution and electing their own representatives. Marin was elected governor, and was re-elected each time until 1968. In addition, the island was given complete freedom in its internal affairs, including maintaining its Spanish heritage and not being required to use English.

To help the island develop economically, the U.S. government launched "Operation Bootstrap" in 1945. Industries were given substantial tax advantages if they made capital investments in Puerto Rico. The tax breaks and abundant supply of low-cost labor resulted in 300 new factories being built by 1953, increasing to 660 by 1960 and creating over 48,000 new jobs. As a result, Puerto Rico became the most advanced and industrialized land in the Caribbean and in most of Central and South America, with the highest per capita income.

THE PUSH-PULL FACTORS

Puerto Rico's unemployment rate has remained at a constant 12 percent since 1946 despite the mass migration and industrial development.[33] Clara Rodriguez points out that Puerto Rico's colonial status and its economic dependence on U.S.-based industries make it particularly vulnerable to changes in the U.S. economy.[34] If unemployment rises on the mainland, it does so even faster in Puerto Rico. A slowdown in the mainland economy just about grinds things to a halt in Puerto Rico, and so the "push" of economic troubles combines with the "pull" of perceived employment opportunities on the mainland. This interlacing of economies affects the migration pattern.

Overpopulation on the island obviously increases the economic pressures. Low-cost three-hour jet flights to New York, rapid communications, and friends and relatives already on the mainland are additional inducements. The Puerto Ricans became the first group to migrate to the United States by air in large numbers. Beginning in the 1940s, many came as migrant farm laborers under contract for the harvest season and returned in time for the sugar cane harvest at home. Like the old Dutch *patroon* and the Greek and Italian *padrone*, the Puerto Rican *padrino* served as the advocate, intermediary, or strategic helper for poor migrants who needed employment or other assistance. This relationship often resulted in exploitation, and the Puerto Rican government had to tighten its supervision to protect the interests of the contract laborers.

PUERTO RICAN COMMUNITIES

The continuous shuttle migration kept an organized community life similar to that of earlier immigrants from developing. Even in New York City and Chicago, where the two largest groups reside, the Puerto Ricans are not densely enough concentrated to become either an effective political force or a cohesive, stable subcommunity like previous immigrants.[35]

Of the 1.7 million Puerto Ricans now living on the mainland, three-fourths of them live in the New York City metropolitan area. Of that number, 25 percent were born in the region and have no first-hand knowledge of island life. The increase in this mainland-born group may help explain the increased visibility of ethnic activities in Puerto Rican neighborhoods.

> Note, for example, the growth of what are today Puerto Rican "cuchifrito" stands, social clubs, and after-hours clubs. These and other institutions did not exist years ago or existed in a very different form. Today they are identifying symbols of a Puerto Rican neighborhood. This same phenomena of change is also reflected in the speech of many second generation Puerto Ricans who no longer speak continuous Spanish, but whose English is decidedly "Rican."[36]

One prominent organization, founded in 1961, is Aspira, which is Spanish for *aspire*, or *strive*. Through guidance, encouragement, and financial assistance, Aspira seeks to develop cultural pride and self-confidence in youth, and to encourage them to further their education and enter the professions, technical fields, and the arts. Begun in New York City, its grass-roots program has achieved national fame, and it has expanded to other cities as well. A more direct community action group is the Puerto Rican Community Development Project, which attempts to promote a sense of identity among Puerto Ricans and to develop community strength. Another organization begun in New York is the Puerto Rican Family Institute, which provides professional social services to Puerto Rican families. Parent action groups, athletic leagues, cultural organizations, and social clubs also exist, providing services and fulfilling community needs.[37]

THE FAMILY

In Puerto Rico, as in all Latin American countries, the individual's identity, importance, and security depend on family membership. There is a deep sense of family obligation that extends to dating and courtship; family approval is necessary because of the emphasis upon a marriage joining two families, not just two individuals. An indication of family importance is the use of both the father's and mother's surnames, but in reverse order to the American practice. José Garcia Rivera, whose father's last name is Garcia and his mother's Rivera, should be called Mr. Garcia, not Mr. Rivera. The sociologist Joseph Fitzpatrick reveals that American confusion about use of these names is a constant source of embarrassment to Spanish-speaking people.[38] José's wife retains her family name and calls herself Maria Gonzalez de Garcia. On formal occasions she may use both sets of family names, such as Maria Gonzalez Medina de Garcia Rivera, while her husband would write his name José Garcia Diaz y Rivera Colon.[39]

Fitzpatrick identifies a fourfold typology among Puerto Rican families: (1) the extended family residing either in the same household or in separate households with frequent visits and strong bonds; (2) the nuclear family, increasingly common among the middle class; (3) the nuclear family plus other children of different names from previous union(s) of husband or wife, a not uncommon pattern among Puerto Ricans; (4) the female-headed household, with children of one or more men, but with no permanent male in the home.[40] The last type is frequently found among welfare families and is thus the target of much criticism.

RELIGION

The Catholic church has traditionally played an important role with immigrant groups, in succession assisting the French, Irish, Germans, Italians, Slavs, Poles, Syrian-Lebanese, and others.[41] This pattern has not been repeated with the Puerto Ricans in terms of representation in the church hierarchy, church leadership in the ethnic community, or immigrant involvement in the church.

> The Puerto Ricans have not created, as others did, national parishes of their own. Thus the capacities of the Church are weak in just those areas in which the needs of the migrants are great — in creating a surrounding, supporting community to replace the extended families, broken by city life, and to supply a social setting for those who feel lost and lonely in the great city. . . .
>
> Most of the Puerto Ricans in the city are Catholic, but their participation in Catholic life is small.[42]

Several factors have contributed to this break in the usual pattern. Because the island was a colony for so long, first Spanish and then American priests predominated within the church hierarchy on the island. Few Puerto Ricans became priests, and what few there were did not come to the mainland with the immigrants. The distant and alien nature of the church in Puerto Rico resulted in the Puerto Ricans having an internalized sense of Catholic identity without formally attending Mass and receiving the sacraments. Baptisms, weddings, and funerals all became important as social occasions, and the ceremony itself was of secondary importance. Throughout all of Latin America, Catholicism means personal relationships with the saints and a community manifestation of faith, not the individual actions and commitments expected in the United States. Another aspect of religious life in Puerto Rico, Brazil, and other parts of Latin America is the widespread belief in spiritualism and superstition. These practices undoubtedly are remnants of old folk rites, but they are still observed by various cults as well as by many Catholics.[43]

On the mainland a few other factors weakened any possibility that the Puerto Ricans would develop a strong ethnic church. Joseph Fitzpatrick indicates that the movement of other third-generation immigrants out of the city left behind clusters of old national churches with few parishioners.[44] Because of these existing church buildings and parochial schools, Cardinal Spellman decided in 1939 that New York City parishes would be integrated to accommodate the newcomers. Instead of having their own churches, the Puerto Ricans had the services of one or more Spanish-speaking priests, with special Masses and services performed in a basement chapel, school hall, or some other area of the parish. Although this practice was cost effective for the Catholic church, it prevented the parish from becoming the basis for a strong, stable community, since the group could not identify with it.

For many lower-class people of all racial and ethnic backgrounds, religion serves as an emotional escape from the harsh realities of everyday life. Pentecostalism is the fastest-growing religious movement among Puerto Ricans; it is the largest Protestant body both on the island and on the mainland. Storefront churches, with small and intimate congregations of about 60 to 100, offer their members a sense of community they cannot find elsewhere. Second-generation participation falls off sharply; Pentecostalism appears to be a first-generation phenomenon and therefore of limited duration.[45]

Church estimates reveal that only 6 percent of the Puerto Rican population on the mainland are involved with any Protestant denomination, including Pentecostalism, and only 20 percent with the Catholic church.[46] It is doubtful, then, that religious identification will be an important factor in either assimilation or cultural pluralism, as it was for earlier immigrant groups.

*"We felt we had all the rights in the world to enjoy all
the privileges others had. We were honest,
hard-working, respectable citizens too. So we took
legal action. . . ."*

"My husband and I bought our own house in Brooklyn after the Second World War, and a few years later we bought other property on Long Island, where we moved to raise our family. In 1956 we were employed by the U.S. Military Academy, West Point, and purchased a lovely home in a so-called exclusive area not too far away. This was a quaint neighborhood where custom-built homes ranged from $40,000 up to $100,000.

"Shortly after we moved in, we went down to Florida on vacation. When we came back, the house was empty. We slept on the floor and the following day our attorney by telephone searched every place high and low until he found our possessions in a warehouse in Nyack. Some of our neighbors had learned we were originally from Puerto Rico, were unhappy to have us as neighbors, and had plotted this against us.

"The harrassment continued for a long time. They threw their garbage every night on our lawn. They even sent the police to intimidate us and even tried to buy us out. We told them they couldn't afford the luxury of buying us out. We felt we had all the rights in the world to enjoy all the privileges others had. We were honest, hard-working, respectable citizens too. So we took legal action and demanded for damages. The judge was fair and ruled for us."

Puerto Rican couple who came to the mainland in 1946
during their twenties

LIVING CONDITIONS

Many Puerto Ricans have replaced the European immigrants in the urban slums and low-status jobs. They often do the work no one else will do because they can find no other work. Unlike their European predecessors, however, they cannot assume that hard manual labor will enable them to improve their lot. The United States is a more technologically advanced society today, and many of the unskilled jobs of the past are no longer available. Many of the blue collar and white collar jobs presently available require skills that the Puerto Ricans do not have.

Living in the cities' worst neighborhoods, Puerto Ricans have the same problems other poor minority peoples have had. There are high levels of tuberculosis, venereal disease, drug addiction, juvenile delinquency, illegitimate births, and chronic unemployment among the Puerto Rican population just as there have been among almost all other ethnic groups in low-income situations. The severity of these social problems is directly related to the low economic status of the Puerto Ricans on the mainland. Rodriguez argues that U.S. technological development in Puerto Rico creates a surplus unskilled labor force that migrates to the mainland. As long as this surplus population remains and there continues to be open migration because of the political ties, Puerto Ricans "will continue to come and join the lower ranks of the working or non-working class."[47]

In October 1976, the federal government reported that "the incidence of poverty and unemployment for Puerto Ricans is more severe than that of virtually any other ethnic group in the U.S."[48] (See Table 10.2.) It added that "the economic situation of Puerto Ricans in the continental United States has deteriorated during the last decade." With a disproportionate number of Puerto Ricans in the low-income group, their median income in 1959 was 71 percent of the national norm, but it had shrunk to 59 percent by 1974.

On the United States mainland, according to other key findings, 33 percent of all Puerto Rican families subsist below the official poverty level, compared with only about 10 percent of all families. Also, almost 25 percent of Puerto Rican families are on welfare, as compared with 5 percent of the total population. The official unemployment rate for Puerto Rican women is three times greater than that for all women.

TABLE 10.2

INDIVIDUALS BELOW GOVERNMENTAL
POVERTY LEVEL IN 1975

All United States	9.7%
Cuban	17.1%
Mexican	26.4%
Puerto Rican	33.5%
Central & South American	18.2%
Other Spanish	13.8%
Non-Spanish	9.0%

SOURCE: U.S. Department of Commerce: Bureau of the Census, "Persons of Spanish Origin in the United States, March 1976," *Current Population Reports*, Series P20, No. 302, November 1976, p. 11.

Puerto Rican men have an even lower rate of "making it" in terms of education, occupation, and income.[49] It thus becomes clear that Puerto Ricans have had great difficulty in achieving upward mobility.

FUTURE PROSPECTS

As noted, because of Puerto Rico's special political and economic relationship with the United States, together with a decline in the number of jobs available in mainland cities, this ethnic community will continue to be distinct and poor. The migratory Puerto Rican poor settle in urban slums, in an area where the cost of living is high and the job opportunities are few. Totally dependent on a cash income because they cannot even partially support themselves by raising crops, as they could in rural areas, they struggle to survive. In the meantime, those who have achieved some economic security return to Puerto Rico for noneconomic reasons.

Reasons for the return migration appear to be retirement; schooling of children (young parents who wish to educate their offspring in an environment less violent, less hostile, and less drug ridden than that in areas where they live in large cities in the four States); homesickness (strong longing for the more family-friend oriented society in which no discrimination against Puerto Ricans exists, in which there is less apparent discrimination against darkness of skin, and in which the sociological and moral fabric of the community is not perceived to be as deteriorated as in the areas of the large cities in the four States where Puerto Ricans live [New York, New Jersey, Connecticut, and Illinois]); and rising expectations about prospects in Puerto Rico.[50]

These structural conditions and sojourner attitudes are usually not conducive to a stable, improving subcommunity. Still, there have been changes, especially among second-generation Puerto Ricans. Activist organizations such as the Young Lords, the Puerto Rican Student Union, and El Comite, and collective community efforts on issues relating to education, antipoverty programs, public welfare, and housing have helped to develop a group consciousness. The problem is that militant actions, ranging from aggressive challenges to the status quo, to the radical FALN bombings dramatizing their demand for Puerto Rican independence, create tension and conflict within the Puerto Rican community and negative responses outside the community. For people who are trying to adjust and improve their life situations, the increased militancy may complicate things rather than improve them. Despite greater community organization, a substantial reduction in structural unemployment and discrimination in the near future is unlikely.

THE CUBANS

Although the United States granted Cuba its independence after the 1898 war with Spain, it continued to exercise control over the island. The United States had Cuba relinquish a naval base at Guantánamo, which it still maintains, and through the Platt Amendment it reserved the right to intervene in Cuba if necessary to protect American interests. The Cubans resented these infringements upon their newly granted sovereignty. Later, in the 1930s, Franklin Roosevelt's Good Neighbor Policy helped to ease relations between the two countries.

Since the government listed Cuban immigrants among those from the West Indies until 1950, exact numbers prior to that time are impossible to determine. Almost 500,000 people came to the United States from the West Indies between 1820 and 1950. Cubans had little impact upon the American scene during that period, although a Cuban community in northern New Jersey that dated back to 1850 did attract many refugees in the 1960s.

POLITICAL REFUGEES

Cuban migration to the United States began, essentially, with the flight of political refugees from the Castro regime. Since 1959, approximately 700,000 Cubans — more than came from the entire West Indies over a 130-year period — have come to the United States. Many came as temporary exiles, hoping to return after the Castro regime was overthrown, and did not immediately seek U.S. citizenship. As that hope faded and they became more adjusted to life in this country, they became citizens. The total Cuban population in the United States is now approximately 900,000.

Unlike those immigrants who came to the United States for economic reasons prior to 1965 (when immigration laws were changed to favor professionals and skilled workers), political refugees (such as the German forty-eighters and the Vietnamese) have usually been more educated and cosmopolitan, with higher occupational skills. So it was with the Cubans, who were mostly middle class, with higher educational levels and skills in the professional, technical, and white collar fields. Many quickly achieved socioeconomic levels proportionately closer to that of the total population than of other Spanish-speaking minorities. In 1976, as shown in Table 10.3, the Census Bureau reported that Cuban median family income in 1975 was $11,772, which was below the national norm but substantial for such a newly arrived group.

TABLE 10.3

MEDIAN FAMILY INCOME OF SPANISH-SPEAKING PEOPLES IN THE UNITED STATES, 1975

All U.S.	$13,719
Cuban	$11,772
Mexican	$ 9,546
Puerto Rican	$ 7,291
Other Spanish	$11,067

SOURCE: U.S. Department of Commerce: Bureau of the Census, "Persons of Spanish Origin in the United States, March 1976." *Current Population Reports*, Series P20, No. 302, November 1976, p. 11.

SOCIETAL REACTION

As resisters and refugees from the first Communist regime in the Western hemisphere, Cubans were sympathetically received. Such saber-rattling confrontations as the Berlin Wall and the Cuban missile crisis reinforced Americans' perception of such groups as victims rather than as threats. Sympathy for the trapped East Berliners who could not flee because of the newly constructed and heavily guarded wall, and for the Cubans, just ninety miles from the mainland, opened people's hearts to those who were able to leave and come to this country. Consequently, these people did not suffer the deprivation and discrimination many other groups had.

Once Fidel Castro relented and allowed anyone who so desired to leave, some Americans had second thoughts about the large influx of political refugees. As the Cubans began concentrating in several major cities in the early 1960s, people in those regions began to fear that the already depressed economy would suffer even more from their unemployment, welfare demands, and educational and social service needs. These concerns were of short duration, as the Cubans made rapid economic progress and became a part of the community.

In some instances Cubans found themselves treated disparagingly because non-Hispanic residents did not differentiate them from other, poorer Spanish-speaking groups such as the Puerto Ricans and Dominicans. Although they had looked upon such other Caribbean peoples with disdain in the past, the Cubans found that it was in their own best interests to work cooperatively with other Hispanic groups. In a pattern reminiscent of the Sephardic and Ashkenazic Jews, who first resisted and then were very helpful to the central and eastern European Jewish immigrants, the Cubans sometimes established closer relations with other Hispanic groups, particularly in New York. These cooperative efforts, where found, have helped to bring greater stability and visible progress to Hispanic neighborhoods.

CUBAN COMMUNITIES

A great many Cubans concentrated in the Miami and New York metropolitan regions. They settled in blighted urban areas, but their motivation, education, and entrepreneurial skills enabled them to bring color, vitality, stability, and improvement to previously declining neighborhoods. Long-time residents of areas heavily populated by Cubans often credit them with restoring and increasing the beauty and vigor of the community.

Miami offers an excellent example. Its climate and closeness to Cuba made it the ideal choice of many exiles, thereby increasing the fears of residents about so large an ethnic group in their midst. Yet, by 1966 an observer could comment:

> Though some ill-feeling still persists in Miami, by and large the city has come to count its new Cuban community as its own good fortune. . . . There is even something of a real-estate boom in Miami — one of the few cities in the U.S. where housing markets are strong — and an estimated 30 percent of the new FHA commitments there are to Cubans. Enterprising Cubans have been credited with bringing a new commerical vigor to much of the downtown area, especially the former commercial center of Flagler Street, which had been rapidly running down. Many of the former Havana cigar manufacturers and their employees have set up nearly a dozen companies in Miami, helping the city to displace Tampa as the hand-rolled-cigar capital of the U.S. At least one cigarette company, Dorsal & Mendes, is thriving; there are also sizable and prosperous Cuban-owned garment companies, shoe manufacturers, import houses, shopping centers, restaurants and night clubs. To the northwest of Miami, Cuban entrepreneurs have set up sugar plantations and mills.[51]

The Cuban impact upon Miami, now dubbed "Little Havana," has been significant. Numbering close to 375,000, the Cuban people make up one-third of the city's population and have given Miami a very definite ethnic flavor.

The New York City metropolitan region has the second largest concentration of Cubans. Over 80,000 Cubans live there, often near groups from other parts of Latin America. Because Cubans have had a high status throughout the Caribbean for a long time, their presence in Hispanic-American neighborhoods has brought a new dimension in intracommunity relations, expectations, and cohesion:

In the Caribbean, the Dominicans, Puerto Ricans and Jamaicans are all highly regarded as entrepreneurs. However, even they acknowledge, sometimes ruefully, that it is the Cubans who are to the tropics what the Parisians are to France and the Genoans to Italy: People who possess that special admixture of diligence and brashness, making the shrewd and prudently risky decisions that are the difference between high success and just making a living.[52]

As the Cubans began to organize within their new communities, their efforts also helped other Hispanics in the neighborhood. In Washington Heights, for example, the Hispanic-American Alliance exerts political pressure to improve local schools and increase police protection, while the Cuban-backed Capital National Bank and Latin American Chamber of Commerce work to encourage successful small business enterprises. Across the Hudson River in New Jersey communities like Union City, West New York, and Elizabeth, as well as in other parts of the United States, Cuban influence has been positive.

Not all Cubans have attained economic security in the United States. The proportion who fell below the poverty level in 1975, while not as high as in many other Spanish-speaking groups, is almost twice the national average. For a group that has arrived so recently, however, the figure is impressive. It remains to be seen whether the number of Cuban poor will decrease further over the next few years through the efforts of ethnic self-help organizations, government assistance, and occupational placement, or whether the 17.1 percent is a hard core of the Cuban poor.

OTHER HISPANIC PEOPLES

Many non-Hispanics either lump all Spanish-speaking people into one group or else think of them only in terms of the major groupings of Mexican, Puerto Rican, and Cuban. A great many other groups exist, sharing a common heritage and tradition, yet distinct in other ways.

SPANISH

Approximately 250,000 immigrants have come to the United States from Spain since 1820. In recent years an average of more than five thousand immigrants have arrived each year. Many of them settle in urban areas, seek employment in a variety of skilled and semiskilled occupations, and keep primarily to themselves. Although they speak the same language and usually have the same religion as other Hispanic groups, they do not, as a rule, interact with them in meaningful primary relationships.

BOX 10.2

"When we needed an escape from Cuba, we only had America. America was the only country that opened the door."

"I have to tell you that the Spanish-speaking people are always talking about brotherhood and the brotherhood of the Latin American countries. They say our brother country Mexico and our brother country Venezuela, and every time they mention a Latin American country, they say the brother country. Well, in reality, it is wrong. When we needed an escape from Cuba, we only had America. America was the only country that opened the door. America is the only place where you can go for freedom and where you can live as a human being.

"I love Cuba very much but I can tell you that we never had the freedom that we have here. I can sincerely say that the opportunities in this country — America — are so great and so many, that no matter how bad they say we are as far as economics right now — they're talking about recession and everything — no matter how bad they say, it will never be as bad as it was and it is, actually, in Cuba.

"America took us in and we are grateful to America and to the Americans. And remember, when we came over, we were looking for freedom and liberty. Now we have freedom, we have liberty, and we have the chance to make money. Many Cubans are doing very well, better than me. I make enough to support my family and to live decently. I am very happy and very grateful.

"Believe me, I am not only speaking for myself, but for a large group of Cubans who feel the same way I feel. We are happy here. We miss Cuba. Sometimes we get tearful when we think about the old friends and the old neighborhoods, but we are lucky. We are lucky because we still can say what we want to say, and we can move around wherever we want, and be what we want to be."

Cuban refugee who came to the United States in 1960
at age 18

One subcultural group from the Spanish mainland is the Basque people, who began coming to the United States in the late nineteenth century. Though never large in number — there are only about ten to fifteen thousand here today, including the second and third generations — they have played an important role in the West. Primarily settling in the bordering regions of Oregon, Idaho, Wyoming, Colorado, Nevada, and California, they came as sheepherders and dominated the sheep industry, including the support services of transportation and marketing, by the end of the nineteenth century. The old Western plot of conflict between cattle ranchers and sheepherders is based on fact, and these conflicts often involved the Basques. An intense hostility sometimes developed between the two groups, resulting in the Basques being stereotyped as "dirty" foreigners who were destroying the open range. But the Basques were a tenacious people who valued achievement in the face of adversity. Their quiet but ironlike determination held them in good stead, and they eventually overcame outgroup hostility. Although many Basques came to this country to stay, a good number also came as sojourners and returned to their native land.[53]

DOMINICANS

Another sizable national group is the Dominicans, who have been arriving here in substantial numbers; they rank third, behind Mexico and Cuba, in the number of Spanish-speaking immigrants. In 1975 a total of 12,526 people emigrated to the United States from the Dominican Republic, slightly more than the yearly average for the past 12 years. Most are dark-skinned, fleeing the poverty of their land. However, because of their skin color and their lack of skills, they have a high unemployment rate. Many live in poor urban neighborhoods, suffering the deprivation and family disruption so common among recent immigrants who are trying to adjust to a new land and to achieve economic security.

OTHER LATIN AMERICANS

Of the other countries in Central and South America, Colombia, Ecuador, and El Salvador — in that order — are the next largest sources of Hispanic newcomers. For example, there may now be more than 300,000 Colombians residing in the United States, many of them illegal aliens.[54] Like other countries in Central and South America, these three countries have been experiencing a population explosion; there simply are not enough resources to support the population, and the result has been increasing emigration to the United States. While not many countries are approaching the 1977 immigration quota of 20,000 from any one country in the Western Hemisphere, the continuing population growth and resulting poverty are likely to cause immigration from the countries to the south to increase proportionately. Some of the immigration is illegal; the Latinos use student or tourist visas to enter, then live a furtive existence in an urban area like New York City, where perhaps as many as 15 percent of the nation's illegal aliens live.[55] If there is a third great wave of immigration, the Caribbean and Central and South America will be most likely to rival Asia as the major sources.

NON-SPANISH CARIBBEAN PEOPLES

From the Caribbean area, where the population growth is especially high, many groups whose background is not Spanish have sought a haven here. Most of them have the same social and economic motivation as the various Hispanic groups.

HAITIANS

Haitians fleeing the Duvalier regime seek both political asylum and economic opportunity. Since 1972 about a thousand have made the dangerous eight-hundred-mile journey in all kinds of small vessels in order to reach the United States. An average of 5,000 a year have been emigrating here through normal channels for the past 12 years. Curiously, our government has not officially classified the Haitians as political refugees, and so they have not had well-funded service centers, as the Cubans did, to help them make the transition to a new life.

Most Haitians are French-speaking Catholics with a fierce pride in themselves and their heritage. As a result, they tend to keep to themselves and do not complain or seek any assistance, particularly welfare. As is usual with political refugees, many are professionals — physicians, lawyers, artisans, accountants — but because of the language barrier and state licensing or union requirements, most are underemployed. Still, they consider themselves far better off than they were in Haiti, and they work so conscientiously that they have a good reputation among employers. New York City, the first residence of hundreds of thousands of immigrants from many different places, is home today to about 200,000 Haitians.

Some immigrants, but relatively few, have also come from the French territories of Guadeloupe, Martinique, and French Guiana.

BRITISH WEST INDIANS

An increasing number of immigrants are coming from the British West Indies. More and more individuals are migrating from Jamaica and Trinidad and Tobago, in particular, but also from Barbados, Guyana, the Bahamas, and the British Virgin Islands. Virgin Islanders from the

BOX 10.3

"I think the melting pot idea . . . is not a workable idea."

"The Colombians here are the poor people. They are the ones who had no chance for an education in Colombia. They are the ones who — because they had no education — their pay was very meager. And so over here they have a better life than they would in Colombia. So over here they really — if you can call it the American Dream — has been fulfilled in them.

"Emotionally they're very attached to their country. See, this is the thing that is very hard for people to understand. They want them to become American and to forget everything. You can't! The ties — the blood ties — are too strong! You just can't become — as I said, I cannot even become an American. I can't! Even if I wanted to. You would have to make me all over again. And I love this country and I choose to stay in this country.

"Now with these people — take some of them. They have come because of necessity — sheer necessity. We criticize them because they don't love America, but I don't think that is the fact. Also, if you notice the kind of people that come here. For instance, I had students who were the children of my father's workers on the coffee plantation. Now in my country they were tilling the soil. You know, the children of the owner go to school. The children of the worker go to till the soil. They had no chance of an education. They had huts up in the mountains where they had no running water, no electricity. Now they come here and they have all the conveniences. If they live poorly, Americans criticize them but they don't realize where they were living before. If they're not clean and spotless and they don't keep the shades the right way — but these people have been doing this for a hundred years! The people who just came in never even had a shade to talk about. They never had a venetian blind. They never even had a window to talk about!" (Laughs.)

"I think we have to be careful because we often make the mistake of imposing our way to the people. Now you could say, we're not going to them, they're coming here. But if you accept them in the country, I think you also have to accept a big risk. I think the melting pot idea is not the prevalent idea. It is not a workable idea. Each one has a culture. Each people has a culture and if you want them in America, if you allow them to stay here, you have to work something by which each one is able to live. I don't mean to say that we have independent little countries, but that they are comfortable. Because you cannot remove — those are strong things that you cannot remove from a person."

Colombian immigrant who came to the United States in 1952
at age 16

United States territory, who are already United States citizens, have also been coming to the mainland, especially New York City, to live. The Caribbean people tend to adapt very easily, except that for most of them the color barrier, unknown in their native country, is a bitter and difficult experience. Their encounters with racial prejudice in housing, jobs, and other opportunities leave them disillusioned about the United States.

MIGRANT WORKERS

Either as contract laborers brought into the country for seasonal employment or as minority-group members living in America, members of racial and ethnic minority groups have long been employed as migrant workers. In other periods, most of the migrant laborers were first-generation Americans from various European countries. Today these hard-working, poverty-stricken people caught in an almost inescapable web are a mixture of blacks, whites, and Hispanics.

Most of the fruits and vegetables harvested in this country are hand-picked by men, women, and children whose yearly income falls well below the government's poverty level. They have no strong pressure groups to speak in their behalf, while the farmers' lobby is one of the most powerful in Washington.

Cesar Chavez has had some success in unionizing farmworkers. After his National Farm Workers Association (NFWA) merged with the AFL-CIO's Agricultural Workers Organizing Committee (AWOC) to form the United Farm Workers Organizing Committee (UFWOC), the *Huelga* movement (use of the boycott) led to signed contracts with many major growers of grapes and lettuce.

Some migrants live in the region and work on whatever farm has work; others travel northward, following the harvest up the Atlantic or Pacific coast or up through the central United States. Most do not qualify for unemployment compensation, welfare benefits, or social security; child labor laws are rarely enforced, if they are enforced at all, for minors working in the fields.

Migrant farm workers are undernourished and often suffer from pesticide poisoning as a result of airplane spraying or from accidental contact between pesticides and their skin or clothing. Their average life expectancy is only 49 years as compared with the national average of 70. Their infant mortality rate is high, and they suffer from many physical and psychiatric illnesses. They tend to be fatalistic, distrustful of outsiders, very permissive about child rearing, and oriented toward immediate gratification.[56] Because they include blacks and whites, native-born and immigrants, they illustrate how material deprivation, social and spatial segregation, and differential treatment can produce varying and sometimes detrimental physical, mental, and cultural effects regardless of race, religion, or national origin.

The United States presently allows alien migrants to come into the country for seasonal farm work, much to the dismay of labor leaders, who argue that this practice leads to high unemployment and depressed wages in farm areas. Most of these alien migrants come from the Caribbean, Mexico, and Canada. About 50,000 workers come in from Mexico each year, and about 10,000 come from Canada. In November 1974 the United States Supreme Court ruled 5–4 that aliens may enter the country on a seasonal basis, provided they have registration cards from the Immigration Service. This practice, opponents believe, makes illegal aliens harder to detect and works to the disadvantage of both United States citizens and legal aliens.

RETROSPECT

In many ways the Hispanic immigrants have been repeating the patterns of earlier racial and ethnic groups. Coming in large numbers from impoverished lands, many have entered the lowest strata of society, clustered together in substandard housing units, and faced the problems of adjustment, deprivation, frustration, and pathology (sickness and crime). Marked as strangers by their language, customs, and physical appearance, they have difficulty being accepted and gaining economic security. Ironically, the Hispanic poor face the same problems and are condemned for them in the same way as earlier groups. They are also condemned for failing to overcome these problems immediately, even though other groups often took three generations to do so. Dominant-minority response patterns are thus quite similar to those of earlier immigrant peoples.

What is particularly significant for the Hispanic immigrants in comparison to other groups is the changed structural conditions. The restrictive immigration laws in the 1920s drastically curtailed the great influx of southern, eastern, and central Europeans. This meant that those immigrants already here did not receive continuous cultural reinforcement from new arrivals. Not only is there a sizable flow of new Hispanic arrivals, but rapid and inexpensive communications and transportation encourage return trips to the not-so-far-away homeland. In addition, the earlier European immigrants encountered sometimes heavy-handed attempts at Americanization, whereas the Hispanics come at a time when pluralism and ethnic resurgence is common among dominant-group members.

Another crucial change in structural conditions has taken place in technology and the job market. When the European poor came to America, they could find many unskilled and semiskilled jobs. There were many evils and abuses in industry, but an immigrant could secure a little piece of the American Dream through hard physical labor. The Hispanic immigrant today enters a contracting labor market, not an expanding one, and so jobs are harder to find. Technology has eliminated a great many low-skill jobs and reduced the total number of blue collar jobs, and the demand now is for skilled blue collar and white collar workers. The poor of the Western Hemisphere are not qualified for these positions; they find they cannot improve their lot through hard physical labor because this labor is no longer there to be found.

During the mass European migration, the fledgling labor unions struggled to improve, and eventually did improve, the economic situation of the immigrant workers. As the economy contracts, the government uses welfare as the answer to the economic problems of today's nonworking poor. In fact, throughout the 1950s and 1960s the government encouraged individuals to apply for welfare by liberalizing eligibility requirements. With structural unemployment leaving no alternative, the system maneuvers many Hispanics into dependence on welfare.

Highly visible because of their numbers, language, culture, and poverty, many Hispanic-Americans find themselves the objects of resentment, hostility, and overt discrimination from the dominant society. The familiar pattern of blaming the victim results in negative stereotyping, social segregation, and all shades of prejudice and discrimination against the Hispanic poor.

Not all Hispanic-Americans are poor, of course, as indicated in Tables 10.2 and 10.3. For those who are not, attaining economic security means a very different life experience. Other positive factors offer some promise of easing the transition to American life: bilingual education, increased public awareness, a greater tolerance for cultural pluralism, civic and governmental programs. Serious problems still remain for a disproportionate number of Hispanic-Americans, however, and it is too soon to tell whether the Carter Administration's efforts to provide full employment, reform welfare, and control illegal aliens will have any impact upon the Hispanic poor.

Even if greater upward mobility occurs, this will not necessarily lead to assimilation. Many variables within both the dominant and minority societies are encouraging cultural and structural pluralism. The present-day public focus is more upon eliminating the problems of poverty among culturally distinct groups than upon eliminating the cultural distinctions. Just how successful these efforts will be has yet to be determined.

QUESTIONS FOR DISCUSSION

1. What changes in American structural conditions have made it more difficult for Hispanic immigrants to find job opportunities?

2. What advantages for retaining their cultural heritage do the Hispanic immigrants have that earlier immigrants did not have?

3. Why is it incorrect to generalize about Mexican-Americans? What factors are prolonging poverty among so many Mexican-Americans?

4. How does the special relationship between Puerto Rico and the United States contribute to Puerto Rican problems on the mainland?

5. Why do many Hispanic immigrants suffer a greater culture shock than other non-English-speaking immigrants?

SUGGESTED READINGS

Chenault, Lawrence. Puerto Ricans in New York. Russell and Russell. New York, 1970.

Fitzpatrick, Joseph P. Puerto Rican Americans. Prentice-Hall, Englewood Cliffs, N.J., 1971.

Glazer, Nathan, and Daniel P. Moynihan. Beyond the Melting Pot. 2nd ed. M.I.T., Cambridge, Mass., 1970.

Gonzalez, Nancie L. The Spanish Americans of New Mexico. University of New Mexico Press, Albuquerque, 1969.

Heller, Celia S. Mexican-American Youth: Forgotten Youth at the Crossroads. Random House, New York, 1966.

Lewis, Oscar. La Vida: A Puerto Rican Family in the Culture of Poverty— San Juan and New York. Random House, New York, 1965.

Madsen, William. The Mexican-Americans of South Texas. Holt, New York, 1964.

McWilliams, Carey. North from Mexico. Greenwood Press, New York, 1968.

Moore, Joan W. Mexican Americans. Prentice-Hall, Englewood Cliffs, N.J., 1970.

Rodriguez, Clara. The Ethnic Queue in the U.S.: The Case of the Puerto Ricans. R & E Research Associates, San Francisco, 1974.

Thomas, Piri. Down These Mean Streets. Knopf, New York, 1967.

Wakefield, Dan. Island in the City: The World of Spanish Harlem. Houghton Mifflin, Boston, 1959.

NOTES

1. Roberta V. McKay, "Americans of Spanish Origin in the Labor Force: An Update," Monthly Labor Review, U.S. Department of Labor, Bureau of Labor Statistics, September 1976, pp. 3–6.

2. Reported in Ronald Hilton, The Latin Americans: Their Heritage and Their Destiny, Lippincott, New York, 1973, p. 16.

3. See Glen H. Beyer, The Urban Explosion in Latin America, Cornell University Press, Ithaca, N.Y., 1967; David Chaplin, Population Policy

and Growth in Latin America, Heath, New York, 1971; Eric R. Wolf and Edward C. Hansen, The Human Condition in Latin America, Oxford University Press, New York, 1972.

4. Hilton, The Latin Americans, pp. 40–41.

5. Celia S. Heller, Mexican-American Youth: Forgotten Youth at the Crossroads, Random House, New York, 1966; William Madsen, The Mexican-Americans of South Texas, Holt, New York, 1964, pp. 15–17.

6. Joseph P. Fitzpatrick, Puerto Rican Americans, Prentice-Hall, Englewood Cliffs, N.J., 1971, p. 91.

7. McKay, "Americans of Spanish Origin in the Labor Force: An Update," pp. 4–5.

8. Clara Rodriguez, The Ethnic Queue in the U.S.: The Case of the Puerto Ricans, R & E Research Associates, San Francisco, 1974, p. 92.

9. Fitzpatrick, Puerto Rican Americans, p. 105.

10. For some excellent cross-cultural analyses of attitudes regarding distance between people, see Edward Hall, The Hidden Dimension, Doubleday, Garden City, N.Y., 1966; E. Hall, Silent Language, Doubleday, Garden City, N.Y., 1959.

11. See "Latinos in U.S." U.S. News and World Report, Dec. 13, 1976, p. 55.

12. U.S. Department of Commerce: Bureau of the Census, "Persons of Spanish Origin in the United States, March 1976," Current Population Reports, Series P20, No. 302, November 1976.

13. Michael T. Malloy, "We Want No Melting Pot," The National Observer, Aug. 7, 1976, pp. 1, 12.

14. Joan W. Moore, Mexican Americans, Prentice-Hall, Englewood Cliffs, N.J., 1970, p. 100.

15. Ed Ludwig and James Santibanex (eds.), The Chicanos, Penguin, Baltimore, 1971, pp. 2–3.

16. Moore, Mexican Americans, p. 43.

17. Ibid.

18. Carey McWilliams, North from Mex-

ico, Greenwood Press, New York, 1968, pp. 247–250.

19. Moore, Mexican Americans, p. 72.

20. See Thomas M. Martinez, "Advertising and Racism: The Case of the Mexican-American," El Grito, Summer 1969.

21. Florence Kluckhohn and Fred L. Strodtbeck, Variations in Value Orientations, Row, Peterson, Evanston, Ill., 1961.

22. See Moore, Mexican Americans, pp. 129–130.

23. Leo Grebler, Joan Moore, and Ralph Guzman, The Mexican American People, Free Press, New York, 1970, pp. 423–439.

24. See the discussion on pp. 82–86.

25. Moore, Mexican Americans, pp. 44–45.

26. Ibid., pp. 57–59.

27. Ibid., p. 75.

28. Ibid., pp. 85–88.

29. U.S. Immigration and Naturalization Service, Annual Report, U.S. Government Printing Office, Washington, D.C., 1976.

30. See James P. Sterba, "From Mexico to Hard Times in the Southwest U.S.," The New York Times, May 1, 1977, p. E3.

31. Rodriguez, The Ethnic Queue in the U.S.: The Case of the Puerto Ricans, pp. 83–85.

32. Ibid., p. 83.

33. Ibid., p. 74.

34. Clara Rodriguez, "Assimilation in the Puerto Rican Communities of the U.S.; A New Focus," presented to the 72nd annual meeting of the American Sociological Association, 1977, pp. 10–12.

35. Fitzpatrick, Puerto Rican Americans, pp. 57, 73.

36. Rodriguez, "Assimilation in the Puerto Rican Communities of the U.S.: A New Focus," p. 8.

37. Fitzpatrick, Puerto Rican Americans, pp. 66–70.

38. Ibid., p. 78.

39. The example is from Fitzpatrick, pp. 78–79.

40. Ibid., pp. 83–84.

41. See Oscar Handlin, *The Uprooted*, Little, Brown, Boston, 1951, p. 135.

42. Nathan Glazer and Daniel P. Moynihan, *Beyond the Melting Pot*, 2nd ed., M.I.T., Cambridge, Mass., 1970, pp. 103–104.

43. For a more detailed discussion of the role of religion among Puerto Ricans, see Fitzpatrick, *Puerto Rican Americans*, pp. 115–129; also Rodriguez, *The Ethnic Queue in the U.S.: The Case of the Puerto Ricans*, pp. 95–99.

44. Fitzpatrick, *Puerto Rican Americans*, pp. 123–127.

45. *Ibid.*, p. 129.

46. *Ibid.*, p. 128.

47. Rodriguez, "Assimilation in the Puerto Rican Communities of the U.S.: A New Focus," p. 15.

48. U.S. Commission on Civil Rights, "Puerto Ricans in the Continental U.S.: An Uncertain Future," October 1976.

49. Rodriguez, "The Ethnic Queue in the U.S.: The Case of the Puerto Ricans," p. 101.

50. Rita M. Maldonado, "Why Puerto Ricans Migrated to the United States in 1947–73," *Monthly Labor Review*, U.S. Department of Labor, Bureau of Labor Statistics, September 1976, p. 14.

51. Tom Alexander, "Those Amazing Cuban Emigres," *Fortune Magazine*, 74 (October 1966), 144–146.

52. Richard Severo, "Spanish Influx Felt in Washington Heights," *The New York Times*, August 12, 1976, p. 33. ©1976 by The New York Times Company. Reprinted by permission.

53. A definitive study on the Basques in America is William A. Douglass and Jon Bilbao, *Amerikanuak: Basques in the New World*, University of Nevada Press, Reno, 1975.

54. Juan de Onis, "From Columbia with Skills and High Hopes," *The New York Times*, May 1, 1977, p. E3.

55. David Vidal, "In New York, They Tend to Stay Together," *The New York Times*, May 1, 1977, p. E3.

56. For an excellent insight into the impact of migrant life upon the formative childhood years, see Robert Coles, *Migrants, Sharecroppers, Mountaineers*, Little, Brown, Boston, 1971, pp. 47–192. See also Robert Coles, *Uprooted Children*, University of Pittsburgh Press, Pittsburgh, 1970; Robert Coles, *Still Hungry in America*, World Publishing, New York, 1969.

ELEVEN

THE AMERICAN MOSAIC

⚑ As a nation of immigrants, the United States has had many different groups of strangers arrive and interact with its people. The strangers have perceived a different world than the native population took for granted, and their reactions have ranged from wonder to bewilderment to dismay, from fulfilled expectations to culture shock. Because their language, appearance, and cultural background often made them conspicuous, the newcomers were categorically identified and judged as a group, rather than individually. Native-born Americans sometimes welcomed these strangers, sometimes were impatient, and sometimes were intolerant; they helped or exploited or ignored the newcomers.

Throughout the nation's history, then, varied patterns of majority-minority relations have existed. Ethnocentric values have prompted the natural development of ingroup loyalty and outgroup hostility among both indigenous and migrant groups. Competition for scarce resources, colonialism, and political dominance by the Anglo-Saxon core groups also provided a basis for conflict. However, the resulting prejudicial attitudes and discriminatory actions varied greatly in intensity. Additionally, both attitudes and social and economic conditions in this country have changed over the years, and this has affected the newcomers' experience.

Not all groups have come for the same reasons, nor have they come from the same backgrounds. Because of variations in social class, education, and occupational skills, not all immigrants have begun at the bottom of the socioeconomic ladder. Some have come as sojourners, intending to stay only long enough to earn enough money for a better life back in their homeland. Some have come with the desire to be American citizens in every sense of the word; others have insisted upon retaining their own culture.

American attitudes toward the newcomers have also varied. Dominant attitudes, as well as sociological analyses, have tended to focus on either assimilation or pluralism as the preferred minority adaptation. Which process the public considers more acceptable will greatly influence dominant-minority relations. For example, if assimilation is held to be the "proper" goal, then evidence of pluralism will probably be a target for negative reaction. In recent years many people, but not all, have been more receptive to pluralism, and government policies and actions have reflected this orientation. Also, there has been a resurgence of ethnicity among the so-called white ethnics and other minority groups. Manifestations of the social processes of pluralism suggest that while minority groups may still encounter problems of adjustment and acceptance, these are not compounded by overt pressures for Americanization to the same extent as in the past.

In this chapter we shall seek some possible explanations for the variations in conflict in intergroup relations. We shall also examine several theories of ethnic consciousness and ethnic behavior, and examine the relative socioeconomic standing of the various groups as a whole.

ETHNIC ANTAGONISM

The term *ethnic antagonism* usually refers to any form of intergroup hostility. This includes ideologies and beliefs (such as racism and prejudice), behavior (such as discrimination, lynchings, and riots), and institutionalized practices (such as segregation laws).[1] Ethnic antagonism can occur in many ways, including among races or among national groupings within a racial category. Another important factor is that the conflict is usually mutual — the outcome of interaction — rather than a one-sided action based on stereotypes.

A number of theorists have advanced the notion of antagonism as a common pattern in dominant-minority relations. Robert E. Park presented a race relations cycle with universal application.[2] Many have challenged the inevitability of Park's cycle (for example, Lipset, 1950; Etzioni, 1959; Lyman, 1972). It was also challenged by Stanley Lieberson, who offered his own explanation based on power distribution.[3] Robert Blauner gave a neo-Marxian analysis of race relations in America, pointing to internal colonialism as a major consideration.[4] Another approach is that of Edna Bonacich, who sees some ethnic antagonism as resulting from a labor market split along ethnic lines.[5] Each of these theories gives additional insights into the group experiences described in this book.

THE UNIVERSAL THEORY

After extensive travel and study, Park concluded that "in the relations of races there is a cycle of events which tends everywhere to repeat itself." Note that in Park's day the term *race* was used to refer to both biological and national groupings, whereas today it is generally used to mean only the former. Therefore, Park's comments should be given the broader application.

Park saw an inevitable process that was irreversible and could take a long period of time. The stages of this cycle were contact between the groups, then competition, followed by some kind of adjustment or accommodation. The final stage was assimilation and amalgamation.

The race relations cycle which takes the form, to state it abstractly, of contact, competition, accommodation, and eventual assimilation, is apparently progressive and irreversible. Customs regulations, immigration restrictions, and racial barriers may slacken the tempo of the movement; may perhaps halt it altogether for a time; but cannot change its direction, cannot, at any rate, reverse it. . . . It does not follow that because the tendencies to the assimilation and eventual amalgamation of races exist, they should not be resisted and, if possible, altogether inhibited. . . . Rising tides of color and oriental exclusion laws are merely incidental evidences of this diminishing distance. . . . In the Hawaiian Islands, where all the races of the Pacific meet and mingle . . . the native races are disappearing and new peoples are coming into existence. Races and cultures die — it has always been so — but civilization lives on.[6]

There are several problems with Park's race relations cycle. By its very nature, this hypothesis of an inevitable cycle is not testable.[7] Park could not cite any racial group that had passed through all four stages. Instead of seeing these negative data as refuting the theory, Park and other cyclical theorists explained the lack of assimilation as the result of obstacles or interference. As a result of such tautological reasoning, this theory lacks an essential element of empirical science: it cannot be proved or disproved.[8] Moreover, the universality of the cyclical theory falters because there are cases in which conflict and competition did not occur when different groups came into contact.

THE POWER THEORY

One of the sociologists who rejected Park's theory was Stanley Lieberson. He pointed to the sharp contrasts between the racial turmoil in South Africa and Indonesia and the relatively harmonious race relations in Brazil and Hawaii as illustrative of the difficulty of proclaiming an inevitable race relations cycle. (Lieberson also used the terms *race* and *ethnic* interchangeably.)

According to Lieberson, the course of race relations depends upon the relative power of the migrant group and the indigenous group. Since the two groups usually do not share the same culture, each will strive to maintain its own institutions. Which group becomes superordinate and which becomes subordinate governs what will follow.

It is here that efforts at a single cycle of race and ethnic relations must fail. For it is necessary to introduce a distinction in the nature or form of subordination before attempting to predict whether conflict or relatively harmonious assimilation will develop. . . .The race relations cycle in areas where the migrant group is superordinate and indigenous group subordinate differs sharply from the stages in societies composed of a superordinate indigenous group and subordinate migrants.[9]

If the newcomers are superior in terms of technology (particularly weapons) and social organization, then conflict may occur at an early stage, and there is likely to be a numerical decline as a result of warfare, disease, or disruption of sustenance activities. The local inhabitants find their institutions undermined or co-opted, and may eventually participate in the institutions of the dominant group. In time a group consciousness may arise, and sometimes the indigenous group will even succeed in ousting the superordinate migrant group. In many former African colonies and in Southeast Asia, when this happened, interethnic fights among the many indigenous groups often led to new forms of superordination and subordination within countries (as was the case in Nigeria and Uganda).

Lieberson maintains that neither conflict nor assimilation is an inevitable outcome of racial and ethnic contact. Instead, the particular relationship between two groups determines which alternative will occur. Conflict between a superordinate migrant group and a subordinate indigenous group can be immediate and violent. If the relationship is the reverse, and the indigenous group is superordinate, conflict will be limited and sporadic, and the host society will exert a great deal of pressure upon the subordinate migrant group to assimilate, acquiesce, or leave. Additionally, the superordinate indigenous group can limit the numbers and groups entering, to reduce any threats of demographic and institutional imbalance. Restrictive immigration laws against the Chinese in 1882 and against all but northern and western Europeans in 1921 and 1924 illustrate this process. Violent union attempts to remove Asian workers, labor union hostility to blacks, efforts to expel foreigners (such as Indians, Japanese, or Pilipinos) or to revolutionize the social order (Indian boarding schools, the Americanization movement) all illustrate the use of power against minority groups.

Another sociologist, William Wilson, has suggested that power relations between superordinate and subordinate groups are different in paternalistic and competitive systems.[10] In the former (such as South Africa and the Old South), the dominant group has almost absolute control over the subordinate group and can exert almost unlimited coercion to maintain societal order. In a competitive system, such as the United States today, there is some degree of power reciprocity, and so society is somewhat vulnerable to political pressures and economic boycotts. Rapid social change — industrialization, unionization, urbanization, migration, political changes — usually loosens the social structure, leading to new tensions as both groups seek new power resources. If the minority group increases its power resources through protective laws and improved economic opportunities, it may foresee even greater improvement in its condition. This heightened awareness is likely to lead to conflict unless additional gains are forthcoming.[11] For example, the civil rights movement of the mid-1960s brought about legislation ensuring minority rights and opportunities in jobs, housing, education, and other aspects of life, but this led to new tensions. In the late 1960s there were urban riots and burnings, protest demonstrations and human barricades to stop construction at low-income housing sites, school busing controversies, and challenges against labor discrimination.

THE INTERNAL COLONIALISM THEORY

In dealing with the issue of black militancy in the late 1960s, Robert Blauner attempted to integrate the factors of caste and racism, ethnicity, culture, and economic exploitation. Though he focused on American black-white relations, he did suggest that the Mexican-Americans might also fit his internal colonialism model, and the Native Americans could be added as another suitable example.

Although in this text we have discussed some similarities between the experiences of blacks and those of other ethnic groups, Blauner rejects any such comparison.

Of course many ethnic groups in America have lived in ghettoes. What makes the Black ghettoes an expression of colonized status are three special features. First, the ethnic ghettoes arose more from voluntary choice, both in the sense of the choice to immigrate to America and the decision to live among one's fellow ethnics. Second, the immigrant ghettoes tended to be a one and two generation phenomenon; they were actually way-stations in the process of acculturation and assimilation. When they continue to persist as in the case of San Francisco's Chinatown, it is because they are big business for the ethnics themselves and there is a new stream of immigrants. The Black ghetto on the other hand has been a more permanent phenomenon, although some individuals do escape it. But most relevant is the third point. European ethnic groups like the Poles, Italians and Jews generally only experienced a brief period, often less than a generation, during which their residential buildings, commercial stores, and other enterprises were owned by outsiders. The Chinese and Japanese faced handicaps of color prejudice that were almost as strong as the Blacks faced, but very soon gained control of their internal communities, because their traditional ethnic culture and social organization had not been destroyed by slavery and internal colonization. But Afro-Americans are distinct in the extent to which their segregated communities have remained controlled economically, politically, and administratively from the outside.[12]

Several of the above statements need to be modified. Chinatowns have persisted not because of any business advantage, but because of racial discrimination. In proportion to the Chinatown population, only a few Chinese actually benefit from the tourist trade. Second, the Chinese and Japanese *always* had "control of their internal communities," although they differ greatly from one another with respect to their structure and cohesiveness.

The exploitation that was limited for other groups, Blauner sees as more permanent for blacks and possibly Chicanos. He believes that conflict and confrontation, as well as real or apparent chaos and disorder, will continue, since this may well be the only way in which an internally colonized group can deal with the dominant society. This conflict orientation suggests that the multigenerational exploitation of certain groups creates both a unique situation in comparison with the situation of other groups, and a basis for the conflict — often violent — that marked the late 1960s.

THE SPLIT LABOR MARKET THEORY

Edna Bonacich theorizes that ethnic antagonism is the result of a combination of economic exploitation by employers and economic competition between two or more groups of laborers that produces a wage differential for labor. She contends that much of the ethnic antagonism is based not on ethnicity and race but on the conflict between higher-paid and lower-paid labor.

> Ethnic antagonism is specifically produced by the competition that arises from a price differential. An oversupply of equal-priced labor does not produce such antagonism, though it too threatens people with the loss of their job. However, hiring practices will not necessarily fall along ethnic lines. . . . All workingmen are on the same footing, competing for scarce jobs. When one ethnic group is decidedly cheaper than another (i.e., when the labor market is split), the higher paid worker faces more than the loss of his job; he faces the possibility that the wage standard in all jobs will be undermined by cheaper labor.[13]

If the higher-paid labor group is racist and is strong enough, it may be able to stop the real or potential cheaper competition through an exclusion movement or caste system. To some degree, America's restriction of Chinese and Japanese immigrant labor, and Australia's restriction of Asian and Polynesian immigrants, are victories for organized labor against lower-paid competition. In a caste system, higher-paid labor controls certain high-paying jobs exclusively and limits the minority group to other, lower-paying jobs. This creates an aristocracy of labor and submerges the labor-market split by stratifying the differentially priced workers. This phenomenon can be seen in the job differentials between blacks and whites in certain trade unions.

Some factors lowering the price of one group's labor might be their exploitation by management, their unfamiliarity with wage standards, their language and customs, their lack of economic resources, all of which force them to take even low-paying jobs to survive, contractual commitments before emigrating, or political support from a labor organization or government.

> Governments vary in the degree to which they protect their emigrants. Japan kept close watch over the fate of her nationals who migrated to Hawaii and the Pacific coast.... In contrast Mexican migrant workers to the United States have received little protection from their government, and African states were unable to intervene on behalf of slaves brought to America.[14]

When a labor market splits along ethnic lines, racial and ethnic stereotyping becomes a key factor in the labor conflict, and prejudice, ethnic antagonism, and racism become overt. The conflict is not the result of religious differences, nor is it a matter of which group was first to move into the area, since there are examples of ethnic antagonism in which these variables have been controlled. Bonacich argues that the one characteristic shared by all societies high in ethnic antagonism is that they have an indigenous working class that earns higher wages than immigrant workers. Not everyone agrees with this theory. In the case of the anti-Chinese movement led by labor unions, racism was the motivating factor, and white workers offered to work for lower wages if this meant that the Chinese would be removed from their jobs.[15]

In applying the split labor market theory to the history of the Chinese in America between 1848 and 1882, Hilton suggested several modifications.[16] If the economy is expanding and labor shortages occur, ethnic antagonisms are disarmed. Most importantly, an ethnic bourgeoisie necessarily evolves because of the existence of an ethnic labor force.

> Native capitalists are seldom equipped to locate and reproduce that ethnic labor force by themselves. Unfamiliarity with the language and customs of Chinese workers made it necessary that white capital rely on an intermediary class of Chinese businessmen for two purposes. First, locating and hiring an adequate number of Chinese workers required that capital act through an intermediate class of Chinese compradors. Second, once obtained, the Chinese labor force

BOX 11.1

DIFFERENT VIEWS OF DOMINANT-MINORITY RELATIONS

THE UNIVERSAL THEORY

1. Minority groups move through progressive and irreversible stages
2. Inevitable cycles are contact, competition, accommodation, assimilation
3. This process occurs among all minority groups

THE POWER THEORY

1. Neither conflict nor assimilation is inevitable
2. Relative power of indigenous and migrant groups determines events
3. If the migrant group is superordinate, early conflict and colonization occur
4. If the indigenous group is superordinate, the result is occasional labor and racial strife, legislative restrictions, and pressures on the minority to assimilate

THE INTERNAL COLONIALISM THEORY

1. Black ghettoes are more permanent than immigrant ghettoes
2. Black ghettoes are controlled economically, politically, and administratively from the outside
3. Continual exploitation means conflict and confrontation

THE SPLIT LABOR MARKET THEORY

1. Ethnic antagonism results more from conflict between higher- and lower-paid workers than from ethnicity and race
2. Racial and ethnic stereotyping and prejudice emerge as key factors in labor conflicts
3. Native labor presses for exclusion of the ethnic group or for a caste resolution restricting ethnic laborers to lowest-paying jobs

MODIFICATIONS OF SPLIT LABOR MARKET THEORY

1. Expanding economy creates labor shortages, which disarm labor antagonism
2. Ethnic bourgeoisie arises as middleman between capitalists and labor
3. Ethnic bourgeoisie can help maintain or challenge the caste labor system

had to be provisioned according to their accustomed tastes. This requirement fostered the development of a class of Chinese merchants.[17]

Hilton also indicates that the ethnic bourgeoisie is both exploitative, in that it benefits from the ethnic worker, and benevolent, in that it solidifies the ethnic community and provides for its social needs. The ethnic bourgeoisie can affect a split labor market because its stronger economic and political base, and often higher educational level, enable it to act on behalf of the ethnic group. Although it does not always do so, the ethnic bourgeoisie can articulate the injustices of a caste system and challenge restrictive institutions.

A bourgeoisie arises from within the ranks of any ethnic group at some stage in their readjustment to life in America. Most notable are the *padroni* among the Italian and Greek immigrants and the *padrinos* among Puerto Rican and Mexican laborers.

LIMITATIONS OF THESE THEORIES

Park's theory, which attempts to be universal, presents problems, for there are instances to which it is not applicable. The power theory offers one variable to explain conflict or acceptance patterns; this does not provide insight into all conflicts, however, such as those between a superordinate indigenous group and a subordinate migrant group. Blauner's internal colonialism theory applies only to three groups — blacks, Chicanos, and Native Americans. Bonacich's emphasis on the labor market is helpful, but her theory does not deal with other sources of prejudice, such as racial or religious antipathy or culture clash. In short, none of these theories can satisfactorily explain most dominant-minority interaction. Many situations are quite complex and defy a single causative explanation. Other instances do show recurring patterns; in these cases, given an understanding of their limitations, theories such as those proposed by Park, Lieberson, Blauner, and Bonacich can provide some insights into the minority experience.

ETHNIC CONSCIOUSNESS

Sociologists have long been interested in the attitudinal and behavioral patterns that emerge when people migrate into a society with a different culture. For example, what factors encourage or discourage ethnic self-awareness or maintenance of one's culture? If succeeding generations supposedly identify less with their country of origin, how do we explain the resurgence of ethnicity among white ethnics in recent years? Are there ethnic differentials in social mobility, social change, and behavior patterns even among third-generation Americans? Sociologists have frequently raised these questions, and a number of sociological theories have been offered in an effort to synthesize the diversity of the ethnic experience.

COUNTRY OF ORIGIN AS A FACTOR

Mary Sengstock believes that focusing on the relationship between the migrant and the country of origin will lead to a better understanding of the degree of assimilation.[18] She contends that the assumption that a migrant group is affected primarily by factors in the receiving country is wrong. This may have been more true of those groups that came here prior to the First World War, when transportation and communication were limited. Furthermore, immigration restrictions in the 1920s sharply curtailed the number of new immigrants, and the assimilation process was less impeded when newcomers were not arriving to reinforce the language and customs of the old country. In today's world, however, an immigrant group can maintain contact with the country of origin not only through air-mail letters but, more importantly, through long-distance telephone calls, rapid transportation, and the continued arrival of newcomers. The Mexican and Puerto Rican communities benefit from geographical proximity, and the mother country can exert more influence over its emigrants than in years past. Where there is greater social contact, cultural transmission is also greater.

The degree of stability or social change in the homeland will have a profound effect on the migrant community's sociocultural patterns and life style.

> Where the country of origin has experienced a relatively stable or gradually changing culture, the effect on the immigrant community will most likely be to encourage retention of the ethnic culture. This is much the same case as has occurred with Puerto Ricans and Mexican-Americans.
>
> Some societies, however, have experienced drastic changes in recent years. When groups of immigrants from such areas experience constant immigration and other types of contact with the mother country, one might expect such contact to produce profound effects on the immigrant community as well.[19]

Sengstock uses a study of Chaldean immigrants from Iraq who settled in Detroit both before and after the Second World War to illustrate her position. Iraq is now an independent nation-state, not a colonial land of different tribes all under the control of another nation. It is struggling to replace centuries-old tribal rivalries with the unity of nationalism. The changes have reached the Detroit community through visitors and immigrants.

> Recent immigrants are less likely to exhibit the traditional family orientation of their predecessors. They are more likely to exhibit the bureaucratic, urban, secular characteristics of the modern nation-state Iraq now is. They are also more likely to identify themselves as Iraqis or Arabs than were the early immigrants. . . . It seems likely that the "modern" pattern will eventually be the established pattern in the Detroit community, since the older immigrants remain the sole repository for the village tradition, and most of them are well advanced in age.[20]

As the Chaldeans illustrate, it appears that recent immigrants who have more education and more experience with urban settings and bureaucracies will be more likely to interact with others. Thus willingness to extend one's social contacts to members of other groups could, suggests Sengstock, produce a more "assimilable" group.

The social structure of an immigrant group's country of origin, then, may help to explain both nationalistic sentiment and social interaction with others in the adopted country.

THE THREE-GENERATION HYPOTHESIS

Historian Marcus Hansen conceptualized a normal pattern of ethnic revival in what he called the "Law of the Return of the Third Generation."[21] The third generation, more secure in its socioeconomic status and American identity, becomes interested in the ethnic heritage that the second generation neglected in its efforts to overcome discrimination and marginality. Simply stated, "What the child wishes to forget, the grandchild wishes to remember." Hansen, who based his conclusions mainly upon Midwestern Swedish-Americans, reaffirmed his position several years later:

> Whenever any immigrant group reaches the third-generation stage in its development a spontaneous and almost irresistible impulse arises which forces the thoughts of many people of different professions, different positions in life and different points of view to interest themselves in that one factor which they have in common: heritage — the heritage of blood.[22]

What Hansen was suggesting here is a pattern in the fall and rise of ethnic identity in succeeding generations of Americans. His hypothesis generated extensive discussion in the academic community, resulting in studies and commentaries that both supported and criticized his views.

SUPPORTERS AND DETRACTORS   Some early studies, using religion as a major criterion of ethnicity, found evidence of continuing or revitalized ethnic consciousness. Ruby Jo Reeves Kennedy's findings of religious endogamy despite intermarriage across national origin lines led her to conclude that assimilation in the United States followed one of three religious routes: a "triple melting pot" pattern.[23] In other words, consciousness of national origin declined, but consciousness of religion remained. Critics of the triple melting pot thesis pointed to places where religious intermarriage does occur, particularly those locations where the Jewish or Catholic population is a very small segment of the community.[24]

Will Herberg blended the Kennedy and Hansen hypotheses into a construct that stressed religion rather than national origin as the basis for a third-generation ethnic revival.[25] Many critics have argued that national-origin endogamy can be just as strong as religious endogamy in many areas. Low national-origin intermarriage rates among Catholics,[26] ethnically balanced political tickets,[27] and the flourishing of many ethnic associations[28] all point to ethnic consciousness regarding national origin.

CONFLICTING FINDINGS   In a study of Irish and Italian Catholics in Providence, Rhode Island, John Goering had mixed results.[29] He found that ethnic consciousness was steadily declining in succeeding generations in some respects, but emerging in a negative sense in other respects as a backlash to the black civil rights movement and the hippie phenomenon. He concluded that this ethnic revival was "less as a source of cultural or religious refreshment than as the basis for organizing the skepticism associated with discontent and racial confrontation."[30] Another interesting observation by Goering was that the ideology of the first- and second-generation Irish- and Italian-Americans living in the ethnic ghetto is more "American" and tolerant of American society than that of the third generation living outside the ghetto:

> Ethnicity is not clearly perceived in the ghetto. The boundaries of the ghetto became the boundaries of the real world. The awareness of ethnicity, and its divisiveness, comes with the "children of the uprooted." All forms of ethnic consciousness are not associated with the ethnic ghetto.[31]

These comments are similar to "Hansen's law" in that they assume that the second generation perceives its ethnicity as a disadvantage in

being accepted in American society. However, Goering perceives growing ethnic awareness not as a progression but as a regression to the "se-
clusiveness of ethnicity in resentment against unattained promises."[32]

Neil Sandburg's study, cited in the section on Polish-Americans,
found that subjects in the Los Angeles area tended to be less ethnic over
several generations.[33] Other writers have suggested that events in one's
homeland or the situation of one's fellow ethnics in other parts of the
world may heighten ethnic awareness.[34]

Perhaps one of the most comprehensive rebuttals of the three-
generation hypothesis was that of Harold Abramson, who argued that
the many dimensions of ethnic diversity preclude any macrosocial
theory about ethnic consciousness.[35] In addition to differences in time
period, which may have influenced the experience, adjustment, and intergenerational conflict or consensus of ethnic groups, there is also a
diversity within the groups themselves. Possibly only the better educated among each ethnic group, being in wider contact with the outside
world and more ambivalent about their identity, experience an ethnic
resurgence, while the majority have quietly progressed in some steady
fashion. The enormous variability of the American social structure also
affects what will happen to the grandchildren of all ethnic groups.

> Here I am talking about the diversity of region, of social stratifica-
> tion, of urban and rural settlement. In other words, the immigrants
> of Old and New and continuing migrations, the blacks of the North
> and the South, the native American Indians, all experience their en-
> counters with America under vastly different conditions. The
> French-Canadians in depressed mill towns of New England, the
> Hungarians and Czechs in company coal towns of Pennsylvania,
> and the Chicanos in migrant labor fields of California, do not ex-
> perience the social mobility or social change of the Irish in Boston
> politics, the Jews in the garment industry of New York, or the
> Japanese in the professions of Hawaii. Not only are there traditional
> cultural factors to explain these phenomena, but there are structural
> reasons of settlement, region, and the local composition of the
> ethnic mosaic as well.[36]

Additionally, the responses of different traditional cultures to the forces
of society vary. For example, the Irish and Italians have different levels
of attachment to Catholicism. Persisting diversity makes it difficult to
describe the American experience in any generalized manner.

THE WHITE ETHNIC REVIVAL

In the late 1960s and 1970s some observers noted an increased ethnic
consciousness among urban Catholic groups, whom they categorized as
"white ethnics." Some, like Goering,[37] saw this as a backlash to the ef-

forts of blacks, hippies, and liberals. Others, such as Andrew Greeley, saw it as an affirmation of Hansen's law.[38] Greeley suggested that the final stage of assimilation included the new generation's interest in its heritage. It had nothing to do with the militant black and Indian social movements, since that was an earlier stage in the assimilation process. Greeley attributed the white ethnic revival to the last phase, when Hansen's law becomes operative. The third generation has a strong interest in the cultural and artistic background of their ethnic tradition. They take trips to the old country out of curiosity and occasional "amused compassion." Greeley saw this increased ethnic awareness as a deliberate, self-conscious effort among young ethnics.[39]

Michael Novak interpreted the ethnic revival not as a part of the assimilation process but as evidence of "unmeltable ethnics," or pluralism.[40] He noted that many working-class ethnics resented the limitations the Protestant Establishment imposed upon their realization of the American Dream.

> Ordinary workers ... resent the liberties, privileges, wealth, and securities of the professional elites based in the universities. They also resent the actual, daily contacts of their own culture with black culture. No amount of good will, theory, or ideology blinds them to the actual experience of that contact: it is very often characterized by economic penalties for both whites and blacks, by rising violence and conflict, by insolence and insult, by mutual stereotype and prejudice.[41]

According to Novak, it is the Anglo-Saxon Protestant, not the working-class ethnic, who harbors strong anti-black sentiment. The white ethnics have discovered their solidarity not for use against blacks, but as a necessary and effective weapon against the established power, which ignores their problems, such as inflation, unemployment, and declining neighborhoods. All of this is to the good, Novak claims, for this ethnic pride allows these groups to feel more a part of America.

> In any case, millions of Americans, who for a long time tried desperately even unconsciously to become "Americanized," are delighted to discover that they no longer have to pay that price; are grateful that they were born among the people destiny placed them in; are pleased to discover the possibilities and the limits inherent in being who they are; and are openly happy about what heretofore they had disguised in silence. There is a creativity and new release, there is liberation, and there is hope.
>
> America is becoming America.[42]

The resiliency of ethnic consciousness makes it endure, observes Perry Weed.[43] Many people have erroneously assumed that acculturation eliminates ethnic identity, but it persists, sometimes intensifies, and has meaning into and beyond the third generation. The majority of ethnic Americans, now that pluralism is tolerated, are recognizing that they have not lost their foreign identity or ethnic consciousness. Many factors have contributed to preserving ethnicity:

> A high level of nationality consciousness has always been maintained by the churches, local newspapers and political organizations wherever there are large concentrations of ethnic groups. Both immigrant neighborhoods and residential movement demonstrate that ethnics prefer to live among those who share their cultural heritage and immigrant experience.[44]

A DISSENTING VIEW   Not everyone agrees that there is a resurgence of ethnicity. Some see the apparent resurgence either as a temporary adjustment, similar to others in the past, or as a much more limited phenomenon. One notable sociologist who has taken this position is Herbert Gans. As one who has long taken exception to the three-generation hypothesis, Gans has seen a steadily diminishing ethnic consciousness and progressive social and cultural assimilation among American Jews[45] and in an Italian-American community in Boston.[46] Gans believes that the so-called ethnic revival is a misnomer, much like the so-called religious revival of the mid-1950s, when many churches and synagogues were constructed in the new suburbs.[47] Since, by and large, American ethnicity today is a working-class ethnicity, ethnic politics is actually an interethnic grouping of members of the same social class to achieve desired goals.

> One reason is the decline of Irish and WASP control of American politics, and the political mobility of Italian-Americans, Polish-Americans, and others into important local and national positions. This political mobility has been developing for a long time and has more to do with the fact that many members of these ethnic groups have achieved middle class status, and thus economic power and political power, than with a new ethnic consciousness. . . .
>
> Second, and far more important, the urban and suburban white working class has also achieved more political power in the last few years, and since many of the members of that class are Catholic ethnics, their new influence has been falsely ascribed to a newly emerging ethnic pride. What has actually happened is that for the first time in a long time, the white working class has become politically visible, but their demands have been labeled as ethnic rather than working class.[48]

Gans sees the so-called ethnic revival as being popularized by a new group of Catholic intellectuals, such as Greeley and Novak. As members of a small academic community that has sometimes had to face covert discrimination from the academic establishment, they may well be expressing their own ethnic consciousness rather than that of all or even many members of their ethnic group. Perhaps, concludes Gans, Hansen's law really applies only to academics and intellectuals, among whom most of the scholarly and theoretical discussions occur, not to the majority of ethnic peoples.

AN ALTERNATIVE VIEW   Recently some sociologists have argued that ethnicity should be regarded not as an ascribed attribute with only the two discrete categories of assimilation and pluralism, but as a continuous variable.[49] In a review of the recent literature, William L. Yancey, Eugene P. Ericksen, and Richard N. Juliani conclude that ethnic behavior is conditioned by occupation, residence, and institutional affiliation — the structural situations in which groups have found themselves. The "old" immigrants, migrating before the Industrial Revolution, had a more dispersed residential pattern than did the "new" immigrants, who were "bunched together" because of concentrated large-scale urban employment and the need for low-cost housing near the place of employment. Similarly, when immigrants arrived, they were drawn to the areas of economic expansion, and the *migration chains* — the subsequent arrival of relatives and friends — continued the concentrated settlement pattern.

> The Germans and Irish, who were earlier immigrants, concentrated in the older cities such as Philadelphia and St. Louis. By contrast, the new immigrants from Poland, Italy and Russia concentrated in Buffalo, Cleveland, Detroit and Milwaukee, as well as in some of the older cities with expanding opportunities. Different migration patterns occurred for immigrants with and without skills. . . . Rewards for skilled occupations were greater, and the skilled immigrant went to the cities where there were opportunities to practice his trade. Less highly skilled workers went to the cities with expanding opportunities. Thus, the Italian concentration in construction and the Polish in steel were related to the expansion of these industries as these groups arrived. The Jewish concentration in the garment industry may have been a function of their previous experience as tailors, but it is also dependent upon the emergence of the mass production of clothing in the late nineteenth century.[50]

Like Gans, these authors conclude that group consciousness is generated and becomes crystallized within the work relationships, common residential areas, interests, and life styles of working-class conditions. Moreover, normal communication and participation in ethnic organizations on a cosmopolitan level can reinforce ethnic identity even among residentially dispersed groups.[51] This "situational ethnicity" may be characterized by such things as:

church and synagogue attendance, marching in a St. Patrick's or Columbus Day parade, voting for a political candidate of a similar ethnicity, or supporting a political cause associated with the country of origin, such as the emigration of Russian Jews to Israel or the reunification of Ireland.[52]

Three observations are of interest to the student in this alternative view: (1) the importance of structural conditions, such as predetermined residential or occupational choices; (2) the existence of ethnic networks among geographically dispersed groups; and (3) ethnicity as the result of a process that continues to unfold, not a constant ascribed trait inherited from the past.

Stanford M. Lyman and William A. Douglass believe that social process offers a more dynamic conception of race and ethnicity, but they suggest that such processes are not necessarily unidirectional or evolutionary, leading to acculturation and assimilation.[53] Instead, there are several different possible strategies as contending ethnic groups attempt to adjust to one another.

A minority might attempt to: (1) become fully incorporated into the larger society; (2) participate actively in the public life of the larger society while retaining significant aspects of its own cultural identity; (3) emphasize ethnic identity in the creation of new social positions and patterned activities not formerly found within the society; (4) retain confederational ties with the larger society at the same time that it secures territorial and communal control for itself; (5) secede from the larger society and form a new state or enter into the plural structure of another state; (6) establish its own hegemony over the society in which it lives.[54]

Not all of these strategies have been used in the United States, but any or all of them may lead to problems and disruption in a pluralistic society. Each of these strategies, it should be added, is in dialectical relationship with patterns in the larger society; a minority's "choice" is heavily dependent upon these prevailing patterns.

ETHNIC BEHAVIOR

Some sociologists, like Gordon and Gans, think that social class is more important than ethnicity. They believe that people of different ethnic backgrounds but the same social class tend to act similarly, more so than people of the same ethnic background but different social classes.[55] Others believe that ethnic differences lead to differences in behavior. Numerous studies have been undertaken to test these hypotheses.

BOX 11.2

REASONS FOR ETHNIC CONSCIOUSNESS

COUNTRY OF ORIGIN

1. Psychological nearness through rapid communications and transportation
2. Geographical proximity
3. Degree of stability or social change in the homeland
4. Social contact with recent immigrants

THREE-GENERATION HYPOTHESIS

1. Second generation emphasizes American ways and neglects own heritage
2. Third generation rediscovers ethnic identity

OTHER EXPLANATIONS

1. Religion replaces national origin as basis of identity
2. Ethnicity less perceived in ethnic community than in real world
3. Outside events may heighten ethnic awareness
4. Only better educated of a group become ethnically self-conscious
5. Variations in time, social structure, and within ethnic groups encourage different types of responses

WHITE ETHNIC REVIVAL

1. Backlash to efforts of blacks, hippies, and liberals
2. Affirmation of Hansen's law
3. Discovery of group consciousness as a reaction to social and economic problems
4. Resiliency of ethnic identity even through acculturation
5. Revival is a misnomer; it is really a temporary structural adjustment reflecting attainment of some political power by working-class ethnics
6. Really a situational ethnicity because of changed structural conditions

---

REACTIONS TO PAIN

In interviewing male patients in a veterans' hospital, Mark Zborowski found some notable differences in responses to pain among Irish, Italians,

Jews, and "Old Americans" (white Protestants).[56] Although definitive patterns emerged, he noted that there were individual differences
within each group as a result of social class, personality differences,
generation (first-, second-, or third-generation American), or the nature
of the disease. Zborowski observed that although these differences affected behavior, the attitudes toward pain were relatively consistent
within each group.

Old Americans suffer pain privately, neither crying nor complaining
because it does no good and they do not want pity. They consider the
body a machine in the hands of a skilled professional; so they prefer
being in a hospital, have confidence in their treatment, and are optimistic about the future. The Irish are also stoic about pain, and almost non-
communicative, making few complaints and forcing the doctor to probe
further to learn the symptoms. For the Irish, pain is a test of manhood,
and they look upon it as a unique personal challenge. The Old American, on the other hand, views pain as useless except as a warning signal
of mechanical failure.

Zborowski found both Italians and Jews to be emotional about pain, to
cry openly and unashamedly, and to believe that pain is something social, something that should be shared with family and friends. Jews are
more skeptical of doctors than are the other three groups, and are interested in the precise diagnosis, something the Old American is reluctant to know. Jews are pessimistic about their health and afraid to take
drugs lest they be habit-forming or mask the source of the pain. Italians
are more present-oriented, and for them the pain is what is important.
Its relief greatly affects their mood, and this buoyancy, along with their
belief that dependency is normal in such a situation, makes them favorite patients among the nurses. Zborowski suggests that these attitudinal
differences are the result of cultural variances in the socialization
process, ranging from parental overprotectiveness to the stressing of
self-reliance.

HOMELAND INFLUENCE

In a 1974 study, Andrew M. Greeley and William C. McCready attempted to measure the extent to which ethnic differences among Irish,
Italians, and Anglo-Saxons are predictable from cultural patterns in the
country of origin.[57] They tested 45 hypotheses comparing personality
variables, political participation, drinking behavior, and sexual attitudes. The hypotheses, established on the basis of the sociological literature about the three homelands, were proven correct 22 times — a
statistically significant level. Six cases, primarily concerning the Irish,
were statistically significant in the opposite direction.

Both Irish and Italians were more fatalistic than Anglo-Saxons. Italians and Anglo-Saxons were more similar in such personality variables as trust, anxiety, conformity, and being authoritarian and moralistic, while the Irish scored lower in these categories. Irish-Americans proved to be the most active politically (in voting, campaigning, and civic activities), Italian-Americans the least active, and Anglo-Saxons in between. The Irish also respected democratic processes much more than did the Anglo-Saxons, who in turn held them in higher regard than did the Italians. Italians were much more conservative in their drinking behavior and more sexually restrictive than either the Irish or the Anglo-Saxons, who tended to be more alike in these areas. The fact that there are similarities and differences among the three groups was just as important to the researchers as the distinctions themselves:

> What have we demonstrated with our exploratory research? It is apparent that we can no longer believe that there are no important differences among native Americans, Irish Americans, and Italian Americans. We are not all alike. On the other hand, we cannot believe that ours is a mosaic society in which differences among the three groups are to be expected on almost every variable. The truth seems to be somewhere in between. We are both alike and different.
>
> ... If one assumes (and many commentators in American life seem to have made this assumption) that European heritages of the American ethnic groups are irrelevant to an understanding of the present attitudes and behaviors of such groups, one can find very little substantiation in the research reported here. The European heritage may not be *all* important, but it is important, probably more so than many of us would have thought.[58]

Michael Novak makes much the same point when he comments on the uniqueness of cultural influences upon particular ethnic groups. It would appear, according to these observers, that subcultural variables tend to shape differences in attitude and behavior in certain areas, although not uniformly throughout an entire group.

> When a person thinks, more than one generation's passions and images think in him. Below the threshold of the rational or the fully conscious, our instincts and sensibilities lead backwards to the predilections of our forebears. More deeply than Americans have been taught to recognize, their own particular pasts live on in their present judgments and actions.[59]

OTHER FACTORS

Obviously, the preceding sections cover only a few aspects of ethnic behavior. Others, such as dating and marriage patterns, male-female relationships, child-rearing practices, actions toward outsiders, education, religion, authority, occupations, eating, drinking, and socializing, are all at least partially dependent upon cultural orientations. If all important forms of social behavior are learned, and if culture shapes our learning experience, then it follows that certain forms of behavior will differ among groups according to cultural variances. To that degree most of us can accept certain generalizations about differences in ethnic behavior.

When we discuss ethnic behavior in any sense, however, we must consider several factors. Is the behavior we are attempting to analyze a reflection of culture, social class, the particular situation only, the prevailing attitudinal climate, or some combination of these or other factors? Does this behavior generally prevail among all members of the group, or is there variance within the group itself? If so, why? Would another ethnic group behave in the same way under the same set of conditions? Is there a more universal explanation for behavioral differences? That is, are behavioral differences attributable to certain idiosyncrasies of one group, or would other groups who shared similar visibility, deprivation, discrimination, generational seniority in America, and rural, tribal, or village life orientations behave in the same fashion? Or is the answer to be found in certain subcultural values and attitudes that are transmitted from one generation to the next despite whatever acculturation or assimilation may have occurred?

These are provocative questions, and not all of them can be easily answered. The basic question is whether it is the degree of minority integration into the society or inherent minority characteristics that determines any ethnic variations in behavior. Some research suggests that there are both similarities and differences among various ethnic groups. More research must be done before we can know the reason for behavioral differences among ethnic groups with any degree of certainty.

ETHNIC STRATIFICATION

Some groups, like the blacks, Hispanics, and American Indians, have received much attention; those findings are reported in the chapters in this book dealing with each specific group. For other ethnic groups, the data are limited, both in frequency of reporting and in recording generational change. Much of the information from the Census Bureau is limited to foreign-born and foreign stock (at least one parent born in another country). Thus the third generation is not broadly measured, except in the regional studies done by social scientists. Also, the Department of Labor's measurement of occupational position and shift does not specifically measure ethnic movement except by race and for

Hispanics. Moreover, many of the more recent Third World immigrants have yet to be included in the data that are collected. Perhaps the 1980 census data will be more helpful. Understanding the limitations, the reader can gain at least a partial insight into the present composition of many ethnic groups in comparison with one another with respect to age, years of schooling, and income.

AGE

Table 11.1 gives the median age of numerous ethnic groups, arranged in descending order by age of those of foreign stock. The median age partly reflects twentieth-century migration patterns, with European immigrants more heavily distributed in the upper age levels and Asian and Western Hemisphere peoples at the lower age levels. One unusual note is the low median age of the German foreign-born in comparison with those from other European countries. The relative youth of certain groups suggests that through marriage and child-bearing those particular ethnic groups will continue to grow in number whether or not immigration continues, depending upon the strength of national endogamy patterns in marriage.

EDUCATION

Recent immigrants from the Western Hemisphere, except those from Mexico, are quite comparable to other groups in years of schooling completed (Table 11.2). Mexico's low position can be partly explained by its geographic nearness and by homeland conditions that encourage poorly educated laborers to seek jobs in the United States, as they have for generations. Laborers from other countries in this hemisphere have little money for transportation. Cultural influences and peak immigration periods help to explain some of the education levels. For example, the Jews (many of whom come from the Soviet Union), Greeks, Chinese and Japanese have traditionally encouraged education for their young. Secondly, as shown in Table 11.1 on median age, many of the second-generation Americans from European countries are considerably older, because of earlier migration patterns, and probably obtained their schooling at a time when a high school diploma was not considered as important as it is today. Economic needs and cultural orientations may also have been important factors limiting their educational attainment. Also, the disparity in educational levels, particularly among the native-born of foreign or mixed parentage, is not especially great. Most groups are quite close in total education received.

TABLE 11.1

MEDIAN AGE BY COUNTRY OF ORIGIN, 1970

COUNTRY OF ORIGIN	NATIVE BORN OF FOREIGN OR MIXED PARENTAGE	FOREIGN BORN
Sweden	58.6	70.5
Germany	58.3	49.6
Norway	57.3	67.2
Denmark	56.4	65.9
Ireland	54.7	61.8
Austria	52.3	68.3
Lithuania	52.0	68.1
Czechoslovakia	51.0	65.2
U.S.S.R.	50.6	68.8
Poland	50.2	64.5
Hungary	49.0	62.8
United Kingdom	48.5	54.6
Italy	46.6	63.2
Netherlands	46.4	47.6
Yugoslavia	45.5	55.2
France	45.1	45.3
Canada	40.2	50.8
Japan	38.3	39.5
Greece	37.6	45.4
Mexico	22.9	37.9
West Indies, except Cuba	18.5	34.4
China	17.9	38.4
Central and South America	10.7	30.7
Cuba	8.8	36.3
All Other	40.8	41.2
U.S. — All Countries	47.3	52.0

SOURCE: U.S. Bureau of the Census, *1970 Census of the Population: National Origin and Language*, Vol. 2, Table 10, pp. 66–71, June 1973.

POVERTY

The most recent available data reporting families below the poverty level by country of origin (Table 11.3) contain a few surprises. Most notable is the comparatively high level of poverty among the Japanese, who for years have been stereotyped as socioeconomically one of the

TABLE 11.2

YEARS OF SCHOOLING COMPLETED BY COUNTRY OF ORIGIN
FOR ADULTS AGED 25 OR OLDER, 1970

Country of origin	MALE		FEMALE	
	Native born	Foreign born	Native born	Foreign born
U.S.S.R.	12.8	8.7	12.5	8.4
Greece	12.8	8.7	12.5	7.7
Central and South America	12.7	12.5	12.5	12.1
China	12.7	12.4	12.7	10.6
Japan	12.6	12.6	12.5	12.2
United Kingdom	12.4	12.3	12.3	12.2
West Indies, except Cuba	12.4	11.7	12.4	10.4
Ireland	12.3	9.4	12.2	9.1
Lithuania	12.3	8.9	12.2	7.8
Canada	12.2	11.4	12.2	11.7
Cuba	12.2	11.3	12.0	9.2
Austria	12.2	8.8	12.1	8.6
Yugoslavia	12.2	8.4	12.1	8.0
France	12.1	12.4	12.1	12.3
Hungary	12.1	10.4	12.1	8.5
Sweden	12.1	8.7	12.2	8.9
Denmark	12.0	10.3	12.2	11.2
Italy	11.9	7.3	11.7	6.6
Poland	11.8	8.4	11.3	7.8
Czechoslovakia	11.6	8.8	11.3	8.5
Netherlands	11.4	12.1	11.8	11.2
Norway	11.3	8.9	12.2	8.9
Mexico	9.4	5.8	9.0	5.8
All Other	12.2	12.2	12.2	11.3
U.S. — All Countries	12.1	9.3	12.1	9.0

SOURCE: U.S. Bureau of the Census, *1970 Census of the Population: National Origin and Language*, Vol. 2, Table 12, pp. 98–123, June 1973.

most successful groups. Also, the relatively high poverty levels of immigrant families from this hemisphere would seem to suggest that, for them at least, there is little correlation between schooling and income. The consistently high percentages for immigrants who arrived before 1925 reflect both the elderly immigrant poor living in the cities and those on small, fixed retirement incomes. What additional support they receive from their children determines greatly their present quality of life.

Not only are there variances between ethnic groups, but there are also variances within the groups themselves. Immigrants continue to come to the United States from all countries, and so each group has its newcomers and its older contingent. Structural conditions in both the host country and the sending countries continually change. Not all immigrants enter the United States at the bottom of the socioeconomic ladder, and not all desire to assimilate. Many recent immigrants have in fact attained better occupational positions than many of the immigrants who preceded them. This is partly because the changed immigration laws give preferential treatment to professionals and skilled workers, and partly a result of occupational shifts and social change throughout much of the world.

WHITE ETHNIC STRATIFICATION

In a composite study of almost 18,000 respondents, Andrew M. Greeley reported some surprising findings in his comparisons of non-Spanish-speaking white ethnics.[60] In terms of occupational stratification and occupational mobility, Jews, Episcopalians, and Presbyterians were the most successful of all religious groups. In terms of educational stratification, the same three groups rank first, second, and third, respectively, but in terms of educational mobility the most successful are Jews, Catholics, and Presbyterians, in that order. For average income, Jews, Catholics, and Episcopalians are in the first three positions, and the standard deviation is far greater among Episcopalians and Presbyterians than for other groups, indicating a much wider range in income levels.

When Greeley refined the data to control for both religion and nationality, the rank order in terms of family income in 1974 was Jews, Irish Catholics, Italian Catholics, German Catholics, Polish Catholics, Episcopalians, Presbyterians, Slavic Catholics, British Protestants, French Catholics, Methodists, German Protestants, Lutherans, Scandinavian Protestants, "American" Protestants, Irish Protestants, Baptists. When only northern metropolitan regions are considered, the Catholic groups do even better. This ranking contrasts with the prevailing stereotype of wealthy WASPs and working-class Catholic ethnic groups. According to this study, the Jewish and Catholic ethnic groups have surpassed the older Protestant ethnic groups in terms of average family income.

One stratification expert, David Featherman, pointed to several misleading interpretations by Greeley.[61] Most importantly, he stresses that Greeley uses family income as a measure of economic achievement and

TABLE 11.3

PERCENT OF FAMILIES BELOW POVERTY LEVEL
BY COUNTRY OF ORIGIN AND YEAR OF IMMIGRATION
BASED ON INCOME FOR 1969

| | | YEAR OF ARRIVAL IN U.S. | | | |
Country of origin	All years	1965–1970	1960–1964	1950–1954	Before 1925
Mexico	26.1	32.3	24.6	26.9	26.3
Japan	17.1	13.6	33.4	18.3	12.8
Cuba	13.1	22.3	7.5	7.8	13.7
West Indies, except Cuba	12.1	13.0	10.0	11.1	14.7
Central & South America	11.6	17.6	7.6	6.5	11.4
China	11.1	21.3	8.4	8.2	19.0
Czechoslovakia	10.9	16.5	6.0	4.5	14.2
France	10.6	16.0	11.9	6.6	11.2
Italy	10.6	10.2	4.7	5.3	13.8
Austria	10.4	5.7	6.9	9.2	12.9
Sweden	10.3	4.8	11.5	5.7	11.9
Greece	9.9	10.3	6.4	7.0	14.7
Denmark	9.7	7.4	4.9	7.0	13.3
U.S.S.R.	9.6	11.5	2.3	5.5	11.0
Norway	9.2	3.4	4.3	1.0	12.6
Lithuania	9.2	—	2.5	—	14.6
Germany	8.8	15.1	12.6	6.8	12.3
Yugoslavia	8.5	13.3	2.6	4.8	12.8
Poland	8.4	6.7	3.1	4.7	11.4
Netherlands	8.3	9.5	5.8	5.0	13.7
Hungary	7.6	10.9	7.8	5.6	11.4
United Kingdom	7.2	7.2	7.6	7.2	8.4
Canada	6.7	7.1	5.7	4.6	8.0
Ireland	6.2	6.9	4.7	4.8	8.5
All Other	10.2	14.9	7.3	6.0	12.8
U.S.— All Countries	10.9	16.1	9.6	8.1	12.7

SOURCE: U.S. Bureau of the Census, *1970 Census of the Population: National Origin and Language*, Vol. 2, Table 14, pp. 150–175, June 1973.

ambition. There is a difference in occupational achievement between income from the full-time employment of the household head only and income from the simultaneous employment of several family members, even if some work only part-time. Larger immigrant families have more potential earners. Higher income from overtime employment taken out of economic necessity or from blue collar union power does not necessarily imply occupational achievement either. Moreover, says Featherman, the data actually show that "few substantive educational and occupational differences remain among white, non-Spanish groups once the disadvantages and advantages of social backgrounds are controlled."[62] Featherman disputes Greeley's interpretation that Catholics have "made it big" economically, instead seeing them from the same data as very close to the national average. Both men agree that many white ethnic groups and denominations have been generally integrated into the American economy.

Each racial and ethnic group is represented at all levels of income, and so one must also be careful in discussing the average incomes Greeley reports. Also, since that study did not include Asians, Indians, Hispanics, and blacks, it does not give a complete picture of ethnic stratification. Increasing intermarriage by national origin, religion, and race, in declining order of frequency, further complicates the measurement of ethnic occupational distribution.

In June 1979, Stanley Lieberson and Donna K. Carter used the rates of inclusion in Who's Who between 1924 and 1974 as a measure of assimilation and achievement of blacks and five white ethnic groups.[63] Since 1944 Jews have moved significantly ahead of the English, who are closely followed by the Scandinavians. Italians and Slavs have also significantly increased their representation, and all five groups are becoming similar. Blacks rank lowest, sharply different from the whites, but have been moving upward since 1944.

IMMIGRANT OCCUPATIONS

Table 11.4 shows, except for a fairly stable level for craftspeople, a gradual upward trend in the percentages of professional and technical workers among immigrants. However, the number of immigrants reporting no occupation now exceeds 50 percent, compared with 26 percent in 1901–1910. This is partly explained by the great numbers of males who came here either as sojourners or ahead of their families in the early twentieth century; fewer dependents came over then. Also, the immigration laws now favor relatives joining the immigrants already here. Then too, for many, it was simpler to report being farm laborers when the entire family participated in that endeavor.

The extent to which other countries begin, continue, or cease to send large numbers of immigrants will partially determine the cultural impact of these immigrants upon American society. Moreover, as different

TABLE 11.4

OCCUPATIONAL DISTRIBUTION OF IMMIGRANTS, 1900–1970

PERIOD	PROFESSIONAL, TECHNICAL, ETC.	CLERICAL, SALES, ETC.	CRAFTSMEN, FOREMEN, OPERATORS, ETC.	LABORERS EXC. FARM	MISC.[a]	NO OCCUPATION
1961–1970	10.2	7.4	11.1	3.9	11.6	55.9
1951–1960	7.3	7.8	14.4	5.3	12.3	52.8
1941–1950	7.9	7.9	13.3	2.4	13.8	54.7
1931–1940	7.2	4.5	8.1	3.6	18.5	58.1
1921–1930	2.7	4.3	14.4	15.0	24.3	39.2
1911–1920	1.7	2.0	12.9	17.9	35.9	29.6
1901–1910	1.0	1.1	13.2	26.1	32.9	25.7

[a]Includes farmers, farm managers, managers, officials, proprietors, private household workers, service workers, farm laborers, and farm foremen.

SOURCE: U.S. Department of Commerce, Bureau of the Census, "We Are the American Foreign Born," June 1973, p. 13.

parts of the world become primary sending areas, the interests of the newly naturalized citizens, and in turn American foreign policy, become increasingly involved in developments in those parts of the world. Table 11.5 shows the leading suppliers of immigrants since 1820, and Table 11.6 shows some recent changes in immigration patterns. The first table shows the past dominance of countries from Europe and the Western Hemisphere in the total numbers, while the second table shows the impact of the current immigration law, with significant shifts in country representation among the leaders. Many immigrants still come from European countries, but there has been a decided increase in the number of immigrants from Asia. As the chain migration process occurs among these immigrants, it is reasonable to assume that there will continue to be large numbers of them among the strangers coming to these shores.

RETROSPECT

The ethnic experience in the United States has been vast and complex. This nation of immigrants has substantial diversity within its population, which has sometimes resulted in antagonism and conflict. Some have struggled to overcome their ethnicity, and others have struggled to preserve theirs, but all have fought to make a better life for themselves and their families in the new country.

TABLE 11.5

LEADING SUPPLIERS OF EMIGRANTS TO THE UNITED STATES, 1820–1977

1. Germany	6,968,216
2. Italy	5,285,354
3. Ireland	4,722,356
4. Austria/Hungary[a]	4,314,266
5. Canada and Newfoundland	4,077,771
6. U.S.S.R.	3,366,886
7. England	3,160,595
8. Mexico	2,014,951
9. West Indies	1,583,720
10. Sweden	1,271,113
11. Norway	855,968
12. Scotland	818,899

[a]Data for Austria/Hungary was not reported until 1861. Austria and Hungary have been reported separately since 1905. From 1938 to 1945, Austria is included in figures for Germany.
SOURCE: U.S. Immigration and Naturalization Service, *Annual Report*, U.S. Government Printing Office, Washington, D.C., 1977, Table 13.

Many differences of opinion exist among sociologists concerning what changes have occurred in the immigrants' value orientations and behavior patterns and whether there is or is not a current ethnic revival, and if so, why. Certainly there is more scholarship and theoretical discussion on the matter than ever before, and many Americans have shown that they are interested in learning more about their own roots. Is this interest the result of curiosity arising out of better education, increased leisure time, affluence, and rapid transportation opportunities, or is it a rediscovery of ethnicity? Is it a temporary phenomenon or part of an ongoing process? Is it based on security in American identity or on uneasiness in a depersonalized society? And what of the new immigrants who have been coming here? What effect will they have upon American society? Will governmental acceptance of pluralism and such controversial practices as bilingual education improve or weaken the fabric of American society?

Most important of all, what kind of society are we becoming? Of the many possibilities, two distinct ones are a pluralistic society that is truly integrated in all respects, or a pluralistic society with the degree of integration dependent upon race and ethnicity. Which of these possibilities is likely to occur, and when? Is there an evolutionary process at work, or is government action necessary? In so complex and dynamic a subject as race and ethnic relations, with so many influencing vari-

TABLE 11.6

MAJOR SOURCES OF NEWCOMERS TO UNITED STATES

1965		1976	
1. Canada	38,327	1. Mexico	57,863
2. Mexico	37,969	2. Philippines	37,281
3. United Kingdom	27,358	3. Korea	30,803
4. Germany	24,045	4. Cuba	29,233
5. Cuba	19,760	5. China and Taiwan	18,823
6. Colombia	10,885	6. India	17,487
7. Italy	10,821	7. Dominican Republic	12,526
8. Dominican Republic	9,504	8. United Kingdom	11,392
9. Poland	8,465	9. Portugal	10,511
10. Argentina	6,124	10. Jamaica	9,026
11. Ireland	5,463	11. Greece	8,417
12. Ecuador	4,392	12. Italy	8,380
13. China and Taiwan	4,057	13. U.S.S.R.	8,220
14. France	4,039	14. Canada	7,638
15. Haiti	3,609	15. Thailand	6,923

SOURCE: U.S. Immigration and Naturalization Service, *Annual Report*, U.S. Government Printing Office, Washington, D.C., 1977, p. 8.

ables, discussing future directions is a challenge. Nevertheless, here are some observations relating to future possibilities:

1. Economic growth is a critical factor in curbing ethnic antagonism and absorbing more minority people into the mainstream of American life. In recent years illegal immigration has led to greater ethnic antagonism, particularly in the Southwest, when the economy has been unable to grow fast enough to absorb the illegal aliens. Moreover, a continuing pattern of illegal immigration also fans antagonism between the illegal and legal aliens with the same heritage who are competing for jobs, an issue over which the Chicano community is currently seriously split.

It would appear that a concentrated federal effort aimed at sustained economic growth, full employment, and urban revitalization would do much to reduce many of the tensions and problems of dominant-minority relations. When economic security for all U.S. residents replaces chronic unemployment, underemployment, dependency, hopelessness, frustration, and despair, then we will have eliminated one of the major causes of negative judgments and treatments of various racial and ethnic groups.

2. Many social scientists feel that more and more Americans are becoming aware of the pluralistic reality of American society and that often their own "hangups" cause them to be prejudiced. If this awareness becomes more widespread and can be translated into action, this may be the beginning of a truly integrated society.

3. It may be argued that heightened racial and ethnic self-awareness will ultimately lead to greater societal cohesion, not to divisiveness. The predominance of an Anglo-conformity assimilationist viewpoint worked to the disadvantage of those who were considered "different" or "unassimilable." An awareness of diversity and an insistence upon acceptance of one's own particular racial and ethnic identity will, hopefully, lead people to allow others that same prerogative. In time, greater tolerance for other groups might even lead to an appreciation of their differences.

4. Racism, which is relatively new in human history but as old as American history, is another critical factor in dominant-minority relations. America is no longer as racist a society as it once was, but it would be naive to think that this ideology has been overcome completely. Again, economic independence would seem to be a key means of overcoming much of the racial condemnation, as it has been to a large extent for the Chinese and Japanese.

5. Finally, young people seem to have an increasing tendency to relate to people as individuals rather than on the basis of race, religion, nationality, or even social class, although they remain interested in those factors. The degree to which that attitude spreads among others and is retained by the young people as they grow older will greatly determine what American society will become.

Economic growth, increased awareness of pluralism, and a greater tendency to relate to individuals as individuals may all allow the strangers in our midst to be perceived more favorably than their predecessors were. When the predominant attitude toward strangers becomes one of acceptance rather than suspicion, and when the newcomers are perceived as equals and sources of cultural enrichment rather than as inferiors and threats to the status quo, then race and ethnic relations will be more positive. Whether this ideal can ever become reality is questionable.

QUESTIONS FOR DISCUSSION

1. What are some of the recent theories that attempt to explain the course of dominant-minority relations? Which do you prefer? Why?
2. What are some of the explanations for the so-called ethnic consciousness of recent years? Which seems most plausible to you? Why?

3. What position do you take regarding the subject of ethnic behavior?

4. What does the stratified distribution of the various racial and ethnic groups say about their realization of the American Dream?

5. Discuss the future state of American society, based on present trends.

SUGGESTED READINGS

Eisenstadt, S. N. *The Absorption of Immigrants.* Routledge, London, 1954.

Glazer, Nathan, and Daniel P. Moynihan, *Ethnicity.* M.I.T., Cambridge, Mass., 1975.

Gordon, Milton M. *Assimilation in American Life.* Oxford University Press, New York, 1964.

Laumann, Edward O. *Bonds of Pluralism.* Wiley, New York, 1972.

Newman, William M. *American Plural-*ism. Harper & Row, New York, 1973.

Novak, Michael. *The Rise of the Unmeltable Ethnics.* Macmillan, New York, 1971.

Park, Robert E. *Race and Culture.* Free Press, Glencoe, Ill., 1950.

Te Selle, Sallie. *The Rediscovery of Ethnicity.* Harper-Colophon Books, New York, 1973.

Weed, Perry L. *The White Ethnic Movement and Ethnic Politics.* Praeger, New York, 1973.

NOTES

1. Edna Bonacich, "A Theory of Ethnic Antagonism: The Split Labor Market," *American Sociological Review,* 37 (October 1972), 549.
2. Robert E. Park, *Race and Culture,* Free Press, Glencoe, Ill., 1949.
3. Stanley Lieberson, "A Societal Theory of Race and Ethnic Relations," *American Sociological Review,* 26 (December 1961), 902–910.
4. Robert Blauner, "Internal Colonialism and Ghetto Revolt," *Social Problems,* 16 (Spring 1969), 393–406.
5. Bonacich, "A Theory of Ethnic Antagonism," pp. 547–559.
6. Park, *Race and Culture,* p. 150.
7. Seymour M. Lipset, "Changing Social Status and Prejudice: The Race Theories of a Pioneering American Sociologist," *Commentary,* 9 (May 1950), 479.
8. Stanford M. Lyman, *The Black American in Sociological Thought: A Failure of Perspective,* Putnam, New York, 1972, pp. 49–50.
9. Lieberson, "A Societal Theory of Race and Ethnic Relations," p. 904.
10. William J. Wilson, *Power, Racism, and Privilege,* Free Press, New York, 1973, pp. 47–65.
11. See Robin M. Williams, Jr., "The Reduction of Intergroup Tensions," *Social Science Research Council Bulletin,* 57 (1947), 61.
12. Blauner, "Internal Colonialism and Ghetto Revolt," p. 397.
13. Bonacich, "A Theory of Ethnic Antagonism," p. 554.
14. *Ibid.,* p. 550.
15. See Alexander Saxton, *The Indispensable Enemy: Labor and the Anti-Chinese Movement in California,* University of California Press,

Berkeley, 1971.

16. Mike Hilton, "The Split Labor Market and Chinese Immigration, 1848–1882," presented at the 72nd annual meeting of the American Sociological Association, 1977.

17. *Ibid.*, pp. 4–5.

18. Mary C. Sengstock, "Social Change in the Country of Origin as a Factor in Immigrant Conceptions of Nationality," *Ethnicity*, 4 (March 1977), 54–69.

19. *Ibid.*, pp. 56–57.

20. *Ibid.*, pp. 61, 64.

21. Marcus L. Hansen, "The Third Generation in America," *Commentary*, 14, No. 5 (November 1952), 492–500.

22. Marcus L. Hansen, "The Third Generation," in Oscar Handlin (ed.), *Children of the Uprooted*, Harper & Row, New York, 1966, pp. 255–271.

23. Ruby Jo Reeves Kennedy, "Single or Triple Melting Pot? Intermarriage in New Haven, 1870–1940," *American Journal of Sociology*, 49 (January 1944), 331–339; also, Ruby Jo Reeves Kennedy, "Single or Triple Melting Pot? Intermarriage Trends in New Haven, 1870–1950, *American Journal of Sociology*, 58 (July 1952), 56–59.

24. Marshall Sklare, *America's Jews*, Random House, New York, 1971, p. 185; John L. Thomas, "The Factor of Religion in the Selection of Marriage Mates," *American Sociological Review*, 16 (August 1951), 487–491.

25. Will Herberg, *Protestant-Catholic-Jew*, Doubleday, Garden City, N.Y., 1955.

26. Harold J. Abramson, *Ethnic Diversity in Catholic America*, Wiley, New York, 1973, pp. 51–68.

27. Mark R. Levy and Michael S. Kramer, *The Ethnic Factor*, Simon and Schuster, New York, 1973.

28. Jerry D. Rose, *Peoples: The Ethnic Dimension in Human Relations*, Rand McNally, Chicago, 1976, p. 21.

29. John M. Goering, "The Emergence of Ethnic Interests: A Case of Serendipity," *Social Forces*, 49 (March 1971), 379–384.

30. *Ibid.*, p. 383.

31. *Ibid.*, pp. 381–382.

32. *Ibid.*, p. 382.

33. Neil C. Sandberg, *Ethnic Identity and Assimilation: The Polish-American Community*, Praeger, New York, 1974.

34. See, for example, Richard O'Connor, *The German Americans*, Little, Brown, Boston, 1968; or Bernard Wasserstein, "Jewish Identification Among Students at Oxford," *Jewish Journal of Sociology*, 13 (December 1971), 131–151.

35. Harold J. Abramson, "The Religioethnic Factor and the American Experience: Another Look at the Three-Generation Hypothesis," *Ethnicity*, 2 (1975), 163–177.

36. *Ibid.*, p. 173.

37. John M. Goering, "The Emergence of Ethnic Interests," pp. 379–384.

38. Andrew M. Greeley, *Why Can't They Be Like Us?*, Dutton, New York, 1971, pp. 148–152.

39. *Ibid.*, p. 152.

40. Michael Novak, *The Rise of the Unmeltable Ethnics*, Macmillan, New York, 1971.

41. *Ibid.*, p. 30.

42. *Ibid.*, p. 291.

43. Perry L. Weed, *The White Ethnic Movement and Ethnic Politics*, Praeger, New York, 1973, p. 48.

44. *Ibid.*

45. Herbert Gans, "American Jewry: Present and Future," *Commentary*, 21 (May 1956), 422–430; and "The Future of American Jewry: Part II," *Commentary*, 21 (June 1956), 555–563.

46. Herbert Gans, *The Urban Villagers*, Free Press, New York, 1962.

47. Herbert Gans, p. xii of Foreword in Sandberg, *Ethnic Identity and Assimilation*.

48. *Ibid.*, p. xi.

49. William L. Yancey, Eugene P. Ericksen, and Richard N. Juliani, "Emergent Ethnicity: A Review and Reformulation," *American Sociological Review*, 41 (June 1976), 391–403.

50. *Ibid.*, p. 393.

51. See also Amitai Etzioni, "The Ghetto: A Re-evaluation," *Social Forces*, 39 (1959), 255–262.

52. Yancey, et al., "Emergent Ethnicity," p. 399.

53. Stanford M. Lyman and William A. Douglass, "Ethnicity: Strategies of Collective and Individual Impression Management," *Social Research*, 40 (Summer 1973), 344–365.

54. *Ibid.*, p. 345.

55. See section on structural pluralism, p. 95.

56. Mark Zborowski, "Cultural Components in Response to Pain," *Journal of Social Issues*, 8 (1952), 16–30; see also M. Zborowski, *People in Pain*, Jossey-Bass, San Francisco, 1969.

57. Andrew M. Greeley and William C. McCready, "Does Ethnicity Matter?," *Ethnicity*, 1 (1974), 91–103.

58. *Ibid.*, p. 102.

59. Novak, *The Rise of the Unmeltable Ethnics*, p. 32.

60. Andrew M. Greeley, *Ethnicity, Denomination, and Inequality*, Sage Research Papers in the Social Sciences, Vol. 4, series 90-029 (Studies in Religion and Ethnicity), Sage Publications, Beverly Hills, Calif., 1976.

61. David L. Featherman in a review of Greeley's book in *Sociological Analysis*, 38 (Summer 1977), 176–179.

62. *Ibid.*, p. 178.

63. Stanley Lieberson and Donna K. Carter, "Making It in America: Differences between Eminent Blacks and White Ethnic Groups," *American Sociological Review*, 44 (June 1979), 347–366.

APPENDIX

IMMIGRATION BY COUNTRY, FOR DECADES 1820–1977[1] *

COUNTRIES	1820	1821–1830	1831–1840	1841–1850	1851–1860	1861–1870	1871–1880
All countries	8,385	143,439	599,125	1,713,251	2,598,214	2,314,824	2,812,191
EUROPE	7,690	98,797	495,681	1,597,442	2,452,577	2,065,141	2,271,925
Austria-Hungary[2] [5]	—	—	—	—	—	7,800	72,969
Belgium	1	27	22	5,074	4,738	6,734	7,221
Denmark	20	169	1,063	539	3,749	17,094	31,771
France	371	8,497	45,575	77,262	76,358	35,986	72,206
Germany[2] [5]	968	6,761	152,454	434,626	951,667	787,468	718,182
Great Britain:							
England	1,782	14,055	7,611	32,092	247,125	222,277	437,706
Scotland	268	2,912	2,667	3,712	38,331	38,769	87,564
Wales	—	170	185	1,261	6,319	4,313	6,631
Not specified[3]	360	7,942	65,347	229,979	132,199	341,537	16,142
Greece	—	20	49	16	31	72	210
Ireland	3,614	50,724	207,381	780,719	914,119	435,778	436,871
Italy	30	409	2,253	1,870	9,231	11,725	55,759
Netherlands	49	1,078	1,412	8,251	10,789	9,102	16,541
Norway }	3	91	1,201	13,903	20,931	{ 71,631	{ 95,323
Sweden[4] }						37,667	115,922
Poland[5]	5	16	369	105	1,164	2,027	12,970
Portugal	35	145	829	550	1,055	2,658	14,082
Romania[12]	—	—	—	—	—	—	11
Spain	139	2,477	2,125	2,209	9,298	6,697	5,266
Switzerland	31	3,226	4,821	4,644	25,011	23,286	28,293
U.S.S.R.[5] [6]	14	75	277	551	457	2,512	39,284
Other Europe	—	3	40	79	5	8	1,001
ASIA	6	30	55	141	41,538	64,759	124,160
China	1	2	8	35	41,397	64,301	123,201
India	1	8	39	36	43	69	163
Japan[7]	—	—	—	—	—	186	149
Turkey	1	20	7	59	83	131	404
Other Asia	3	—	1	11	15	72	243
AMERICA	387	11,564	33,424	62,469	74,720	166,607	404,044
Canada & New-foundland[8]	209	2,277	13,624	41,723	59,309	153,878	383,640
Mexico[9]	1	4,817	6,599	3,271	3,078	2,191	5,162
West Indies	164	3,834	12,301	13,528	10,660	9,046	13,957
Central America	2	105	44	368	449	95	157
South America	11	531	856	3,579	1,224	1,397	1,128
AFRICA	1	16	54	55	210	312	358
AUSTRALIA & NEW ZEALAND	—	—	—	—	—	36	9,886
PACIFIC ISLANDS (U.S. ADM.)	—	—	—	—	—	—	1,028
NOT SPECIFIED	301	33,032	69,911	53,144	29,169	17,969	790

*From 1820–1867, figures represent alien passengers arrived; from 1868–1891 and 1895–1897, immigrant aliens arrived; from 1892–1894 and 1898 to the present time, immigrant aliens admitted. Data for years prior to 1906 relates to country whence alien came; thereafter, to country of last permanent residence. Because of changes in boundaries and changes in lists of countries, data for certain countries is not comparable throughout.

See notes and source at end of table.

COUNTRIES	1881–1890	1891–1900	1901–1910	1911–1920	1921–1930	1931–1940	1941–1950
All countries	5,246,613	3,687,564	8,795,386	5,735,811	4,107,209	528,431	1,035,039
EUROPE	4,735,484	3,555,352	8,056,040	4,321,887	2,463,194	347,552	621,124
Albania[11]	—	—	—	—	—	2,040	85
Austria	353,719	529,707	2,145,266	453,649	32,868	3,563	24,860
Hungary[2][5]				442,693	30,680	7,861	3,469
Belgium	20,177	18,167	41,635	33,746	15,846	4,817	12,189
Bulgaria[10]	—	160	39,280	22,533	2,945	938	375
Czechoslovakia[11]	—	—	—	3,426	102,194	14,393	8,347
Denmark	88,132	50,231	65,285	41,983	32,430	2,559	5,393
Estonia	—	—	—	—	—	506	212
Finland[11]	—	—	—	756	16,691	2,146	2,503
France	50,464	30,770	73,379	61,897	49,610	12,623	38,809
Germany[2][5]	1,452,970	505,152	341,498	143,945	412,202	114,058	226,578
Great Britain:							
England	644,680	216,726	388,017	249,944	157,420	21,756	112,252
Scotland	149,869	44,188	120,469	78,357	159,781	6,887	16,131
Wales	12,640	10,557	17,464	13,107	13,012	735	3,209
Not specified[3]	168	67	—	—	—	—	—
Greece	2,308	15,979	167,519	184,201	51,084	9,119	8,973
Ireland	655,482	388,416	339,065	146,181	220,591	13,167	26,967
Italy	307,309	651,893	2,045,877	1,109,524	455,315	68,028	57,661
Latvia[11]	—	—	—	—	—	1,192	361
Lithuania[11]	—	—	—	—	—	2,201	683
Luxembourg[15]	—	—	—	—	—	565	820
Netherlands	53,701	26,758	48,262	43,718	26,948	7,150	14,860
Norway[4]	176,586	95,015	190,505	66,395	68,531	4,740	10,100
Poland[5]	51,806	96,720	—	4,813	227,734	17,026	7,571
Portugal	16,978	27,508	69,149	89,732	29,994	3,329	7,423
Romania[12]	6,348	12,750	53,008	13,311	67,646	3,871	1,076
Spain	4,419	8,731	27,935	68,611	28,958	3,258	2,898
Sweden[4]	391,776	226,266	249,534	95,074	97,249	3,960	10,665
Switzerland	81,988	31,179	34,922	23,091	29,676	5,512	10,547
U.S.S.R.[5][6]	213,282	505,290	1,597,306	921,201	61,742	1,356	548
Yugoslavia[10]	—	—	—	1,888	49,064	5,835	1,576
Other Europe	682	122	665	8,111	22,983	2,361	3,983
ASIA	69,942	74,862	323,543	247,236	112,059	16,081	32,360
China	61,711	14,799	20,605	21,278	29,907	4,928	16,709
India	269	68	4,713	2,082	1,886	496	1,761
Japan[7]	2,270	25,942	129,797	83,837	33,462	1,948	1,555
Turkey	3,782	30,425	157,369	134,066	33,824	1,065	798
Other Asia	1,910	3,628	11,059	5,973	12,980	7,644	11,537
AMERICA	426,967	38,972	361,888	1,143,671	1,516,716	160,037	354,804
Canada & New-foundland[8]	393,304	3,311	179,226	742,185	924,515	108,527	171,718
Mexico[9]	1,913	971	49,642	219,004	459,287	22,319	60,589
West Indies	29,042	33,066	107,548	123,424	74,899	15,502	49,725
Central America	404	549	8,192	17,159	15,769	5,861	21,665
South America	2,304	1,075	17,280	41,899	42,215	7,803	21,831
Other America[13]	—	—	—	—	31	25	29,276
AFRICA	857	350	7,368	8,443	6,286	1,750	7,367
AUSTRALIA & NEW ZEALAND	7,017	2,740	11,975	12,348	8,299	2,231	13,805
PACIFIC ISLANDS (U.S. ADM.)	5,557	1,225	1,049	1,079	427	780	5,437
NOT SPECIFIED[14]	789	14,063	33,523	1,147	228	—	142

See notes at end of table.

COUNTRIES	1951–1960	1961–1970	1971	1972	1973
All countries	2,515,479	3,321,677	370,478	384,685	400,063
EUROPE	1,325,640	1,123,363	91,509	86,321	91,183
Albania[11]	59	98	4	8	99
Austria[2][5]	67,106	20,621	1,945	2,251	1,589
Hungary [2][5]	36,637	5,401	488	475	1,008
Belgium	18,575	9,192	577	530	438
Bulgaria[10]	104	619	44	40	212
Czechoslovakia[11]	918	3,273	734	1,152	910
Denmark	10,984	9,201	492	503	439
Estonia[11]	185	163	5	12	10
Finland[11]	4,925	4,192	331	341	283
France	51,121	45,237	2,844	2,870	2,587
Germany[2][5]	477,765	190,796	8,646	7,760	7,565
Great Britain:					
England	156,171	174,452	11,125	10,036	10,450
Scotland	32,854	29,849	740	947	790
Wales	2,589	2,052	62	85	99
Not specified[3]	3,884	3,675	375	453	521
Greece	47,608	85,969	15,002	10,452	10,348
Ireland	57,332	37,461	1,173	1,423	1,588
Italy	185,491	214,111	22,818	22,413	22,264
Latvia[11]	352	510	27	28	14
Lithuania[11]	242	562	20	25	18
Luxembourg[15]	684	556	46	26	26
Netherlands	52,277	30,606	1,092	979	966
Norway[4]	22,935	15,484	409	375	394
Poland[5]	9,985	53,539	1,928	3,770	4,136
Portugal	19,588	76,065	10,545	9,465	10,019
Romania[12]	1,039	2,531	687	354	1,106
Spain	7,894	44,659	3,661	4,284	5,538
Sweden[4]	21,697	17,116	648	654	597
Switzerland	17,675	18,453	1,066	999	704
U.S.S.R.[5][6]	584	2,336	303	400	874
Yugoslavia[10]	8,225	20,381	3,265	2,767	5,213
Other Europe	8,155	4,203	407	444	378
ASIA[16]	150,106	427,771	98,062	115,978	119,984
China[17]	9,657	34,764	7,597	8,511	9,153
India	1,973	27,189	13,056	15,589	11,975
Japan[7]	46,250	39,988	4,649	5,037	6,104
Turkey	3,519	10,142	1,147	1,531	1,447
Other Asia	88,707	315,688	71,613	85,310	91,305
AMERICA	996,944	1,716,374	171,680	173,165	179,604
Canada and New-					
foundland[8]	377,952	413,310	22,709	18,596	14,800
Mexico[9]	299,811	453,937	50,324	64,209	70,411
West Indies	123,091	470,213	66,552	60,386	62,830
Central America	44,751	101,330	8,870	8,407	9,125
South America	91,628	257,954	22,678	21,393	22,423
Other America[13]	59,711	19,630	547	174	15
AFRICA	14,092	28,954	5,844	5,472	5,537
AUSTRALIA AND					
NEW ZEALAND	11,506	19,562	2,357	2,550	2,466
PACIFIC ISLANDS					
(U.S. ADM.)[16]	4,698	1,769	158	235	176
NOT SPECIFIED[14]	12,493	3,884	868	964	1,113

See notes at end of table.

COUNTRIES	1974	1975	1976	1977	TOTAL 158 YEARS 1820–1977
All countries	394,861	386,194	398,613	462,315	47,959,847
EUROPE	80,407	72,774	73,035	74,048	36,108,166
Albania[11]	33	12	25	51	2,514
Austria[2][5]	669⎫	507⎫	519⎫	459⎫	4,314,266
Hungary [2][5]	897⎭	534⎭	561⎭	475⎭	
Belgium	432	437	537	531	201,643
Bulgaria[10]	131	83	107	98	67,669
Czechoslovakia[11]	381	267	267	273	136,535
Denmark	454	342	400	403	363,636
Estonia[11]	10	8	10	1	1,122
Finland[11]	243	215	232	227	33,085
France	2,160	1,816	2,030	2,651	747,123
Germany[2][5]	7,238	5,861	6,642	7,414	6,968,216
Great Britain:					
England	10,233	10,662	11,444	12,579	3,160,595
Scotland	918	1,015	997	884	818,899
Wales	85	134	105	139	94,953
Not specified[3]	425	433	424	438	804,369
Greece	10,590	9,799	8,553	7,792	645,694
Ireland	1,306	1,069	962	967	4,722,356
Italy	15,045	10,966	7,993	7,369	5,285,354
Latvia[11]	16	5	20	8	2,533
Lithuania[11]	20	11	21	11	3,814
Luxembourg[15]	45	21	17	27	2,833
Netherlands	988	755	850	1,039	358,171
Norway[4]	413	372	287	344	855,968
Poland[5]	3,492	3,482	3,192	3,331	509,181
Portugal	10,696	11,291	11,031	9,977	432,144
Romania[12]	1,184	825	1,670	1,506	168,923
Spain	4,704	2,573	2,758	5,568	254,660
Sweden[4]	637	507	568	576	1,271,113
Switzerland	671	673	776	812	348,056
U.S.S.R.[5][6]	921	4,713	7,417	5,443	3,366,886
Yugoslavia[10]	4,952	2,942	2,310	2,315	110,733
Other Europe	418	424	310	340	55,122
ASIA[16]	127,003	129,196	146,725	150,842	2,572,439
China[17]	10,038	9,201	9,925	12,513	510,241
India	11,694	14,336	16,130	16,849	140,425
Japan[7]	5,408	4,807	4,789	4,545	400,723
Turkey	1,433	1,071	956	991	384,271
Other Asia	98,430	99,781	114,925	115,944	1,136,779
AMERICA	178,846	174,732	169,180	223,174	8,739,969
Canada and New- foundland[8]	12,301	11,215	11,439	18,003	4,077,771
Mexico[9]	71,863	62,552	58,354	44,646	2,014,951
West Indies	61,284	66,975	65,734	109,959	1,583,720
Central America	9,431	9,800	10,097	16,892	289,522
South America	23,964	24,183	23,555	33,671	664,582
Other America	3	7	1	3	109,423
AFRICA	5,227	5,868	5,723	9,612	119,756
AUSTRALIA AND NEW ZEALAND	1,978	1,804	2,133	2,544	115,237
PACIFIC ISLANDS (U.S. ADM.)[16]	168	198	195	195	24,374
NOT SPECIFIED[14]	1,232	1,622	1,622	1,900	279,906

See notes at end of table.

[1]Since July 1, 1868, the data is for fiscal years ending June 30. Prior to fiscal year 1869, the periods covered are as follows: from 1820–1831 and 1843–1849, the years ended on September 30—1843 covers 9 months; and from 1832–1842 and 1850–1867, the years ended on December 31 — 1832 and 1850 cover 15 months. For 1868, the period ended on June 30 and covers 6 months.

[2]Data for Austria-Hungary was not reported until 1861. Austria and Hungary have been recorded separately since 1905. From 1938–1945, Austria is included in Germany.

[3]Great Britain not specified. From 1901–1951, included in other Europe.

[4]From 1820–1868, the figures for Norway and Sweden are combined.

[5]Poland recorded as a separate country from 1820–1898 and since 1920. From 1899–1919, Poland is included with Austria-Hungary, Germany, and Russia.

[6]From 1931–1963, the U.S.S.R. is broken down into European U.S.S.R. and Asian U.S.S.R. Since 1964 total U.S.S.R. has been reported in Europe.

[7]No record of immigration from Japan until 1861.

[8]Prior to 1920, Canada and Newfoundland are recorded as British North America. From 1820–1898, the figures include all British North American possessions.

[9]No record of immigration from Mexico from 1886–1893.

[10]Bulgaria, Serbia, and Montenegro were first reported in 1899. Bulgaria has been reported separately since 1920; also in 1920, a separate enumeration was made for the Kingdom of Serbs, Croats, and Slovenes. Since 1922, the Serbs, Croat, and Slovene Kingdom has been recorded as Yugoslavia.

[11]Countries added to the list since the beginning of World War I are included with the countries to which they belonged. Figures available since 1920 for Czechoslovakia and Finland and, since 1924, for Albania, Estonia, Latvia, and Lithuania.

[12]No record of immigration from Romania until 1880.

[13]Included with countries not specified to 1925.

[14]The figure 33,523 in column headed 1901–1910 includes 32,897 persons returning in 1906 to their homes in the United States.

[15]Figures for Luxembourg are available since 1925.

[16]Beginning with the year 1952, Asia includes the Philippines. From 1934–1951, the Philippines are included in the Pacific Islands. Prior to 1934, the Philippines are recorded in separate tables as insular travel.

[17]Beginning with the year 1957, China includes Taiwan.

SOURCE: U.S. Immigration and Naturalization Service, Annual Report, U.S. Government Printing Office, Washington, D.C., 1977, Table 13.

GLOSSARY

Abstract typification the generalization of people or things into broad categories.

Acceptance a minority response to prejudice and discrimination; it is based on powerlessness, fear for personal safety or economic security, or fatalism.

Accommodation a tendency to accept the situation as it exists, without seeking to change it or make others conform.

Acculturation the process by which a group changes its distinctive cultural traits to conform with those of the host society.

Achieved status one's socially defined position in a society based on individual accomplishments or failings.

Action-orientation level of prejudice a positive or negative predisposition to engage in discriminatory behavior toward a member or members of other groups.

Amalgamation the biological and cultural blending of two or more groups of people into a distinct new type; the melting-pot theory.

Americanization the effort to have ethnic groups quickly give up their cultural traits and adopt those of the dominant American group.

Anglo-conformity a physical and behavioral adherence to the established white Anglo-Saxon Protestant prototype; what many ethnocentric Americans mean by assimilation.

Annihilation the extermination of a specific group of people.

Ascribed status one's socially defined, unchangeable position in a society based on such arbitrary factors as age, sex, race, or family background.

Assimilation the process by which members of racial or ethnic minorities are able to function within a society without indicating any marked cultural, social, or personal differences from the people of the majority group.

Authoritarian personality a set of distinct personality traits, including conformity, insecurity, and intolerance, said to be common among many prejudiced people.

Avoidance a minority-group response to prejudice and discrimination in which the minority group migrates or withdraws to escape further problems; a majority-group attempt to minimize contact with specific minority groups through social or spatial segregation.

Categoric knowing a stereotype of others based merely on information obtained visually and perhaps verbally.

Chain migration a sequential flow of immigrants to a locality previously settled by friends, relatives, or other compatriots.

Cognitive level of prejudice a group's beliefs and perceptions about another racial or ethnic group.

Conflict view a theoretical perspective of society that emphasizes conflict as an important influence and permanent feature of social life.

Convergent subculture a subgroup that gradually becomes completely integrated into the dominant culture.

Culture the values, attitudes, customs, beliefs, and habits that are shared by members of a society.

Culture of poverty a controversial school of thought that argues that the disorganization and pathology of lower-class culture is self-perpetuating through cultural transmission.

Cultural assimilation also called acculturation, the change of cultural patterns to those of the host society.

Cultural determinism a theory that a group's culture explains its position in society and its achievements or lack of them.

Cultural differentiation those differences in culture that make one group distinguishable from another.

Cultural diffusion the spread of ideas, inventions, and practices from one culture to another.

Cultural drift a gradual change in the values, attitudes, customs, and beliefs of the members of a society.

Cultural pluralism two or more culturally distinct groups coexisting in relative harmony.

Cultural relativism the perception and judging of another culture or subculture from the perspective of the other culture rather than that of one's own culture.

Cultural transmission the passing on of a society's culture from one generation to another.

Cumulative causation Gunnar Myrdal's term for the vicious-circle process in which prejudice and discrimination each mutually "cause" the other, thereby continuing and intensifying the cycle.

De facto discrimination unequal and differential treatment of a group or groups that is entrenched in social customs and institutions.

Defiance a peaceful or violent action to challenge openly what a group considers a discriminatory practice.

De jure discrimination unequal and differential treatment of a group or groups that is established by law.

Deviance characteristics or behavior that violates social norms and is therefore negatively valued by many people in that society.

Dialectical process the situation in which one force meets a countervailing force and the result is a synthesis of the two.

Differentiation the social theory that societies tend to treat their members differently because of race, religion, age, sex, or other factors.

Discrimination differential and unequal treatment of other groups of people, usually along racial, religious, or ethnic lines.

Displaced aggression hostility directed against a powerless group rather than against the more powerful cause of the feelings of hostility.

Dysfunction a disruption of the equilibrium in a social system or of the functioning of some unit within the system.

Economic determinism a theory that a society's economic base establishes its culture and general characteristics.

Emotional level of prejudice the feelings aroused in a group by another racial or ethnic group.

Endogamy the tendency for people to marry only within their own social group.

Ethclass a social group classification based on a combination of race, religion, social class, and regional residence.

Ethnic antagonism various forms of intergroup hostility, including ideologies, beliefs, behavior, and institutionalized practices.

Ethnic behavior a concept that members of different ethnic groups behave differently in similar situations.

Ethnic consciousness a self-awareness of ethnic identity; the deliberate maintenance of one's culture in another cultural environment.

Ethnic group a group of people who share a common religion, nationality, culture, and/or language.

Ethnicity a cultural concept in which a large number of people who share learned or acquired traits and close social interaction regard themselves and are regarded by others as a single group on that basis.

Ethnocentrism a tendency to judge other cultures or subcultures by the standards of one's own culture.

Ethnography the study of the way of life of a people.

Ethnophaulism a derogatory word or expression used to describe or refer to a racial or ethnic group.

Exogamy the tendency for people to marry outside their own social group.

Expulsion the forced removal of a group of people from an area.

Fatalism a belief that events are determined by fate and thus beyond human control.

First-generation American someone born in another country who migrated to the United States.

Folkways norms that a society considers useful but not essential; their violation evokes only a mild negative response.

Frustration a behavioral response when expectations remain unsatisfied; sometimes linked to scapegoating.

Functionalist view a theoretical perspective about society that focuses primarily on the processes of order and stability, and on the functional interrelationships among the various elements within the society.

Gemeinschaft a small, tradition-dominated community characterized by intimate primary relationships and strong feelings of group loyalty.

Group a collectivity of people closely interacting with one another on the basis of shared expectations about behavior.

Hansen's law a theory that what the child of an immigrant wishes to forget, the grandchild wishes to remember; also called the three-generation hypothesis.

Hegemony leadership or predominant influence exercised by one group over others, whether on a racial, religious, cultural, or linguistic basis.

Historicity historical actuality or authenticity; past experiences.

Ideology a generalized set of beliefs that explains and justifies the interests of those who hold them.

Ingroup the group to which an individual belongs and feels loyalty.

Institution patterns of behavior organized to meet a basic need of a society, such as family, education, religion, economics, or politics.

Institutionalized discrimination differential and unequal treatment of a group or groups that deeply pervades social customs and institutions, and is usually subtle and informal.

Interactionist view a theoretical perspective that emphasizes the everyday routines of the micro order and the meanings and interpretations of the social interaction between individuals.

Intergenerational mobility the change in social status within a family from one generation to the next.

Internal colonialism theory a concept that seeks to explain the black experience, and possibly those of the Chicanos and American Indians, in terms of economic exploitation and rigid stratification.

Invasion-succession the ecological process in which one group displaces another group in a residential area or business activity.

Jim Crow laws Southern state segregation laws, passed in the 1890s and early twentieth century, which covered use of all public facilities, including schools, restaurants, transportation, waiting rooms, rest rooms, drinking fountains, and parks.

Linguistic relativity the recognition that different languages dissect and present reality differently.

Marginality the situation of individuals who are the product of one culture but are attempting to live within another, and therefore are not fully a part of either one.

Melting-pot theory an idealistic idea that many diverse peoples would blend both biologically and culturally and form a distinct new breed: the American.

Middleman minority a minority group that occupies an intermediate occupational position in trade or commerce between producer and consumer — the elite and the masses.

Minority group a group of people lacking socioeconomic power and different from the dominant group in physical or cultural traits, or both.

Mores norms that society considers essential; their violation evokes a strong negative response.

Nativist one who advocates a policy of protecting the interests of native inhabitants against those of immigrants.

Negative self-image the result of social conditioning or differential treatment or both that causes people or groups to believe themselves inferior.

"New" immigrants a term used by the Dillingham Commission (1907–1911) to identify immigrants from southern, central, and eastern Europe.

Norms the internalized rules of conduct that embody the fundamental expectations of society.

Objectivity disciplining oneself to examine and interpret reality with the least possible amount of personal bias and distortion.

"Old" immigrants a term used by the Dillingham Commission (1907–1911) to identify immigrants from northern and western Europe.

Outgroup any group to which an individual does not belong, in contrast to the ingroup, to which the individual belongs and toward which he or she feels loyalty.

Persistent subculture a subgroup that adheres to its own way of life and resists absorption into the dominant culture.

Personality an individual's typical patterns of thought, feeling, and action.

Pluralism a state in which minorities can maintain their distinctive subcultures and simultaneously interact with relative equality in the larger society.

Power differential the uneven distribution of power, whether economic, political, or social, in a society.

Power theory a concept in race and ethnic relations that the relative power of the migrant group and the indigenous group is the key variable determining the outcome of their interaction.

Prejudice a system of negative beliefs, feelings, and action-orientations regarding a certain group or groups of people.

Primary group a small number of people who interact with one another in close, personal, and meaningful relationships.

Push-pull factors the forces that encourage migration from one country to another.

Race a biological concept in which a large number of people who share visible physical characteristics regard themselves or are regarded by others as a single group on that basis.

Racial stratification differences in socioeconomic status within a society that is structured according to race.

Racism an ideology that establishes a link between the biological conditions of a human organism and its sociocultural capabilities and behavior.

Random sample a scientific selection of people from a larger population in which everyone has an equal chance to be chosen.

Reciprocal typifications people's categorizations of one another based upon their shared experiences.

Reference group a group to which people may or may not belong, but to which they refer when evaluating themselves and their behavior.

Relative deprivation a lack of resources, or rewards, in one's standard of living in comparison with others in the society.

Role behavior determined by the status the individual occupies.

Scapegoating placing blame on others for something that is not their fault.

Second-generation American a child born in the United States of immigrant parents; can also refer to a child born elsewhere but raised from a young age in the United States by immigrant parents.

Secondary group a collectivity of people who interact on an impersonal or limited emotional basis for some practical or specific purpose.

Selective perception a tendency to see or accept only that information that agrees with one's value orientations or is consistent with one's attitude about other groups.

Self-fulfilling prophecy a prediction that so influences behavior that the consequence is a realization of the prediction.

Self-justification a defense mechanism whereby people denigrate another person or group to justify maltreatment of them.

Situational ethnicity ethnic consciousness generated by residence, special events, work relationships, or working-class life style.

Social change any alteration, whether gradual or swift, in the patterns of social behavior or the social structure.

Social class a categorization designating people's places in the stratification hierarchy on the basis of similarities in income, property, power, status, and life style.

Social conditioning a socialization process through which people are molded to fit into the social system.

Social distance the degree to which ingroup members do not engage in social or primary relationships with members of various outgroups.

Social hierarchy the stratified levels of status within a group or society.

Social interaction the reciprocal process by which people act and react toward one another.

Social mobility the change from one status to another in a stratified society.

Social norms generally shared rules or expectations of what is and is not proper behavior.

Social organization any grouping formed to provide a means of social interaction among individuals.

Social segregation a situation in which participation in social, fraternal, service, and other types of activities is confined to members of the ingroup.

Social stratification the hierarchy within a society based upon the unequal distribution of resources, power, or prestige.

Social structure the organized patterns of behavior in a social system governing people's interrelationship with one another.

Socialization the process of social interaction by which people acquire personality and learn the culture or subculture of their group.

Society a group of individuals who share a common culture and territory.

Socioeconomic status (SES) a social prestige ranking as determined by numerous factors, including occupation, income, educational background, and place of residence.

Spatial segregation the physical separation of a minority group from the rest of society, such as in housing or education.

Split labor market theory a concept that explains ethnic antagonism on the basis of conflict between higher-paid and lower-paid labor.

Status a socially defined position in society.

Stereotype an oversimplified generalization by which we attribute certain traits or characteristics to any person in a group without regard to individual differences.

Structural assimilation the large-scale entrance of minority-group members into primary-group relationships with the host society in its social organizations and institutions.

Structural conditions those large-scale factors that affect the society, such as industrialization, economic vitality, and stratification.

Structural differentiation status distinctions for different racial and ethnic groups entrenched within the social system.

Structural discrimination differential treatment of groups of people that is entrenched in the institutions of a society.

Structural pluralism coexistence of

racial and ethnic groups in separate subsocieties that are also divided along social class and regional boundaries.

Subculture a group that shares in the overall culture of a society while retaining its own distinctive traditions and life style.

Subjectivity observing the world from one's own viewpoint, as shaped by cultural input, personal opinion, emotions, and experiences.

Subordinate less powerful than another group that possesses political, economic, or technological advantages.

Superordinate possessing superior power, whether political, economic, or technological.

Symbol anything that can be understood to signify something else, such as a word or gesture that symbolizes an attitude or feeling.

Symbolic interaction the use of symbols such as signs, gestures, and language through which people interact with one another.

Third-generation American someone born in the United States whose grandparents migrated to the United States.

Three-generation hypothesis see Hansen's Law.

Thomas theorem an observation that if people define situations as real, then they are real in their consequences.

Triple-melting-pot theory the concept that intermarriage is occurring among various nationalities within the three major religious groupings.

Universal theory a concept in race and ethnic relations of an inevitable cycle of contact, competition, accommodation, and assimilation.

Value judgment a personal or subjective opinion based on the values of the observer.

Value neutrality an ideal state, never fully possible, in which the observer eliminates all personal bias in order to be completely objective.

Values shared general concepts regarding what is good, right, useful, or desirable.

Vertical mobility a change to a higher or lower social or occupational status than previously held.

Vicious circle a self-perpetuating process in human behavior, as when a negative attitude influences a negative action, which results in a reaction that reaffirms or intensifies the negative attitude.

Victimological approach blaming the victim for his or her situation, rather than looking for other causes for the problem.

Xenophobia an irrational fear of or contempt for strangers or foreigners.

INDEX

Abramson, Harold, 446
Acadia: "Cajuns" expelled from, 55, 127
Acceptance, as minority response, 46–47
Accommodation theory, 93. See also
  Pluralism
Acculturation, 70, 95
  Cherokee, 239–240
  East Indian, 336
  Japanese, 289
  Native American, 79, 95, 97, 259–260
  non-Western immigrant, 317–319
  Vietnamese, 305–306
  See also Americanization; Culture
Adams, John, 124, 129, 149
Adams, John Quincy, 136
Adorno, T. W., 28–29
Africans, 9, 338, 346
  attitudes of, toward each other, 340,
    341
  in "smelting pot," 117
  social organization of (in Africa),
    353–354
  Spanish enslavement of, 230
  value orientations of, 339
  See also Blacks
Age, ethnic stratification by, 455, 456
Aggression: displaced, 29
  free-floating, 33
Agricultural Workers Organizing Com-
  mittee, 427
Alcatraz Island, 46, 228
  Indian takeover of, 251–252
Alien and Sedition Acts, 57, 112
Aliens, see Illegal aliens
Allport, Gordon, 18, 30, 48, 49
Amalgamation, 93, 97–100. See also
  Melting-pot theory
American Creed, 37–38, 100
American Dream, 82
American Indian Movement (AIM), 251
American Indian Policy Review Com-
  mission, 249, 258
American Indians, see Native Americans
Americanization, 95, 135, 447
  of Indians, 228, 242–243

of Jews, 199
of non-Westerners, 318
of Puerto Ricans, 411–412
of southern and eastern Europeans,
  165–166
See also Acculturation
American Protective Association, 34
Americans, 7
  stereotypes of, 22–24
  See also Native Americans
Amin, Idi, 14, 55
Amish, the, 79
Anglicans, 148
Anglo-Chinese War, 271
Anglophobia, 122. See also Xenophobia
Anglo-Saxon(s): "complex," 97
  values of, 434, 452–453
  See also English immigrants
Annihilation, 57–61, 191, 224
  accidental, 61, 230–231
  of Armenians, 58, 213, 333
  of gypsies, 179
  See also Massacre(s)
Ansari, Abdoulmaboud, 326–328
Antagonism, see Ethnic antagonism
Anti-Semitism, see Jews
Apache Indians, 237, 239
Arabs, 77, 317, 329–332
  Israelis as, 190
  as "race," 14
  value orientations of, 330–331
Arawak Indians, 229, 411
Armenians, 156, 204, 212–215, 327
  annihilation of, 58, 213, 333
  and ethnic identity, 215
  as refugees, 213
Aryans, as "race," 14
Asch, Solomon, 29
Ashkenazic Jews, see Jews
Asians, 268–312, 460
  as minority groups, 14, 34, 97
  racist hostility toward, 34, 225, 270,
    335
  refugees among, 269, 270
  sexual ratio among, 269

New York Times, 273, 274
Nipmuc Indians, 225
Nixon, Richard, 245, 256, 258
Nizza, Father Marcos da, 200
Nonez, Benjamin, 190
Nonintercourse Act (1790), 255. *See also*
    Legislative controls
Nonverbal communication, 72
Non-Western immigrants: acculturation
    of, 317–319
    Americanization of, 318
    push-pull factors for, 316–317
    social distance toward, 319, 333
    *See also individual countries and
    peoples*
Norms, 70
    between blacks and whites, 347
    social, 35
Northern Ireland, 15
Norwegians, 142–145
Novak, Michael, 447, 453

Oakes, Michael, 252
OAS (Organization of American States),
    7
Objectivity, 10
Occupational mobility: defined, 90. *See
    also* Social mobility
O'Kane, James M., 91
Oneida Indians, 234, 245
Onondaga Indians, 234
Osage Indians, 260
Outgroup, 5
    defined, 4
    ethnocentrism and, 434
    meaning of, to gypsies, 178
    See also Ethnocentrism

Pacific Islanders, 307
Padrino: Mexican, 442
    Puerto Rican, 413, 442
Padrone (Greek and Italian), 413, 442
Pain, reactions to, 450, 452
Palmer, Albert W., 279
Palmer, A. Mitchell: and Palmer raids
    (1917), 57, 186
Palmore, Erdman, 24
Pan-Indianism, 228, 251, 263. *See also*
    Native Americans
Parenton, Vernon, 130
Park, Robert E., 39, 50, 95–96, 286,

435–436, 442
Parks, Rosa, 368
Parsons, Talcott, 31
Passamaquoddy Indians, 255
Paterson, New Jersey, 120
Patroons (Dutch), 124, 413
Pavalko, Ronald M., 163–165
Pelley, William, 194
Penn, William, 109, 131
Pennsylvania Dutch, 109. *See also* Dutch
Penobscot Indians, 255
Perry, Matthew, 283
Persians, ancient, 7
Persistent subculture, *see* Subcultures,
    ethnic
Personality, authoritarian, 28–30
Pettigrew, Thomas, 35
Philip, Indian king, 225
Philosophical difference, 11
Phuc duc concept, 303–304
Pickering, Timothy, 135
Picture brides: among Japanese, 285
    among Koreans, 297
Pierce, Franklin, 117
Pilgrims, 42, 110, 118–119, 346
    culture shock among, 119
Pilipinos, 293–296, 334
    labor hostility toward, 294
    occupations of, 294
    sexual ratio among, 294–295
    stereotypes of, 307
Plains Indians, 251
Plato, 39–40
Platt Amendment, 419
Plessy v. *Ferguson,* 361
Pluralism, 79, 93, 97, 100–102, 462
    attitude toward, 434, 464
    among Dutch, 125–127
    among French, 130–131
    among Germans, 133, 135
    among Greeks, 209
    among Hispanics, 400
    among Portuguese, 211
Plymouth, Massachusetts, 118
Pogroms, 191, 333. *See also* Annihilation
Poles, 117, 156, 171, 207, 212, 356
    Catholics, 175, 458
    community, 175–176
    culture shock among, 174–175
    and education, 175–176
    ethnocentrism of, 174, 446
    stereotypes of, 19
    upward mobility of, 91

STRANGERS TO THESE SHORES
PARRILLO

Your comments on this book will help us in developing other new textbooks and future editions of this book. We would appreciate it if you could take a few minutes to answer the following questions. You can then mail this page to:

> *College Marketing Services*
> *Houghton Mifflin Company*
> *One Beacon Street*
> *Boston, MA 02107*

1. What was your overall impression of the book? _____

_____

_____

2. Did you find the text interesting and readable? ☐ Yes ☐ No

If not, what problems did you have? _____

_____

_____

3. Did the illustrations clarify the text in a useful way?

_____

4. How would you rate the following features of the text?

	Excellent	Very good	Good	Fair	Poor
Writing style	☐	☐	☐	☐	☐
Reading level	☐	☐	☐	☐	☐
Photographs	☐	☐	☐	☐	☐
Firsthand immigrant stories	☐	☐	☐	☐	☐
Coverage of many different groups	☐	☐	☐	☐	☐
Retrospects	☐	☐	☐	☐	☐
Questions for discussion	☐	☐	☐	☐	☐
Glossary	☐	☐	☐	☐	☐

Feel free to comment on any of the above items. _____

_____

5. Which chapters were required reading for your class?

_____

6. Did you read any chapters on your own that were not required reading?

_____

7. Are there any topics or immigrant groups that you think should have been covered in the text, but were not?

_____

_____

8. Did your instructor assign any additional books for this course?
☐ Yes ☐ No If so, what were they? _____

_____

9. Which chapters were especially interesting to you?

_____

10. Would you omit any chapters from future editions of the text?

_____

11. Do you have any suggestions that might help make this a better textbook?

_____

_____

Name of your school: _____

Course title: _____

Level: ☐ Sophomore ☐ Junior ☐ Senior ☐ Graduate

Prerequisite for the course: _____

Number of students in the class: _____

Your age: _____

Your major: _____